Mrs BEETON'S

MAIN COURSE
COOKBOOK

Mrs BEETON'S
MAIN COURSE COOKBOOK

Consultant Editor **Bridget Jones**

WARD LOCK

First published 1992 by Ward Lock
Villiers House, 41/47 Strand, London WC2N 5JE

First paperback edition 1993

A Cassell imprint

© Text and illustrations Ward Lock Limited 1992

Designed by Cherry Randell
Edited by Jenni Fleetwood
Photography by Sue Atkinson
Home Economists Jacqui Hine and Sarah Maxwell
Illustrations by Tony Randell and John Woodcock

The publishers are grateful to The Token House,
Windsor and Pine Place, St Leonard's Road, Windsor
for the loan of material for use in photography.

Typeset by Best-set Typesetter Ltd., Hong Kong
Printed and bound in Great Britain by The Bath
Press.

British Library Cataloguing in Publication Data
Beeton, *Mrs., 1836–1865*
    Mrs Beeton's main course cookbook.
    I. Title.   II. Jones, Bridget
    642.1

ISBN 0-7063-7177-1

CONTENTS

USEFUL WEIGHTS AND MEASURES

USING METRIC OR IMPERIAL MEASURES

Throughout the book, all weights and measures are given first in metric, then in Imperial. For example 100 g/4 oz, 150 ml/¼ pint or 15 ml/1 tbsp.

When following any of the recipes use either metric or Imperial – do not combine the two sets of measures as they are not interchangeable.

EQUIVALENT METRIC/IMPERIAL MEASURES

Weights The following chart lists some of the metric/Imperial weights that are used in the recipes.

METRIC	IMPERIAL
15 g	½ oz
25 g	1 oz
50 g	2 oz
75 g	3 oz
100 g	4 oz
150 g	5 oz
175 g	6 oz
200 g	7 oz
225 g	8 oz
250 g	9 oz
275 g	10 oz
300 g	11 oz
350 g	12 oz
375 g	13 oz
400 g	14 oz
425 g	15 oz
450 g	1 lb
575 g	1¼ lb
675 g	1½ lb
800 g	1¾ lb
900 g	2 lb
1 kg	2¼ lb
1.4 kg	3 lb
1.6 kg	3½ lb
1.8 kg	4 lb
2.25 kg	5 lb

Liquid Measures The following chart lists some metric/Imperial equivalents for liquids. Millilitres (ml), litres and fluid ounces (fl oz) or pints are used throughout.

METRIC	IMPERIAL
50 ml	2 fl oz
125 ml	4 fl oz
150 ml	¼ pint
300 ml	½ pint
450 ml	¾ pint
600 ml	1 pint

Spoon Measures Both metric and Imperial equivalents are given for all spoon measures, expressed as millilitres and teaspoons (tsp) or tablespoons (tbsp).

All spoon measures refer to British standard measuring spoons and the quantities given are always for level spoons.

Do not use ordinary kitchen cutlery instead of proper measuring spoons as they will hold quite different quantities.

METRIC	IMPERIAL
1.25 ml	¼ tsp
2.5 ml	½ tsp
5 ml	1 tsp
15 ml	1 tbsp

Length All linear measures are expressed in millimetres (mm), centimetres (cm) or metres (m) and inches or feet. The following list gives examples of typical conversions.

METRIC	IMPERIAL
5 mm	¼ inch
1 cm	½ inch
2.5 cm	1 inch
5 cm	2 inches
15 cm	6 inches
30 cm	12 inches (1 foot)

OVEN TEMPERATURES

Whenever the oven is used, the required setting is given as three alternatives: degrees Celsius (°C), degrees Fahrenheit (°F) and gas.

The temperature settings given are for conventional ovens. If you have a fan oven, adjust the temperature according to the manufacturer's instructions.

°C	°F	GAS
110	225	¼
120	250	½
140	275	1
150	300	2
160	325	3
180	350	4
190	375	5
200	400	6
220	425	7
230	450	8
240	475	9

MICROWAVE INFORMATION

Occasional microwave hints and instructions are included for certain recipes, as appropriate. The information given is for microwave ovens rated at 650-700 watts.

The following terms have been used for the microwave settings: High, Medium, Defrost and Low. For each setting, the power input is as follows: High = 100% power, Medium = 50% power, Defrost = 30% power and Low = 20% power.

All microwave notes and timings are for guidance only: always read and follow the manufacturer's instructions for your particular appliance. Remember to avoid putting any metal in the microwave and never operate the microwave empty.

NOTES FOR AMERICAN READERS

In America dry goods and liquids are conventionally measured by the standard 8 oz cup. When translating pints, and fractions of pints, Americans should bear in mind that the U.S. pint is equal to 16 fl oz or 2 cups, whereas the Imperial pint is equal to 20 fl oz.

EQUIVALENT METRIC/AMERICAN MEASURES

METRIC/IMPERIAL	AMERICAN
Weights	
450 g/1 lb butter or margarine	2 cups (4 sticks)
100 g/4 oz grated cheese	1 cup
450 g/1 lb flour	4 cups
450 g/1 lb granulated sugar	2 cups
450 g/1 lb icing sugar	3½ cups confectioners' sugar
200 g/7 oz raw long-grain rice	1 cup
100 g/4 oz cooked long-grain rice	1 cup
100 g/4 oz fresh white breadcrumbs	2 cups
Liquid Measures	
150 ml/¼ pint	⅔ cup
300 ml/½ pint	1¼ cups
450 ml/¾ pint	2 cups
600 ml/1 pint	2½ cups
900 ml/1½ pints	3¾ cups
1 litre/1¾ pints	4 cups (2 U.S. pints)

Terminology Some useful American equivalents or substitutes for British ingredients are listed below:

BRITISH	AMERICAN
aubergine	eggplant
bicarbonate of soda	baking soda
biscuits	cookies, crackers
broad beans	fava or lima beans
chicory	endive
cling film	plastic wrap
cornflour	cornstarch
courgettes	zucchini
cream, single	cream, light
cream, double	cream, heavy
flour, plain	flour, all-purpose
frying pan	skillet
grill	broil
minced meat	ground meat
prawn	shrimp
shortcrust pastry	basic pie dough
spring onion	scallion
sultana	golden raisin
swede	rutabaga

INTRODUCTION

The very words – main course – suggest a grand affair, and in Mrs Beeton's day this part of the meal would have held significant importance no matter what the occasion. In all but the humblest of households, eating was a serious business, to be undertaken in a formal fashion, at table, from breakfast right through to dinner. The main course, be it mixed grill, a hearty pot of stewed meat with vegetables or a dainty dish for entertaining, commanded forethought and preparation.

Times have changed and formal 'occasions' have become less frequent, but many meals still retain the old form, with one central dish in pride of place. This is reflected by the wide range of recipes and ideas gathered in this book, covering all meal occasions, from breakfast or lunch to formal dinners, cooking ahead and cooking for one. Complementary side dishes, sauces and other accompaniments are included, with helpful advice on planning and serving meals. Menu planning is discussed in the opening pages of the book, with follow up advice provided throughout.

The principles of preparing fish, meat, poultry and game are explained and illustrated. Vegetarian cooking is rightfully acknowledged and a concise glossary of vegetables provides valuable background information.

If you find the process of organizing main dishes a daunting one, you will appreciate the variety of recipes that follow; on the other hand, if your quest is to broaden your existing repertoire or experiment with new foods, Mrs Beeton's classic dishes and detailed techniques will satisfy that need.

PLANNING THE MAIN COURSE

The key points to consider when planning a menu, apart from the likes and dislikes or dietary restrictions of the diners, are the flavours, textures, colour and weight of the meal. A well-planned menu balances all these elements. Additional, practical, aspects to consider are your ability and confidence as a cook; the budget for one meal or for a weekly – or monthly – run of meals; and the cooking facilities available.

When planning a menu, it is usual to consider the main course of the meal first, then to fit the starter, fish course or dessert around it. This does not always have to be the rule – if you have a particularly splendid starter or dessert which you want to serve at a dinner party, or even for a family meal, there is absolutely no reason why you should not work the rest of the meal around it. If, for example, you wanted to serve a chocolate fondue as the finale of a dinner party, it would be logical to keep the preceding courses light. Equally, traditional steamed sponge pudding with custard is a real family treat but is not suitable for serving after a very filling main course, so a light salad and grilled fish would be the better option.

The recipes in this book include comments on the results you may expect to achieve. Notes, tips and variations all offer ideas about the flavours, textures and colour of a finished dish. Most recipes also include suggestions or comments about suitable accompaniments. This advice is useful when you are planning to incorporate one course into a more complicated menu.

FLAVOURS AND TEXTURES

As well as considering the accompaniments for the main dish, remember that a strongly flavoured starter will put a delicate main course in the shade, just as a very spicy main course will ruin the palate for a delicate dessert. Balance strong flavours and aim to accentuate delicate dishes.

Texture is a less obvious but equally important characteristic of food. A meal that consists solely of soft food is dull, and three courses of dry or crunchy dishes can be a disaster, leaving everyone gasping for water. Balance soft and smooth mixtures with crunchy textures; combine moist dishes with dry ones. Offer crisp salads with zesty dressings to counteract rich fried foods; serve plain, crunchy, lightly cooked vegetables with heavily sauced casseroles.

COLOUR AND WEIGHT

The food should be arranged and garnished to look appealing. The ingredients used, the quality of cooking juices and sauces and the choice of accompaniments are all factors in achieving a menu that includes colourful vegetables with rich-looking sauces or a succulent appearance. Some cooked foods inevitably look beige and uninteresting; this is when the choice of vegetable accompaniments and salads is vital to the success of the meal. Remember, that flavour and texture must be considered as well as colour.

The overall weight of the meal is important. Light dishes should balance richer foods. A filling dish should always be flanked by delicate courses.

FISH AND SHELLFISH

There is a seafood dish for every occasion, from inexpensive herring or mackerel for mid-week meals, to luxurious salmon or shellfish for celebration dinners.

It makes very good sense to choose fish for the main course. Not only is it versatile, very good value, nutritious and quick-cooking, but it also tends to be considerably lighter and more digestible than meat, allowing the cook greater rein in choosing starters and desserts that will be compatible while offering variations in texture and colour.

In the chapter that follows you will find detailed information on buying, cleaning and preparing fish and seafood, with illustrated instructions for some of the more tricky techniques. There are suggestions on what you can – and should – expect from a good fishmonger, and some sound advice on home freezing.

The many ways of cooking fish are explored in dishes that range from simple Battered Cod to Poached Trout with Prawn Sauce, Creamed Salmon in Pastry and Stuffed Squid.

Never overcook fish – this is the classic culinary crime, resulting in dry, tasteless and disappointing meals. The flesh should be just firm; white fish should be opaque when cooked. Unless the fish is cooked and cooled before it is eaten, perhaps as the basis of an interesting salad, it should always be served freshly cooked and piping hot.

Fried fish should be coated with flour, egg and breadcrumbs, batter or some other protective layer to protect it from the high temperature of the cooking fat. When grilling, make sure that the grill is hot before starting to cook the portions, and never leave them unattended.

Marry flavoursome sauces and vegetables with poached and steamed fish or seafood. Offer crisp salads or garnishes with smooth and lightly sauced dishes.

When casting fish in a leading role on the menu, take advantage of the wide variety of quality frozen fish and seafood available. Remember, too, the array of versatile canned products, since both are extremely practical for everyday dishes or when planning ahead for special meals.

PREPARATION TECHNIQUES

The basic techniques outlined in the pages that follow are, on the whole, interesting rather than essential because the majority of good fishmongers will prepare the fish for you. However, the advice below on handling mussels, oysters and scallops should always be followed carefully. If you are lucky enough to have a fisherman in the family, you may find the advice on cleaning fish (page 14) useful.

PREPARING MUSSELS

Thoroughly scrub the shells and scrape off any barnacles. Discard any open shells which do not close when tapped. Pull away the dark hairy 'beard' which protrudes slightly from the shell.

Cook mussels in a small amount of boiling liquid over high heat. Put a tight-fitting lid on the saucepan. Shake the pan occasionally and cook for about 5 minutes, until all the shells have opened. The mussels cook in the steam of the liquid. They should not be overcooked or they will toughen. Discard any shells that have not opened after cooking.

Note: The above method is also used for cockles and clams. Bought farmed shellfish should not be sandy; however leaving the shellfish in a cold place in a bucket of salted water overnight allows time for them to expel any sand they may contain.

OPENING OYSTERS

Ideally a special, short-bladed, tough oyster knife should be used. Do not use your favourite light kitchen knife as the blade may break. Select a fairly blunt, short, strong knife or similar implement. Hold the oyster with the curved shell down. Insert the point of the knife into the hinged end of the shell and prise it open. Take care as the tough shell is difficult to open and a knife which slips can cause a nasty injury.

OPENING SCALLOPS

Scallops are usually sold prepared. To open them at home place them in a warm oven for a few moments, until the shells part slightly. Then prise the shells apart and cut the nugget of white muscle and coral free.

ASK THE FISHMONGER

Knowing the basics of fish preparation makes it easier when shopping. Always ask the fishmonger to clean (gut) whole fish (trout, mackerel, bass, mullet and so on), stating clearly whether you want the head and tail on or off. Filleting is a task for the fishmonger. Most will also bone, scale and skin fish. Some fishmongers may even cut large fillets into serving portions.

These are not attributes of the model fishmonger; they are services you can reasonably expect, for no extra charge, but you must be sensible in making a request. At busy times, select your purchase, explain the preparation required and call back later. A polite request achieves a lot more than a haughty demand. Most fishmongers are highly skilled and only too ready to help.

SEAFISH QUALITY AWARD

Look out for the symbol above. It is displayed by fishmongers who have satisfied the judges that they not only sell quality fish, but also score in terms of quality and operation of the premises, storage, equipment, staff, handling and presentation.

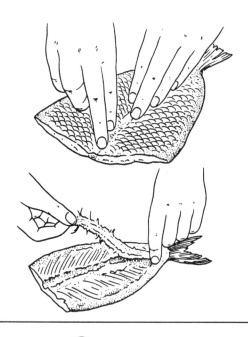

BONING ROUND FISH

1 Ensure that the cleaned fish has been slit right down to the tail. The head must be removed. Lay the fish, skin up, flat on a board. Press the flesh firmly along the backbone.

2 Turn the fish over and lift the backbone off from the tail end. It should come away easily, lifting most of the bones with it. Remove any stray bones.

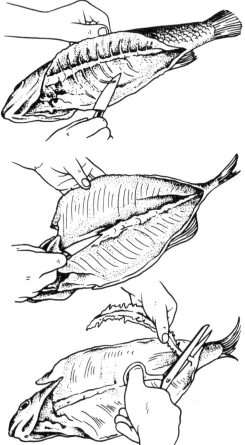

BONING WHOLE ROUND FISH

This is a technique for removing the bones while keeping the head and tail intact, for instance when stuffing the body cavity of a whole fish.

1 Make sure the body cavity of the fish is slit all along its length. Slide the point of a knife under each bone to free it from the flesh. Work from the backbone outwards.

2 Use a pair of kitchen scissors to snip through the backbone at the head and tail ends. Use the point of a knife to free the backbone, and lift it away. Remove any stray bones.

SKINNING FISH FILLETS

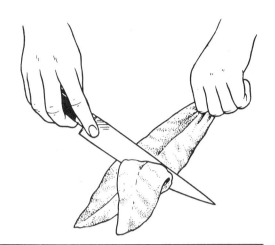

1 Lay the fillet on a board, skin down. Rub your fingers in salt. Hold the tail end firmly, then cut the flesh away from the skin. Hold the knife at an acute angle and use a sawing motion to remove the flesh in one piece, folding it back as you cut from the tail end towards the head.

SCALING FISH

1 Hold the fish in a clean sink and have cold water running slowly to wash away the scales as you work. Scrape off the scales from the tail towards the head, occasionally rinsing the knife and fish. A messy task, also known as descaling.

BONING FISH STEAKS OR CUTLETS

1 Use a thin, pointed knife and cut down around the bone to free the flesh from it. In the case of cutlets it is sometimes easier to snip the end of the bone free with kitchen scissors.

CLEANING FISH

If possible, ask the fishmonger or fisherman to clean (gut) fish for you. If you have to do this at home, lay several thicknesses of clean newspaper on the work surface and place the fish on greaseproof paper on top. Slit the fish down its belly, then scrape out the innards. Transfer the fish to a plate; repeat with other fish. Wrap the newspaper tightly around the innards at once, and place in an outdoor waste bin. Wash down all surfaces, utensils and your hands. Thoroughly rinse the fish, then pat it dry with absorbent kitchen paper.

Other Methods Round fish may also be cleaned through the gills to avoid splitting the body open. Similarly, whole flat fish (plaice and Dover or lemon sole) have only small pockets of innards that are removed through a small slit below the head. The fishmonger will clean fish in this way for you but always remember to ask for a specific cleaning method such as through the gills.

RULES TO REMEMBER

Buying Fish and Seafood

■ Buy from a reputable source – the premises should look clean and smell fresh.

■ Wet fish should look moist and fresh. All eyes should be bright and moist, markings on skin should be bright. Fish fillets should be moist, clean and unbroken.

■ Ready-to-eat fish and seafood (for example, smoked mackerel) should never be handled immediately after raw fish. The fishmonger should pick up the ready-to-eat fish with an implement or in a bag. This rule is particularly important if the fishmonger has been cleaning raw fish. He should either wear gloves for this operation or wash his hands thoroughly.

■ Make fish the last item you buy on a shopping trip, take it home quickly (in a chiller bag on hot days) and unpack it at once.

■ Rinse and dry the fish, then put it in a dish and cover it with cling film. Place in the refrigerator and cook it within 24 hours.

Handling Fish

■ Use a clean board, preferably made of plastic material. Wooden boards should always be scrubbed and rinsed in boiling water, then allowed to dry after use.

■ Use a sharp, narrow-bladed, pointed knife for preparing fish.

■ Kitchen scissors are useful for snipping off fins and for cutting bones. Wash them well after use.

■ Never prepare raw fish and cooked food using the same utensils, unless the utensils have been thoroughly washed and dried.

■ Always keep fish covered and chilled before cooking.

Freezing Fish

■ Bought frozen fish is frozen soon after it is taken from the sea. It is frozen speedily at low temperatures for best results.

■ Fish for home freezing should be freshly caught or bought fresh from a reputable fishmonger. Do not freeze bought fish which has been frozen and thawed before sale. Freeze fish immediately after purchase. This applies particularly to oily fish such as mackerel.

■ Always clean and prepare fish for cooking before freezing it.

Pack fish in heavy polythene bags, excluding as much air as possible.

■ White fish may be stored for 3-4 months; oily fish keeps for 2-3 months in a domestic freezer at −18°C/0°F.

BASIC FISH STOCK

This simple fish stock is a valuable ingredient in main course fish dishes and may also be used in batters for frying fish. It should always be freshly made and will not keep unless frozen.

fish bones and trimmings without gills
    which cause bitterness
5 ml/1 tsp salt
1 small onion, sliced
2 celery sticks, sliced
4 white peppercorns
1 bouquet garni

Break up any bones and wash the fish trimmings, if used. Put the bones, trimmings or heads in a saucepan and cover with 1 litre/1¾ pints cold water. Add the salt.

Bring the liquid to the boil and add the vegetables, peppercorns and bouquet garni. Lower the heat, cover and simmer gently for 30-40 minutes. Do not cook the stock for longer than 40 minutes or it may develop a bitter taste.

Strain the stock through a fine sieve into a clean saucepan or measuring jug and use as required.

MAKES 1 LITRE/1¾ PINTS

COURT BOUILLON

This is the traditional stock used for poaching salmon, salmon trout or any other whole fish. It is discarded after use.

500 ml/17 fl oz dry white wine or dry
    cider
30 ml/2 tbsp white wine vinegar
2 large carrots, sliced
2 large onions, sliced
2-3 celery sticks, chopped
6 parsley stalks, crushed
1 bouquet garni
10 peppercorns, lightly crushed
salt and pepper

Put the wine in a large stainless steel or enamel saucepan. Add 1 litre/1¾ pints water, with the remaining ingredients.

Bring the liquids to the boil, lower the temperature and simmer for 30 minutes. Cool, then strain and use as required.

MAKES 1.5 LITRES/2¾ PINTS

> **MRS BEETON'S TIP** Parsley stalks impart valuable flavour to stocks and other simmering liquids. The leaves and sprigs may be cut off and saved.

FISHERMAN'S HOT POT

2 slices of white bread
25 g/1 oz butter
45 ml/3 tbsp oil
50 g/2 oz piece of white cabbage,
    shredded
2 leeks, trimmed, sliced and washed
1 large onion, chopped
225 g/8 oz white fish fillet, skinned and cut
    into 2.5 cm/1 inch cubes
150 ml/¼ pint Muscadet or other dry
    white wine
45 ml/3 tbsp tomato purée
1 chicken stock cube
1 bouquet garni
1 garlic clove, crushed
salt and pepper
chopped parsley to garnish

Remove the crusts from the bread, cut it into cubes and spread on a baking sheet. Dry out in a 150°C/300°F/gas 2 oven for 10-15 minutes, then set aside.

Melt the butter in the oil in a large saucepan. Add the vegetables, cover and cook gently for 7-8 minutes until soft. Do not allow the leeks and onions to colour.

Add the fish cubes and fry for 3 minutes, turning occasionally, until firm on all sides. Pour in the wine and add 1 litre/1¾ pints water. Stir in the tomato purée and crumble in the stock cube. Add the bouquet garni, crushed garlic and salt and pepper to taste.

Heat the stew to simmering point and cook for 20 minutes. Discard the bouquet garni. Pour into a serving dish and sprinkle with the chopped parsley. Serve with the toasted bread cubes.

SERVES 4

CASSEROLE OF LING

Ling is one of the largest fish in the cod family. It is a long fish, with a bronze-green or brown skin and firm white flesh. Cod or haddock may be substituted for ling fillet.

575 g/1¼ lb ling fillet, skinned and cut
    into 5 cm/2 inch pieces
25 g/1 oz butter
1 large onion, sliced
25 g/1 oz plain flour
400 ml/14 fl oz tomato juice
pinch of mixed herbs
salt and pepper

Set the oven at 200°C/400°F/gas 6. Arrange the ling pieces in a shallow oven-proof dish.

Melt the butter in a saucepan, add the onion and mushrooms and fry for 3-4 minutes until the onions start to colour. Sprinkle in the flour and cook for 1 minute, stirring.

Stir in the tomato juice and bring to the boil, stirring constantly. Add the herbs, with salt and pepper to taste, then pour the sauce over the fish. Cover the dish with foil and bake for 30 minutes. Serve at once.

SERVES 4

MRS BEETON'S TIP Do not peel or wash the mushrooms; simply wipe them clean with a piece of absorbent kitchen paper. Trim the base of each stem and cut in half or quarters if large.

COD WITH CREAM SAUCE

6 (100 g/4 oz) cod steaks or portions
75 g/3 oz butter
250 ml/8 fl oz Basic Fish Stock (page 15)
milk (see method)
25 g/1 oz plain flour
30 ml/2 tbsp double cream
15 ml/1 tbsp lemon juice
salt and pepper

Rinse the fish and pat dry on absorbent kitchen paper. Melt half the butter in a frying pan, add the cod and fry quickly on both sides to seal without browning.

Add the stock, cover the pan and simmer gently for 20 minutes. Drain the fish, reserving the cooking liquid in a measuring jug, place on a warmed dish and keep hot. Make the cooking liquid up to 300 ml/ ½ pint with milk.

Melt the remaining butter in a saucepan, add the flour and cook for 1 minute, stirring. Gradually add the reserved cooking liquid and milk mixture, stirring constantly. Bring to the boil, lower the heat and simmer for 4 minutes, stirring occasionally.

Remove the pan from the heat and stir in the cream and lemon juice. Add salt and pepper to taste and spoon a little sauce over each fish portion. Serve at once.

SERVES 6

> **MRS BEETON'S TIP** The stock used as the basis for this recipe should be pale in colour. Avoid adding the skin of the fish when making it, as this would darken it.

CURRIED COD

800 g/1¾ lb cod fillets, skinned
50 g/2 oz butter
1 large onion, sliced
15 ml/1 tbsp plain flour
10 ml/2 tsp curry powder
500 ml/17 fl oz Basic Fish Stock (page 15)
15 ml/1 tbsp lemon juice
salt and pepper
cayenne pepper

Rinse the fish and pat dry. Cut into pieces about 2.5 cm/1 inch square. Melt the butter in a saucepan and fry the cod lightly for 2-3 minutes. Using a slotted spoon, transfer the pieces to a warmed dish and keep hot.

Add the onion to the butter remaining in the pan and fry gently for 3-4 minutes until soft. Stir in the flour and curry powder and fry for 5 minutes, stirring constantly to prevent the onion from becoming too brown.

Pour in the stock and bring to the boil, stirring constantly. Lower the heat and simmer for 15 minutes. Strain the sauce into a clean saucepan, adding lemon juice, salt and pepper and cayenne to taste. Carefully add the fish to the pan, stir gently and bring to simmering point.

Simmer for about 10 minutes, until the fish has absorbed the flavour of the sauce. Stir occasionally to prevent sticking. Serve at once, with boiled rice if liked.

SERVES 6

VARIATION

QUICK COD CURRY Use cold cooked fish, omitting the preliminary frying. Serve with a mixture of plain yogurt and chopped cucumber.

*H*ADDOCK FLORENTINE

50 g/2 oz butter
1 kg/2¼ lb fresh spinach
salt and pepper
100 ml/3½ fl oz Basic Fish Stock (page 15)
100 ml/3½ fl oz dry white wine
1 kg/2¼ lb haddock fillets, skinned
1.25 ml/¼ tsp grated nutmeg
50 g/2 oz Parmesan cheese, grated

MORNAY SAUCE
  1 small onion
  1 small carrot
  1 small celery stick
  600 ml/1 pint milk
  1 bay leaf
  few parsley stalks
  1 thyme sprig
  1 clove
  6 white peppercorns
  1 blade of mace
  50 g/2 oz butter
  50 g/2 oz plain flour
  1 egg yolk
  25 g/1 oz Gruyère cheese, grated
  25 g/1 oz Parmesan cheese, grated
  60 ml/4 tbsp single cream
  pinch of grated nutmeg

Start by making the sauce. Combine the onion, carrot, celery and milk in a saucepan. Add the herbs and spices, with salt to taste. Heat to simmering point, cover, turn off the heat and allow to stand for 30 minutes to infuse. Strain into a measuring jug.

Melt the butter in a saucepan. Stir in the flour and cook over low heat for 2-3 minutes, without allowing the mixture to colour. Remove the pan from the heat and gradually add the flavoured milk, stirring constantly.

Return the pan to moderate heat, stirring until the mixture boils and thickens to a coating consistency. When the mixture boils, lower the heat and simmer for 1-2 minutes, beating briskly. Cool slightly.

Beat the egg yolk in a small bowl. Add a little of the sauce and mix well. Add the contents of the bowl to the sauce and heat gently, stirring. Do not allow the sauce to boil. Stir in the cheeses until melted. Add the cream and nutmeg. Cover the surface of the sauce closely with damp greaseproof paper and set aside.

Using 25 g/1 oz of the butter, grease a shallow ovenproof serving dish. Tear the spinach leaves from the stalks and place in a large saucepan with the remaining butter. Add salt and pepper to taste. Cover with a tight-fitting lid and cook gently for about 15 minutes, shaking the pan occasionally.

Meanwhile, combine the stock and white wine in a large saucepan. Bring to simmering point, add the fish and poach for 7-10 minutes.

Drain the spinach throughly in a colander, pressing out all free liquid with the back of a wooden spoon. Put the spinach on the base of the prepared dish. Remove the fish fillets with a slotted spoon and arrange them on top. Keep hot.

Boil the fish stock until reduced by half. Reheat the sauce, stirring frequently. Add the reduced fish stock, season with salt, pepper and nutmeg and pour the sauce over the fish. Sprinkle with the grated Parmesan and brown under a hot grill. Serve at once.

SERVES 4

CAPE COD PIE

This simple potato-topped pie would make an ideal main course for a family supper. Serve with Stir-fried Beans with Savory (page 211) for colour and texture contrast.

fat for greasing
450 g/1 lb potatoes, halved
salt and pepper
90 g/3½ oz butter
30-45 ml/2-3 tbsp single cream
25 g/1 oz plain flour
300 ml/½ pint milk
salt and pepper
450 g/1 lb cooked cod, skinned, boned and
 flaked
50 g/2 oz Cheddar cheese, grated
few grains of cayenne pepper
1 egg, beaten
pinch of grated nutmeg

Grease a 1 litre/1¾ pint pie dish. Cook the potatoes in a saucepan of salted boiling water for about 30 minutes or until tender. Drain thoroughly and mash with a potato masher, or beat with a hand-held electric whisk until smooth. Beat in 25 g/1 oz of the butter and the cream. Set aside until cold.

Set the oven at 190°C/375°F/gas 5. Melt 25 g/1 oz of the remaining butter in a saucepan. Stir in the flour and cook over low heat for 2-3 minutes, without allowing the mixture to colour. Gradually add the milk, stirring constantly until the sauce boils and thickens. Add salt and pepper to taste. Stir in the flaked cod, half the cheese and 15 g/½ oz of the remaining butter. Check the seasoning and add the cayenne. Remove from the heat.

Set aside about 10 ml/2 tsp of the beaten egg for glazing. Stir the remaining egg into the cold mashed potato. Melt the remaining butter and stir it into the potato with the nutmeg. Line the prepared dish with half the potato mixture.

Heat the fish mixture until it bubbles. Pour it into the lined pie dish and cover evenly with the rest of the potato. Press the edge with the tines of a fork. Glaze with the reserved egg and sprinkle with the remaining cheese. Bake for 8-12 minutes until well browned.

SERVES 4 TO 5

———————— ◇ ————————

HADDOCK IN CIDER

fat for greasing
575 g/1¼ lb haddock fillet, skinned and
 cubed
225 g/8 oz tomatoes, peeled and sliced
150 g/5 oz mushrooms, sliced
125 ml/4 fl oz dry cider
salt and pepper
30 ml/2 tbsp chopped parsley
25 g/1 oz Cheddar cheese, grated
30 ml/2 tbsp fresh white breadcrumbs

Grease a large ovenproof baking dish. Set the oven at 190°C/375°F/gas 5. Spread out the fish cubes in an even layer on the base of the dish and top with the tomatoes and mushrooms.

Pour the cider over the fish and sprinkle with salt and pepper. Mix the parsley, cheese and breadcrumbs together in a small bowl. Scatter over the fish and bake for 30-35 minutes. Serve at once.

SERVES 4

COD AU GRATIN

fat for greasing
4 (100 g/4 oz) portions of cod fillet
25 g/1 oz butter
2 large onions, finely chopped
100 g/4 oz mushrooms, sliced
salt and pepper
1 green pepper, seeded and diced
450 g/1 lb tomatoes, peeled, seeded and
    sliced
50 g/2 oz Cheddar cheese, grated
75 g/3 oz fresh white breadcrumbs

Grease a fairly deep ovenproof dish. Set the oven at 190°C/375°F/gas 5. Arrange the cod portions on the base of the dish.

Melt the butter in a frying pan, add the onions and fry gently for 4-5 minutes until slightly softened. Remove the onions with a slotted spoon and place on top of the fish. Cook the mushrooms in the same way.

Meanwhile bring a small saucepan of salted water to the boil, add the diced green pepper and blanch for 2 minutes. Drain and add to the fish, followed by the mushrooms. Top with the tomato slices, generously sprinkled with salt and pepper.

Combine the cheese and breadcrumbs in a bowl, mix well, then sprinkle over the fish and vegetables. Bake for 30 minutes. Serve at once.

SERVES 4

SMOKED COD AND CORN CASSEROLE

1 (326 g/11½ oz) can sweetcorn kernels,
    drained
450 g/1 lb smoked cod fillet, skinned and
    cut in 1 cm/½ inch strips
pepper
25 g/1 oz butter
125 ml/4 fl oz single cream

Set the oven at 180°C/350°F/gas 4. Drain the corn and spread a layer on the base of an ovenproof dish. Add a layer of cod strips. Season with pepper and dot with butter.

Repeat the layers until all the corn and cod have been used, then pour over the cream. Cover and bake for 25 minutes. Serve at once.

SERVES 3 TO 4

VARIATION

CORN 'N' COD Poach the smoked cod fillets, then drain and flake. Make a white sauce, using 50 g/2 oz each of butter and plain flour and 600 ml/1 pint milk (or milk mixed with the drained liquid from the can of sweetcorn). Add salt and pepper to taste and stir in the flaked cod and the corn. Spoon into a dish, top with grated Cheddar cheese and bake for 15-20 minutes at 180°C/350°F/gas 4.

COD CUTLETS WITH SHRIMP STUFFING

Illustrated on page 66

4 cod cutlets
15 ml/1 tbsp oil

STUFFING
25 g/1 oz butter
1 onion, chopped
50 g/2 oz fresh white breadcrumbs
15 ml/1 tbsp chopped parsley
150 g/5 oz peeled cooked shrimps or
    prawns, chopped
juice of ½ lemon
salt and pepper

GARNISH
lemon twists (see Mrs Beeton's Tip)
watercress sprigs
whole prawns

Make the stuffing. Melt the butter, add the onion and fry gently for 10 minutes until soft but not browned. Remove from the heat and stir in the breadcrumbs and parsley, with the shrimps or prawns and lemon juice. Add salt and pepper to taste.

Rinse the fish cutlets, pat them dry with absorbent kitchen paper and remove their bones. Arrange the fish neatly on a flame-proof platter or baking sheet and fill the centre spaces with the stuffing.

Sprinkle the oil over the stuffed fish and cook under a moderate grill for 15-20 minutes or until the fish is cooked through. If the stuffing begins to brown too fiercely before the fish is cooked, then reduce the heat. Garnish with lemon twists, watercress sprigs and whole prawns, and serve at once.

SERVES 4

SPICY FISH SLICES

Illustrated on page 67

675 g/1½ lb cod or hake fillets
7.5 ml/1½ tsp salt
5 ml/1 tsp turmeric
5 ml/1 tsp chilli powder
90 ml/6 tbsp oil
coriander sprigs to garnish

Cut the fish into 2 cm/¾ inch slices and spread it out in a shallow dish large enough to hold all the slices in a single layer. Mix the salt and spices in a bowl. Stir in enough water to make a thick paste. Rub the paste into the fish, cover and leave to marinate for 1 hour.

Heat the oil in a large frying pan. Add as much of the spiced fish as possible, but do not overfill the pan. Fry the fish for 5-10 minutes, until golden brown all over, then remove from the pan with a slotted spoon. Drain on absorbent kitchen paper and keep hot while cooking the rest of the fish.

Garnish and serve hot, with rice or a small salad, if liked.

SERVES 4 TO 5

> **MRS BEETON'S TIP** To prepare the lemon twists (for the recipe, left), use a canelle knife to score a lemon from top to bottom at regular intervals. Cut lengthwise halfway through the fruit, using one of the pared lines as a guide, then cut the lemon in slices. Twist each slice away from the cut.

GOLDEN GRILLED COD

margarine or butter for greasing
4 cod cutlets or steaks, about 2 cm/¾ inch
    thick
4 small tomatoes, halved
chopped parsley to garnish (optional)

TOPPING
    25 g/1 oz margarine or butter
    50 g/2 oz mild Cheddar or Gruyère
        cheese, finely grated
    30 ml/2 tbsp milk (optional)
    salt and pepper

Grease a shallow flameproof dish with margarine or butter, then arrange the fish in the dish. Grill under moderate heat for 2-3 minutes on one side only.

Meanwhile make the topping. Cream the margarine or butter with the grated cheese in a small bowl. Work in the milk, a few drops at a time, if using, and add salt and pepper to taste.

Turn the fish cutlets or steaks over, spread the topping on the uncooked side and return them to the grill. Lower the heat slightly and grill for 12-15 minutes until the fish is cooked through and the topping is golden brown. Arrange the tomatoes around the fish about 5 minutes before the end of the cooking time.

Serve the fish piping hot with the lightly grilled tomatoes. A little chopped parsley may be sprinkled over the fish for colour and flavour, if liked.

SERVES 4

COATING BATTER

This is a firm batter, suitable for cod fillets and other large fish portions.

    100 g/4 oz plain flour
    pinch of salt
    1 egg
    125 ml/4 fl oz milk

Sift the flour and salt into a bowl and make a well in the centre.

Add the egg and a little milk, then beat well, gradually incorporating the flour and the remaining milk to make a smooth batter.

MAKES ABOUT 150 ML/¼ PINT

COD IN BATTER

4 portions cod fillet, skinned
salt and pepper
flour for dusting
Coating Batter
oil for deep frying

Remove any bones from the fish, sprinkle the portions with salt and pepper and dust them with flour. Make up the coating batter.

Heat the oil for deep frying to 180°C/ 350°F or until a day-old cube of bread browns in 30-60 seconds. Dip a piece of cod in the batter to coat it completely, allow the excess to drip off, then lower the fish into the hot oil. Repeat with another piece of cod. Fry the cod until crisp and golden, turning once.

◇

Drain the cod on absorbent kitchen paper and keep hot under a low to medium grill while cooking the remaining pieces.

SERVES 4

SWEET AND SOUR HAKE

Illustrated on page 68

450 g/1 lb hake fillet, skinned and cut into
    2.5 cm/1 inch cubes
cornflour for coating
oil for deep frying
1 green pepper, seeded and finely
    chopped

MARINADE
  2 spring onions, finely chopped
  15 ml/1 tbsp medium-dry sherry
  30 ml/2 tbsp soy sauce
  15 ml/1 tbsp finely chopped peeled fresh
    root ginger

SAUCE
  1 (227 g/8 oz) can pineapple cubes in
    natural juice
  30 ml/2 tbsp cornflour
  30 ml/2 tbsp soy sauce
  15 ml/1 tbsp medium-dry sherry
  5 ml/1 tsp malt vinegar
  5 ml/1 tsp oil

Make the marinade by combining all the ingredients in a shallow dish large enough to hold all the fish cubes in a single layer.

Add the fish cubes, cover the dish and marinate for 1-2 hours, stirring several times.

Meanwhile make the sauce. Drain the pineapple cubes, reserving the juice in a measuring jug. Make up to 90 ml/6 tbsp with orange juice or water if necessary. Reserve the pineapple cubes.

Put the cornflour in a small saucepan. Add about 30 ml/2 tbsp of the pineapple juice and mix to a smooth paste, then stir in the remaining pineapple juice, soy sauce, sherry, vinegar and oil. Bring to the boil, stirring constantly, then lower the heat and simmer for 3 minutes.

Drain the fish cubes, discarding the marinade. Spread the cornflour for coating in a shallow bowl, add the fish cubes and shake the bowl until all the cubes are well coated.

Put the oil for frying into a deep wide saucepan to a depth of at least 7.5 cm/3 inches. Heat the oil to 180-190°C/350-375°F or until a cube of bread added to the oil browns in 30 seconds. If using a deep-fat fryer, follow the manufacturer's instructions.

Fry the fish cubes, a few at a time, for 2-3 minutes until evenly browned. Drain on absorbent kitchen paper, transfer to a warmed serving dish and keep hot.

Add the reserved pineapple cubes to the sweet and sour sauce and heat through. Pour the sauce over the fish, sprinkle with the chopped green pepper and serve at once.

SERVES 4

PLAICE MORNAY

Illustrated on page 65

fat for greasing
350 ml/12 fl oz milk
1 onion, finely chopped
1 carrot, finely chopped
1 celery stick, finely chopped
1 bouquet garni
salt and pepper
8 plaice fillets
25 g/1 oz butter
25 g/1 oz plain flour
100 g/4 oz Gruyère cheese, grated
50 g/2 oz Parmesan cheese, grated
1.25 ml/¼ tsp mustard powder
chervil sprigs to garnish

Grease a shallow flameproof dish. Combine the milk, vegetables and bouquet garni in a saucepan. Add salt and pepper to taste. Bring to the boil, lower the heat and simmer for 10 minutes. Set aside to cool.

Fold the plaice fillets in three, skin side inwards. Strain the flavoured milk into a deep frying pan and heat to simmering point. Add the fish and poach for 6-8 minutes or until the fish is cooked. Using a slotted spoon, transfer the fish to the prepared dish. Cover with buttered greaseproof paper and keep warm. Reserve the cooking liquid in a jug.

Melt the butter in a saucepan, add the flour and cook for 1 minute, stirring. Gradually add the reserved cooking liquid, whisking constantly until the sauce thickens.

Mix the cheeses and stir half the mixture into the sauce, with the mustard. Remove the buttered paper from the fish, pour the sauce over the top and sprinkle with the remaining cheese mixture. Brown briefly under a hot grill. Garnish and serve.

SERVES 4

SOLE VERONIQUE

Illustrated on page 65

4 large lemon sole fillets
2 shallots, chopped
50 g/2 oz mushrooms, finely chopped
2 parsley sprigs · 1 bay leaf
salt and pepper
125 ml/4 fl oz dry white wine
25 g/1 oz butter
30 ml/2 tbsp plain flour
125 ml/4 fl oz milk
100 g/4 oz small seedless white grapes,
    halved
juice of ½ lemon
30 ml/2 tbsp single cream

GARNISH
Fleurons (see Mrs Beeton's Tip, page 216)
chopped parsley

Set the oven at 190°C/375°F/gas 5. Arrange the fillets in a shallow ovenproof dish. Sprinkle the shallots, mushrooms, herbs and seasoning over. Pour in the wine, with 125 ml/4 fl oz water. Cover the dish and bake for 15 minutes.

Using a slotted spoon and a fish slice, carefully transfer the fish to a warmed serving dish and keep hot. Tip the cooking liquid into a saucepan and boil until reduced to about 125 ml/4 fl oz.

Meanwhile melt the butter in a clean pan and stir in the flour. Cook for 1 minute, stirring, then gradually add the reduced cooking liquid with the milk, stirring constantly until boiling. Set aside a few grapes and stir the rest into the sauce.

Remove the sauce from the heat and stir in the lemon juice and cream. Pour over the fish, garnish with the reserved grapes, fleurons, and parsley.

SERVES 4

*P*LAICE STUFFED WITH PRAWNS

fat for greasing
8 (75 g/3 oz) plaice fillets, skinned
100 ml/3½ fl oz white wine
250 ml/8 fl oz Basic Fish Stock (page 15)
25 g/1 oz butter
100 g/4 oz button mushrooms, halved if
    large
25 g/1 oz plain flour
juice of 1 lemon
salt and pepper
100 ml/3½ fl oz double cream
puff pastry fleurons (see Mrs Beetons's
    Tip, page 216)
chopped parsley

STUFFING
    50 g/2 oz fresh white breadcrumbs
    50 g/2 oz butter, softened
    50 g/2 oz peeled cooked prawns, chopped

Grease a shallow ovenproof baking dish and a piece of foil large enough to cover it. Set the oven at 190°C/375°F/gas 5. Make the stuffing by mixing all the ingredients together in a bowl.

Spread the stuffing over the plaice and roll up. Place the plaice rolls in the prepared dish and pour the wine and fish stock over. Cover loosely with the foil and bake for 20 minutes. Using a slotted spoon, transfer the fish to a warmed serving dish. Keep hot. Tip the cooking liquid into a jug.

Meanwhile melt the butter in a saucepan. Add the mushrooms and fry gently for 3-4 minutes. Stir in the flour and cook for 1 minute. Gradually add the cooking liquid, stirring constantly until the mixture boils and thickens. Lower the heat and stir in the lemon juice, with salt and pepper to taste.

Remove the pan from the heat, cool slightly, then stir in the cream. Pour the sauce over the fish, garnish with the pastry fleurons and sprinkle with chopped parsley. Serve at once.

SERVES 4

*P*LAICE PORTUGAISE

fat for greasing
25 g/1 oz butter
2 shallots, sliced
4 tomatoes, peeled, seeded and chopped
100 g/4 oz mushrooms, halved if large
8 (75 g/3 oz) plaice fillets
100 ml/3½ fl oz dry white wine
salt and pepper

Grease a shallow ovenproof baking dish and a piece of foil large enough to cover it. Set the oven at 190°C/375°F/gas 5.

Melt the butter in a frying pan, add the shallots and fry for 2-3 minutes until slightly softened. Stir in the tomatoes and mushrooms and fry for 3-4 minutes. Spread the mixture in the prepared dish.

Fold each fillet into 3, skin side inwards, and arrange on the tomato mixture. Pour the wine over the fish, sprinkle with salt and pepper to taste and cover loosely with the foil. Bake for 25 minutes. Spoon the sauce mixture over the fish and serve at once.

SERVES 4

> **MRS BEETON'S TIP** If you grow fresh herbs, add a few chopped leaves of marjoram, basil or oregano to the tomato mixture for extra flavour.

SOLE DIEPPOISE

In this classic dish, the sole is poached in white wine with mussels and shrimps.

fat for greasing
1 (800 g/1¾ lb) sole, cleaned and trimmed
1 small onion, thinly sliced
1 bouquet garni
150 ml/¼ pint dry white wine
12 mussels, scrubbed and bearded
15 ml/1 tbsp white wine vinegar
12 peeled cooked prawns or shrimps
15 ml/1 tbsp butter
15 ml/1 tbsp plain flour
1 egg yolk
90 ml/6 tbsp single cream
salt and pepper
pinch of grated nutmeg
juice of ½ lemon
pinch of cayenne pepper or paprika

Grease a shallow ovenproof baking dish and a piece of foil large enough to cover it. Set the oven at 190°C/375°F/gas 5.

Skin and fillet the sole. Put the bones, skin and head in a saucepan with the onion, bouquet garni and white wine. Put the mussels into the pan, bring to the boil, lower the heat and simmer for 6 minutes.

Using a slotted spoon, remove the mussels. Discard any that remain shut. Shell the mussels and set them aside. Add 150 ml/¼ pint water to the pan and stir in the vinegar. Reduce the liquid by boiling gently for 15 minutes, uncovered, then strain into a jug.

Fold each fillet in half and place in a single layer in the prepared dish. Pour in the reserved cooking liquid and arrange the shelled mussels and prawns or shrimps around the fish. Cover with the foil and bake for 20 minutes.

Drain the stock from the fish into a saucepan and heat to simmering point. Keep the fish and shellfish hot. In a small bowl, cream the butter to a paste with the flour.

Add the butter and flour paste to the fish stock, a little at a time, whisking after each addition. Raise the heat and bring the sauce to the boil, whisking constantly. Boil for 10 minutes. Lower the heat.

Mix the egg yolk and cream in a bowl and stir in about 100 ml/3½ fl oz of the thickened sauce. Add the contents of the bowl to the sauce and bring the mixture to just below boiling point. Add salt, pepper and nutmeg and pour the sauce evenly over the fish and shellfish. Sprinkle with the lemon juice and dust with the cayenne or paprika. Serve at once.

SERVES 4

FILLETS OF SOLE BONNE FEMME

fat for greasing
16 lemon sole fillets
275 g/10 oz mushrooms
50 g/2 oz butter
12 black peppercorns
2-3 parsley stalks
25 g/1 oz plain flour
300 ml/½ pint Basic Fish Stock (page 15)
salt and pepper
lemon juice
2 shallots, sliced
15 ml/1 tbsp chopped parsley
250 ml/8 fl oz dry white wine

Grease a shallow ovenproof baking dish and a piece of foil large enough to cover it. Arrange the sole fillets on the base. Set the oven at 180°C/350°F/gas 4. Cut off the mushroom stems and set them aside. Slice the mushroom caps and scatter them over the fish.

Melt 25 g/1 oz of the butter in a saucepan, add the mushroom stems, peppercorns and parsley stalks. Cook over gentle heat for 10 minutes. Add the flour and cook over low heat for 2-3 minutes, without allowing the mixture to colour. Gradually add the stock and simmer, stirring, for 3-4 minutes. Rub the sauce through a sieve into a clean saucepan. Add salt, pepper and lemon juice to taste. Cover the surface with damp greaseproof paper and set aside.

Sprinkle the shallots and parsley over the fish, sprinkle with salt and pepper and pour in the wine. Cover with the foil and bake for 20 minutes.

Using a slotted spoon and fish slice, transfer the fish to a warmed serving dish and keep hot. Strain the cooking liquid into a saucepan. Boil it rapidly until reduced by half.

Meanwhile return the sauce to a gentle heat and bring to simmering point. Stir the sauce into the reduced cooking liquid with the remaining butter. As soon as the butter has melted, pour the sauce over the fish. Place under a hot grill until lightly browned. Serve at once.

SERVES 8

SOLE WITH PRAWNS

100 g/4 oz peeled cooked prawns, finely
    chopped
50 g/2 oz fresh white breadcrumbs
1 egg
salt and pepper
12 Dover sole or lemon sole fillets
125 ml/4 fl oz dry white wine
125 ml/4 fl oz Basic Fish Stock (page 15)
50 g/2 oz butter
50 g/2 oz plain flour
250 ml/8 fl oz milk
salt and pepper

GARNISH
  whole cooked prawns
  parsley sprigs
  lemon slices or wedges

Set the oven at 190°C/375°F/gas 5. Mis the prawns, breadcrumbs and egg in a bowl, with salt and pepper to taste. Spread the mixture over each fillet and roll up. Pour over the wine and stock and bake for 20 minutes.

Using a slotted spoon, transfer the stuffed fish rolls to a warmed serving dish and keep hot. Tip the cooking juices into a jug.

Melt the butter in a saucepan. Stir in the flour and cook over low heat for 2-3 minutes, without allowing the mixture to colour. Gradually add the reserved cooking juices and the milk, stirring constantly until the sauce boils and thickens. Add salt and pepper to taste.

Pour the sauce over the fish and garnish before serving.

SERVES 6

TURBOT MARENGO

fat for greasing
4 (1 cm/½ inch thick) turbot steaks
350 ml/12 fl oz Basic Fish Stock (page 15)
50 g/2 oz butter
1 onion, sliced
1 carrot, sliced
1 turnip, sliced
5 ml/1 tsp dried mixed herbs
25 g/1 oz plain flour
1 (70 g/2½ oz) can tomato purée
salt and pepper

GARNISH
stuffed green olives
chopped parsley
lemon slices

Grease a shallow ovenproof baking dish. Set the oven at 180°C/350°F/gas 4. Arrange the fish in the dish, add 75 ml/5 tbsp of the fish stock and bake for 20 minutes.

Meanwhile melt 25 g/1 oz of the butter in a frying pan. Add the onion, carrot and turnip and fry gently for 5 minutes until soft. Sprinkle over the herbs, add the remaining stock and cover the pan. Simmer for 20 minutes. Strain the stock into a jug, discarding the solids in the strainer.

Melt the remaining butter in a saucepan, add the flour and cook for 1 minute. Gradually add the reserved cooking liquid, stirring constantly, then stir in the tomato purée and seasoning. Simmer the sauce, stirring occasionally, for 10 minutes.

When the fish is cooked, transfer it to warmed serving dish. Pour over the sauce, garnish with olives, parsley and lemon slices and serve at once.

SERVES 4

TURBOT DUGLERE

fat for greasing
1 (1.5 kg/3¼ lb) turbot, cleaned and trimmed
40 g/1½ oz butter
30 ml/2 tbsp oil
1 small onion, finely chopped
225 g/8 oz tomatoes, peeled and chopped
30 ml/2 tbsp white wine vinegar
200 ml/7 fl oz dry white wine
salt and pepper
1 bouquet garni
10 ml/2 tsp plain flour

Skin and fillet the turbot, reserving the trimmings in a saucepan. Grease a shallow ovenproof baking dish. Set the oven at 190°C/375°F/gas 5.

Melt 25 g/1 oz of the butter in the oil in a frying pan. Add the onion and fry for 2-3 minutes until soft but not coloured. Add the chopped tomatoes, vinegar and white wine. Simmer for 10 minutes; set aside.

Lay the fish fillets in the prepared dish. Sprinkle with salt and pepper and pour over the tomato mixture. Cover the dish with a lid or foil and bake for 20 minutes.

Meanwhile add 300 ml/½ pint water and the bouquet garni to the fish trimmings. Bring to the boil, lower the heat and simmer for 15 minutes. Remove from the heat. Strain the liquid into a small saucepan. In a small bowl, cream the remaining butter to a paste with the flour.

Add the butter and flour paste to the fish stock, a little at a time, whisking after each addition. Return to the heat and bring the sauce to the boil, whisking constantly until the sauce thickens. Add salt and pepper to taste and pour the sauce over the fish.

SERVES 4

APRICOT-STUFFED TROUT

The apricots for the stuffing need to be soaked overnight, so start preparation the day before cooking – or use ready-to-eat fruit.

fat for greasing
6 trout, cleaned and trimmed
2 onions, finely chopped
salt and pepper
300 ml/½ pint dry white wine
75 g/3 oz butter
25 g/1 oz plain flour
250 ml/8 fl oz Basic Fish Stock (page 15)
2 egg yolks
juice of ½ lemon
chopped parsley to garnish

STUFFING
75 g/3 oz dried apricots
75 g/3 oz fresh white breadcrumbs
pinch of dried thyme
pinch of ground mace
pinch of grated nutmeg
1 celery stick, finely chopped
25 g/1 oz butter

Make the stuffing. Soak the apricots overnight in a small bowl with water to cover. Next day, drain the fruit, reserving the soaking liquid, and chop finely. Mix the apricots in a bowl with the breadcrumbs, salt, pepper, thyme, spices and celery. Melt the butter in a small saucepan and stir it into the mixture. Moisten further with a little of the reserved soaking liquid.

Grease a shallow ovenproof baking dish. Set the oven at 180°C/350°F/gas 4. Fill the trout with the apricot stuffing. Spread out the onions on the base of the prepared dish, arrange the trout on top and sprinkle with plenty of salt and pepper. Pour 250 ml/ 8 fl oz of the wine into the dish, dot the fish with 25 g/1 oz of the butter, cover and oven-poach for 25 minutes.

Meanwhile, melt 25 g/1 oz of the remaining butter in a saucepan. Stir in the flour and cook over low heat for 2-3 minutes, without allowing the mixture to colour. Gradually add the fish stock, stirring constantly until the sauce boils and thickens. Add salt and pepper to taste. Lower the heat, add the remaining wine and simmer for 10 minutes.

Bring the sauce to just below boiling point and whisk in the remaining butter, a little at a time. Remove the pan from the heat. Blend the egg yolks and lemon juice in a small bowl, add a little of the hot sauce and mix well. Add the contents of the bowl to the sauce and mix well. Cover with damp greaseproof paper and set aside.

Using a slotted spoon and fish slice, carefully transfer the fish to a wooden board. Strain the cooking liquid into a saucepan. Skin the trout, then arrange them on a warmed flameproof serving dish and keep hot.

Boil the cooking liquid until it is reduced by a quarter, then add it to the white wine sauce. Place over moderate heat and warm through, stirring the sauce until it thickens. Do not allow it to boil. Pour the hot sauce over the fish. Place under a moderate grill for 4-5 minutes to brown lightly. Garnish with chopped parsley and serve at once.

SERVES 6

> **MRS BEETON'S TIP** If you use ready-to-eat dried apricots, moisten the stuffing with a little chicken stock.

TROUT HOLLANDAISE

6 trout, cleaned, heads left on
1 litre/1¾ pints Court Bouillon (page 15)
chopped parsley to garnish
250 ml/8 fl oz Hollandaise Sauce (page
    261), to serve

Put the trout in a saucepan large enough to hold them in a single layer. Add the court bouillon, bring to simmering point and poach the fish gently for 15 minutes.

Carefully remove the fish from the stock and arrange on a heated serving dish. Garnish with parsley and serve at once, with the sauce.

SERVES 6

POACHED TROUT WITH PRAWN SAUCE

125 ml/4 fl oz red wine
1 clove
1 bay leaf
4 trout, cleaned, heads left on
salt and pepper
25 g/1 oz butter
25 g/1 oz plain flour
125 ml/4 fl oz milk
100 g/4 oz peeled cooked prawns
45 ml/3 tbsp double cream

GARNISH
    parsley sprigs
    lemon wedges

Set the oven at 160°C/325°F/gas 3. Combine the red wine, clove and bay leaf in a shallow ovenproof dish large enough to hold all the trout in a single layer. Add the fish, with salt and pepper to taste. Cover tightly with foil to keep in all the moisture and place in the oven for 15-20 minutes, or until cooked. The fish poach in the wine and moisture in the gentle oven heat.

Using a slotted spoon and a fish slice, carefully transfer the fish one at a time to a platter or board. Remove the skin, then put the fish on a warmed serving dish, cover and keep hot. Strain the cooking liquid.

Melt the butter in a clean saucepan, add the flour and cook for 1 minute, stirring constantly. Gradually add the cooking liquid, stirring all the time until the mixture begins to thicken, then gradually add the milk, still stirring and bring to the boil. Lower the heat and simmer for 2-3 minutes, stirring occasionally.

Remove the sauce from the heat and stir in the prawns and cream. Pour the hot sauce over the fish, garnish and serve.

SERVES 4

MICROWAVE TIP The trout may be cooked in the microwave. Arrange them in alternate directions in a shallow dish. Pour over the wine and add the clove and bay leaf. Cover loosely and cook on High for 12 minutes, turning once. Strain off the cooking liquid as suggested above. Make the sauce in a large bowl by whisking the cooking liquid into the flour, then adding the milk and finally the butter. Cook on High for 10 minutes, whisking twice during cooking. Whisk again and stir in the prawns and cream. Reheat the fish for 1 minute on High if necessary, pour over the sauce, garnish and serve.

MACKEREL WITH GOOSEBERRY SAUCE

Gooseberry sauce is such a classic accompaniment to mackerel that in France the fruit is known as groseille à maquereau.

50 g/2 oz plain flour
salt and pepper
8 mackerel fillets
50 g/2 oz butter
juice of 1 lemon
45 ml/3 tbsp chopped parsley

SAUCE
450 g/1 lb gooseberries, topped and tailed
45 ml/3 tbsp dry still cider
25 g/1 oz butter
15 ml/1 tbsp caster sugar

Make the sauce by combining the gooseberries, cider and butter in a small pan. Bring the liquid to simmering point and poach the fruit, stirring occasionally, until soft. Purée the mixture by passing it through a sieve set over a small saucepan. Stir in the sugar.

Spread the flour in a shallow bowl, season with salt and pepper, and coat the fish lightly all over.

Melt the butter in a large frying pan, add the fish and fry gently for 5-7 minutes or until browned, turning once. Using a slotted spoon and a fish slice, transfer the fish to a warmed serving dish and keep hot.

Heat the gooseberry sauce. Continue to heat the butter in the frying pan until it becomes light brown. Stir in the lemon juice and parsley and pour over the fish. Pour the gooseberry sauce into a jug or sauceboat and serve at once, with the fish.

SERVES 4

SABO-NO-TERIYAKI

This dish can also be made with herring, salmon or bream.

150 ml/¼ pint soy sauce
45 ml/3 tbsp mirin (see Mrs Beeton's Tip)
pinch of chilli powder
15 ml/1 tbsp grated fresh root ginger
2 garlic cloves, crushed
4 mackerel fillets

Mix the soy sauce, mirin, chilli powder, ginger and garlic in a bowl. Stir well. Arrange the mackerel fillets in a shallow dish large enough to hold them all in a single layer. Pour the soy sauce mixture over, cover the dish and marinate for 2 hours.

Drain the fish, reserving the marinade. Cook under a hot grill for 5-10 minutes brushing the fish several times with the reserved marinade during cooking. Serve at once.

SERVES 4

> 🥄 **MRS BEETON'S TIP** If you cannot obtain mirin, which is a sweet Japanese rice wine, use a mixture of 45 ml/3 tbsp dry sherry and 10 ml/2 tsp sugar.

STUFFED HERRINGS

butter for greasing
4 large herrings

STUFFING
   50 g/2 oz butter
   225 g/8 oz onions, finely chopped
   225 g/8 oz cooking apples
   15 ml/1 tbsp cider or white wine vinegar
   salt and pepper

Grease a flat ovenproof dish and a piece of foil large enough to cover it. Set the oven at 190°C/375°F/gas 5. Scale the herrings, cut off the heads and remove the bones without breaking the skin.

Make the stuffing. Melt the butter in a large frying pan, add the onions and fry gently for about 10 minutes until soft. Peel, core and grate the apples and add them to the pan. Mix well, then add the vinegar, with salt and pepper to taste.

Divide the stuffing between the herrings, filling the cavities and then reshaping the fish. Lay them on the prepared dish, cover loosely with the foil and bake for 25 minutes. Serve at once.

SERVES 4

☀ **MICROWAVE TIP** Arrange the stuffed herrings in alternate directions in a suitable dish. Cover with microwave film and cook on High for 7-8 minutes.

HERRINGS STUFFED WITH SHRIMPS

4 herrings
salt and pepper
1 egg, beaten
toasted breadcrumbs
25 g/1 oz butter

STUFFING
   15 ml/1 tbsp fresh white breadcrumbs
   15 ml/1 tbsp milk
   50 g/2 oz peeled cooked shrimps, chopped
   cayenne pepper
   few drops of anchovy essence

Set the oven at 190°C/375°C/gas 5. Scale the herrings, cut off the heads and remove the bones without breaking the skin. Sprinkle with plenty of salt and pepper.

Make the stuffing by combining all the ingredients in a small bowl. Mix well. Spread the filling on the flesh side of the fillets and roll up tightly. Fasten each with a small skewer.

Pack the herrings tightly in an ovenproof dish. Brush with the egg, sprinkle with the toasted breadcrumbs, dot with the butter and bake for 30-35 minutes. Serve at once.

SERVES 4

BAKED HERRINGS

butter for greasing
4 herrings, cleaned and scaled
salt and pepper
25 g/1 oz butter
2 onions, finely sliced
450 g/1 lb tomatoes, peeled and sliced
30 ml/2 tbsp malt vinegar
parsley to garnish

Grease an ovenproof dish. Set the oven at 190°C/375°F/gas 5. Make 3 cuts on either side of each herring and season.

Melt half the butter in a frying pan. Add the onions and fry gently for 5 minutes. Place the tomato slices on the base of the prepared dish. Add the onions and sprinkle with salt and pepper, and the vinegar.

Arrange the fish on top and dot with the remaining butter. Cover and bake for 45 minutes. Garnish with parsley.

SERVES 4

RED MULLET BAKED IN FOIL

6 red mullet, cleaned and trimmed
50 g/2 oz butter
salt and pepper
juice of ½ lemon

GARNISH
lemon wedges • parsley sprigs

Set the oven at 190°C/375°F/gas 5. Lay each mullet on a piece of foil large enough to enclose it completely. Dot with butter, sprinkle with salt and pepper and add a little lemon juice. Fasten the packages by folding the edges of the foil firmly together.

Put the fish packages on a baking sheet and bake for 20-30 minutes. Remove from the foil, taking care to save the cooking juices. Transfer the fish to a warmed platter, pour over the cooking juices, garnish and serve.

SERVES 6

RED MULLET WITH MUSHROOMS

25 g/1 oz butter
6 small red mullet, cleaned and trimmed

STUFFING
25 g/1 oz butter
1 large onion, chopped
225 g/8 oz mushrooms, finely chopped
50 g/2 oz fresh white breadcrumbs
25 g/1 oz parsley, chopped
salt and pepper

GARNISH
baby tomatoes • watercress sprigs

Use the butter to grease an ovenproof baking dish large enough to hold all the fish in a single layer. Set the oven at 190°C/375°F/gas 5.

Make the stuffing. Melt the butter in a small saucepan and fry the onion for 3-4 minutes or until soft. Transfer to a bowl and add the chopped mushrooms, breadcrumbs and parsley, with salt and pepper to taste. Stuff the fish with this mixture.

Place the stuffed fish in the prepared baking dish, cover and bake for 30 minutes. Garnish with baby tomatoes and watercress sprigs and serve at once.

SERVES 6

PRAWN CURRY

Illustrated on page 67

15 ml/1 tbsp ground coriander
2.5 ml/½ tsp ground cumin
2.5 ml/½ tsp chilli powder
2.5 ml/½ tsp turmeric
1 garlic clove, crushed
250 ml/8 fl oz Basic Fish Stock (page 15)
30 ml/2 tbsp oil
1 large onion, finely chopped
45 ml/3 tbsp tomato purée
2 tomatoes, peeled, seeded and chopped
450 g/1 lb peeled cooked prawns
juice of ½ lemon
10 ml/2 tsp coconut cream (optional)
coriander sprigs to garnish

Mix all the spices in a small bowl. Add the garlic and mix to a paste with a little of the stock. Set aside.

Heat the oil in a frying pan, add the onion and fry for 4-5 minutes until golden brown. Add the tomato purée and spice mixture, then cook for 1-2 minutes. Stir in the remaining stock and tomatoes, cover the pan and simmer gently for 20 minutes.

Add the prawns and lemon juice to the pan, with the coconut cream, if used. Stir until the coconut cream dissolves, then simmer for 5 minutes more. Garnish with coriander sprigs and serve with basmati rice.

SERVES 4

SWEET AND SOUR PRAWNS

225 g/8 oz peeled cooked prawns
15 ml/1 tbsp medium-dry sherry
salt and pepper
30 ml/2 tbsp oil
2 onions, sliced in rings
2 green peppers, seeded and sliced in rings
125 ml/4 fl oz chicken or vegetable stock
1 (227 g/8 oz) can pineapple cubes, drained
15 ml/1 tbsp cornflour
30 ml/2 tbsp soy sauce
125 ml/4 fl oz white wine vinegar
75 g/3 oz sugar
whole cooked prawns to garnish

Spread out the prawns on a large shallow dish. Sprinkle with the sherry, salt and pepper, cover and set aside to marinate for 30 minutes.

Towards the end of the marinating time, heat the oil in a frying pan or wok. Add the onions and peppers and fry gently for 5-7 minutes. Add the stock and pineapple cubes. Cover and cook for 3-5 minutes.

In a small bowl, blend the cornflour, soy sauce, vinegar and sugar together. Stir the mixture into the pan or wok and bring to the boil, stirring, then simmer for 2 minutes until thickened. Lower the heat, add the prawns with the marinating liquid and heat for 1 minute.

Serve hot on a bed of rice, if liked. Garnish with the whole cooked prawns, in their shells.

SERVES 4

MOULES MARINIERE

Illustrated on page 69

1.6 kg/3½ lb mussels
1 onion, sliced
2 garlic cloves, cut in slivers
1 carrot, sliced
1 celery stick, sliced
1 bouquet garni
125 ml/4 fl oz white wine
25 g/1 oz butter
25 g/1 oz plain flour
salt and pepper
chopped parsley to garnish

Wash, scrape and beard the mussels following the instructions on page 11. Put them in a large saucepan. Tuck the sliced vegetables among the mussels and add the bouquet garni.

Pour over 125 ml/4 fl oz water and the wine. Place over moderate heat and bring to the boil. As soon as the liquid begins to boil, shake the pan 2 or 3 times, cover it tightly and cook for about 5 minutes until the mussels have opened. Discard any that remain shut. With a slotted spoon transfer the mussels to a deep dish and keep hot.

Strain the cooking liquid through muslin or a very fine sieve into a smaller saucepan. In a cup, cream the butter with the flour.

Place the small saucepan over moderate heat and add the butter mixture in small pieces, whisking thoroughly. Bring to the boil, whisking, then add salt and pepper.

Pour the thickened cooking liquid over the mussels, sprinkle with chopped parsley and serve with plenty of chunky bread.

SERVES 4 TO 6

MUSSELS IN WHITE SAUCE

1.6 kg/3½ lb mussels
50 g/2 oz butter
25 g/1 oz plain flour
1 egg yolk
30 ml/2 tbsp double cream
lemon juice
chopped parsley to garnish

Wash, scrape and beard the mussels following the instructions on page 11. Put them in a large saucepan with 250 ml/8 fl oz water. Place over moderate heat and bring to the boil. As soon as the liquid boils, shake the pan 2 or 3 times, cover it tightly and cook for about 5 minutes until the mussels have opened. Discard any that remain shut. Remove the mussels with a slotted spoon, shell them and keep them hot.

Strain the cooking liquid through muslin or a very fine sieve into a measuring jug. Reserve 250 ml/8 fl oz of the liquid.

Melt half the butter in a saucepan, add the flour and cook for 1 minute over low heat, stirring constantly. Do not allow the flour to colour. Remove from the heat and gradually add the reserved cooking liquid, whisking constantly.

Over moderate heat, bring the sauce to the boil. Lower the heat and simmer for 5 minutes. Beat the egg yolk and cream together in a small bowl, then add to the sauce with lemon juice to taste. Stir in the remaining butter with the reserved shelled mussels. Heat through but do not allow to boil. Serve immediately, garnished with chopped parsley.

SERVES 2 TO 3

QUEENS OF THE SEA

Queens are small scallops. They have good texture and flavour and are well worth looking for. They are usually sold shelled, as small round nuggets of white flesh.

75 g/3 oz butter
30 ml/2 tbsp dry white wine
16 queen scallops
30 ml/2 tbsp plain flour
pinch of paprika
250 ml/8 fl oz milk
salt and pepper
4 hard-boiled eggs
1 egg yolk
15 ml/1 tbsp double cream

Melt half the butter in a large frying pan. Add the wine and scallops and cook very gently for 3 minutes or until just cooked. Do not boil. Set the pan aside.

Melt the remaining butter in a saucepan, add the flour and paprika and cook for 1 minute, stirring constantly. Gradually add the milk, stirring until the sauce boils and thickens. Simmer, still stirring, for 2 minutes. Add salt and pepper.

Spoon 60 ml/4 tbsp of the sauce into a shallow dish. Add the remaining sauce to the scallop mixture and heat gently, shaking the pan to blend the ingredients. Cut each of the eggs into 8 segments and arrange them on the sauce in the dish.

Beat the egg yolk and cream in a small bowl. Add to the scallops in sauce and heat gently, stirring. Do not allow the sauce to boil. As soon as the sauce has heated through, pour it over the hard-boiled eggs and place under a hot grill to brown slightly. Serve at once.

SERVES 4

COQUILLES ST JACQUES MORNAY

Great care must be taken not to overcook the scallops. Their delectable flavour and texture is easily spoiled by high heat.

fat for greasing
450 g/1 lb potatoes, halved
salt and pepper
50 g/2 oz butter
90 ml/6 tbsp single cream
8-12 large scallops, shelled, with corals
1 small onion, sliced
1 bay leaf
45 ml/3 tbsp dry white wine
juice of ½ lemon
25 g/1 oz plain flour
125 ml/4 fl oz milk
45 ml/3 tbsp dry white breadcrumbs
60 ml/4 tbsp grated Parmesan cheese
watercress sprigs to garnish

Cook the potatoes in a saucepan of salted boiling water for about 30 minutes or until tender. Drain thoroughly and mash with a potato masher, or beat with a hand-held electric whisk until smooth. Beat in 25 g/1 oz of the butter and 15 ml/1 tbsp of the cream to make a creamy piping consistency.

Grease 4 scallop shells or shallow individual ovenproof dishes. Spoon the creamed potato into a piping bag fitted with a large star nozzle and pipe a border of mashed potato around the edge of each shell. Set the oven at 200°C/400°F/gas 6.

Combine the scallops, onion, bay leaf, wine and lemon juice in a saucepan. Add 75 ml/5 tbsp water. Bring to simmering point and poach the scallops gently for 5 minutes. Using a slotted spoon remove the scallops and cut into slices. Strain the cooking liquid into a jug.

Melt the remaining butter in a saucepan, add the flour and cook for 1 minute, stirring constantly. Gradually add the reserved cooking liquid, stirring all the time, until the sauce starts to thicken. Add salt and pepper to taste and stir in the milk. Bring to the boil, stirring, then lower the heat and simmer for 2-3 minutes. Remove from the heat and stir in the remaining cream.

Divide the sliced scallops between the prepared scallop shells or dishes. Coat with the sauce and sprinkle lightly with the breadcrumbs and Parmesan.

Stand the scallop shells or dishes on a large baking sheet and bake for 10 minutes until the breadcrumbs are crisp and the potatoes browned. Garnish with the watercress sprigs and serve at once.

SERVES 4

STUFFED SQUID

8 squid, cleaned and trimmed
25 g/1 oz butter
1 small onion, finely chopped
1 garlic clove, crushed
grated rind and juice of ½ lemon
50 g/2 oz mushrooms, diced
50 g/2 oz fresh white breadcrumbs
30 ml/2 tbsp chopped parsley
5 ml/1 tsp dried marjoram
salt and pepper
a little oil for brushing
Fresh Tomato Sauce (page 352)
lemon wedges to garnish

Rinse the squid well, drain and dry on absorbent kitchen paper. Set aside. Melt the butter in a frying pan, add the onion and garlic and cook, stirring occasionally, until the onion is soft but not browned.

Add the grated lemon rind and mushrooms to the pan and continue to cook until the mushrooms have reduced and most of the liquid has evaporated – this takes some time but is important to avoid making the stuffing too moist.

Remove the pan from the heat and stir in the breadcrumbs and herbs, with salt and pepper to taste. Add lemon juice to taste but avoid making the stuffing too moist.

Use a teaspoon to fill the squid pouches with stuffing – they should not be too full as the breadcrumb mixture expands on heating. Thread a small meat skewer through the open end of each squid to keep the stuffing enclosed, then pass the skewer through the pointed end of the body.

Brush the squid with oil and grill under moderate heat, turning occasionally, until they are golden brown all over. This will take about 15 minutes. Do not let the squid cook too quickly or the stuffing will not be cooked.

Heat the tomato sauce if necessary, then pour it into a serving dish. Arrange the squid in it and add lemon wedges for garnish. Any remaining lemon juice may be drizzled over the squid. Offer a mill of black pepper with the squid.

SERVES 4

> **MRS BEETON'S TIP** To clean squid, if the tentacles are to be used, cut them off first and set them aside. Cut off and discard the beak from the centre of the tentacles. Pull the head and the attached parts out of the sac: discard the head parts. Remove the transparent 'pen' from inside the body. Rub off the mottled skin under running water, at the same time rubbing off the small flaps on either side of the body, leaving the body clean and white.

CREAMED SALMON IN PASTRY

125 ml/4 fl oz white wine
1 bouquet garni
1 onion, sliced
salt and pepper
450 g/1 lb salmon pieces or steaks
50 g/2 oz butter
25 g/1 oz plain flour
150 g/5 oz mushrooms, sliced
75 ml/5 tbsp double cream
450 g/1 lb puff pastry, thawed if frozen
plain flour for rolling out
beaten egg to glaze

GARNISH
lemon wedges
dill sprigs

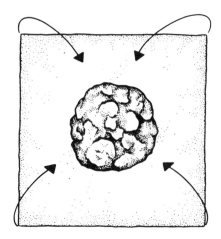

Put the wine in a saucepan with 125 ml/ 4 fl oz water. Add the bouquet garni and onion slices, with salt and pepper to taste. Bring to the boil, lower the heat and simmer for 5 minutes. Strain into a clean pan, add the salmon and poach gently for 10-15 minutes or until cooked. Using a slotted spoon, transfer the fish to a wooden board. Remove the skin and any bones and flake the flesh. Reserve the cooking liquid.

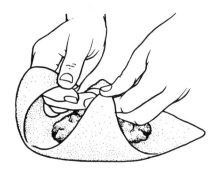

Melt half the butter in a saucepan. Stir in the flour and cook over low heat for 2-3 minutes, without allowing the mixture to colour. Gradually add the reserved cooking liquid, stirring constantly until the sauce boils and thickens. Lower the heat and simmer for 3-4 minutes. Stir in the flaked salmon and remove from the heat.

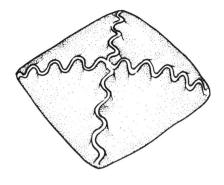

Melt the remaining butter in a frying pan. Add the mushrooms and fry for 3-4 minutes. Using a slotted spoon, add the mushrooms to the salmon mixture. Stir in the cream, cover the surface of the mixture with damp greaseproof paper and set aside.

Set the oven at 200°C/400°F/gas 6. Roll out the pastry 3 mm/⅛ inch thick on a floured surface. Cut to a 25 cm/10 inch square, reserving the pastry trimmings. Place the salmon mixture in the middle and brush the edges of the pastry with beaten egg. Lift the corners of the pastry to the middle, enclosing the filling. Seal with beaten egg. Make leaf shapes from the trimmings and use to hide the seal on the top of the pastry envelope. Glaze with egg.

Place the pastry envelope on a baking sheet and bake for 15 minutes. Lower the temperature to 190°C/375°F/gas 5 and bake for 20 minutes more. Serve hot, garnished with lemon wedges and dill.

SERVES 4 TO 6

SALTBURN FISH PIE

Although haddock is traditionally used for this dish, cod or any other firm white fish is equally suitable.

butter for greasing
450 g/1 lb haddock fillet
60 ml/4 tbsp grated onion
salt and pepper
30 ml/2 tbsp lemon juice
2 gammon steaks, trimmed and cut into
    7.5 cm/3 inch squares
3 hard-boiled eggs, sliced
30 ml/2 tbsp chopped parsley

SHORT CRUST PASTRY
150 g/5 oz plain flour
1.25 ml/¼ tsp salt
65 g/2½ oz margarine
plain flour for rolling out

Grease a 750 ml/1¼ pint pie dish. Set the oven at 200°C/400°F/gas 6. Make the pastry. Sift the flour and salt into a bowl, then rub in the margarine until the mixture resembles fine breadcrumbs. Add enough cold water to make a stiff dough. Press the dough together with your fingertips, wrap in a polythene bag and chill until required.

Put the haddock in a large frying pan. Sprinkle the onion over the top, with salt and pepper to taste, and add the lemon juice. Pour enough water into the pan to almost cover the fish. Heat the liquid to simmering point and simmer for 8-15 minutes or until the fish is just tender. Using a fish slice and slotted spoon, transfer the fish to a wooden board. Remove any fins, bones or skin and flake the fish. Reserve the cooking liquid.

Put a layer of fish into the prepared pie dish. Cover with a layer of gammon, then a layer of sliced egg. Sprinkle with salt and parsley. Continue layering until all the ingredients have been used. Moisten with a little of the reserved cooking liquid.

Roll out the pastry on a lightly floured surface and use to make a crust for the pie. Dampen the edges of the dish, lay the pastry crust on the dish and press down firmly to seal. Bake for 25-30 minutes. Serve hot.

SERVES 4

> **MRS BEETON'S TIP** When the pastry has been rolled to a round large enough to cover the pie, place the rolling pin in the middle of the pastry, lop half the pastry over it, then use the rolling pin to lift the pastry into position.

POULTRY

Poultry is ideal for all occasions, for light everyday dishes or
celebration meals; from popular chicken and festive turkey
to the traditional Christmas goose, duck and guineafowl. The
recipes in this chapter range from homely favourites to
exotic new ideas.

Poultry is the term used for domestic birds
specially bred for food, as opposed to birds
caught in the wild, which are game. Except
at small country markets, when birds may
be 'rough-plucked', all poultry is sold ready
for cooking; plucked and drawn. If you do
have to carry out any such basic preparation, follow the information given for game
birds. Unlike game, poultry should be
plucked and drawn when freshly killed and
the birds are not hung for lengthy periods.

CHICKEN

Chicken is lean, tender and easy to digest.
The majority of the fat content is found in or
under the skin, so trimming and skinning
renders chicken meat ideal for low-fat
meals. The vast majority of chickens are
roasting birds, under a year old; birds over
this age are referred to as boiling fowl but
these are no longer popular. Although they
taste good boiling fowl require 1½-2 hours'
boiling to tenderize the meat, after which
time they have to be sauced for pies or
similar recipes or used in soup.

Chickens are sold ready for cooking,
most often without their giblets. If the
giblets are included, they will be sealed in a
packet in the body cavity of the bird; this
will be clearly marked on the outside of the
packaging.

Corn Fed Chicken This has a distinct
yellow tinge when raw and the skin browns
to a golden colour when roasted. The meat
has a fine flavour, resulting from the high
proportion of corn in the birds' feed.

Poulet Noir A popular French breed of
black-feathered bird. Poulet noir has a mild
gamey flavour.

Poussins Young birds, 4-8 weeks old,
these are ideal for grilling, steaming or
speedy roasting. They are usually served as
individual portions, but larger birds (up to
675 g/1½ lb) may be split to provide two
servings.

Spring Chickens Small chickens, weighing 900 g-1.4 kg/2-3 lb, these are 8-12
weeks old.

Chicken Portions There is a good choice of
prepared portions, including skinned boneless breasts or thin fillets of breast meat,
chicken quarters, drumsticks, thighs and
wings.

TURKEY

Uncooked turkey portions, whole birds and
turkey products are available throughout
the year. Significantly larger than other
poultry, weighing 2.25-11.3 kg/5-25 lb,
turkey has a high meat yield for the carcass.

The white, tender, delicately flavoured breast meat is the prized portion. Leg meat is dark and tougher, also veined with sinews. Like chicken, whole birds are sold ready for cooking, with or without giblets. Larger birds are not as popular as they were when turkey was reserved as a Christmas speciality.

In addition to whole birds, whole breast fillets are sold boned and tied into neat joints. These are usually barded with a thin coating of fat, or rolled so that the skin forms a neat covering. Breast fillets and a variety of white-meat products are available. Drumsticks are also sold separately – these are useful for casseroling.

DUCKS AND DUCKLINGS

Although larger than chickens, ducks do not have a high yield of meat for their carcass size. They range in weight from 1.5 kg/3¼ lb to 2.5 kg/5½ lb and yield 2-4 servings. Duck has a higher fat content than either turkey or chicken. However, birds are now reared to have far less fat so this once off-putting characteristic of duck is no longer as relevant as at once was. It is, however, advisable to prick the skin on a whole bird all over before roasting to release the fat.

As well as whole birds, which are mainly sold frozen (usually with giblets), quarters, breast portions and legs are available.

GOOSE

Goose is probably the most expensive of the poultry birds. Available all year, most often to order, goose yields little meat and a large quantity of fat for its carcass size of 3-7 kg/ 6½-15¼ lb. The main area of meat is on the breast, where it is dark and flavoursome. The high fat content means that goose requires long roasting to render the fat; small birds are therefore not the best buy.

GUINEAFOWL

Although guineafowl is a domestic bird, originally from West Africa it does have a hint of game to its flavour. Available all year, the birds range from 675 g/1½ lb to 2 kg/4½ lb, depending on maturity. Sold ready for cooking, guineafowl should be treated in the same way as chicken.

FREEZING AND THAWING POULTRY

Poultry for freezing should be absolutely fresh. Never buy poultry and allow the use-by date to expire before freezing it; when buying from a butcher always check that the bird is suitably fresh for freezing, or that portions have not previously been frozen.

Never re-freeze poultry once it has been thawed.

Prepare birds as for cooking and pack them in heavy-quality airtight bags, labelled with the date and weight or number of portions. Breasts, drumsticks, fillets or other portions may be individually wrapped in freezer film before being packed in bags. Cubed meat or strips of meat should be loosely packed in sealed bags. The bags should then be spread out thinly on a baking sheet until the meat is hard. When hard the meat may be shaken down in the bag and any extra air extracted – this method creates a 'free-flow' pack, permitting some of the meat to be used as required and the rest replaced in the freezer without thawing. If available, use the fast freeze facility on your freezer to process the poultry as speedily as possible. Follow the freezer manufacturer's instructions.

Always allow sufficient time for thawing poultry in the refrigerator before cooking. It is also possible to thaw poultry in the microwave oven; follow the manufacturer's instructions. Both chicken and turkey *must* be cooked through before serving; if the whole bird or portions are not thoroughly thawed before cooking, thick areas of meat may not cook through. Due to its size, turkey is the most difficult poultry to thaw.

Always unwrap poultry and place it in a covered deep dish in the refrigerator, preferably on a low shelf, ensuring that it will not drip on any other food. Occasionally, drain off the liquid which seeps from the poultry as it thaws. Allow several hours or up to 24 hours for portions and smaller birds to thaw. Large poultry such as turkeys, are usually purchased fresh; when buying frozen birds always read and follow the recommendations listed on the wrapping. The following is a guide to recommended thawing times by weight in the refrigerator: these times are not exact and they can only act as a guide. As soon it is possible to do so, remove the giblets, and cook them to make stock. Cool the stock and freeze it until required. This is preferable to storing the stock in the refrigerator for several days while the turkey continues to thaw.

Weight of turkey	Thawing time in refrigerator
2.5-3.5 kg/5½-8 lb	up to 2½ days
3.5-5.5 kg/8-12 lb	2½-3 days
5.5-7.25 kg/12-16 lb	3-4 days
7.25-9 kg/16-20 lb	4-4½ days

PREPARING POULTRY FOR COOKING

Ensure that the bird is free from any small feathers or hairs. If necessary, singe the bird to remove hairs: use long matches or a taper and allow the flame to burn for a few seconds until it has stopped smoking. Trim away any lumps of fat from the body cavity. Rinse the bird inside and out under cold water and dry it well on absorbent kitchen paper.

NOTE

Always thoroughly wash surfaces, the sink and all utensils that come in contact with raw poultry immediately after use. Scrub cutting boards after use. Wash your hands well, paying attention to nails, and dry them thoroughly before preparing other food.

STUFFING POULTRY

Never stuff a bird more than an hour before cooking it. The stuffing may be prepared in advance and kept separately in a covered container in the refrigerator. Stuffing may be placed in the body cavity of the bird or under the skin covering the breast.

To insert stuffing under the skin, first loosen the skin by inserting the point of a knife between it and the flesh at the neck end of the bird. Once the skin is loosened, wash and dry your hands, then work your fingers up between the flesh and skin to form a pocket over the breast meat. Take care not to split the skin. Thoroughly clean your hands.

Use a spoon to insert the stuffing into the prepared pocket, easing it in place by moulding it with the skin on the outside. When the stuffing is in place, use a skewer to secure the end of the skin to the bird.

ROASTING POULTRY

The cooking time should be calculated according to the weight of the prepared bird, with stuffing, if used. Place the bird in a roasting tin; using a rack or trivet if liked. A goose should always be cooked on a rack over a deep tin so that the large amount of fat drips away. Brush the bird with a little melted butter or oil if required and sprinkle with seasoning (see individual recipes for more detailed information). A large chicken or turkey may have its breast covered with streaky bacon to prevent the meat from drying out. Turkey should be covered with foil for part of the cooking time to prevent overbrowning.

Chicken does not usually require turning during cooking. Duck may be turned once or twice but this is not essential. Goose and turkey should be turned several times, depending on size, to promote moist, even cooking. All poultry should be basted during cooking. The following times are a general guide but may vary according to the exact ingredients used and the oven temperature, as when a bird is marinated and coated with seasonings that affect the browning.

Chicken and Guineafowl Allow 20 minutes per 450 g/1 lb plus 20 minutes at 180°C/350°F/gas 5.

Duck Prick the duck all over with a fork or skewer to release the fat. Roast on a rack, allowing 15-20 minutes per 450 g/1 lb at 190-200°C/375-400°F/gas 5-6.

Goose Allow 20-25 minutes per 450 g/1 lb at 180°C/350°F/gas 4.

Turkey This requires long, slow cooking to ensure that the meat is thoroughly cooked. This is particularly important if the body cavity of the bird is stuffed. The following times are at 180°C/350°F/gas 4. Keep the bird covered with foil until the final 30-45 minutes of cooking. These times are a guide only, based upon the bird's weight excluding stuffing, since it is not easy to weigh a stuffed turkey. Birds without stuffing will take slightly less time to cook.

Weight (before stuffing)	Time at 180°C/ 350°F/gas 4
2.5 kg/5½ lb	2½-3 hours
2.75-3.5 kg/6-8 lb	3-3¾ hours
3.5-4.5 kg/8-10 lb	3¾-4½ hours
4.5-5.5 kg/10-12 lb	4½-5 hours
5.5-11.4 kg/12-25 lb	20 minutes per 450 g/ 1 lb plus 20 minutes

Microwave Cooking Lean, tender poultry cooks well in the microwave, although whole chickens and ducks benefit from being partially cooked by this method, then placed in a conventional oven to crisp the skin. Consult your manufacturer's handbook for more information.

TESTING FOR COOKING PROGRESS

It is essential that chicken and turkey are thoroughly cooked right through. With large birds, increasing the cooking temperature will not necessarily speed up the process as lengthy cooking must be allowed to ensure the thick areas of meat and the body cavity reach a high temperature.

To test, pierce the meat at a thick point – for example on the thigh behind the drumstick. Check for any signs of blood in the juices and for any meat that appears pink or uncooked. When the bird is cooked, the juices will run clear and the meat will be firm and white right through to the bone. On a large bird test in at least two places to ensure that all the meat is well cooked.

PREPARATION TECHNIQUES

The majority of poultry is sold ready for cooking. If any special preparation is required, a good butcher will almost certainly do this willingly, given sufficient notice, but it is useful to know the basics of trussing and jointing poultry. Detailed instructions for trussing are given under Game, see page 90.

JOINTING

You need a large, heavy cook's knife. A pair of poultry shears or strong kitchen scissors are also useful and a meat mallet or rolling pin may be necessary to tap the blade of the knife through areas of bone. There are many ways of jointing poultry; this is one method.

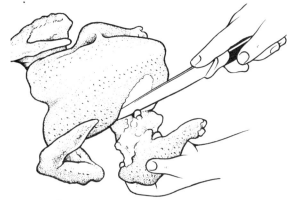

Pull the leg away from the body, cut through the skin, then break the joint away above the thigh.

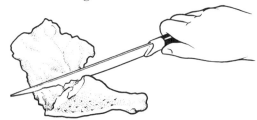

Cut through the meat between the thigh and drumstick and separate the two portions.

Cut through the breast down to the wing

joint, taking a portion of breast meat and removing it with the whole wing joint.

Turn the bird over, so that the breast is down. Cut the carcass in half through the middle, tapping the knife with a meat mallet. Cut away the ends of the breast bone and any small pieces of bone. Turn the breast over and split it in half.

SPATCHCOCK

Turn the bird breast down. Cut off the parson's nose. Using a heavy cook's knife, cut through the skin, flesh and bone down the length of the bird to open the carcass. Do not cut right through to the breast. Open the carcass out and turn it over so that the breast is uppermost.

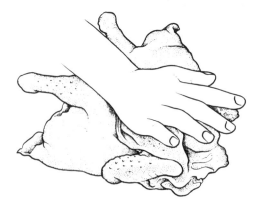

Place the palm of your hand on the top of the breast and flatten the bird by pressing down firmly with your other hand. The spatchcocked bird may be kept flat by threading two metal skewers through it.

SKINNING RAW POULTRY

It is sometimes necessary to skin a whole chicken. The technique is sometimes used to allow the full flavour of a marinade to permeate the flesh, notably when spicing a whole chicken for baking covered and serving cold. The technique is not difficult and there are no hard and fast rules about how it should be done. The method described below, however, is an organized and practical approach to the task, which avoids damaging the meat.

Use a sharp knife to slit the skin down the back of the bird. Pull it off, using a pointed knife to separate the skin from the membrane covering the flesh. Use scissors to cut the skin free around the joints. Turn the bird over and loosen the skin at the neck end, then pull it away from the breast meat, easing it off and cutting it free around the joints and at the parson's nose.

Skin the drumsticks individually with the help of scissors or a sharp pointed knife. Do the same with the first part of the wing joint, nearest the body. It is not easy to remove the skin from the wing ends and they are best removed. The parson's nose may be left in place or cut off as required.

BONING A BIRD

Have ready a sharp, pointed cook's knife. A pair of kitchen scissors is also useful for snipping flesh and sinew free from joint ends.

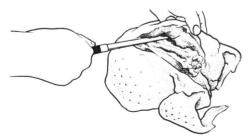

Lay the bird breast down. Cut through the skin and flesh right in to the bone along the length of the back. Beginning at one end of the slit, slide the point of the knife under the flesh and skin. Keeping the knife close to the bone, cut the meat off the bone. Work all the meat off the bone on one side of the carcass, going down the rib cage as far as the breast. Leave the breast meat attached to the soft bone.

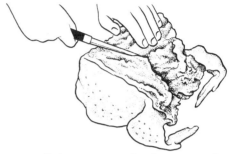

Cut off the wing ends, leaving only the first part of the joint in place. To free the flesh from the wing joint, carefully scrape the meat off the first part, using scissors or the point of the knife to cut sinews. Pull the

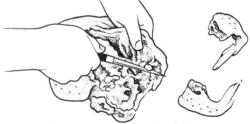

bones and meat apart as though removing an arm from a sleeve. Again use the point of a knife or scissors to cut sinew and skin attached at the bone end. This leaves the flesh and skin turned inside-out and the bones free but attached to the carcass. Turn the flesh and skin back out the right way. Repeat the process with the leg.

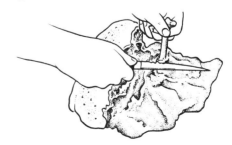

Turn the bird around and repeat the process on the second side, again leaving the breast meat attached to the soft bone. When all the meat is removed from the second side, and the joints have been boned, the carcass will remain attached along the breast bone. Taking care not to cut the skin, lift the carcass away from the meat and cut along the breast bone, taking the finest sliver of soft bone to avoid damaging the skin.

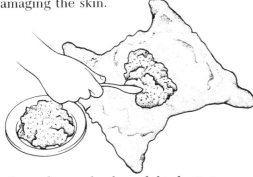

Spread out the boned bird. It is now ready for stuffing. To reshape it, simply fold the sides over the stuffing and sew them with a trussing needle and cooking thread. Turn the bird over with the seam down and plump it up into a neat shape, tucking the boned joint meat under at the sides.

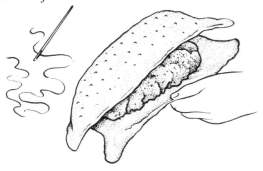

CARVING

The same rules apply to all poultry: the breast meat is carved in neat slices, working at an angle to the carcass to yield several slices of a similar size from each side. The wings and legs are then removed. To make it easier to carve the breast meat on chickens and smaller birds, the wings and legs are usually cut off first and served as individual portions. This is not necessary when carving larger birds, such as turkey, as the breast meat can easily be sliced off with the joints still in place.

GALANTINE OF CHICKEN

1 (2.25 kg/5 lb) chicken
salt and pepper
450 g/1 lb sausagemeat
100 g/4 oz cooked ham, cut in 1 × 2.5 cm/
    ½ × 1 inch strips
2 hard-boiled eggs, sliced
6 flat mushrooms, chopped
25 g/1 oz pistachio nuts, blanched,
    skinned and chopped
750 ml/1¼ pints chicken stock

CHAUDFROID SAUCE
    125 ml/4 fl oz aspic jelly
    10 ml/2 tsp gelatine
    300 ml/½ pint Béchamel sauce (see Mrs
        Beeton's Tip), cooled until tepid
    5 ml/1 tsp white wine vinegar or lemon
        juice
    15 ml/1 tbsp double cream

GARNISH
    125 ml/4 fl oz aspic jelly
    canned or bottled pimiento strips
    lemon rind strips
    hard-boiled egg slices

Using a sharp knife, cut down the back of the bird, then remove all the bones neatly, using the technique described on previous page. Open out the boned bird and season with plenty of salt and pepper.

Spread half the sausagemeat evenly over the inner surface of the bird. Arrange the ham strips, egg slices, chopped mushrooms and nuts on top. Add salt and pepper to taste, then top with the remaining sausage-meat. Carefully lift the two halves of the bird and bring them together so that it is as near the original shape as possible. Wrap the bird tightly in foil.

Heat the chicken stock in a pan large enough to hold the stuffed bird. Carefully lower the bird into the hot stock and sim-mer gently for 2½ hours. Allow to cool for 30 minutes in the stock. Remove and drain the package, tighten the foil to allow for any shrinkage during cooking, then press the foil-wrapped chicken between two large plates or boards and cool. Chill until quite cold.

Meanwhile make the chaudfroid sauce. Melt the aspic jelly in a bowl placed over hot water. Add the gelatine and continue to stir over heat until dissolved. Cool the mixture until tepid, then fold it into the Béchamel sauce. Add salt and pepper to taste. Stir in the vinegar or lemon juice. Rub the sauce through a fine sieve into a clean bowl, then fold in the cream. Leave to cool and thicken slightly but do not allow to set.

Unwrap the chicken, remove the skin from the bird and wipe away any excess grease. Place the chicken on a wire rack and stand this on a sheet of foil. Slowly spoon the chaudfroid sauce over the chicken, teasing it down the sides to coat the bird evenly. Work quickly before the sauce sets and use a spatula to retrieve the excess which drops on the foil. If the sauce becomes too thick to coat the chicken

evenly, stand the bowl over hot water for a few seconds and stir the sauce until it is smooth and more fluid. Chill until the coating is set.

For the garnish, have the aspic jelly cooled and just beginning to set: it should resemble syrup in consistency. The chaud-froid coating must be chilled. Dip the strips of pimiento and lemon rind in the aspic, then arrange them on the chicken. Care-fully arrange the egg slices on the chicken, then spoon the aspic all over the bird to coat it in a thin, even glaze. Catch the excers aspic as before, tip it into a small saucepan, and warm it until just fluid. Pow it nto a small rectangular dish. Chill the chicken and remaining aspic until set. Chop the aspic and arrange it around the chicken on a serving platter.

SERVES 8 TO 10

> 🥣 **MRS BEETON'S TIP** To make a classic Béchamel sauce, infuse 600 ml/ 1 pint milk for 30 minutes with 3-4 onion slices, 1 small sliced carrot and 1 small sliced celery stick. Add 1 bay leaf, a few parsley stalks, 1 thyme sprig, 1 clove, 6 white peppercorns and 1 blade of mace. Add salt to taste. Melt 50 g/2 oz butter in a saucepan, stir in 50 g/2 oz plain flour and cook for 2-3 minutes. Gradually add the strained milk, stirring constantly. Bring to the boil, stirring all the time until the sauce thickens. Lower the heat and simmer for 1-2 minutes, beating briskly to give the sauce a gloss. Use half quantities of butter, flour and milk for the recipe above.

ROAST CHICKEN WITH HONEY AND ALMONDS

Illustrated on page 70

1 (1.5-1.8 kg/3½-4 lb) oven-ready
    roasting chicken
½ lemon
salt and pepper
45 ml/3 tbsp honey
50 g/2 oz flaked almonds
a pinch of powdered saffron
30 ml/2 tbsp oil
watercress sprigs to garnish (optional)

Set the oven at 180°C/350°F/gas 4. Rub the chicken all over with the cut lemon, then sprinkle with salt and pepper. Line a roasting tin with a piece of foil large enough to enclose the bird completely.

Put the bird into the foil-lined tin, then brush it all over with the honey. Sprinkle the nuts and saffron over, then trickle the oil very gently over the top. Bring up the foil carefully, tenting it over the bird so that it is completely covered. Make sure that the foil does not touch the skin. Seal the package by folding the edges of the foil over.

Roast for 1½-2 hours or until the chicken is cooked through. Open the foil for the last 10 minutes to allow the breast of the bird to brown. Transfer the chicken to a heated serving dish and garnish it with watercress if liked.

SERVES 4 TO 6

CHICKEN KIEV

The original chicken Kiev was a boned and flattened chicken breast with a simple herb – usually chive – butter filling. Today the butter is frequently flavoured with garlic, as in the version below.

4 chicken breast and wing joints
salt and pepper
plain flour for coating
1 egg, beaten
about 75 g/3 oz dry white breadcrumbs
oil for deep frying

BUTTER FILLING
100 g/4 oz butter, softened
finely grated rind of ½ lemon
15 ml/1 tbsp chopped parsley
2 small garlic cloves, crushed

GARNISH
lemon wedges
parsley sprigs

Make the butter filling. Beat the butter lightly in a bowl. Gradually work in the lemon rind, parsley and garlic, with salt and pepper to taste. Form the butter into a roll, wrap it in greaseproof paper and chill well.

To prepare the chicken, cut off the wing ends and remove the skin from the breast meat. Turn the joints flesh side up and cut out all bones except the wing bone, which is left in place. Do not cut right through the flesh. To slightly flatten the boned meat, place it between greaseproof paper and beat lightly with a cutlet bat or rolling pin.

Cut the flavoured butter into four long pieces and place one on each piece of chicken. Fold the flesh over the butter to enclose it completely, and secure with wooden cocktail sticks. The wing bone should protrude at one end of each cutlet.

Spread out the flour in a shallow bowl and season with salt and pepper. Put the beaten egg in a second bowl and stir in a little water. Place the breadcrumbs on a sheet of foil. Coat the chicken in flour, then in egg and breadcrumbs. Repeat the coating at least once more, using more egg and breadcrumbs, so that the chicken and butter filling are well sealed. Chill lightly.

Heat the oil to 160°C/325°F or until a cube of bread added to the oil browns in 2 minutes. Deep fry the chicken, turning or basting the cutlets until golden brown and firm to the touch, as necessary for even cooking. Allow 15-20 minutes to ensure the flesh is cooked through. Drain thoroughly and keep hot, if necessary, while frying any remaining cutlets. To serve, place the cutlets on a heated serving dish. Remove the cocktail sticks and garnish with lemon wedges and parsley.

SERVES 4

SPATCHCOCKED CHICKENS WITH BACON AND CORN FRITTERS

2 spring chickens
50 g/2 oz butter
salt and pepper
bacon rolls (see Mrs Beeton's Tip) and
 parsley sprigs, to garnish

CORN FRITTERS
 1 (275 g/10 oz) can sweetcorn, drained
 2 eggs, separated
 75 g/3 oz self-raising flour
 2.5 ml/½ tsp salt
 oil for frying

Split the birds through the back only, following the instructions on page 44.

Flatten out each bird, removing the breast bone if necessary. Break the joints and remove the tips from the wings, to make flattening easier. Use skewers to keep the birds in shape while cooking.

Melt the butter and brush it on both sides of the birds. Sprinkle lightly with salt and pepper. Grill under moderate heat – or over medium coals – for about 20 minutes on each side, or until cooked through. Brush the chickens with more butter and turn occasionally while grilling to ensure even cooking.

Meanwhile make the corn fritters. Combine the corn, egg yolks and flour in a bowl. Whisk the egg whites and the salt until they form soft peaks, then fold them into the corn mixture.

Pour oil to a depth of about 1 cm/½ inch into a large deep saucepan. Heat to 180-190°C/350-375°F or until a cube of bread browns in 30 seconds. Gently drop in spoonfuls of the corn mixture, a few at a time. As each corn fritter browns, turn it over with a slotted spoon and cook the other side. When cooked, remove the fritters, drain on absorbent kitchen paper and keep hot while cooking the remainder.

When the chickens are cooked, remove the skewers, arrange on a heated platter and serve, surrounded by the corn fritters, bacon rolls and parsley sprigs.

SERVES 4

> **MRS BEETON'S TIP** To make the bacon rolls, roll up 8 rindless streaky bacon rashers, threading them in pairs on short metal skewers. Grill for about 5 minutes, turning frequently, until crisp.

CHICKEN CHASSEUR

butter for greasing
1 (1.6 kg/3½ lb) roasting chicken
25 g/1 oz plain flour
salt and pepper
50 g/2 oz butter
15 ml/1 tbsp oil
1 small onion, finely chopped
175 g/6 oz button mushrooms, sliced
150 ml/¼ pint dry white wine
15 ml/1 tbsp tomato purée
275 ml/9 fl oz chicken stock
1 sprig each of fresh tarragon, chervil and
    parsley, chopped

Divide the chicken into 8 serving portions. Mix the flour, salt and pepper in a sturdy polythene bag. Add the chicken portions and toss until well coated. Shake off excess flour.

Melt the butter in the oil in a large frying pan. When hot, add the chicken pieces and fry until browned all over and cooked through, see Mrs Beeton's Tip. Using a slotted spoon, remove the chicken pieces from the pan, drain on absorbent kitchen paper and transfer to a warmed serving dish. Cover and keep hot.

Add the onion to the fat remaining in the pan and fry gently until soft but not coloured. Add the mushrooms and fry briefly. Pour in the wine and add the tomato purée and stock. Stir until well blended, then simmer gently for 10 minutes. Stir in two thirds of the chopped herbs, with salt and pepper to taste.

Pour the sauce over the chicken portions and sprinkle with the remaining herbs. Serve hot.

SERVES 4 TO 6

BARBECUED CHICKEN DRUMSTICKS

Illustrated on page 71

75 g/3 oz butter
12 chicken drumsticks
60 ml/4 tbsp vinegar
15 ml/1 tbsp Worcestershire sauce
15 ml/1 tbsp tomato purée
5 ml/1 tsp soy sauce
5 ml/1 tsp grated onion
5 ml/1 tsp paprika
2.5 ml/½ tsp salt

Melt the butter in a small saucepan. Brush a little of it over the chicken drumsticks to coat them thoroughly, then arrange on a rack in a grill pan.

Stir the remaining ingredients into the leftover butter in the pan. Simmer for 2 minutes, then brush a little of the mixture over the chicken. Grill or barbecue over medium coals, turning occasionally and brushing with more sauce until cooked through. Serve with rice or salad.

SERVES 4

MRS BEETON'S TIP Do not rush the cooking process when frying chicken. Keep the heat moderate to prevent the butter from burning and turn the chicken portions frequently to ensure they cook evenly. The cooking temperature and size of the portions affects the timing – even the size of the pan contributes to the result. Allow at least 15-20 minutes but always check the thickest areas of meat to ensure they are cooked before serving.

*F*RITOT OF CHICKEN

1 (1.4-1.6 kg/3-3½ lb) cooked chicken
oil for deep frying
watercress to garnish

MARINADE
¼ onion, finely chopped
1 parsley sprig, finely chopped
30 ml/2 tbsp olive oil
15 ml/1 tbsp lemon juice
2.5 ml/½ tsp dried mixed herbs
salt and pepper

BATTER
15 ml/1 tbsp oil
100 g/4 oz plain flour
2 egg whites

Cut the chicken into 8 serving portions. Remove the skin and any fat, then place the pieces in a bowl large enough to hold them all in a single layer. Mix all the ingredients for the marinade in a bowl, pour over the chicken, cover and marinate for 1½ hours.

Make the batter. Mix the oil with 125 ml/ 4 fl oz tepid water in a jug. Mix the flour and salt in a bowl. Make a well in the centre, add the liquid and mix well, gradually incorporating the flour to make a smooth batter. Leave to stand for 1 hour.

Drain the chicken portions and pat dry with absorbent kitchen paper. Whisk the egg whites in a clean grease-free bowl until stiff; fold into the batter.

Heat the oil for deep frying to 180-190°C/350-375°F or until a cube of bread browns in 30 seconds.

Dip each piece of chicken in batter, add to the hot oil and fry until golden on all sides. Turn once or twice during cooking. Drain on absorbent kitchen paper and keep hot while frying any remaining portions, reheating the oil if necessary. Garnish with watercress. Serve with Courgettes with Almonds (page 225) and plain boiled or baked potatoes, if liked. Alternatively, add some fresh orange segments to a plain green salad to make a zesty accompaniment.

SERVES 4 TO 6

*D*EVILLED CHICKEN

Illustrated on page 71

4 chicken breasts
30 ml/2 tbsp oil
50 g/2 oz butter, softened
15 ml/1 tbsp tomato purée
2.5 ml/½ tsp mustard powder
few drops of Tabasco sauce
10 ml/2 tsp Worcestershire sauce
lemon or lime wedges to serve

Place the chicken breasts on a rack in a grill pan. Brush generously with oil and grill under moderate heat for 5 minutes on each side.

Meanwhile prepare the devilled mixture. Beat the butter in a small bowl and gradually work in the tomato purée, mustard powder, Tabasco and Worcestershire sauce. Spread half the mixture over the chicken and grill for 5 minutes more, then turn the breast over carefully, spread with the remaining mixture and grill for a further 5 minutes or until the chicken is thoroughly cooked. Transfer the chicken to plates or a serving dish and add lemon or lime wedges: the fruit juice may be squeezed over just before the chicken is eaten. Serve with Baked Jacket Potatoes (page 308) and French Bean and Tomato Salad (page 338).

SERVES 4

BRAISED CHESTNUT CHICKEN

1 (1.4-1.6 kg/3-3½ lb) chicken
flour for coating
salt and pepper
45 ml/3 tbsp oil
1 onion, sliced
3 rindless streaky bacon rashers, cut into
    strips
300 ml/½ pint chicken stock
30 ml/2 tbsp plain flour
25 g/1 oz butter
450 g/1 lb chipolata sausages, fried or
    grilled, to garnish

STUFFING
450 g/1 lb chestnuts
250-300 ml/8-10 fl oz chicken stock
50 g/2 oz cooked ham, finely chopped
100 g/4 oz fresh white breadcrumbs
grated rind of 1 lemon
2-3 parsley sprigs, chopped
25 g/1 oz butter, melted
1 egg, beaten

Start by making the stuffing. Remove the shells and skins of the chestnuts (see Mrs Beeton's Tip). Place the cleaned nuts in a saucepan, just cover with stock and bring to the boil. Cover, lower the heat until the liquid is only just boiling, and cook for about 20 minutes or until the nuts are tender. Drain and mash them, or press them through a fine sieve into a bowl.

Stir in the ham, breadcrumbs, lemon rind and parsley, with salt and pepper to taste. Add the melted butter with enough of the beaten egg to bind. Stuff the chicken with this mixture and truss it.

Spread out the flour in a large shallow bowl. Season with salt and pepper. Add the chicken, turning and rolling it in the mixture until well coated. Heat the oil in a large, heavy-bottomed flameproof casserole or saucepan with a lid. Fry the bird on all sides until lightly browned, then remove it.

Add the onion and bacon to the oil remaining in the pan and fry for 4-5 minutes over gentle heat until the onion is slightly softened but not coloured. Replace the chicken in the pan. Pour in the stock, cover the pan and bring just to the boil. Lower the heat and simmer for 1½ hours or until the chicken is cooked through, adding more chicken stock or water as necessary.

Carefully remove the chicken from the pan. Use a large spoon to skim the fat from the cooking liquid, then process the remaining juices in a blender or food processor, or push them though a sieve into a clean saucepan. In a small bowl, blend the butter with the flour. Bring the sieved liquid to the boil, then reduce the heat so it simmers steadily. Gradually add small pieces of the flour and butter mixture to the cooking juices remaining in the pan, whisking thoroughly after each addition. Whisk until the sauce is thickened. Simmer for 3 minutes, whisking occasionally, season to taste and pour into a sauceboat.

Serve the chicken surrounded by fried or grilled chipolatas. Offer the sauce separately.

SERVES 4 TO 6

> 🥣 **MRS BEETON'S TIP** To shell chestnuts, make a small slit in the shell of each, then place the nuts in a saucepan of boiling water. Cook for 5 minutes. Drain, carefully removing the shells and skins while the chestnuts are still hot.

TURKEY WITH WALNUTS

Serve this nutty, Oriental-style turkey dish with plain cooked rice and a fresh green salad topped with diced avocado.

60 ml/4 tbsp cooking oil
225 g/8 oz shelled walnuts, roughly chopped
4 thick turkey fillets, skinned and diced
15 ml/1 tbsp cornflour
pinch of salt
pinch of sugar
45 ml/3 tbsp soy sauce
45 ml/3 tbsp dry sherry
100 g/4 oz button mushrooms, sliced

Heat the oil in a heavy-bottomed frying pan, add the walnuts and fry for 2-3 minutes until browned. Using a slotted spoon, remove them from the pan and drain on absorbent kitchen paper.

Add the diced turkey to the oil remaining in the pan. Fry, stirring gently, until pale golden and cooked. Mix the cornflour, salt, sugar, soy sauce and sherry to a smooth paste in a small bowl. Stir in 30 ml/2 tbsp water and pour the mixture into the pan, then add the mushroom slices.

Cook the mixture, stirring, over moderate heat until the sauce boils. Simmer for 2-3 minutes, stirring frequently to prevent the mixture from sticking to the base of the pan. Remove from the heat, stir in the walnuts and serve at once.

SERVES 4

CHICKEN WINGS WITH GINGER

oil for greasing
12 chicken wings
juice of 1 lemon
2.5 ml/½ tsp sesame oil
45 ml/3 tbsp plain flour
10 ml/2 tsp ground ginger
salt and pepper

SAUCE
60 ml/4 tbsp preserved ginger in syrup, drained and chopped
30 ml/2 tbsp medium-dry sherry
25 g/1 oz butter

Remove and discard the ends from the chicken wings. Mix the lemon and oil together in a small bowl. Brush the mixture all over the chicken wings. Reserve the remaining lemon/oil mixture.

Spread out the flour in a shallow bowl and flavour with the ginger, salt and pepper. Add the chicken wings and turn them in the mixture until well coated.

Set the oven at 190°C/375°F/gas 5. Spread out the chicken wings on a greased baking sheet and bake for 50-60 minutes, or until crisp and golden. Turn the wings occasionally during cooking.

Meanwhile, make the sauce. Add the ginger, sherry and butter to the remaining lemon/oil mixture, tip into a small saucepan and bring to the boil. Arrange the cooked chicken wings on a heated serving platter and pour the sauce over them. Serve with noodles or rice, if liked, and some stir fried mixed vegetables.

SERVES 4

LEMON CHICKEN

Illustrated on page 72

6 chicken breasts
salt and pepper
50 g/2 oz butter
15 ml/1 tbsp oil
1 onion, sliced
1 lemon, sliced
60 ml/4 tbsp plain flour
250 ml/8 fl oz chicken stock
2-3 bay leaves
5 ml/1 tsp caster sugar

Set the oven at 190°C/375°F/gas 5. Season the chicken breasts with salt and pepper. Melt the butter in the oil in a large frying pan, add the chicken and fry until golden brown all over. Using tongs or a slotted spoon, transfer to a casserole.

Add the onion and lemon slices to the fat remaining in the pan and fry over very gentle heat for about 15 minutes. Using a slotted spoon, transfer the onion and lemon to the casserole. Sprinkle the flour into the fat remaining in the pan. Cook for 1 minute, then blend in the stock. Bring to the boil, stirring all the time. Add the bay leaves and sugar, with salt and pepper to taste. Pour over the chicken breasts in the casserole, cover and bake for about 45 minutes or until the chicken is tender. Remove the casserole lid 5 minutes before the end of the cooking time.

Remove the bay leaves before serving or reserve them as a garnish. Potatoes Dauphine (page 233) and Glazed Carrots (page 214) would be ideal accompaniments.

SERVES 6

CHICKEN AND BACON CASSEROLE

25 g/1 oz plain flour
salt and pepper
1 (1.6 kg/3½ lb) chicken, cut in serving
    portions
30 ml/2 tbsp cooking oil
125 g/4 oz rindless streaky bacon rashers,
    cut into strips
100 g/4 oz mushrooms, sliced
1 onion or 100 g/4 oz shallots, finely
    chopped
500 ml/17 fl oz chicken stock

Mix the flour, salt and pepper in a sturdy polythene bag. Add the chicken portions and toss until well coated. Shake off and reserve excess flour.

Heat the oil in a flameproof casserole. Add the chicken pieces and fry them until golden on all sides, turning frequently. Remove from the pan, then add the bacon, mushrooms and onion or shallots to the fat remaining in the pan. Cook for 5 minutes, stirring frequently, then stir in the reserved flour and half the stock. Replace the chicken in the pan.

Pour in enough stock to cover the chicken pieces. Bring to the boil, then reduce the heat. Cover the casserole and simmer for 1-1½ hours or until the chicken portions are cooked through. Taste and add more seasoning if required. Serve from the casserole, with Potatoes Lyonnaise (page 232) and Petits Pois à la Française (page 230), if liked. Alternatively, serve buttered noodles and plain green beans with the casserole.

SERVES 4 TO 6

COQ AU VIN

Illustrated on page 72

The best coq au vin is made by marinating the chicken overnight in the red wine before cooking.

1 (1.6 kg/3½ lb) chicken with giblets
1 bouquet garni
salt and pepper
75 g/3 oz unsalted butter
15 ml/1 tbsp oil
150 g/5 oz belly of pickled pork or green (unsmoked) bacon rashers, rind removed and chopped
150 g/5 oz button onions or shallots
30 ml/2 tbsp brandy
175 g/6 oz small button mushrooms
2 garlic cloves, crushed
575 ml/19 fl oz Burgundy or other red wine
15 ml/1 tbsp tomato purée
25 g/1 oz plain flour
croûtes of fried bread, to serve

Joint the chicken and skin the portions if liked. Place the giblets in a saucepan with 450 ml/¾ pint water. Add the bouquet garni, salt and pepper. Cook gently for about 1 hour, then strain. Measure the stock and set aside 275 ml/9 fl oz.

Set the oven at 150°C/300°F/gas 2. Melt 50 g/2 oz of the butter in the oil in a flameproof casserole. Add the pork or bacon, with the onions. Cook over gentle heat for about 10 minutes until the onions are lightly coloured. Using a slotted spoon, transfer the bacon and onions to a plate.

Add the chicken portions to the fat remaining in the pan and brown lightly all over. Ignite the brandy (see Mrs Beeton's Tip). When the flames die down, pour it into the casserole. Add the reserved bacon and onions, with the mushrooms and garlic. Stir in the wine, giblet stock and tomato purée. Cover and cook in the oven for 1-1½ hours or until the chicken is tender.

Using a slotted spoon, transfer the chicken portions to a heated serving dish. Arrange the bacon, mushrooms and onions over them. Cover with buttered greaseproof paper and keep hot. Return the casserole to the top of the stove and simmer the liquid until reduced by about one third.

Meanwhile make a beurre manié by blending the remaining butter with the flour in a small bowl. Gradually add small pieces of the mixture to the stock, whisking thoroughly after each addition. Continue to whisk the sauce until it thickens. Pour it over the chicken. Garnish with croûtes of fried bread and serve at once.

SERVES 4 TO 6

> **MRS BEETON'S TIP** To flame the brandy, either pour it into a soup ladle and warm over low heat or warm it in a jug in the microwave for 15 seconds on High. Ignite the brandy (if warmed in a soup ladle it may well ignite spontaneously) and when the flames die down, pour it into the casserole.

CHICKEN SUPREME

1 (1.4-1.6 kg/3-3½ lb) chicken
1 litre/1¾ pints chicken or vegetable
    stock
chopped truffle or poached mushrooms to
    garnish

SAUCE
    50 g/2 oz butter
    4 button mushrooms, finely chopped
    6 black peppercorns
    4-5 parsley stalks
    25 g/1 oz plain flour
    250 ml/8 fl oz chicken or vegetable stock
    salt and pepper
    lemon juice (see method)
    150 ml/¼ pint single cream
    1 egg yolk
    grated nutmeg

Truss the chicken neatly, put it into a large saucepan and pour over the stock. Bring the liquid to the boil, lower the heat, cover the pan and simmer for 1½-2 hours or until tender. After 1 hour, strain off 250 ml/8 fl oz of the chicken stock. Blot the surface with a piece of absorbent kitchen paper to remove excess fat, then set the stock aside for use in the sauce.

Melt half the butter in a saucepan. Add the mushrooms, peppercorns and parsley stalks. Cook gently for 10 minutes, then stir in the flour. Cook over gentle heat for 2-3 minutes. Gradually add the reserved stock, stirring well to prevent the formation of lumps. Raise the heat and simmer the sauce, stirring constantly, until it thickens. Rub through a sieve into a clean pan, add salt, pepper and lemon juice to taste and stir in half the cream. Cool the sauce slightly.

Beat the egg yolk and remaining cream with a little of the cooled sauce in a bowl. Add the contents of the bowl to the sauce and stir over gentle heat until the mixture thickens. Do not boil. Whisk in the remaining butter, adding a knob at a time. Add nutmeg to taste.

Drain the cooked chicken, joint it into serving portions and transfer these to a heated serving dish. Pour the sauce over, garnish with truffles or mushrooms and serve.

SERVES 4 TO 6

SPRING CHICKENS WITH PARSLEY

50 g/2 oz parsley sprigs
100 g/4 oz butter
salt and pepper
2 spring chickens
300 ml/½ pint double cream

GARNISH
    1 lemon, cut in wedges
    4 parsley sprigs

Roughly chop the parsley leaves. Soften half the butter in a bowl, beat well, then mix in half the parsley, with salt and pepper to taste. Place half the mixture in the body cavity of each bird.

Melt the remaining butter in a large frying pan, add the chickens and brown them lightly all over. Add 150 ml/¼ pint water, bring just to the boil, cover and cook gently for 40 minutes or until the chickens are cooked through. Transfer the chickens to a plate and cut them in half. Arrange on a heated serving dish and keep hot.

Add the cream to the stock remaining in the pan and cook over low heat, stirring until the sauce is hot. Do not allow it to boil. Add the remaining parsley, taste the sauce, and add more salt and pepper if required. Pour the sauce over the chicken and garnish with lemon wedges and parsley sprigs.

SERVES 4

> **MRS BEETON'S TIP** If baby chickens are not available, substitute 1 (1.4 kg/3 lb) roasting chicken. Stuff it with the parsley butter. Cook for about 1½ hours, adding extra water as necessary. When cooked, cut into quarters.

POACHED CHICKEN WITH OYSTERS

24 oysters
1 (1.4-1.6 kg/3-3½ lb) chicken
1 blade of mace
salt and pepper

SAUCE
50 g/2 oz plain flour
50 g/2 oz butter
1 egg, beaten
30 ml/2 tbsp single cream

Open the oysters (see Mrs Beeton's Tip), reserving the liquor. Reserve 12 of the oysters. Put the rest inside the chicken, then truss the bird and put it in a large saucepan with a tight-fitting lid. Add water to a depth of about 2.5 cm/1 inch, then add the mace, salt and pepper. Bring the liquid to the boil, lower the heat, cover the pan and cook for 1½ hours or until the chicken

is cooked through, adding more water during cooking if required.

Remove the trussing string from the chicken, put the bird on a heated platter and keep hot while making the sauce. Strain the cooking liquid into a measuring jug and make up to 600 ml/1 pint with water, if necessary.

Place the flour in a saucepan. Gradually whisk in the chicken stock and add the butter, then whisk over moderate heat until the mixture comes to the boil. Lower the heat and simmer for 3-4 minutes, whisking constantly until the sauce is thick, smooth and glossy. Add salt and pepper to taste. Cool the sauce slightly.

Beat the egg and cream with a little of the cooled sauce in a bowl. Add the contents of the bowl to the sauce and stir over gentle heat until the mixture thickens a little more. Do not allow it to boil.

Meanwhile, put the reserved oysters in a small saucepan with the oyster liquor and poach very gently for 10 minutes. To assemble the dish, pour half the sauce over the chicken portions. Stir the oysters and their liquor into the remaining sauce and serve separately, in a sauceboat.

SERVES 4 TO 6

> **MRS BEETON'S TIP** A short-bladed tough oyster knife should ideally be used for opening these shellfish, but any fairly blunt, short strong knife will do. Hold the oyster with the curved shell down. Insert the point of the knife into the hinged end of the shell and prise it open. Take care as the tough shell is difficult to open and a knife which slips can cause a nasty injury.

MRS BEETON'S CHICKEN PIE

fat for greasing
1 (1.6 kg/3½ lb) chicken with giblets
1 onion, halved
salt and pepper
1 bouquet garni
1 blade of mace
2.5 ml/½ tsp grated nutmeg
2.5 ml/½ tsp ground mace
6 slices lean cooked ham
3 hard-boiled eggs
flour for dredging
150 g/5 oz puff pastry, thawed if frozen
beaten egg for glazing

HERB FORCEMEAT
  50 g/2 oz shredded beef suet or
      margarine
  100 g/4 oz fresh breadcrumbs
  pinch of grated nutmeg
  15 ml/1 tbsp chopped parsley
  5 ml/1 tsp chopped fresh mixed herbs
  grated rind of ½ lemon
  1 egg, beaten

Lightly grease a 1.5 litre/2¾ pint pie dish. Make the herb forcemeat. Melt the margarine, if using. Mix the breadcrumbs with the suet or margarine in a bowl. Add the nutmeg, herbs and lemon rind. Add salt and pepper to taste, then bind with the beaten egg.

Skin the chicken and cut it into small serving joints. Put the leftover bones, neck and gizzard into a small pan with 250 ml/8 fl oz water. Add the onion to the pan with salt, pepper, bouquet garni and mace. Half cover and simmer gently for about 45 minutes until the liquid is well reduced and strongly flavoured. Put to one side.

Set the oven at 220°C/425°F/gas 7. Put a layer of chicken joints in the bottom of the prepared dish. Sprinkle with salt, pepper, nutmeg and ground mace. Cover with a layer of ham, then with forcemeat; add salt and pepper to taste. Slice the eggs, place a layer over the forcemeat, and season again. Repeat the layers until the dish is full and all the ingredients are used, ending with a layer of chicken joints. Pour in 150-200 ml/5-7 fl oz water and dredge lightly with flour.

Roll out the pastry on a lightly floured surface to the same shape as the dish but 2.5 cm/1 inch larger all round. Cut off the outside 2 cm/¾ inch of the pastry. Lay the pastry strip on the rim of the dish. Dampen the strip and lay the lid on top. Knock up the edge, trim, then use any trimmings to garnish the crust with pastry leaves. Make a pastry rose and put to one side. Brush the pastry with the beaten egg. Make a small hole in the centre of the pie.

Bake for 15 minutes to set the pastry, then reduce the oven temperature to 180°C/350°F/gas 4, and cover the pastry loosely with greaseproof paper. Bake for 1-1¼ hours. Bake the pastry rose with – but not on – the pie for the final 20 minutes. Test whether the joints are cooked through by running a small heated skewer into the pie through the central hole. It should come out clean with no trace of blood.

Just before the pie is cooked, reheat the stock and strain it. When the pie is cooked, pour the stock in through the central hole, then cover with the pastry rose.

SERVES 6 TO 8

*T*ANDOORI CHICKEN

1 (1.4-1.6 kg/3-3½ lb) chicken
15 ml/1 tbsp cumin seeds
30 ml/2 tbsp grated fresh root ginger
1 onion, grated
4 garlic cloves, crushed
5 ml/1 tsp salt
5 ml/1 tsp chilli powder
2.5 ml/½ tsp turmeric
5 ml/1 tsp garam masala
few drops of red food colouring (optional)
juice of 2 lemons
150 ml/¼ pint plain yogurt
30 ml/2 tbsp oil

Skin the chicken. Keep it whole or cut it into 4 or 8 pieces. Toast the cumin seeds in a small ungreased frying pan over moderate heat for 1 minute. Grind them in a pepper mill, or use a pestle and mortar. Set the seeds aside.

Combine the ginger, onion, garlic, salt, chilli powder, turmeric and garam masala in a small bowl. Add the colouring, if used, then stir in the lemon juice and yogurt.

Prick the chicken with a fork and cut a few slits in the legs and breast. Rub the bird with the paste, pressing it deeply into the slits. Place in a shallow dish, cover tightly with foil and a lid and marinate for 12 hours or overnight.

Set the oven at 180°C/350°F/Gas 4. Put the chicken on a rack in a shallow roasting tin. Baste it with the oil and any remaining paste. Bake for 1½-2 hours, spooning over the oil and pan juices from time to time. When cooked, sprinkle with the toasted cumin seeds. Serve with rice and a tomato and onion salad.

SERVES 4

MRS BEETON'S TIP There are many versions of garam masala, authentically dry, although some are mixed to a paste with water. They vary according to region and the cook's preference but the sweet spices are used to make the fragrant mixtures. Garam masala may be used in a wide variety of dishes, either added towards the end of the cooking time or combined with other spices in a paste. It may also be sprinkled over the food during the final stages before serving. To make your own garam masala, toast 60 ml/4 tbsp coriander seeds in a small ungreased frying pan, stirring all the time, for a few minutes until they give off their aroma. Tip the seeds into a bowl and repeat the process with 30 ml/2 tbsp cumin seeds, 15 ml/1 tbsp black peppercorns, 10 ml/2 tsp cardamom seeds, 3 cinnamon sticks and 5 ml/1 tsp whole cloves, toasting each spice separately. When all the spices have been toasted and cooled, grind them to a powder in a coffee grinder (reserved for the purpose) or in a mortar with a pestle. Stir in 30 ml/2 tbsp freshly grated nutmeg. Store in an airtight jar.

MRS BEETON'S ROAST TURKEY

The recipe that follows is based upon a 6 kg/ 13 lb bird. Timings for birds of different weights are given in the introduction to this section, which also includes information on thawing frozen birds, tips for successful cooking and advice on what to do with leftovers.

fat for basting
1 turkey
450 g/1 lb Mrs Beeton's Forcemeat (page 349)
675 g/1½ lb seasoned sausagemeat
225 g/8 oz rindless streaky bacon rashers

Set the oven at 180°C/350°F/gas 4. Weigh the turkey. Trim it, and wash it inside and out in cold water. Pat dry with absorbent kitchen paper. Immediately before cooking, stuff the neck of the bird with forcemeat. Put the sausagemeat inside the body cavity. Cover the breast of the bird with the bacon rashers.

Place the prepared turkey in a roasting tin. Cover with foil and roast for 15 minutes. Lower the oven temperature to 180°C/350°F/Gas 4 and roast for 20 minutes per 450 g/1 lb (unstuffed weight) plus 20 minutes, or until cooked through. Remove the foil for the last hour of cooking and the bacon strips for the final 20 minutes to allow the breast to brown.

Serve on a heated platter, with roasted or grilled chipolata sausages, bacon rolls (see page 49), bread sauce and lemon and cranberry cups (see Mrs Beeton's Tip).

SERVES 14 TO 16

> **MRS BEETON'S TIP** Lemons, cut in half and with all flesh and pulp removed, make ideal containers for individual portions of cranberry sauce. Arrange them around the turkey and add a touch of contrasting colour with a watercress garnish, if liked.

ROAST TURKEY WITH CHESTNUTS

1 (4.5-5.5 kg/10-12 lb) turkey
salt and pepper
225 g/8 oz rindless streaky bacon rashers

HERB FORCEMEAT
50 g/2 oz margarine
100 g/4 oz fresh white breadcrumbs
pinch of grated nutmeg
15 ml/1 tbsp chopped parsley
5 ml/1 tsp chopped fresh mixed herbs
grated rind of ½ lemon
salt and pepper
1 egg, beaten

CHESTNUT STUFFING
1 kg/2¼ lb chestnuts
275 ml/9 fl oz turkey or chicken stock
50 g/2 oz butter
1 egg, beaten
single cream or milk (see method)

Make the chestnut stuffing first. Shell and skin the chestnuts (see Mrs Beeton's Tip, page 52). Put them in a saucepan, add the stock and simmer for 20 minutes or until tender. Drain the chestnuts and chop them finely, or press through a sieve into a clean bowl. Melt the butter in a small saucepan. Remove from the heat and add to the bowl containing the chestnuts. Stir in the beaten egg, with enough cream or milk to moisten the mixture.

Make the forcemeat. Melt the margarine in a small saucepan. Add the breadcrumbs, nutmeg, herbs and lemon rind. Stir in salt and pepper to taste and sufficient beaten egg to bind the mixture.

Set the oven at 180°C/350°F/gas 4. Trim the turkey and wash it inside and out in cold water. Pat dry with absorbent kitchen paper and season inside with salt and pepper. Immediately before cooking, fill the neck end of the bird with chestnut stuffing and the body with the forcemeat. Truss, if wished, and cover the bird with the bacon.

Place the bird in a roasting tin and roast for 4½-5 hours or until cooked through, removing the bacon towards the end to allow the breast to brown. (For a larger bird, see the chart on page 43 for cooking times.) Serve with giblet Gravy (see page 352).

SERVES 14 TO 16

MRS BEETON'S TIP Overcooked turkey tastes dry and uninteresting, so it is important to test it frequently towards the end of the cooking time. Pierce the deepest part of the thigh with a sharp skewer. The juices should run clear. Pink-tinged juices indicate that more cooking time is required.

TURKEY AND PRUNE CASSEROLE

2 turkey drumsticks
25 g/1 oz plain flour
50 g/2 oz butter
2 onions, chopped
2 red peppers, seeded and chopped
1-3 garlic cloves, crushed
5 ml/1 tsp mustard powder
5 ml/1 tsp mixed herbs
450 ml/¾ pint chicken or turkey stock
100 g/4 oz ready-to-eat prunes
2 bay leaves
salt and pepper

Set the oven at 160°C/325°F/gas 2. Skin the turkey portions and sprinkle with the flour. Melt the butter in a large flameproof casserole, add the turkey and fry gently until browned on all sides. Reserve any remaining flour.

Add the onions, red pepper and garlic and fry gently for about 5 minutes. Sprinkle in the mustard and herbs with the reserved flour, then add the stock, stirring it into the vegetables. Add the prunes, bay leaves and salt and pepper to taste. Bring just to the boil, then cover and transfer to the oven.

Cook for 1½ hours or until the turkey is very tender. Remove the turkey from the casserole and cut all the meat off the bone in bite-size pieces. Replace the turkey in the casserole, discard the bay leaves and taste for seasoning. Serve at once, with rice, pasta or baked potatoes.

SERVES 4

BRAISED TURKEY BREAST

50 g/2 oz butter
1 onion, finely chopped
1 carrot, thinly sliced
1 leek, trimmed, sliced and washed
2 celery sticks, sliced
½ small turnip, finely chopped
2 rindless streaky bacon rashers, chopped
1 (800 g/1¾ lb) turkey breast 'joint'
600 ml/1 pint chicken or turkey stock
300 ml/½ pint dry white wine
pinch of dried thyme
1 bay leaf
3 parsley sprigs
salt and pepper
25 g/1 oz plain flour
60 ml/4 tbsp double cream

Melt 25 g/1 oz of the butter in a large heavy-bottomed saucepan, add the chopped vegetables and bacon and fry for about 10 minutes over gentle heat until lightly browned all over. Add the turkey. Pour the stock and wine over, and add the herbs, salt and pepper. Cover the pan tightly with foil and a lid. Simmer very gently for about 2 hours, basting the breast joint occasionally with the stock, until tender.

In a small bowl, blend the remaining butter with the flour. Transfer the turkey joint to a heated serving platter and keep hot. Discard the bay leaf and parsley from the cooking liquid. Gradually add small pieces for the butter mixture to the simmering stock, whisking after each addition, until thickened.

Simmer for 5 minutes, whisking, until the sauce is thick and smooth. Stir in the cream and remove from the heat. Garnish the turkey joint with vegetables. Serve the sauce separately.

SERVES 4

BLANQUETTE OF TURKEY

bones from a cooked turkey
1 onion, sliced
1 blade of mace
salt and pepper
40 g/1½ oz butter
40 g/1½ oz plain flour
450 g/1 lb cooked turkey, diced
pinch of nutmeg
30 ml/2 tbsp single cream
1 egg yolk

Combine the turkey bones, onion and mace in a saucepan. Add enough water to cover, with a good sprinkling of salt and pepper. Bring to the boil, lower the heat and cover the pan. Simmer for 1½ hours, or longer, to obtain well-flavoured stock. Strain stock, setting aside 400 ml/14 fl oz.

Melt the butter in a saucepan, stir in the flour and cook for 1 minute without browning. Gradually stir in the measured stock. Bring to the boil, stirring constantly, and cook for 10 minutes. Stir in the turkey and nutmeg.

Heat the turkey in the sauce over gentle heat for about 20 minutes. Mix the cream or milk and egg yolk in a small bowl. Stir in a little of the hot sauce and mix well. Add the contents of the bowl to the saucepan and heat gently; do not boil. Taste for seasoning and serve at once, with boiled rice or noodles.

SERVES 4

VARIATION

TURKEY WITH CASHEW NUTS AND BACON Add 2 crumbled grilled bacon rashers and 100 g/4 oz cashew nuts to the blanquette just before serving. Sprinkle with chopped parsley or lightly sautéed leek rings.

TURKEY BREASTS IN PASTRY

2 turkey breasts (about 500 g/18 oz each)
25 g/1 oz butter
175 g/6 oz mushrooms, finely chopped
50 g/2 oz onion, finely chopped
225 g/8 oz belly of pork, minced
50 g/2 oz sage and onion stuffing mix
salt and pepper
1 egg, beaten
225 g/8 oz puff pastry, thawed if frozen
flour for rolling out

Set the oven at 220°C/425°F/gas 7. Remove the skin from the turkey breasts, then cut each across to make 2 thinner slices. Place each slice between sheets of greaseproof paper and flatten with a cutlet bat or rolling pin.

Melt the butter in a saucepan and gently cook the mushrooms and onion until the onion is soft but not brown. Remove from the heat. Add the pork, stuffing mix, salt, pepper and half the beaten egg to the pan. Allow to stand for a few minutes for the crumbs to swell.

Roll out the pastry on a lightly floured surface into a 30 cm/12 inch square. Place 2 turkey pieces in the centre and spread the stuffing over them. Lay the remaining 2 turkey breasts on top to enclose the stuffing. Dampen the edges of the pastry lightly and fold it over the turkey, pinching the edges together to seal firmly. Place on a baking sheet with the seam under neath. Brush with the remaining egg and garnish with any pastry trimmings. Bake for 20 minutes, then reduce the oven temperature to 180°C/350°F/gas 4. Continue baking for a further 35 minutes. Serve hot, in slices.

SERVES 8

ENGLISH ROAST DUCK

fat for basting
Sage and Onion Stuffing (page 349)
1 (1.8 kg/4 lb) oven-ready duck
salt and pepper
30 ml/2 tbsp plain flour
300 ml/½ pint duck or chicken stock (see
     Mrs Beeton's Tip)

Set the oven at 190°C/375°F/gas 5. Spoon the stuffing into the duck and truss it. Weigh the duck and calculate the cooking time at 20 minutes per 450 g/1 lb. Sprinkle the breast with salt. Put the duck on a wire rack in a roasting tin and prick the skin all over with a fork or skewer to release the fat. Roast for the required time, basting the duck occasionally with the pan juices. Test by piercing the thickest part of the thigh with the point of a sharp knife. The juices should run clear.

Transfer the duck to a heated platter, remove the trussing string and keep hot. Pour off most of the fat from the roasting tin, sprinkle in the flour and cook, stirring, for 2 minutes. Blend in the stock. Bring to the boil, then lower the heat and simmer, stirring, for 3-4 minutes. Add salt and pepper to taste. Serve in a gravyboat, with the duck.

SERVES 4

> **MRS BEETON'S TIP** If you have the duck giblets, use them as the basis of your stock. Put them in a saucepan with 1 sliced onion and 1 sliced carrot. Add 600 ml/1 pint water. Simmer, covered, for 1 hour, then strain.

DUCK WITH ORANGE SAUCE

1 (1.6-1.8 kg/3½-4 lb) oven-ready duck
salt and pepper
5 oranges
15 ml/1 tbsp caster sugar
15 ml/1 tbsp white wine vinegar
30 ml/2 tbsp brandy
15 ml/1 tbsp plain flour

Set the oven at 190°C/375°F/gas 5. Weigh the duck and calculate the cooking time at 20 minutes per 450 g/1 lb. Sprinkle the breast with salt. Put the duck on a wire rack in a roasting tin and prick the skin all over with a fork or skewer to release the fat. Roast for the required time, basting the duck occasionally with the pan juices.

Meanwhile, thinly peel the rind from one of the oranges, taking care not to include any of the bitter pith. Cut the rind into strips, then cook these in boiling water for 1 minute. Drain and set aside on absorbent kitchen paper. Slice one of the remaining oranges and set the slices aside for the garnish. Squeeze the rest of the oranges, including the one with the rind removed, and set the juice aside.

Put the sugar in a saucepan with the vinegar. Heat gently, stirring until the sugar has dissolved, then bring to the boil and boil rapidly without stirring until the syrup turns a golden caramel colour. Remove from the heat and carefully add the orange juice and brandy. Return to the heat and stir until just blended, then add the reserved orange rind.

When the duck is cooked, transfer it to a platter, remove the trussing string and cut it into serving portions. Transfer to a heated serving dish and keep hot. Pour off the fat from the roasting tin, sprinkle in the flour and cook, stirring, for 2 minutes. Blend in the orange mixture. Bring to the boil, then lower the heat and simmer, stirring, for 3-4 minutes. Add salt and pepper to taste. Spoon the sauce over the duck, garnish with the reserved orange slices and serve.

SERVES 4

SALMIS OF DUCK

1 (2.25 kg/5 lb) duck
1 Spanish onion, sliced
1 carrot, quartered
25 g/1 oz butter
25 g/1 oz plain flour
350 ml/12 fl oz well-flavoured duck or
    chicken stock
150 ml/¼ pint burgundy
12 stoned green olives
salt and pepper

Set the oven at 200°C/400°F/gas 6. Prick the duck all over with a fork. Spread the onion slices on the base of a roasting tin, add the carrot quarters and put the duck on top. Roast for 1-1½ hours or until tender. Cut into portions and keep hot. Discard vegetables.

Pour off the fat from the roasting tin, add the butter and melt over gentle heat. Stir in the flour and cook for 1 minute, then gradually add the stock and wine, stirring until the sauce boils and thickens. Stir in the olives, with salt and pepper to taste.

Return the duck to the sauce and heat through gently for 10-15 minutes, stirring frequently. Serve at once. Potato Croquettes (page 232) would be a suitable accompaniment.

SERVES 4

Plaice Mornay and Sole Veronique (both on page 24)

Cod Cutlets with Shrimp Stuffing (page 21)

Spicy Fish Slices (page 21) and Prawn Curry (page 34)

Sweet and Sour Hake (page 23)

Moules Marinière (page 35)

Roast Chicken with Honey and Almonds (page 48)

Barbecued Chicken Drumsticks (page 50) and Devilled Chicken (page 51)

Coq au Vin (page 55) and Lemon Chicken (page 54)

FILLETS OF DUCK WITH RICH CHERRY DRESSING

Creamy mashed potatoes or plain cooked noodles and crisp, lightly cooked green beans are suitable accompaniments for this simple, yet rich dish.

4 boneless duck breasts
salt and pepper
2.5 ml/½ tsp ground mace
4 bay leaves
4 thyme sprigs
125 ml/4 fl oz red wine
60 ml/4 tbsp port
25 g/1 oz butter
15 ml/1 tbsp finely chopped onion
225 g/8 oz cherries, stoned
5 ml/1 tsp grated lemon rind
10 ml/2 tsp arrowroot

Prick the skin on the duck breasts all over, or remove it, if preferred. Rub plenty of salt, pepper and mace into the breasts, then place them in a shallow dish, skin uppermost, with a bay leaf and thyme sprig under each. Pour the wine and port over the duck, cover and allow to marinate for at least 2 hours; it may be chilled overnight.

Melt the butter in a frying pan and add the onion with the herbs from the duck. Cook over low heat for 5 minutes. Meanwhile, drain the duck breasts, reserving the marinade. Place them skin down in the pan and increase the heat to moderate. Cook until the skin is well browned, then turn the breasts and cook the second side. Allow about 15 minutes on each side to cook the duck breasts.

Using a slotted spoon, transfer the cooked duck to a heated serving dish or individual plates. Keep hot. Leaving the herbs in the pan, add the cherries and lemon rind. Toss the cherries in the cooking juices for about a minute, until the heat causes them to begin to change colour.

Pour in the reserved marinade and heat gently until just boiling. While the sauce is heating, put the arrowroot in a cup and blend to a paste with 15-30 ml/1-2 tbsp cold water. Add it to the pan, stirring. Bring to the boil and remove the pan from the heat.

Discard the thyme sprigs but arrange the bay leaves on the duck. Use a slotted spoon to divide the cherries between the duck breasts, then pour the sauce over and serve the once.

SERVES 4

VARIATION

FILLETS OF DUCK BIGARADE (*Illustrated on page 137*) Cut the pared rind from 1 Seville orange into fine strips and simmer these in water until tender; drain and set aside. Marinate the duck as above, adding the juice of the orange but omitting the port. Continue as above, stirring 30 ml/ 2 tbsp plain flour into the cooking juices from the duck, then add 250 ml/8 fl oz duck or chicken stock and 5 ml/1 tsp tomato purée. Bring to the boil, stirring, add the reserved marinade and simmer rapidly for 10 minutes. Stir in the juice of ½ lemon and 5 ml/1 tsp redcurrant jelly. Taste for seasoning and pour over the duck.

> **MRS BEETON'S TIP** For presentation purposes, cut each cooked duck fillet across into thick slices. Separate the slices slightly on individual plates before finishing with the bay leaves, cherries and sauce.

STUFFED BONED DUCK

25 g/1 oz butter
1 onion, finely chopped
100 g/4 oz long-grain rice
275 ml/9 fl oz chicken stock
1 bay leaf • salt and pepper
1 small red pepper, seeded
225 g/8 oz cooked ham
50 g/2 oz seedless raisins
50 g/2 oz peanuts, roughly chopped
1 egg, beaten
1 (1.6-1.8 kg/3½-4 lb) oven-ready duck
30 ml/2 tbsp oil

Melt the butter in a small saucepan, add the onion and fry for about 5 minutes until soft but not brown. Stir in the rice and cook until translucent. Pour on the stock and add the bay leaf, with salt and pepper to taste. Cook for 12-15 minutes or until the rice is tender and the stock has been absorbed.

Put the red pepper in a saucepan with water to cover. Bring to the boil and cook for 5 minutes, then drain, cool quickly under cold water and drain again. Mince the ham, raisins, blanched pepper and peanuts together or process briefly in a food processor. Stir in the rice, with enough of the beaten egg to bind the stuffing. Add salt and pepper to taste.

Set the oven at 190°C/375°F/gas 5. Following the general instructions on page 45, bone the duck. Spread the stuffing over the inside of the bird. Carefully lift the two halves of the duck and bring them together. Sew the skin together.

Heat the oil in a roasting tin. Put the duck, breast side up, in the tin. Baste with the hot oil. Transfer to the oven and roast for 1½-2 hours. Serve hot or cold.

SERVES 6 TO 8

DUCKLING IN RED WINE

1 (1.8 kg/4 lb) duckling
salt and pepper
2 onions, chopped
1 bay leaf
250 ml/8 fl oz red wine
30 ml/2 tbsp oil
100 g/4 oz rindless streaky bacon rashers, chopped
400 ml/14 fl oz chicken or duck stock
1 carrot, sliced
2 celery sticks, sliced
grated rind of 1 orange
100 g/4 oz small button mushrooms

Cut the duckling into quarters. Arrange in a shallow dish large enough to hold all the pieces of duckling in a single layer. Sprinkle with plenty of salt and pepper. Add the onions, bay leaf and wine, cover the dish and marinate for 2 hours.

Remove the duckling portions from the marinade and pat dry on absorbent kitchen paper. Strain the marinade and set it aside. Heat the oil in a large frying pan, add the bacon and fry over gentle heat for 3-4 minutes. Add the duckling portions and brown them all over. Using tongs and a slotted spoon, transfer the duckling portions and bacon to a casserole.

Heat the stock in a small saucepan or in the microwave, pour it into the casserole and bake for 15 minutes. Add the carrot and celery slices, the orange rind, mushrooms amd reserved marinade. Cover and cook for 1½-2 hours or until the duck is cooked through and very tender. Skim off any surplus fat from the surface before serving.

SERVES 4

DUCK WITH GREEN OLIVES

1 set duck giblets
4 carrots
2 onions, roughly chopped
1 bouquet garni
salt and pepper
1 (2.25 kg/5 lb) duck
30 ml/2 tbsp goose fat or oil
2 slices of stale white bread, crusts removed
24 stuffed green olives

Set aside the duck liver for use in another recipe. Put the rest of the giblets in a small saucepan. Add 500 ml/17 fl oz water. Roughly chop 2 of the carrots and add them to the pan with the onions, bouquet garni and salt and pepper to taste. Bring to the boil, lower the heat and simmer for 40 minutes or until the stock is reduced by about one third. Set aside.

Season the inside of the duck. Heat the fat in a heavy flameproof casserole, put in the duck, and brown it on all sides. Lower the heat, cover the casserole and cook slowly for 15 minutes. Remove the duck, cut it into neat joints and return the joints to the casserole.

Crumble the bread over the duck and strain the stock into the casserole. Add the olives. Slice the remaining carrots thinly; stir them into the stock. Cover the casserole and simmer over moderate heat for 45 minutes or until the duck is cooked through. Skim off as much fat from the surface of the stock as possible.

Serve the duck with saffron rice. Celeriac Purée (page 215) and Petits Pois à la Française (page 230) would complement the rich flavour of the duck.

SERVES 4

DUCK WITH GREEN PEAS

1 kg/2¼ lb fresh peas
12 button onions, peeled but left whole
50 g/2 oz butter
225 g/8 oz rindless bacon rashers, halved
1 (2.25 kg/5 lb) duck
450 ml/¾ pint chicken stock
1 bouquet garni
salt and pepper

Set the oven at 180°C/350°F/gas 4. Shell the peas and set them aside. Bring a small saucepan of water to the boil, add the onions and cook for 2–3 minutes. Drain.

Melt the butter in a large flameproof casserole, add the onions and bacon and stir fry until the onions are pale brown and the bacon is beginning to crisp. Using a slotted spoon, set the onions and bacon aside.

Add the duck to the fat remaining in the pan. Brown it quickly on all sides over moderate heat, then carefully lift it out of the pan. Put on a plate and reserve. Pour away the fat from the pan, add a third of the stock and boil down to half its quantity, then add the rest of the stock.

Return the duck to the pan and add the reserved onions and bacon. Stir in the bouquet garni and season lightly with salt and pepper. Bring to the boil, then cover the casserole and transfer it to the oven. Bake for 1¼ hours. Stir in the peas. Replace the cover, return the casserole to the oven and bake for about 45 minutes, basting occasionally.

Using a slotted spoon, remove the duck, peas, onions and bacon and keep hot. Skim off any fat from the surface of the liquid, then boil until reduced to a coating sauce. Pour over the duck and serve.

SERVES 4 TO 5

BRAISED DUCK WITH TURNIPS

100 g/4 oz butter
1 (2.25 kg/5 lb) duck
1 bouquet garni
6 black peppercorns
2 cloves
about 600 ml/1 pint well-flavoured duck
    or chicken stock
450 g/1 lb young turnips, sliced
75 ml/5 tbsp medium-dry sherry
    (optional)

MIREPOIX
2 onions, sliced
1 small turnip, sliced
2 carrots, sliced
1 celery stick, sliced

Melt 50 g/2 oz of the butter in a large saucepan, add the mirepoix ingredients and turn until well coated. Lay the duck on this bed of vegetables, cover the pan and cook very gently for 20 minutes, shaking the pan occasionally. Add the bouquet garni and spices, then pour in enough stock to cover three quarters of the mirepoix. Cover the pan with foil and a tight-fitting lid. Simmer gently for 1¼ hours, adding more stock if necessary to prevent the vegetables from burning.

Set the oven at 220°C/425°F/gas 7. Put a baking sheet in the oven to heat up. Melt the remaining butter in a frying pan, add the turnips and toss over moderate heat for 4-5 minutes. Add the contents of the pan to the pan containing the duck and cook for 45 minutes more, until the duck is tender.

Remove the duck from the pan, place it on the hot baking sheet and put it in the oven for 10 minutes to crisp the skin. Using a slotted spoon, transfer the turnips from the saucepan to a heated bowl. Keep hot.

Remove the excess fat from the top of the stock. Strain it into a clean pan, boil it quickly until reduced by half, and stir in the sherry, if used. Serve the duck on a hot platter, with turnips piled at either end. Offer the sauce separately.

SERVES 4 TO 5

DUCK AND RED CABBAGE

The trimmings from 2 roast ducks should yield enough meat for this flavoursome dish.

50 g/2 oz butter
450 g/1 lb red cabbage, shredded
salt and pepper
well-flavoured stock (see method)
about 400 g/14 oz cold roast duck,
    shredded
15 ml/1 tbsp red wine vinegar
15 ml/1 tbsp demerara sugar

Melt the butter in a heavy-bottomed saucepan and add the red cabbage. Stir lightly to coat the cabbage in butter, then season with salt and pepper. Cover the pan tightly and simmer for 1 hour. Shake the pan from time to time to prevent the cabbage from sticking to the base, and add just enough stock when required to prevent it from burning.

In another pan, combine the duck with enough stock to moisten. Place over gentle heat until the duck is heated through. Add the vinegar and sugar to the cabbage, mix well, then turn on to a heated dish. Drain the duck and arrange it on the top. Serve with a mixture of brown rice and wild rice, if liked. Beans with Soured Cream (page 210) would be an appropriate accompaniment.

SERVES 4 TO 6

DUCK AND ORANGE CURRY

1 (2.25 kg/5 lb) duck, jointed
salt and freshly ground black pepper
30 ml/2 tbsp ghee, clarified butter (see
    Mrs Beeton's Tip, page 313) or oil
2 large onions, chopped
2 garlic cloves, crushed
2.5 ml/½ tsp cardamom seeds
10 ml/2 tsp finely grated fresh root ginger
5 ml/1 tsp ground cumin
5 ml/1 tsp turmeric
10 ml/2 tsp ground coriander
5 cm/2 in piece of cinnamon stick
6 cloves
750 ml/1¼ pints unsweetened orange juice

Sprinkle the duck generously with salt. Heat the ghee, fat or oil in a large deep frying pan, add the duck and fry over moderate heat for 15-20 minutes, turning frequently. Using tongs, transfer the duck portions to a plate and set aside.

Add the onions and garlic to the fat remaining in the pan and fry for 4-6 minutes until transparent. Add the spices and fry for 2-3 minutes, stirring constantly, then pour in the juice. Bring to the boil, stirring.

Replace the duck in the pan, cover and simmer for 1¼-1½ hours. Season with a little extra salt if required. Serve with rice.

SERVES 4

MRS BEETON'S TIP Cardamom seeds are the tiny black seeds found inside the pale green pods. Slit each pod with the point of a knife, holding it over a small bowl, then scrape out the seeds.

DUCK ON CROUTES

50 g/2 oz butter
2 onions, finely chopped
25 g/1 oz plain flour
600 ml/1 pint well-flavoured stock
2 cloves
1 blade of mace
6 allspice berries
6 small mushrooms
salt and pepper
350 g/12 oz cold roast duck, cut into neat
    pieces
oil for shallow frying
8 rounds of bread, crusts removed
Apple Sauce (page 351) to serve

Melt the butter in a saucepan, add the onions and fry until lightly browned. Stir in the flour and cook slowly until nut-brown, then add the stock. Bring to the boil, stirring constantly, then lower the heat and simmer for 10 minutes.

Tie the spices in muslin and add with the mushrooms to the pan. Stir in salt and pepper to taste. Add the duck pieces to the sauce, then simmer gently for 20 minutes. Just before serving, make the croûtes. Heat the oil in a large frying pan. Add the rounds of bread and fry quickly until golden on both sides. Remove from the heat, drain on absorbent kitchen paper and arrange on 4 heated plates.

Arrange the pieces of duck on the croûtes, discarding the spices from the sauce. Spoon the remaining sauce over the duck. Serve the apple sauce separately.

SERVES 4

———————— ◆ ————————

DUCK RAGOUT

Based on a flavoursome recipe from the first edition of Mrs Beeton's Book of Household Management, this is ideal for today's birds that are bred to be less fatty. The duck may be served whole but it is often more practical to joint it for ease of serving, particularly when presenting the ragout at a dinner party.

1 (1.8 kg/4 lb) oven-ready duck with
　giblets
salt and pepper
1 bay leaf
1 small carrot, sliced
1 celery stick, sliced
3 onions, sliced
4 large fresh sage leaves or small sprigs,
　or 10 ml/2 tsp dried sage
2 lemon thyme sprigs or a strip of lemon
　peel and thyme sprigs
25 g/1 oz butter
25 g/1 oz plain flour

Set the oven at 220°C/425°F/gas 7. Place the duck breast down on a rack or trivet in a roasting tin, prick the skin all over and rub it with plenty of salt and pepper. Roast the duck for 15 minutes, then turn it over and roast it for a further 15 minutes with the breast uppermost.

Meanwhile, place the giblets, bay leaf, carrot, celery and 1 onion (or about a third of the slices if already prepared) in a saucepan with plenty of water to cover. Bring to the boil, skim off any scum and reduce the heat. Cover the pan and cook the giblets for 45 minutes.

When the duck is browned all over, remove it from the oven and reduce the temperature to 180°C/350°F/gas 5. The duck may be placed whole in a large oven-proof casserole or, more practically, cut into four portions. To joint the duck, place it breast down on a large board and split it in half. Use a meat mallet or rolling pin to tap the knife through the bones. Cut both halves into two portions, splitting the breast meat so that most of it rests with the wing joint. Use scissors or a pointed knife to trim away any small bones and the ends of the breast bone.

Pour a little of the roasting fat into a frying pan and fry the remaining onions until they are evenly browned, stirring occasionally. This will take 20-30 minutes but the long cooking time is important for the colour and flavour of the finished dish.

Add the onions to the casserole with the herbs. Strain the giblet stock straight over the duck. Add plenty of salt and pepper and return the ragout to the oven. There should be plenty of stock, so the casserole should not need to be covered. Cook for 1 hour, turning the joints halfway through cooking, and basting if necessary. The duck should be very tender and the cooking liquid should be richly flavoured.

Transfer the joints to a serving dish or plates. Pour the stock into a pan, discarding the herbs – there should be about 600 ml/1 pint. Reduce it by boiling if necessary or add a little more water. If adding water, swirl it around the casserole to incorporate all the cooking sediment. Cream the butter and flour to a paste.

Heat the cooking liquor until just simmering, then whisk it constantly as you add knobs of the butter mixture. Continue whisking until the sauce boils for 2-3 minutes and thickens.

Taste for seasoning, then pour the sauce over the duck and serve at once.

SERVES 4

VARIATIONS

DUCK WITH ORANGE AND CLARET Pare the rind and squeeze the juice from 1 orange. Add both to the duck in the casserole, with the herbs and onions. Pour over 300 ml/½ pint claret and 300 ml/½ pint of the giblet stock. Cover and continue as above. Serve with pasta or rice and a garnish of orange slices.

DUCK WITH CHESTNUTS Soak 100 g/4 oz dried chestnuts in plenty of cold water overnight. Drain and simmer in fresh water for 15 minutes. Add the chestnuts to the casserole with the onions. Use a slotted spoon to transfer the chestnuts to a serving dish with the duck. Add 125 ml/4 fl oz port and 15 ml/1 tbsp redcurrant jelly to the cooking juices and stir until melted before thickening. (Boiled and peeled fresh chestnuts may be added directly to the casserole.)

ROAST GOOSE WITH FRUIT STUFFING AND RED CABBAGE

1 goose with giblets
½ lemon
salt and pepper
350 g/12 oz prunes, soaked overnight in
    water to cover
450 g/1 lb cooking apples
15 ml/1 tbsp redcurrant jelly

RED CABBAGE
50 g/2 oz butter
1.5 kg/3¼ lb red cabbage, finely
    shredded
50 g/2 oz demerara sugar
75 ml/5 tbsp malt or cider vinegar
salt and peper

Remove the giblets from the goose and put them in a saucepan. Add 1.5 litres/2¾ pints water and bring to the boil. Lower the heat and simmer until the liquid is reduced by half. Strain and set aside.

Set the over at 230°C/450°F/gas 8. Weigh the goose and calculate the cooking time at 20 minutes per 450 g/1 lb. Remove the excess fat usually found around the vent. Rinse the inside of the bird, then rub the skin with lemon. Season with salt and pepper.

Drain the prunes, remove the stones and roughly chop the flesh. Put it in a bowl. Peel, core and chop the apples. Add them to the prunes, with salt and pepper to taste. Use the mixture to stuff the body of the bird. Put the goose on a rack in a roasting tin. Place in the oven, immediately lower the temperature to 180°C/350°F/gas 4 and cook for the calculated time. Drain away fat from the roasting tin occasionally during cooking.

Meanwhile, melt the butter in a large flameproof casserole, add the red cabbage and sugar and stir well. Pour in 75 ml/ 5 tbsp water and the vinegar, with salt and pepper to taste. Cover and cook in the oven for about 2 hours, stirring occasionally.

When the goose is cooked, transfer it to a heated serving platter and keep hot. Drain off the excess fat from the roasting tin, retaining the juices. Stir in the reserved giblet stock and cook over fairly high heat until reduced to a thin gravy. Stir in the redcurrant jelly until melted. Serve the gravy and red cabbage separately.

SERVES 6 TO 8 (depending on size of bird)

◆

ROAST GOOSE WITH APPLES AND ONIONS

1 goose with giblets
salt and pepper
1 orange
1 lemon
13 small onions
7 bay leaves
1 large thyme sprig
30 ml/2 tbsp dried sage
1 cinnamon stick
4 cloves
50 g/2 oz butter
12 Cox's Orange Pippin apples
5 ml/1 tsp lemon juice
45 ml/3 tbsp port
45 ml/3 tbsp crab apple or redcurrant jelly

Remove the giblets from the goose and put them in a saucepan. Add 1.5 litres/2¾ pints water and bring to the boil. Lower the heat and simmer until the liquid is reduced by half. Strain and set aside.

Set the oven at 230°C/450°F/gas 8. Weigh the goose and calculate the cooking time at 20 minutes per 450 g/1 lb. Trim away excess fat and rinse the bird, then rub it all over with plenty of salt and pepper. Pare the rind from the fruit and place it in the body cavity with 1 onion, 2 bay leaves and the thyme sprig. Rub the sage over the outside of the bird and tuck a bay leaf behind each of the wing and leg joints.

Place the goose on a rack in a roasting tin. Place it in the oven and immediately reduce the heat to 180°C/350°F/gas 4. Cook for the calculated time, draining away fat from the roasting tin occasionally.

Peel the remaining onions but leave them whole. Place them in a saucepan and pour in boiling water to cover. Add a little salt. Simmer for 15 minutes, then drain well. Squeeze the juice from the orange and lemon, and mix together in a small saucepan. Add the cinnamon, cloves and remaining bay leaf, then heat gently until simmering. Cover and cook for 15 minutes. Off the heat, stir in the butter.

Peel and core the apples. As each apple is prepared, place it in a bowl of iced water to which the lemon juice has been added. This will prevent discoloration. Drain the apples, put them in an ovenproof dish and spoon the fruit juice and spice mixture over them to coat them completely. Add the onions, then toss them with the apples so all are coated in juices.

Place the dish of apples and onions in the oven 1 hour before the goose is cooked. Turn them occasionally during cooking so that they are evenly browned and tender. About 10 minutes before the goose is cooked, heat the port and jelly gently in a saucepan or in a bowl in the microwave until the jelly has melted. Spoon this over the apple and onion mixture for the final 5 minutes.

When the goose is cooked, transfer it to a heated serving platter and keep hot. Drain off the fat from the tin. Stir the flour into the cooking juices and cook over low heat for 5 minutes, scraping in all the sediment from the base of the pan. Pour in the reserved giblet stock and bring to the boil, stirring all the time. Taste for seasoning and pour or strain into a sauceboat.

Serve the goose surrounded by the glazed apples and onions, with their juices. Roast potatoes, Brussels Sprouts with Chestnuts (page 212) and Celeriac Purée (page 215) are all excellent accompaniments.

SERVES 6 (with meat to spare, depending on the size of the goose)

GUINEAFOWL WITH GRAPES

The guineafowl may be stuffed with Wild Rice Stuffing (page 350), if liked. Select the longer cooking time.

1 guineafowl with giblets
1 bouquet garni
salt and pepper
50 g/2 oz butter
1 parsley sprig
6 rindless streaky bacon rashers
25 g/1 oz plain flour
125 ml/4 fl oz dry white wine
225 g/8 oz seedless white grapes
lemon juice (see method)

GARNISH
　　filled lemon cups (see Mrs Beeton's Tip, page 60), seedless red grapes or redcurrant jelly

Put the guineafowl giblets in a saucepan. Add 250 ml/8 fl oz water, the bouquet garni, salt and pepper. Bring to the boil, lower the heat and simmer for 40 minutes to make a good stock. Strain the stock and reserve 150 ml/¼ pint.

Set the oven at 180°C/350°F/gas 4. Put a knob of butter and the parsley inside the bird; spread the rest of the butter over the breast. Cover with the bacon.

Put the bird in a roasting tin and roast for 1-1½ hours, basting frequently. Remove the bacon rashers for the last 15 minutes to allow the breast to brown.

Remove the guineafowl from the roasting tin. Cut it into neat serving portions, arrange on a heated serving dish and keep hot. Drain the fat from the tin, leaving just sufficient to absorb the flour. Sprinkle the flour into the tin and brown it lightly. Stir in the wine and reserved stock. Bring the gravy to the boil, stirring constantly, then add the grapes. Add a little lemon juice to bring out the flavour and heat through, stirring all the time. Taste the sauce and add more salt and pepper if required. Pour the sauce over the guineafowl. Garnish with lemon cups filled with small red seedless grapes or redcurrant jelly and serve.

SERVES 3 TO 4

ROAST GUINEAFOWL

50 g/2 oz butter
salt and pepper
1 guineafowl
2 rindless fat bacon rashers
flour for dredging
watercress sprigs to garnish

Set the oven at 180°C/350°F/gas 4. Mix the butter in a small bowl with plenty of salt and pepper. Put most of the seasoned butter inside the body of the bird. Spread the rest on the thighs. Lay the bacon rashers over the breast.

Put the bird in a roasting tin and roast for 1-1½ hours or until cooked through, basting frequently. When the bird is almost cooked, remove the bacon rashers, dredge the breast with flour, baste with the pan juices and finish cooking.

Wash and dry the watercress. Put it in a bowl, add about 30 ml/2 tbsp French dressing and toss lightly. Remove any trussing strings from the bird, place it on a serving dish and garnish.

SERVES 2 TO 3

GAME

Game refers to wild birds and animals which are hunted for sport as well as for food. The hunting, killing and selling of game is strictly controlled in Great Britain and the majority of game is protected by law, the exceptions being rabbits and woodpigeons.

There are certain times of the year when game cannot be shot and these 'seasons' vary slightly according to the nesting and mating patterns of the individual species. Outside of the season, not only is it illegal to kill game but it is also an offence to sell game; unless it has been imported into the country when already dead. Only licensed butchers and poulterers are allowed to deal in game and it can be offered for sale up to ten days after the end of the season. The restrictions on the sale of home-reared game apply to frozen animals as well as to fresh ones. However, there are companies that specialise in importing game for out-of-season sale. Some game, notably venison, is now farmed. Certain birds must not be killed and these include wild geese, Garganey teal, Long-tailed duck and Scaup duck.

A note of the season for each type of game is given in the following pages, along with advice on identifying birds and the best cooking methods to use. In the section which follows, the details of preparing and cooking game are outlined; however you will find that game is readily available dressed for the oven, not only from specialist butchers but also from good supermarkets where it is often sold frozen.

CAPERCAILLIE

Season: October 1st to January 31st.

The capercaillie is a member of the grouse family, originating from Scandinavia. It is found today in small numbers in the northern areas of Scotland where it has been re-introduced following previous extinction from this country. It is not a common game bird but when available it should be treated in the same way as grouse, and grouse can be substituted for it in recipes. This is a large bird which can weigh up to 4 kg/9 lb. It should be hung for 3-4 days, depending on conditions and personal preference.

GROUSE

Season: August 12th to December 10th.

In addition to the capercaillie (above) there are several other members of the grouse family, including the blackcock (also known as the heathpoult or black grouse) and the ptarmigan which comes from Europe and North America. However, the smaller Scottish grouse or red grouse (weighing about 675 g/1½ lb each) is considered to be the finest for flavour.

Young grouse shot early in the season are the most tender. They can be slightly tough at the beginning of December, just before the season ends. Look for birds with pointed flight feathers and soft pliable feet, also a downy breast. Hang for about 3-4 days, depending on conditions and preference. The young birds are ideal for roasting or grilling and the older ones can be casseroled. An average-sized grouse serves 1-2.

PARTRIDGE

Season: September 1st to February 1st.

This bird is related to the pheasant. There are two main varieties of partridge: the grey partridge which is the most common and considered to be the better bird and the red-legged, or French, partridge. When selecting birds, look for pliable, yellow-brown feet as they turn grey when the bird is older. The flight feathers should have pointed tips and the under feathers should be rounded. The beak of a young bird is fairly sharp. The best birds are obtained in October and November.

As a guide, partridges should be hung for about a week. Young birds can be roasted, older ones should be casseroled. It is usual to serve one partridge per person or one bird can be split before cooking to serve 2. The average weight for a partridge is 350-400 g/12-14 oz.

PHEASANT

Season: October 1st to February 1st.

The pheasant is probably the best known and most readily obtainable of the game birds. Pheasants are sold dressed, ready for the oven, or they can be purchased in the traditional brace, consisting of a male and female bird. The male bird is easily distinguished by its bright plumage but the hen pheasant is rather dull by comparison, with pale brown feathers. However, the hen pheasant is the most tender and has the best flavour; the cock pheasant can be rather dry and slightly tough.

When looking for a bird, notice the feet which should be fairly smooth on a young bird. They tend to become scaly in appear-ance as the pheasant ages. The breast of a young bird should still be downy. Pheasants can be hung for some time, anything from a few days to two weeks, but this is a matter of taste and a source of great controversy among gourmets and cooks alike. The best months for buying pheasant are November and December.

The younger birds or tender hen pheasants can be roasted but if they are older or likely to be tough, they should be braised or casseroled. An average weight for pheasant is about 1.4 kg/3 lb and the hen is smaller than the cock. A smaller bird will serve 3; a larger one can be made to serve 4, depending on the way in which it is prepared and served.

PIGEON

Season: Available all year.

There are two types of pigeon: the wood-pigeon which is larger and has dark flesh and the stronger flavour, and the tame pigeon which has pale flesh and resembles young chicken more than game. The average weight for a pigeon is just over 450 g/1 lb and they are at their best from August to October. Look for birds with pink legs as they tend to be younger. Pigeons are best cooked by moist methods, braised or casseroled or in pies.

QUAIL

Season: Available all the year.

Quail are protected by law in Britain and are not shot in the wild; however, they are farmed and are therefore available all year round, both fresh and frozen. They are very small birds, weighing about 150 g/5 oz, and are often sold – and served – in pairs.

They are tender and delicate in flavour and much esteemed by gourmets. Suitable for grilling or roasting, quails are not hung. They are usually cooked whole, without being drawn.

SNIPE

Season: August 12th to January 31st.

Small birds, not widely available in shops, and best killed when plump, in November. Related to the woodcock, snipe live only in marshy land.

Weighing about 100 g/4 oz each, snipe are considered a delicacy. They are cooked whole, trussed with their long, pointed beaks skewered through their legs. Hang the birds for a few days, or up to a week. The gizzard can be removed before roasting or grilling. Serve 1 snipe per person.

WILD DUCK

Season: September 1st to January 31 st.

There are many varieties of wild duck. The mallard is the most common and is also the largest. Other common varieties include the pintail, teal and widgeon; the teal being the smallest. The best months for wild duck are November and December. They should be eaten fresh, without hanging. A mallard will serve 2-3; the teal serves 1.

WOODCOCK

Season: October 1st to January 31st.

A relative of the snipe, the woodcock is found in woodland as well as marshy land. Seldom available in the shops, this bird is prized for its flavour. Weighing about 150 g/5 oz serve 1 woodcock per person. Hang these birds for up to a week, then cook them by roasting or braising.

VENISON

Season: England and Wales

Red deer, stags: August 1st to April 30th.
hinds: November 1st to February 28/29th.

Fallow deer, bucks: August 1st to April 30th.
does: November 1st to April 30th.

Roe deer, bucks: April 1st to September 30th.
does: November 1st to February 28/29th.

Scotland
Red deer, stags: July 1st to October 20th.
hinds: October 21st to February 15th.

Fallow deer, bucks: August 1st to April 30th.
does: October 21st to February 15th.

Roe deer, bucks: April 1st to October 20th.
does: October 21st to March 31st.

The red deer is the largest and most splendid-looking beast; the meat of the roe deer is paler and the least gamey; and the fallow deer is considered to have the best flavour. The meat of any type should be fine-grained and dark, with firm white fat. Young animals or fawns up to 18 months old produce delicate meat which should not be marinated before cooking. The meat of the male is preferred to that of the female and older venison is usually marinated, larded or barded before cooking as it is dry.

Venison is always hung, otherwise it would have little flavour. The whole carcass is hung for 10-14 days, depending on the weather and the strength of flavour required. Small cuts need hanging for about a week; however, if you buy the meat from a butcher, it will have been hung in advance. If you prefer well-hung venison, ask your butcher if he advises hanging the meat for a while longer before cooking.

If you have fresh venison, inspect the meat thoroughly before hanging it. If there is any musty smell, the meat should be washed in lukewarm water and dried thoroughly. Rub the meat with a mixture of ground ginger and black pepper, then hang it in a cool, dry, well-ventilated place. Check the venison daily and wipe off any moisture. To test if the meat is ready, run a sharp knife into the flesh near the bone. If it smells very strong, cook the meat at once or wash it with warm milk and water, then dry it and cover it with plenty of ginger and pepper. Wash the spices off before cooking. Haunch, saddle and loin are the prime cuts for roasting, or they can be cut into cutlets or steaks for grilling. Shoulder is a fairly tender cut which can be roasted or braised. The neck and other pieces of meat are either stewed, minced or made into sausages. The fat should always be removed from venison before cooking as it has an unpleasant flavour.

HARE

Two types of hare are fairly common in Britain, the English or brown hare and the Scottish or blue hare; the brown hare is considered to have the best flavour. An animal under a year old is known as a leveret. It is distinguished by a small bony knot near the foot, a short neck, long joints, smooth sharp claws, a narrow cleft in its lip and soft ears.

Hare should be hung, whole, for 7-10 days, depending on the weather. It should hang from the back legs in a cool, dry, well-ventilated place. Catch its blood in a dish. Add one or two drops of vinegar to the blood to prevent clotting; store, covered, in the refrigerator.

The back, saddle and the hind legs can be roasted; the shoulders or forelegs are better cooked by braising or casseroling, or they can be jugged.

RABBIT

Wild and tame rabbit are closely related but the difference in flavour is derived from the diet and habitat.

The meat of wild rabbit is darker and it has a more gamey flavour. A freshly killed rabbit is treated in the same way as hare but it must be paunched (gutted) immediately it is killed. There is no need to hang the animal for any length of time. Although the skin of the rabbit is usually left on once it is paunched, there is opinion which suggests skinning the animal immediately will eliminate the slightly musty taste which is often associated with wild rabbit.

Three to four month old rabbit is best, with thick foot joints, smooth claws, a flexible jaw and soft ears. The eyes should be bright, the fat whitish and the liver bright red. Average weight 2-2.25 kg/ 4½-5 lb but can be up to 4 kg/9 lb.

PREPARING AND COOKING GAME

All water birds should be eaten as fresh as possible but most other game birds of any size should be hung before being eaten. This process serves two purposes: to tenderize the meat and to give the characteristic gamey flavour. The birds should be hung in a cool place where air can circulate freely. The hanging time depends on the weather, the type of bird and individual taste. Birds which are considered to be over-hung for most tastes have a distinct greenish or blueish tinge to the skin. In this case they should be washed with salted water which contains a little vinegar, then rinsed before cooking.

PLUCKING

The first stage in the preparation of game, once it has been hung, is to pluck out all feathers and down, away from the direction of growth. Ducks should be plucked as soon as possible after they are killed, preferably while still warm. To avoid unnecessary mess, pluck birds in a draught-free place, preferably a shed or outhouse.

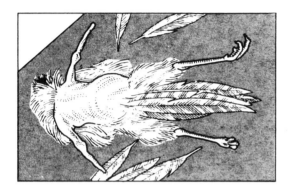

1 Extend one wing and pull out the under feathers. Work down towards the breast, leaving the feathers on the very tips of the wings. Repeat with the other wing, turning the bird over to pluck the other side of each wing. Pull off the feathers on the back, leaving just the tail feathers. Snap off the large feathers at the ends of the wings.

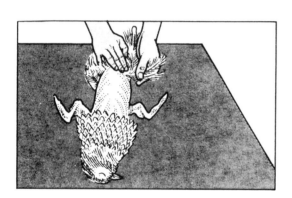

2 Next pluck the breast of the bird, holding the skin to keep it taut. Again pull out just a few feathers at a time and work down from the head towards the tail.

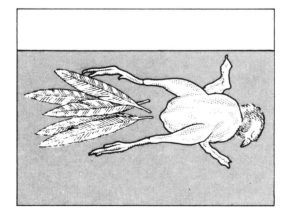

3 Pluck the legs and the lower half of the neck. The head and top part of the neck will be cut off (except in the case of snipe if the bird is to be skewered on its beak). Remove the tail feathers.

4 Cut off the wing tips at the joint and cut off the feet, or trim them if you want to leave them on for cooking. Remember that the wing tips may be used, along with other trimmings or a carcass, for making stock. The feet are usually discarded if not roasted with the bird.

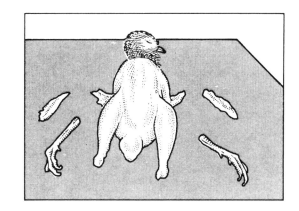

5 Cut off the head about half-way along the neck. Cut a ring round the outer skin, then pull or cut off the head, leaving the skin neatly severed.

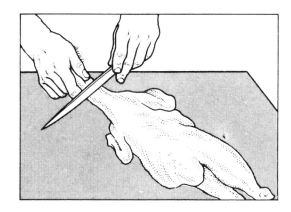

6 Singe the bird all over to remove any trace of down. Do this by passing the bird over a gas flame, or use matches. Long matches are best; light the match and let the smoke burn away, then move it over the bird, just above the skin. If the match is allowed to smoke as the bird is singed, then the skin will be tainted with a 'smoked' flavour.

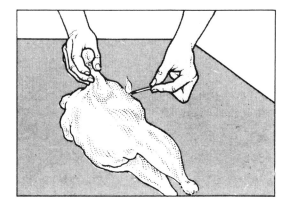

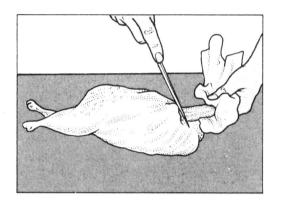

DRAWING

1 Cover the surface with several layers of newspaper and top with greaseproof paper. Hold the neck with a clean dry cloth, pull the skin back from it to leave it bare. At the base of the neck cut through the meat only.

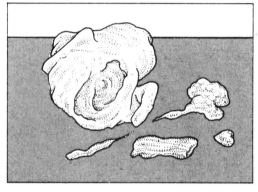

2 Still using the cloth to hold the neck, twist it around to break the bone. Cut through the bone to neaten the end, then draw the neck out from the skin and set it aside. It can be used to make stock.

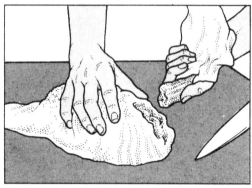

3 Push one finger inside the neck cavity to loosen the wind pipe. Pull away the wind pipe and the gullet. Remove the crop – a small pouch filled with food which has not travelled further into the bird. Discard the crop.

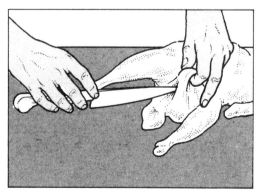

4 Make a small slit above the vent, between it and the tail. Do not cut too far into the bird as the intestines should not be cut.

Note: Thin, surgical-style, rubber gloves may be worn when drawing a bird. Thoroughly clean all areas when the task is finished.

5 At the neck end loosen the gizzard (the bird's second stomach) with one finger so that it will pull away easily. Use one or two fingers of your other hand and insert them into the slit at the vent of the bird. Gently feel inside the cavity and loosen the contents, then draw out all the intestines and the gizzard – they should come out fairly cleanly and all in one piece.

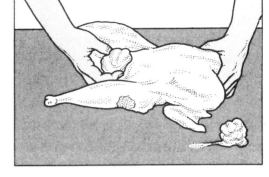

6 Wipe the inside of the bird with absorbent kitchen paper, then rinse it out thoroughly with plenty of running water. Smaller birds need less rinsing and should be handled carefully to avoid damage.

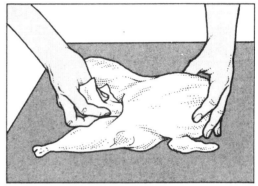

7 Separate the liver from the gall bladder, taking care not to split the bladder as it has a strong, bitter flavour that will spoil the flesh of the bird if it comes in contact with it. Split the gizzard and rinse it out to remove all grit. The liver, gizzard, neck and heart are the giblets and they can be used to make stock.

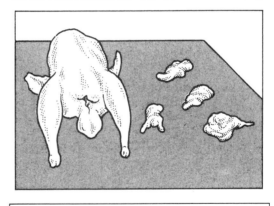

8 Wrap all waste innards in plenty of paper and tie them in a polythene bag before placing in the outdoor bin. Wash and dry all surfaces and utensils.

MRS BEETON'S TIP Larger birds can be boned out in the same way as poultry. Given sufficient notice, the butcher will do this. If you bone the bird yourself, follow the instructions on page 45, taking care not to break the skin of the bird, particularly on the breast.

TRUSSING

Birds are trussed to keep them in a neat shape while they are cooking and to secure any stuffing. The technique is the same for poultry and game birds. The easiest method is with a large needle and strong thread or fine string. Special, long, thick trussing needles are available from cook's shops. There are several ways of trussing birds, using one or two pieces of string inserted through the thighs, then wrapped back around the wings. Tying the legs neatly in place is adequate trussing for small game birds. If one piece is used, longer ends must be left and the string taken from the legs around the wings, then back to the legs.

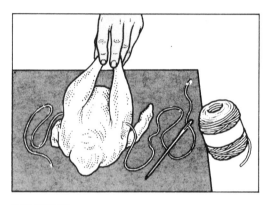

1 Put the bird on its back and hold the legs together forming a 'V' shape pointing towards the neck end. Insert the trussing needle into one leg, then push it through the body and out through the other leg. The string should pass through just above the thigh bone. Leave good lengths of string to tie the legs firmly in place.

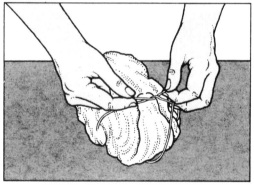

2 Tie the leg ends neatly, then re-thread the needle and thread it through the wings. Leave a long end of string and secure the flap of skin at the wing end of the bird to keep it neatly in place.

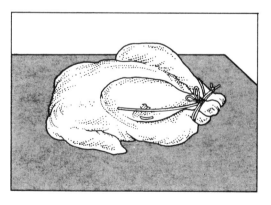

3 Take the string round underneath the body and towards the leg end of the bird. Tie off the ends to keep the whole body in a neat, secure shape.

BARDING

Barding is the term used for wrapping or covering the birds (or a joint) with pieces of fat. This prevents the breast meat from drying out during cooking. It is used for birds which have dry meat, containing little fat. Pork fat, from the belly, is usually used. Alternatively use fatty streaky bacon.

1 For barding cut thin, even and neat slices of fat from belly of pork. The bird should be ready trussed. Lay the fat over the breast side of the bird, using as many slices as necessary to cover the breast completely.

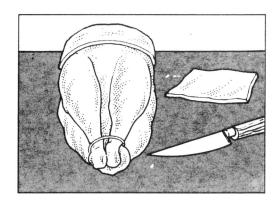

2 Tie the fat neatly in place. The bird is now ready for cooking: the fat should be removed shortly before the end of the cooking time so as to brown the skin.

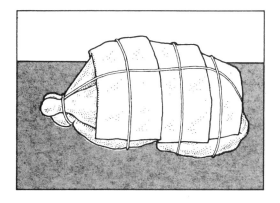

ROASTING TIMES FOR GAME BIRDS

The following times are a guide for roasting unstuffed birds. For a small stuffed bird up to 375 g/13 oz in weight allow up to 10 minutes extra; for a larger stuffed bird allow between 15-18 minutes extra cooking time.

Blackcock 40-50 minutes
Grouse 25-30 minutes
Pheasant 45-60 minutes
Partridge 20-30 minutes
Teal 15-20 minutes
Widgeon 25-30 minutes
Pintail 20-30 minutes
Mallard 30-45 minutes

Tame pigeon 30-40 minutes
Squab 15-25 minutes
Woodpigeon 35-45 minutes
Other small birds 10-15 minutes

SKINNING RABBIT OR HARE

Rabbits are paunched or drawn before they are skinned and they are not hung. Hares are hung and skinned before they are drawn. The method of skinning is the same for both animals. This is a task which you can expect the butcher to complete if the animal is purchased. In fact, both paunching and skinning are only carried out at home if a freshly killed animal is obtained. This is not to be recommended to those who are squeamish. The process is not as messy as paunching the animal but you should equip yourself with a sharp, pointed knife, and a pair of kitchen scissors are useful.

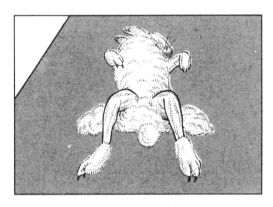

1 Start with the hind legs of the animal. Lay it on its back and slit the skin down each leg, then pull it off so that it hangs down towards the back of the animal.

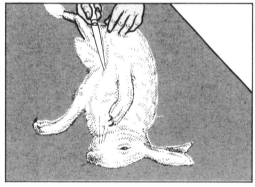

2 Cut the skin down the length of the belly of the animal, from the slits made down the hind legs. A rabbit will already have been paunched but take care not to split the belly of a hare.

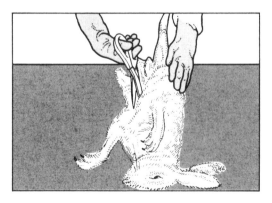

3 Loosen the skin from the meat on either side of the slit, then ease it away from the flesh, up towards the spine on both sides, until the centre of the body is completely free from its skin.

4 Turn the animal over and hold the hind legs firmly with one hand, then carefully pull the skin off the back of the animal to leave the rear end skinned.

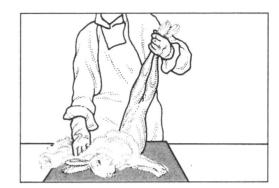

5 To remove the skin from the fore legs, carefully cut around it just above both paws. Peel the skin off each leg, using the point of a knife to ease it off like sleeves.

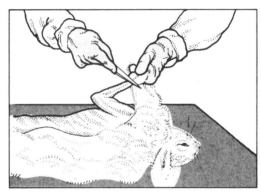

6 Ease the skin off the neck, then carefully cut it free all around below the head. The head can be chopped off at this stage.

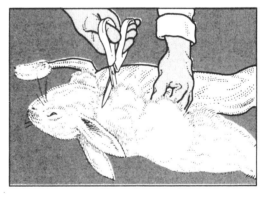

Note: For a traditional roast the head is skinned and the ears are left with their fur. Skinning the head is difficult and it is best to ask the butcher to do this if you want to roast it on the animal. The skin has to be cut around the eyes, mouth and the base of the ears but it should be left attached to the body skin. It can be peeled off from the body end. If you do this, have a small, sharp, pointed knife at the ready and use the point to ease the skin carefully off the head as you pull it free.

Alternatively, the head can be left with its fur on, in which case it should be covered with cooking foil during roasting. The most acceptable method is to chop off the head before cooking.

PAUNCHING HARE OR RABBIT

Paunching is the term used for gutting a rabbit or hare. Rabbits are paunched when they are freshly killed but hares are hung whole. Any blood that drips out of the hare as it hangs should be collected and chilled (see page 111) but blood also collects inside the animal, in the chest. Before paunching the hare have a bowl ready to catch the blood when you split the chest. The blood is used to thicken the sauce of jugged hare. Protect the work surface with newspaper and lay clean greaseproof paper on top. When finished, thoroughly rinse the animal.

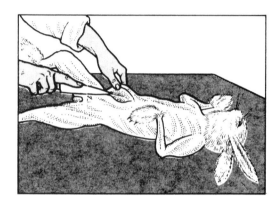

1 Using a sharp knife, slit the hare down its belly towards the rear end. Do not cut in too far or you may slit the intestines.

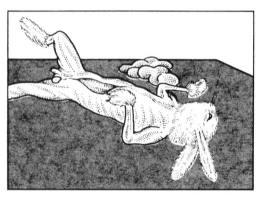

2 Open out the slit and ease your fingers round the intestines to loosen them. Pull the innards out, leaving the kidneys in place. They should come out roughly in one piece.

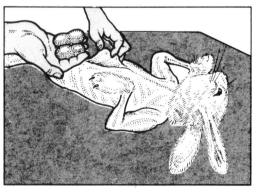

3 The liver is higher up near the rib cage. Gently pull it out with your fingers. Rinse the liver in cold water, pat it dry and use it in stuffings or sauces.

4 Have ready a bowl to catch the blood and tilt the animal so that the head end is downwards. Cut down into the chest where the blood will have collected during hanging, then tip it into a bowl.

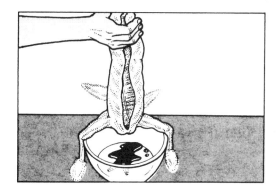

5 Remove the heart. Cut the gall bladder off the liver, taking care not to split it, then discard the bladder. Reserve the heart and lungs, the kidneys are left in place if the hare is to be roasted. The liver and heart can be chopped and used for a stuffing.

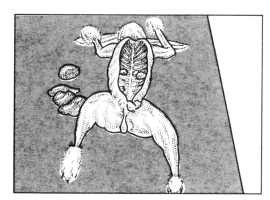

TRUSSING HARE OR RABBIT

The simplest method of trussing is to cut off the head and neck, leaving a flap of skin which can be skewered over the cut surface like the skin over the neck end of a chicken. The front and back legs are tied together, or skewered to keep them neatly in place under the body. If the head is left on, cover the ears with foil. If it is not skinned, remove the eyes and cover the head with foil.

1 A trussed hare with the unskinned head left on and covered with foil.

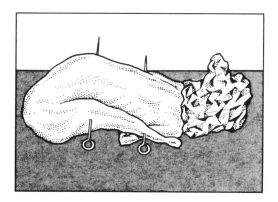

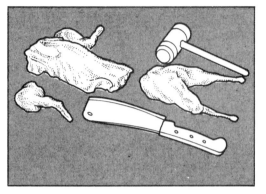

JOINTING HARE OR RABBIT

1 The head should be removed. Cut off each foreleg in one piece. Cut off the hind legs where they join on to the back (or saddle) of the animal. First cut straight across. You will need a heavy cook's knife and a mallet or rolling pin to tap the knife through the bones.

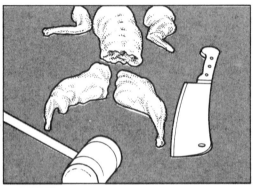

2 Cut between the hind legs to make two separate joints. The hind legs of rabbit are usually left whole unless they are to be used in a pie in which case they can be cut into two portions.

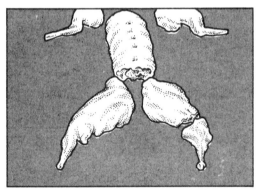

3 The hind legs of a hare should be split into thigh portions and lower leg portions, cutting through at the joint, again tapping the knife through the bones if necessary.

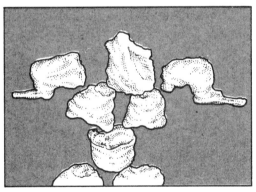

4 Separate the rib cage from the saddle, cutting through the spine as before, about a third of the way down the back. Cut the saddle across to give two joints. The front joint from the saddle can be chopped in half lengthways to split it into two joints.

CARVING HARE OR RABBIT

1 Carve the hare before arranging it on a plate for serving. Make short cuts across the spine in two or three places, then cut through down the length of the spine, from head to tail.

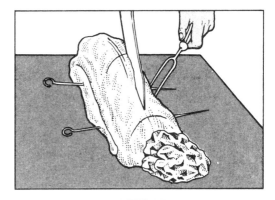

2 Cut across the spine towards the hind-quarters, then cut between the legs to make two serving portions. This releases any stuffing in the body cavity and it can be scooped out at this stage.

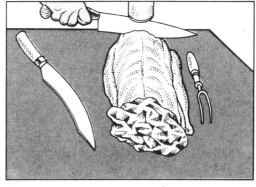

3 Divide the thigh and lower leg from the body meat to cut each of the two hind portions into two separate pieces.

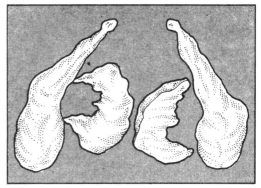

4 Cut across the spine just behind the shoulders to separate the saddle from the fore quarters. The saddle can be cut across into two or three portions. Cut off the head and cut fore legs into two further portions if preferred.

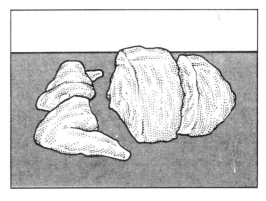

LARDING VENISON

Larding is the term used for threading strips of fat through meat before cooking. The fat is cut from belly of pork in neat slices, then the slices are cut into strips. A special larding needle is available, with a grip to hold a strip of fat at one end. Larding is used for very lean cuts of meat that tend to become dry on cooking. The strips of fat moisten the meat as it cooks.

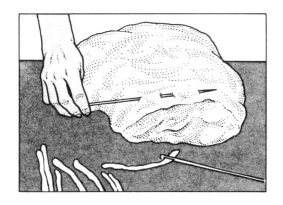

1 Cut neat strips of fat: they do not have to be too long but they should be fairly even in thickness. Larding is made easier if a fine skewer is first used to pierce the meat, this helps to prevent the fat from breaking as you pull it through with the larding needle. Pierce the meat as though sewing running stitches, inserting a fine skewer, then pushing it out about 2.5-5 cm/1-2 inches along.

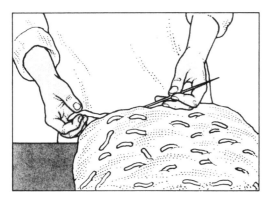

2 Put a piece of fat in the larding needle, then thread it through the meat, following the line cut by the skewer. Leave a short piece of fat protruding at each end of the stitch, then continue to lard the piece of meat all over, keeping the spaces between the fat even.

> 🥣 **MRS BEETON'S TIP** The process of larding meat is not a difficult one but it is time consuming. The fat should be evenly cut into narrow strips measuring about 5 mm/¼ inch wide and up to 5 cm/2 inches long. Larding bacon is specially prepared without saltpetre but pork fat can be used. Pierce and lard a small area at a time, working in a methodical pattern over the joint.

PREPARING A HAUNCH OF VENISON FOR COOKING

A haunch of venison can be boned out completely, then tied neatly in place before cooking. The butcher will usually do this for you but should you want to attempt the task yourself it is not very difficult but it is time consuming. You will need a very sharp pointed knife. Start from the wide end, cutting the meat off the bone. Work very closely to the bone, easing the meat away with your fingers. Alternatively, split the haunch down one side, then cut out the bone.

1 If the butcher has not already done so, chop off the bone end close to the meat and pull away any tendons. Trim all fat off the meat, cutting it away thinly using a sharp knife.

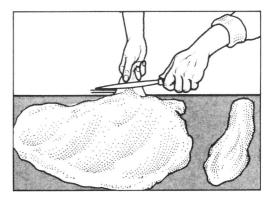

2 Once the meat is trimmed it should be larded, then marinated. Place the joint in a suitable dish, one which is large enough to hold the venison and deep enough to hold the marinade. A large gratin dish, lasagne dish or similar is ideal. During marinating the meat should be turned frequently and basted.

> **MRS BEETON'S TIP** Dry meats are marinated before they are roasted to moisten them. The marinade imparts the flavour of the chosen ingredients to the meat and, where necessary, it can help to tenderize the joint. Rich marinades can be used with venison and they can include red wine, spices and fresh herbs. Juniper berries, mace and cinnamon are all suitable spices. Bay leaves, parsely, thyme or rosemary can be used.

CARVING A SADDLE OF VENISON

The easiest way to prepare and serve saddle of venison is to ask the butcher for a boned and rolled joint which will include the tender fillet. Boned and rolled joints can be obtained in a variety of sizes, to cater for individual requirements. However, joints on the bone tend to be far larger and they may have the fillets left on. The fillets should be cut off in one piece and sliced. A rolled joint can be cut across into thick slices. The following steps are a guide to the more difficult process of carving the whole, unboned, saddle joint.

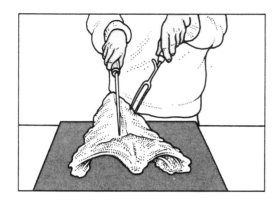

1 First carve the meat off the top, or loin, of the saddle. Starting in the middle to one side of the bone, cut downwards as near to the bone as possible.

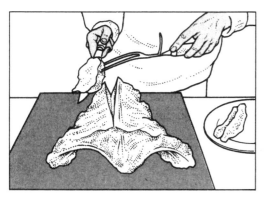

2 The next cut should be at a slight angle but down to meet the base of the first cut and release the first slice of meat.

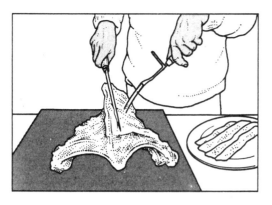

3 When one slice has been removed the carving is simplified and the rest of the same side of the haunch should be carved in neat, long slices. Carve the opposite side in the same way.

4 If the fillets were not removed before cooking, remove each in one piece: to do this, first slice down as near to the bone as possible, then cut outwards from the base to remove the fillet in one piece. Remove the fillet from the second side in the same way.

5 Cut the fillets into neat slices and serve them with the long slices taken from the top of the saddle.

CARVING A HAUNCH OF VENISON

A haunch of venison on the bone is not as difficult to carve as a saddle joint. The meat is taken off the sides, working on both sides of the joint to cut away large, even slices. The remaining small pieces of meat can be sliced off in small pieces but these are not prime portions. A boned haunch can be cut across into slices. Venison differs from beef in that the meat should be cut into fairly thick slices.

1 Holding the joint firmly by the bone end, cut neat slices off one side, then turn the leg slightly to carve the meat off the other side. The remaining meat can be cut off in small slices.

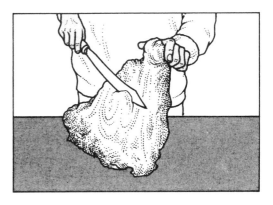

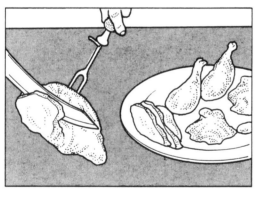

CARVING ROAST PHEASANT

1 Remove the legs by cutting between the breast and the point where the legs join the body. The bones should be cleanly cut and a pair of stout kitchen scissors may be useful. The legs can be cut into two portions, the thigh and the lower leg, although they are best left whole.

2 Next the wings should be removed, cutting them off close to the body and again using a pair of kitchen scissors to snip through awkward bones.

3 Lastly the breast meat should be carved off, first one side then the other. Cut the meat into neat, even slices, as thinly as possible.

ACCOMPANIMENTS FOR GAME

The traditional accompaniments for roast game are the same for all types.
■ Fried breadcrumbs may be served with large birds. Small to medium birds may be served on a croûte of fried bread.
■ Thin gravy or giblet gravy.
■ Bread Sauce (page 351) for grouse, pheasant and partridge.
■ Sharp fruit jelly, such as redcurrant or crab apple jelly.
■ Watercress sprigs for garnish.
■ Green vegetables, particularly Brussels sprouts, or a crisp salad.
■ Game chips are made by thinly slicing potatoes, rinsing and patting dry, then frying in hot deep fat until golden.

PHEASANT·WITH MUSHROOM STUFFING

2 pheasants
½ onion
50 g/2 oz butter

STUFFING
25 g/1 oz butter or margarine
100 g/4 oz finely chopped onion
100 g/4 oz mushrooms, chopped
50 g/2 oz cooked ham, chopped
75 g/3 oz fresh white breadcrumbs
salt and pepper
15 ml/1 tbsp game or chicken stock
(optional)
watercress sprigs to garnish

Wash the pheasant giblets. Put them in a saucepan, and cover with cold water. Add the half onion and simmer gently for 40 minutes to make stock for the gravy.

Make the stuffing. Melt the butter or margarine in a frying pan and cook the onion until soft. Add the mushrooms to the onion; cook for a few minutes. Stir in the ham and breadcrumbs, then add salt and pepper. If the stuffing is too crumbly, add the stock.

Set the oven at 190°C/375°F/gas 5. Divide the stuffing between the birds, filling the body cavities only. Truss the birds neatly and put them in a roasting tin; spread with the butter. Roast for 45-60 minutes, depending on the size of the birds. Baste occasionally while roasting. Transfer the birds to a heated serving dish and remove the trussing strings. Garnish with watercress and serve with gravy made from the giblet stock (see page 352). Wild mushrooms, tossed in butter, are good with this dish.

SERVES 6

PHEASANT VERONIQUE

Illustrated on page 139

2 pheasants
salt and pepper
75 g/3 oz butter
600 ml/1 pint chicken stock
7.5-10 ml/1½-2 tsp arrowroot
225 g/8 oz seedless white grapes, peeled
60 ml/4 tbsp double cream
5 ml/1 tsp lemon juice

Set the oven at 180°C/350°F/gas 4. Wipe the pheasants, season and rub well all over with butter. Put a knob of butter inside each bird. Place the pheasants, breast side down, in a deep pot roaster or flameproof casserole. Cover with stock and buttered paper. Cook for 1-1¼ hours, until tender, turning the birds breast side up after 25 minutes.

When cooked, remove the pheasants from the stock and cut into convenient portions for serving; keep hot. Boil the liquid in the casserole to reduce it a little. Strain into a saucepan. Blend the arrowroot with a little water, then stir it into the hot stock. Bring to the boil and stir until the sauce thickens and clears. Add the grapes, cream and lemon juice, then heat through without boiling. Check the seasoning. Arrange the pheasants on a serving dish, spoon the sauce over and serve.

SERVES 4

🍲 **MRS BEETON'S TIP** When seedless grapes are not available, halve ordinary fruit and remove all the seeds. Unfortunately, this is a tedious task which is essential. Use a small, pointed knife to peel the grapes.

RAISED PHEASANT PIE

Illustrated on page 138

450 g/1 lb plain flour
2.5 ml/½ tsp salt
225 g/8 oz butter or margarine
2 egg yolks
1 hen pheasant, boned with carcass (see page 45)
grated nutmeg
1.25 ml/¼ tsp ground allspice
salt and pepper
2 quantities Basic Forcemeat (page 349)
2 veal escalopes
1 thick slice cooked ham (about 50-75 g/2-3 oz)
beaten egg to glaze
1 small onion, quartered
1 bay leaf
1 carrot, quartered lengthways
10 ml/2 tsp gelatine

To make the pastry, mix the flour and salt in a large bowl. Add the butter or margarine and rub it into the flour until the mixture resembles fine breadcrumbs. Make a well in the middle and add the egg yolks with about 60 ml/4 tbsp water. Mix the pastry to a smooth, fairly soft dough, adding extra water as necessary. The pastry should have a little more water than ordinary short crust dough but it must not be sticky.

Set the oven at 160°C/325°F/gas 3. Grease a 23 cm/9 inch raised pie mould with a little oil and place it on a baking sheet. Set aside one third of the pastry for the lid and garnish, then roll out the remainder into an oblong shape, about twice the size of the top of the mould. Do not be tempted to roll the pastry out into a sheet large enough to completely line the mould as it may break when you lift it into the mould. Carefully lift the pastry into the mould, then use the back of your fingers and knuckles to press it into the base of the mould, smoothing it up the sides to line the mould completely. Take plenty of time to ensure that the mould is well lined with pastry and that there are no breaks in the lining.

Open out the pheasant and sprinkle it with a little nutmeg, the allspice, salt and pepper. Set aside half the forcemeat, then divide the remainder into two portions. Spread one portion over the middle of the pheasant and lay the veal escalopes on top. Lay the cooked ham on top of the veal, then spread the second portion of forcemeat over the ham. Fold the sides of the boned pheasant around the stuffing to enclose it completely.

Put half the reserved forcemeat into the base of the pie, particularly around the edges. Put the pheasant in the pie, placing the join in the skin downwards (there is no need to sew up the opening as the pie will keep the filling inside the bird). Use the remaining forcemeat to fill in around the pheasant, packing it neatly into all the gaps.

Cut off a small piece of the remaining pastry and set it aside to make leaves for garnish. Roll out the rest to a shape slightly larger than the top of the pie. Dampen the rim of the pastry lining with a little water, then lift the lid on top of the pie and press the edges to seal in the filling. Trim off any excess pastry – you may find that snipping it off with a pair of kitchen scissors is the easiest method. Pinch up the pastry edges. Roll out the trimmings with the reserved pastry and cut out leaves to garnish the top of the pie. Cut a small hole to allow steam to escape, then glaze the pie with beaten egg.

Bake the pie for 3 hours. Check it frequently and cover it loosely with a piece of foil after the first hour to prevent the pastry from overcooking. Increase the oven temperature to 190°C/375°F/gas 5, uncover the pie and glaze it with a little more egg. Cook for a further 20-30 minutes, until the pastry is golden and glossy.

While the pie is cooking, simmer the pheasant carcass in a saucepan with the onion, bay leaf and carrot for 1½ hours. Make sure that there is plenty of water in the saucepan to cover the carcass and keep the pan covered. Strain the stock into a clean pan, then boil it hard, uncovered, until it is reduced to 300 ml/½ pint. Strain it through a muslin-lined sieve, then taste and season it.

When the pie is cooked, heat the stock and sprinkle the gelatine into it. Remove the pan from the heat and stir until the gelatine has dissolved completely. Set this aside to cool. When the pie has cooled until it is just hot and the stock is cold, pour the stock slowly in through the vent in the top crust.

Leave the pie to cool in the tin, then carefully remove the clips which hold the sides of the tin together; ease the sides away from the pie. Have a small pointed knife ready to ease away any small pieces of pastry that are stuck.

SERVES 6 TO 8

NORMANDY PARTRIDGES

Serve simple, but interesting, vegetables to accompany this old-fashioned French dish. Tiny scrubbed potatoes, baked in their jackets, lightly steamed French beans and carrots cut into thin, julienne strips are all ideal.

100 g/4 oz unsalted butter
2 young partridges
salt and pepper
2 rindless streaky bacon rashers
675 g/1½ lb eating apples
125 ml/4 floz double cream
30 ml/2 tbsp Calvados or brandy
chopped parsley to garnish

Set the oven at 180°C/350°F/gas 4. Heat half the butter in a flameproof casserole, add the partridges and brown them on all sides. Sprinkle with salt and pepper. Place a bacon rasher on each bird's breast. Peel, core and cut the apples into wedges. Melt the remaining butter in a frying pan, add the apples and cover the pan. Cook gently for 5 minutes, then add to the casserole.

Cook in the oven for 20-30 minutes. Transfer the partridges and apples to a hot serving dish.

Mix the cream and the Calvados or brandy, then season to taste. Heat the mixture over a low heat, stirring well, and taking care that the mixture does not boil. Pour this sauce over the partridges and apples, and sprinkle with chopped parsley before serving.

SERVES 2

> 🥄 **MRS BEETON'S TIP** Calvados is a brandy which is prepared by distilling cider. It is made in the French, Auge region.

*P*IGEON PIE

2 pigeons
45 ml/3 tbsp plain flour
salt and pepper
45 ml/3 tbsp corn oil
100 g/4 oz chuck steak, cubed
100 g/4 oz button onions
30 ml/2 tbsp sage and onion stuffing mix
1 small cooking apple, peeled, cored and
    sliced
250 ml/8 fl oz beef stock
225 g/8 oz prepared puff pastry, thawed if
    frozen
flour for rolling out
beaten egg for glazing

Cut the pigeons into quarters. Remove the feet and backbone. Put the flour in a stout polythene bag, with salt and pepper to season. Add the pigeon joints and shake the bag to coat them in seasoned flour. Heat the oil and fry the joints for about 10 minutes, turning as required, until lightly browned all over.

Add the steak to the bag and coat in the remaining seasoned flour. Remove the pigeons from the pan and drain on absorbent kitchen paper. Add the steak and onions to the pan and cook for 5 minutes, turning frequently.

Make up the stuffing according to the packet directions. Form into small balls and fry in the pan until lightly browned all over. Remove and drain.

Set the oven at 220°C/425°F/gas 7. In a large casserole or pie dish, layer all the filling ingredients, adding salt and pepper to taste. Pour in the stock. Roll out the pastry on a lightly floured surface to fit the dish. Moisten the rim of the pie dish and cover the pie with the pastry. Brush the crust with the egg.

Cook for 20 minutes, until the pastry is risen and golden. Reduce the heat to 180°C/350°F/gas 4, and cook for a further 2 hours, or until the pigeons are tender when pierced with a skewer through the crust. Cover the pie crust with buttered grease-proof paper if necessary to prevent it over-browning or drying out.

SERVES 4 TO 5

PIGEONS IN RED WINE

Illustrated on page 139

75 g/3 oz butter
3 woodpigeons
salt and pepper
1 large onion or 3 shallots, sliced

SAUCE
    25 g/1 oz dripping or lard
    1 small carrot, sliced
    1 onion, sliced
    25 g/1 oz plain flour
    600 ml/1 pint game or chicken stock
    salt and pepper
    300 ml/½ pint red wine

Start by making the sauce. Melt the dripping or lard in a saucepan. Fry the vegetables slowly for about 10 minutes until the onion is golden brown. Stir in the flour and cook very gently until golden, then gradually add the stock, stirring constantly until the sauce boils and thickens. Lower the heat and simmer for 30 minutes, then strain the sauce into a large clean pan. Add salt and pepper to taste, stir in the wine and bring the mixture to simmering point.

Meanwhile melt two-thirds of the butter and fry the pigeons, turning as required, until browned on all sides. Add the pigeons to the wine sauce and simmer with the pan half-covered for about 45 minutes, or until the birds are tender. Taste and season just before serving.

Melt the remaining butter in a frying pan and fry the onion or shallots. Drain well and keep hot. Split the cooked pigeons in half. Serve with the onions and the sauce poured over.

SERVES 6

ROAST QUAIL IN A VINE-LEAF COAT

Illustrated on page 137

8 oven-ready quail
8 fresh or canned vine leaves
8 rindless streaky bacon rashers
4 large slices of bread fron a tin loaf
butter for spreading
small bunches of black and green grapes
   to garnish

Set the oven at 200°C/400°F/gas 6. Wrap each quail in a vine leaf. Wrap one bacon rasher around each quail. Secure with thread or wooden cocktail sticks. Place on a rack in a roasting tin and roast for 10-20 minutes.

Meanwhile, cut the crusts off the bread, cut each slice in half and toast lightly on both sides. Spread the toast with drippings from the quail and a little butter. Serve each quail on toast and garnish with grapes.

SERVES 4

CASSEROLE OF RABBIT

Illustrated on page 140

1 rabbit
salt and pepper
60 ml/4 tbsp plain flour
65 g/2½ oz butter
1 onion, sliced
225 g/8 oz cooking apples, peeled, cored
   and sliced
1 (213 g/7½ oz) can prunes
1 chicken stock cube

GARNISH
   chopped parsley
   crescents of fried bread

Set the oven at 180°C/350°F/gas 4. Joint the rabbit and discard the lower forelegs and rib-cage, or keep for stock. Put half the flour in a shallow bowl, season and coat the rabbit lightly. Melt 50 g/2 oz butter in a flameproof casserole and brown the rabbit on all sides; transfer to a plate. Add the onion and fry until soft. Stir in the apples.

Drain the prunes and make the juice up to 250 ml/8 fl oz with water. Add the stock cube, crumbling it finely. Return the rabbit to the casserole with the prunes and stock. Cover and cook in the oven for 1½ hours, or until the rabbit is tender.

When the rabbit is cooked, arrange the joints on a warmed serving dish with the apples and prunes; keep hot. In a small bowl, blend the remaining butter with the remaining flour. Gradually add small pieces of the mixture to the liquid in the casserole, whisking thoroughly after each addition. Bring to the boil and stir all the time until the sauce thickens. Check the seasoning before pouring the sauce over the rabbit. Garnish and serve.

SERVES 4

MARINATED VENISON STEAKS

4 venison slices (from haunch)
salt and pepper
25 g/1 oz plain flour
butter or dripping
1 small onion, chopped
6-8 juniper berries, crushed
150 ml/¼ pint game or chicken stock
chopped parsley to garnish

MARINADE
about 300 ml/½ pint red wine
1 bouquet garni
6 peppercorns
4 onion slices
30 ml/2 tbsp olive oil
10 ml/2 tsp red wine vinegar

Make the marinade first. Combine all the ingredients in a saucepan and boil for 1 minute. Allow to cool completely. Put the venison steaks in a shallow dish large enough to hold them all in a single layer. Pour the marinade over them. Cover and leave overnight.

Set the oven at 180°C/350°F/gas 4. Take the venison out of the marinade and pat dry. Reserve the marinade. Snip the edges of the venison slices with scissors to prevent curling. Season the flour with salt and pepper and rub it over both sides of the venison steaks. Heat the fat in a large flameproof casserole or roasting tin until it hazes. Sear the steaks on both sides in the fat. Add the onion when searing the second side.

Pour off all but a film of fat from the pan. Sprinkle the steaks with the crushed juniper. Pour the stock and a little of the marinade round them, to a depth of about 1 cm/½ inch. Cover the casserole or tin tightly with foil and bake for 30 minutes, or until the steaks are tender. Drain and serve, sprinkled with chopped parsley.

Drain off the excess fat from the stock, pour it into a heated sauceboat and serve with the steaks.

SERVES 6 TO 8

ROAST VENISON WITH BAKED APPLES

4 small sharp cooking apples
juice of 1 lemon
30 ml/2 tbsp gooseberry, rowanberry or
    redcurrant jelly
15 ml/1 tbsp butter
10 ml/2 tsp soft light brown sugar
1 kg/2¼ lb young venison
about 45 ml/3 tbsp oil

SAUCE
150 ml/¼ pint game or beef stock
30 ml/2 tbsp gooseberry, rowanberry or
    redcurrant jelly
small pinch of ground cloves
salt and pepper
10 ml/2 tsp cornflour
30 ml/2 tbsp sherry

Set the oven at 190°C/375°F/gas 5. Peel and core the apples. Put them in a saucepan, add a little water and the lemon juice and simmer for 10-15 minutes. Drain and arrange in an ovenproof dish. Fill the core holes with the gooseberry, rowanberry or redcurrant jelly. Dot each apple with a small piece of butter, and sprinkle with the brown sugar.

Put the venison in a roasting tin. Brush with 30 ml/2 tbsp of the oil and roast for 40 minutes, basting with extra oil from time to time. Bake the apples at the same time.

Meanwhile make the sauce. Combine the stock, jelly, ground cloves, salt and pepper in a small pan. Heat gently to dissolve the jelly. In a cup, blend the cornflour with 15 ml/1 tbsp water, add to the stock and bring to the boil, stirring all the time. Cook for 2 minutes to thicken the sauce.

Slice the meat and arrange it on a warm dish with the apples; keep both hot. Place the roasting tin over the heat, add the sauce and the sherry and stir vigorously. Strain over the meat and serve at once.

SERVES 4 TO 6

*O*RANGE-SCENTED BRAISED VENISON

1-1.25 kg/2-2¾ lb haunch or shoulder of
    venison
25 g/1 oz dripping
1 onion, thickly sliced
2 carrots, thickly sliced
2 celery sticks, thickly sliced
1 orange
game or chicken stock (see method)
25 g/1 oz butter • 25 g/1 oz plain flour
30 ml/2 tbsp redcurrant jelly
salt and pepper

RED WINE MARINADE
   1 onion, chopped
   1 carrot, chopped
   1 celery stick, sliced
   6-10 parsley sprigs, chopped
   1 garlic clove, crushed
   5 ml/1 tsp dried thyme
   1 bay leaf • 6-8 peppercorns
   1-2 cloves
   2.5 ml/½ tsp ground coriander
   2.5 ml/½ tsp juniper berries
   250 ml/8 fl oz chicken stock
   150 ml/¼ pint each red wine and oil

GARNISH
   watercress sprigs
   orange slices
   Forcemeat Balls (page 349)

Combine all the ingredients for the marinade in a deep dish. Stir in 150 ml/¼ pint water and add the venison. Leave for about 12 hours or overnight, basting and turning occasionally. Dry the venison on absorbent kitchen paper and trim if required. Reserve the marinade.

Set the oven at 190°C/375°F/gas 5. Melt the dripping in a large frying pan and brown the venison on all sides. Remove and keep on one side.

Add the vegetables to the fat remaining in the pan and cook briefly, then place in a large casserole. Pare off a few thin strips of rind from the orange and add to the casserole. Strain in the marinade and add enough stock just to cover the vegetables. Place the venison on top, cover with a well-greased piece of greaseproof paper and a lid. Cook for 1¼ hours. Meanwhile cream the butter and flour together in a small bowl. Set aside.

Carve the meat into slices. Arrange them on a heated serving dish and keep hot. Strain the stock from the casserole into a small saucepan, discarding the vegetables. Squeeze the orange and strain the juice into the pan. Add the redcurrant jelly, salt and pepper, and bring to the boil. Lower the heat and stir until the jelly has melted, then add knobs of the prepared butter and flour paste, whisking well after each addition. Simmer for 2-3 minutes, whisking.

Pour the sauce over the venison and garnish with the watercress, orange and forcemeat balls. Serve at once.

SERVES 6 TO 8

BIGOS

There are many ways of preparing what is in effect Poland's national dish. The essence of them all is that they should consist of a mixture of sauerkraut and smoked sausage and the game secured by the hunter. Duck or any type of game can be used instead of venison.

1 kg/2¼ lb sauerkraut
450 g/1 lb boneless shoulder of venison
175-225 g/6-8 oz smoked pork sausage
50 g/2 oz lard
1 large onion, sliced
30 ml/2 tbsp tomato purée
125 ml/4 fl oz red wine
salt and pepper
1 large green apple
2 bay leaves
250 ml/8 fl oz game or chicken stock
25 g/1 oz butter
15 ml/1 tbsp plain flour

Thoroughly squeeze the sauerkraut, then shred it. Wipe the venison, trim off all the fat and cut into 2.5 cm/1 inch cubes. Slice the sausages into pieces 1 cm/½ inch thick.

Melt half the lard in a large frying pan and brown the onion until golden. Add the venison and cook, stirring for 5 minutes. Stir in the tomato purée and the wine. Season to taste and mix in the sausage.

Set the oven at 180°C/350°F/gas 4. Place half the sauerkraut in a large casserole, then top with the meat. Peel, core and dice the apple. Add it to the casserole with the bay leaves and place the remaining sauerkraut on top. Pour half the stock over the bigos. Dot with flakes of butter, cover and cook for 2½-3 hours, or until the venison is tender. Stir occasionally during cooking.

About 10 minutes before the end of cooking time, melt the remaining lard in a frying pan, add the flour and stir over low heat for 2-3 minutes, without allowing the mixture to colour. Gradually add the remaining stock, stirring all the time, until the sauce boils and thickens. Simmer for 2 minutes, stirring, then season to taste. Mix the sauce into the bigos, which should be moist. Serve piping hot.

SERVES 4

> **MRS BEETON'S TIP** Use a large Polish boiling sausage for bigos, for example *wiejska*, available from larger supermarkets and delicatessens. The sauerkraut is usually squeezed and shredded before being added to the stew; however, if preferred it may be rinsed and squeezed first. Another traditional ingredient is dried mushrooms: soak 2-4 in boiling water to cover for 15 minutes, then drain and chop them before adding to the bigos at the beginning of cooking. Strain the soaking water through muslin and add that too.

HIGHLAND GROUSE

The availability of frozen raspberries allows for this dish to be prepared while grouse is in season – even if the fresh fruit is long finished.

50 g/2 oz butter
2 young grouse
salt and pepper
225 g/8 oz raspberries
grated rind of 1 lemon

GARNISH
whole raspberries (optional)
herb sprigs or watercress

Set the oven at 200°C/400°F/gas 6. Place half the butter inside each bird and sprinkle well with salt and pepper. Mix the raspberries and lemon rind together in a bowl and fill the cavities in the birds with the mixture. Put 5 mm/¼ inch water in a deep ovenproof dish with a lid which will just hold the birds. Place the birds and any remaining raspberry mixture in the dish, and cover. Cook for 35-45 minutes. Remove the lid and cook for a further 10 minutes, to brown the birds.

Serve with creamed potatoes and a green vegetable. Garnish with a few whole raspberries and herb sprigs or watercress.

SERVES 4

JUGGED HARE

Jugged hare is thickened with the blood which is saved when the animal is paunched.

1 hare
liver of the hare (optional)
blood of the hare
5 ml/1 tsp vinegar (see method)
30 ml/2 tbsp plain flour
salt and pepper
100 g/4 oz butter or margarine
3 whole cloves
1 onion
1 bouquet garni
good pinch of ground mace
good pinch of freshly grated nutmeg
beef stock to moisten
150 ml/¼ pint port or claret
50 g/2 oz redcurrant jelly

GARNISH
   heart-shaped or triangular sippets of
      toasted bread
   Mrs Beeton's Forcemeat Balls (page 349)

Joint the hare. Reserve the liver and the blood in a bowl, adding the vinegar to the blood to prevent it coagulating. Set the oven at 180°C/350°F/gas 4. Put the flour in a bowl, season with salt and pepper, then dust the hare joints with it. Melt the butter or margarine in a frying pan and brown the hare joints all over. Remove the hare joints from the pan and put them in a deep ovenproof pot or cooking jar, preferably earthenware. Press the cloves into the onion. Add the onion, bouquet garni, spices and just enough stock to cover about a quarter of the joints. Cover the pot or jar very securely with foil and stand it in a roasting tin. Add boiling water to come halfway up the sides of the pot or jar and cook for about 3 hours, depending on the age and toughness of the hare.

Meanwhile, prepare the liver. When the hare is cooked, remove the meat to a serving dish and keep hot. Pour off the juices into a saucepan. If using the hare's liver, mash it into the hot liquid. Add the port or claret and redcurrant jelly. Add the hare's blood to the liquids in the pan and reheat, stirring all the time; do not allow the sauce to boil. If the blood is not available, thicken the sauce with a beurre manié (see Mrs Beeton's Tip). Sharpen with a few drops of lemon juice, if liked.

Pour the thickened sauce over the hare joints and serve garnished with the sippets and forcemeat balls.

SERVES 6

MRS BEETON'S TIP To thicken the sauce without using the blood, blend 15 ml/1 tbsp butter with 15 ml/ 1 tbsp plain flour in a bowl. Gradually add small pieces of the mixture to the sauce, whisking thoroughly after each addition. Bring the sauce to the boil, lower the heat and simmer for 5 minutes, stirring.

MEAT AND OFFAL

This chapter concentrates on the essential aspects of meat cookery, from hints on buying and storing or carving to classic dishes and contemporary, international favourites.

Always buy meat from a reputable supplier to ensure that it has been properly handled and prepared before sale. Local butchers offer a personal service and expert advice. They will prepare exactly the amount or cut you want, or offer advice on the best buy if you are not sure what you need, and trim, truss or bone the meat for you, often more economically than the pre-packed product.

All meat should look moist and fresh. Fat should be firm and pale. There should be no unpleasant smell, slimy texture, softening or wet feel or appearance to the fat, nor any tinge of green or yellow to either meat or fat. Beef ranges from bright red to a darker colour when well hung. Lamb is neither as bright nor as dark as beef and it tends to be slightly drier. Its skin should look clean and pale and any fat should be creamy-white. Pork is a paler meat and the fat is softer and creamier in appearance. Liver, kidney and heart should all be firm, moist and evenly coloured and they should smell fresh without any hint of a strong or 'off' smell.

Bacon and ham should be firm and even in colour, with pale, creamy, firm fat. Avoid any fat which is yellowing, soft or slightly slimy in appearance; and meat which has a yellow-green tint or sheen.

Remember that meat should be kept chilled until sold – either in a butcher's cold room or refrigerator or in a refrigerated display cabinet. It should not be displayed unchilled (pre-packed or otherwise).

Chill meat as soon as possible after purchase. Leave sealed packs closed; transfer wrapped meat to a large covered container. Place the meat on a low shelf in the refrigerator, making sure that it does not drip over the edges of the container. Cook the meat before the date on the packet, or within 1-2 days if bought loose. Use minced meat and offal within a day of purchase.

COOKING METHODS

The selection of meat depends on the cooking method; some methods are suitable for certain cuts and not appropriate to others.

Roasting This is a dry cooking method for tender cuts. Originating from spit roasting over an open fire, the traditional method is to cook the joint uncovered on a rack in a tin. Modern cooks may dispense with the rack, placing the meat directly in the tin. It may be loosely covered for part of the cooking time to prevent overbrowning.

Grilling A quick cooking method for tender, small cuts such as steak and chops.

Frying Shallow, deep or stir frying are all suitable methods for tender cuts. Deep frying, like stir frying, is used only for meat which has been cut into small pieces. Chops and steaks are typical candidates for shallow frying, whereas tender pork, trimmed and cut into small pieces, is perfect for stir frying.

Pot Roasting This is a form of roasting, usually on a bed of vegetables, in a tightly covered container. A little liquid may be added to the container. This is not strictly necessary; the condensation from the ingredients will be retained in the cooking pot. This method is suitable for less tender cuts but it is not a moist method and will not be successful with tough cuts.

Braising This is a part-moist method. The meat is cooked with some liquid, usually on a bed of vegetables, but is not submerged in liquid. It is suitable for less tender cuts as well as chops and steaks but not for tough meats.

Stewing This is a moist cooking method for tough cuts of meat. The meat should be submerged in liquid and the container covered. Stews may be cooked on the hob or in the oven but it is important that the process is slow and lengthy, allowing time for the meat to become tender.

Casseroling This is a slightly ambiguous term used for moist cooking. It is similar to braising, but usually has more liquid; however it is not usually used to denote cooking periods as long as for stewing.

Microwave Cooking The majority of meat does not cook particularly well in the microwave oven. Sauces, such as Bolognese, which are based upon minced meat, can be cooked by this method, but microwave cooking is not suitable for any of the cuts that require long, slow cooking. Consult your manufacturer's handbook for more information.

CUTS OF MEAT

A wide variety of cuts is available, including the traditional portions listed here and Continental-style cuts which are cut quite differently, often with the grain of the meat instead of across it. Most supermarkets and butchers also offer a range of trimmed meats which are ready for grilling, frying or baking. These include skewered meats, rolled portions, thin escalopes or slices of meat and fine strips or cubes.

The value of becoming familiar with different cuts is in learning how best to cook them. Meat is muscle tissue: if it is taken from the most active part of the animal, for example the leg, it will have more connective tissue and be tougher than meat from less active muscles on the back and around the rib areas. Long, moist cooking is necessary to soften connective tissue and make the meat tender. Tender cuts which do not have much connective tissue may be cooked by the quicker, fiercer and dry methods.

CARVING MEAT

A sharp, long-bladed knife is essential for carving and a two-pronged carving fork is useful but not vital.

Remove any trussing string and skewers. Holding the joint with the fork, use a sawing action to slice across the grain of the meat. Cutting across the grain is important as it makes the meat more tender to eat. If the joint has an 'L' shaped bone (such as in a rib of beef), then cut between the meat and bone, as close to the bone as possible, on the shortest side of the bone. Carve the meat in slices down towards the bone, either straight down or at an angle, whichever is best for giving large, neat slices. When the majority of the meat is removed from one side, turn the joint, if necessary, and remove meat from the other side. Any remaining small areas of meat should be cut in small pieces.

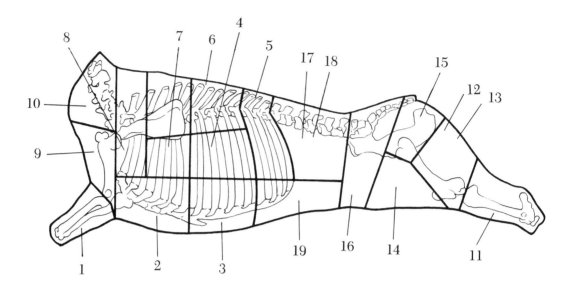

BEEF

1 Shin A tough cut with much gristle, this must be cooked by a slow moist method. It is ideal for flavoursome stews, soups and stocks, particularly on the bone, when it will yield stock which sets well on chilling.

2 Brisket Usually sold boned and rolled. This used to be a fatty cut, but modern breeding methods have reduced the fat content considerably. Suitable for pot roasting or braising, brisket may also be casseroled or boiled. It has good flavour.

3 Flank A comparatively fatty joint which requires long, slow cooking, by boiling, stewing or braising.

4 Flat Rib Taken from between the flank and forerib, this is not commonly available. If found it should be pot roasted or braised, as it is not a tender cut.

5 Wing Rib Cut from between the rib and sirloin, this is a succulent, expensive cut for roasting.

6 Forerib A roasting joint, at its best cooked on the bone. A well-hung joint, roasted fairly slowly will yield full-flavoured, tender results. Since a joint on the bone has to be large in order to be practical, forerib is often sold boned and rolled.

7 Top Rib With back rib, this is also known as middle rib, thick rib or, traditionally, leg-of-mutton cut. Top rib and back rib may be sold separately, the former being an excellent cut for braising to soften the gristle which runs through the meat.

8 Chuck and Bladebone Both braising cuts, also used for making succulent stews. Chuck steak may also be purchased in one piece and pot roasted to give excellent results. In some areas chuck may also be known as chine. In Scotland chuck and blade combined are known as shoulder.

9/10 Clod or Front Chest and Sticking or Neck of Beef Although these inexpensive cuts do not have a lot of connective tissue, they tend to contain significant amounts of gristle. Use for boiling or stewing.

11 Leg Suitable for long slow stewing and boiling, leg has good flavour and yields tender results when cooked correctly. Leg may be sliced across the muscle in large round nuggets of meat. It may be stewed in this form, or cut into cubes before cooking.

12 Topside This is taken from the inside of the leg. It is lean and boneless and the rolled joint is usually wrapped in a thin sheet of fat (barded) to keep it moist during cooking. Although topside is often regarded as a roasting joint, it is best pot roasted.

13 Silverside From the thigh and buttock, this is suitable for roasting, but benefits from pot roasting or braising. Silverside is also suitable for boiling; salted silverside is an excellent boiling joint.

14 Top Rump or Thick Flank Although this is generally regarded as a braising joint (whole or in slices) it may be pot roasted to give full-flavoured results.

15 Aitchbone This is a large joint on the bone lying over the rump. It is an old fashioned cut which can be boned and rolled and prepared in smaller joints. It may be roasted or braised.

16 Rump Next to the sirloin, this is a popular cut for grilling and frying, but it is not the most tender of steaks. Rump has a thin covering of fat but it is free of gristle.

17 Sirloin The prime, traditional roasting joint, sirloin includes the fillet. Tender and flavoursome, sirloin is one of the most expensive cuts of beef. A well-hung rib of beef is less expensive and offers equal if not better flavour when cooked with care.

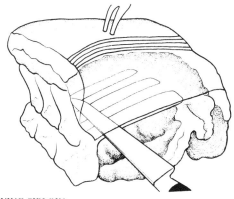

CARVING SIRLOIN
ON THE BONE

18 Fillet Tucked underneath the bone, the fillet is a long, slim piece of very tender meat with a good flavour. As it is expensive, it is usually reserved for special dishes, such as Beef Wellington, or it may be sliced into small, thick steaks for grilling or frying.

19 Hindquarter Flank The belly of the animal. A braising and stewing cut which has a high fat content and is therefore often trimmed and minced.

BEEF STEAKS

Fillet Small steaks off the fillet which cook quickly to give succulent, tender results.

Tournedos A 2.5 cm/1 inch thick slice off the fillet, trimmed and tied neatly.

Châteaubriand A thick centre cut from the fillet, weighing about 250 g/9 oz and measuring about 5 cm/2 inches thick, this may be served as a portion for two.

Rump Flavoursome steak for grilling, frying, or braising, this is not the most tender but it is economical with good texture.

Sirloin Large tender steak on the bone, this may be cut in several ways and served under several names.

Porterhouse A 2.5 cm/1 inch thick steak from the thick end of the sirloin, this is tender and ideal for grilling.

T-bone On the T-shaped bone, this large steak cut through the sirloin includes a slice each of the loin meat and of the fillet.

Entrecôte A boneless steak consisting of the eye of the loin meat from the sirloin, but without fillet. Usually cut 2.5-4 cm/1-1½ inches thick.

Minute Steak A thin slice of steak of good quality which may be fried or grilled very quickly. This may be taken from the sirloin, or even from the fillet. It is trimmed of all fat and may be beaten out very thinly.

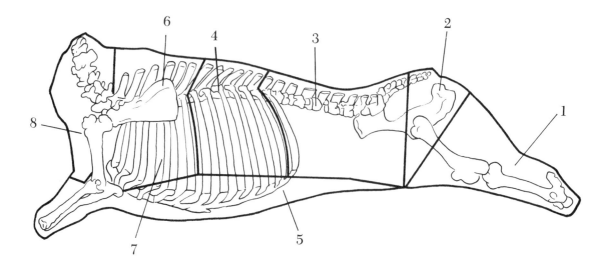

VEAL

1 Leg The lower part of the leg, the knuckle or shin, this is jointed on the bone for stewing or boned and cubed to be sold as pie veal. The upper part of the leg provides a large roasting joint. Continental escalopes are cut along the muscle on the topside area of the joint; however British escalopes may be cut across the grain of the meat on the fleshy part of the leg in the form of steaks which are beaten out thinly to make escalopes.

2 Fillet The most expensive and tender cut, either sliced into steaks or cooked whole.

3 Loin For roasting on the bone or boned, this may be cut into chops for grilling or frying. The leg end of the loin may be referred to as the chump end.

4 Best End of Neck For roasting or braising, this is also chopped into cutlets for grilling and frying.

5 Breast Usually boned for stuffing, rolling and roasting. An economical cut with a good flavour.

6 Shoulder On the bone or boned and rolled, for roasting. If the fore knuckle is removed, this is called the oyster of veal.

7/8 Middle Neck and Scrag For stewing and braising, these have a high proportion of bone to meat.

9 Cutlets Cut from the best end of neck, providing 6 per carcass, each weighing about 175 g/6 oz.

10 Chops Cut from the loin, these may have a slice of kidney included. The chops may be cut in various ways; they usually weigh about 225 g/8 oz each.

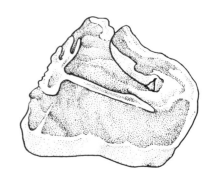

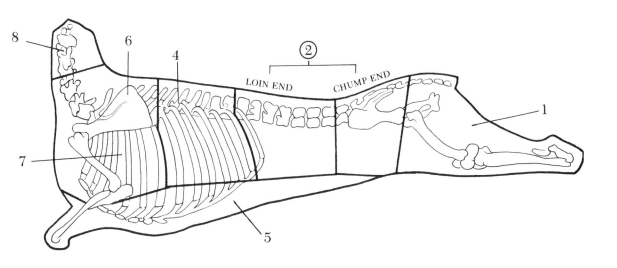

LAMB

1 Leg Known as gigot in Scotland, the leg may be divided into fillet and shank end. Leaner than shoulder, the leg may be roasted whole or boned and stuffed. Slices chopped off the leg are known as lamb steaks.

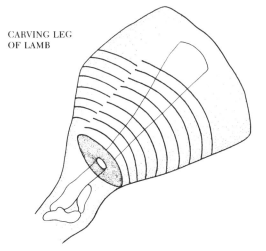

CARVING LEG OF LAMB

2 Loin A roasting joint for cooking on the bone or boned and rolled. Divided into loin and chump ends, the joint may be separated into loin and chump chops.

3 Saddle The whole loin from both sides of the lamb, with a central bone.

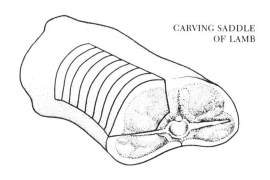

CARVING SADDLE OF LAMB

4 Best End of Neck This may be boned and rolled, then sliced into noisettes. The individual bones may be separated with their eye of meat to make cutlets or the whole rack roasted on the bone. Two racks may be interlocked to make a guard of honour, or they may be trussed into a circular crown roast.

5 Breast One of the most economical cuts of meat, the breast may be separated into riblets on the bone for treating like pork spareribs. More commonly, the boned joint is stuffed and rolled for slow roasting, pot roasting or braising.

6 Shoulder An economical roasting joint which may be separated into the blade end or best end and the knuckle end. Shoulder may be roasted on the bone or the whole joint may be boned and trussed neatly. Boned shoulder is an excellent joint for stuffing.

CARVING SHOULDER OF LAMB

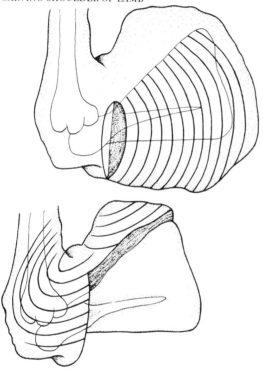

7 Middle Neck Usually chopped into portions for stewing; however 2-3 chops of grilling quality may be taken from the meat closest to the best end of neck.

8 Scrag End of Neck Economical for stewing.

9 Chops Each carcass yields 4-6 chump chops, 6 loin chops and 4-6 neck chops (cutlets with the rib bone removed). Leg chops or cutlets, also known as steaks, may be cut from the fillet end of the leg.

PORK

The majority of pork meat is tender and therefore suitable for quick cooking as well as braising. The important differences between the cuts is in the proportion of fat to lean and the presence of sinews, gristle or skin which must be trimmed before the meat is subjected to quick or dry cooking methods.

1 Leg Divided into the fillet end, from the top of the leg, or knuckle end, from the lower half of the leg. Popular for roasting, on the bone or boned and rolled.

2 Loin A popular roasting cut, either on the bone or boned and rolled (in which case the joint may be stuffed). Tenderloin is the meat from the inside of the loin bone, also known as the fillet.

CARVING LOIN OF PORK

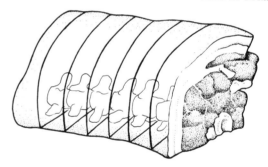

3 Belly Also known as flank or draft of pork, this used to be regarded as a very fatty cut. Animals bred for leaner meat yield belly that has a better proportion of lean to fat. The flat joint may be roasted or sliced into rashers for grilling.

4 Bladebone Boned and stuffed or roasted on the bone.

5 Sparerib A cut which is equivalent to the middle neck of lamb. This is marbled with fat, but overall it provides a lean roasting joint or slices (known as sparerib chops) for grilling and frying.

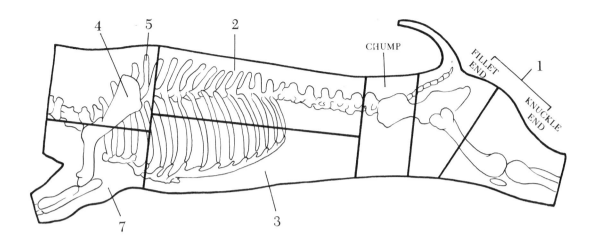

6 Spare Ribs These are cut from the belly once the main joint has been removed to include only the bones with their covering of meat. The amount of meat left on the bone can vary considerably, so always look for meaty ribs when buying.

7 Hand and Spring A large, economical cut which yields a generous amount of meat. Ideal for slow roasting, it can be divided into hand which may be boned and stuffed, and shank which may be trimmed and cubed for braising. With careful trimming of sinews, the joint provides a large quantity of meat which may be used for different purposes: a fair-sized portion for roasting, cubes for braising and strips or small cubes for frying and stir frying.

8 Head The head contains a considerable quantity of meat, notably the cheeks which are traditionally boiled and crumbed to be sold as Bath Chaps, small hams on the bone. The whole head may be boiled and cleaned for making brawn, or a prepared half head purchased from butchers.

Trotters or Pettitoes The may be boiled, skinned and the meat removed. The meat is flavoursome and the stock sets to a firm jelly. Unskinned trotters may be boned and stuffed, then roasted.

10 Chops Taken from the loin or spare rib. Chump chops are the first 2-3 chops from the leg-end of the loin. They are large and meaty. Middle loin chops are sometimes sold with the kidney, whereas foreloin chops have a curved shape and no kidney.

CHUMP CHOP

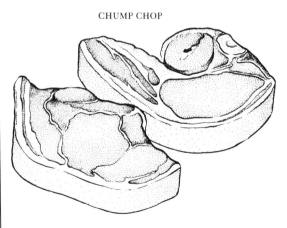

MIDDLE LOIN CHOP

OFFAL

Offal is the term used for internal organs and other, less valuable, edible parts of the carcass. The term embraces brains, tongue, head, sweetbreads, heart, liver, kidneys, lights, tripe, melts, caul, marrow bones, tail and feet. Most offal is highly nutritious and low in fat, and many types cook quickly.

Liver Calf's liver is considered to have the best and most delicate flavour, followed by lamb's, pig's and ox liver, in that order. Calf's liver and lamb's liver are both suitable for grilling, frying or braising. Although pig's liver has a fine texture, its flavour is strong, so it is usually used in pâtés or combined with other ingredients in mixed dishes. Ox liver is the least popular since it is both strongly flavoured and coarse textured. It is seldom used except in casseroles which include plenty of other ingredients.

Liver is covered with a fine membrane which should be removed before cooking. When rinsed and dried on absorbent kitchen paper, the liver may be sliced, cut in strips or diced. All sinews and any blood vessels should be removed. Before frying or grilling, liver is usually coated in well-seasoned flour.

Kidneys These have a distinct flavour, strongest in ox and pig's kidneys. Lamb's kidneys are milder. Lamb's, pig's and calf's kidneys may be grilled, fried or braised; ox kidney is suitable for stewing and for adding to pies and savoury puddings.

Kidneys are usually sold with the outer covering of fat removed. The fine membrane surrounding them should be removed, and they should then be cut open so that the core, tubes and sinews may be cut out. A pair of kitchen scissors is the best implement for this.

Hearts Ox, calf's, lamb's and sheep's hearts are all lean and firm. They require careful preparation to remove all tubes, then long, slow cooking. The outer covering of fat and any membrane should be removed, then the tubes, fat and tough tissue should be cut away to leave only the trim, dark meat. The heart may be split and stuffed, then neatly sewn to enclose the stuffing before long slow braising.

Sweetbreads The thymus gland. Ox, calf's and lamb's sweetbreads are sold in pairs, each pair serving two people. Sweetbreads should be soaked in cold water for 15 minutes, then thoroughly washed in several changes of cold water. They must be simmered gently until firm – 2-5 minutes, depending on type – then drained and rinsed in cold water. The outer membrane should be removed and the sweetbreads pressed by placing in a dish, covering with scalded muslin and placing a weight on top. Chill until firm – this takes several hours. The sweetbreads will then be ready for cooking: they may be cut into pieces or sliced and coated in egg and breadcrumbs for frying. Alternatively, they may be coated in well-seasoned flour, browned in butter and served in a creamy sauce.

Oxtail This is sold ready jointed. Excess fat should be trimmed off and the joints stewed with vegetables and stock or water for several hours, until tender. The meat may be served on the bone or the joints may be picked over for meat and the bones discarded. Oxtail has a rich, beefy flavour, ideal for winter stews and soups.

Tongue Lamb's, ox and calf's tongues require boiling, skinning and trimming. Ox tongue may be purchased pickled in brine or unsalted, the former requiring soaking before cooking. Tongue should be simmered gently with vegetables, bay leaves, mace and other herbs in plenty of water to cover until tender. This will take about 45 minutes for lamb's tongues, 1 hour for a calf's tongue and 2 or more hours for an ox tongue. For detailed instructions on how to prepare (and press) tongue, see page 185. Pressed tongue may be served with mustard. Hot Béchamel sauce flavoured with mustard is the ideal accompaniment for a freshly boiled tongue.

Tripe This is the lining of the stomach. Smooth, or blanket tripe comes from the first stomach cavity and honeycomb tripe comes from the second stomach cavity. The latter has a distinct honeycomb texture. Tripe is usually sold prepared, blanched and cleaned, or dressed, ready for cooking in a sauce. The preparation process is long, involving much washing, scrubbing, blanching and rinsing. The prepared tripe is white with a glutinous texture. It should be further cooked for anything from 30 minutes to 2 hours, depending on the dish.

Brains Lamb's and calf's brains have a delicate flavour, although they are not a popular food. Their preparation is similar to that of sweetbreads, involving soaking and rinsing, blanching and removing the covering membrane, then pressing and chilling before coating or cooking as required.

Heads Pig's head is used for making brawn and is the only head sold with the animal carcass to the butcher. They are easily obtainable from proper butchers (as opposed to meat sellers). The boiled head is used to make brawn, although a half head may be a more practical buy in view of its size. Calf's heads are also traditionally, although less commonly, used for brawn. Sheep's head may be split, boiled, casseroled and served in a variety of ways but these are not popular in British cookery.

Feet Pig's and calf's trotters and cow heel are all traditionally boiled for their jellied stock. Pig's trotters, both fresh or smoked, are more readily available than calf's. They are delicious for making soups and stews and yield a good portion of flavoursome meat.

Bones and Other Offal Marrow bones should be chopped by the butcher ready for baking and boiling at home to make stock.

In various countries and regions many other animal parts are eaten, including the lungs (lights) and melts (spleen) or even the testicles, ears and intestines. However, these are not popular for home cooking, even though they may be encountered as well-seasoned specialities at Continental charcuteries. Perhaps the nearest British equivalent is the Scottish haggis, although the modern version makes less use of offal than the old-fashioned stuffed sheep's stomach did.

ROASTING TIMES FOR MEAT

The following times are a guide for roasting meat at 180°C/350°F/gas 4. Weights and timings are for oven-ready joints, including any stuffing. Small joints weighing less than 1 kg/2¼ lb may need an extra 5 minutes per 450 g/1 lb.

Personal preferences play an important role when roasting, and there are many methods. For example, the joint may be placed in an oven preheated to a higher temperature than that recommended for general roasting. The temperature may be turned down immediately or after the first 5-15 minutes. This method is popular for pork (to crisp the rind) and for sealing and browning the outside of larger joints of beef or lamb. Small to medium joints may need less time than that calculated below, if they are started off at a high temperature, but thick or large joints will still require the full calculated time to ensure they are cooked.

Attitudes towards roasting pork have changed considerably, based on professional guidance on food safety. Pork is usually served cooked through, not rare or medium; however, the meat may be roasted until it is succulent rather than very dry; hence the two recommended timings.

BEEF

Rare	–	20 minutes per 450 g/1 lb plus 20 minutes
Medium	–	25 minutes per 450 g/1 lb plus 25 minutes
Well Done	–	30 minutes per 450 g/1 lb plus 30 minutes

LAMB

Medium	–	20-25 minutes per 450 g/ 1 lb plus 20-25 minutes
Well Done	–	25-30 minutes per 450 g/ 1 lb plus 25-30 minutes

PORK

Medium	–	20-25 minutes per 450 g/ 1 lb plus 25-30 minutes
Well Done	–	25-30 minutes per 450 g/ 1 lb plus 25-30 minutes

VEAL

Well Done	–	30 minutes per 450 g/ 1 lb plus 30 minutes

USING A MEAT THERMOMETER

A meat thermometer may be inserted into the joint before cooking, ready to register the internal temperature and indicate the extent of cooking. Preheat the thermometer in the oven from cold. Pierce the meat at the thickest point with a skewer and insert the hot thermometer into it. At any stage during cooking the reading on the thermometer may be checked to assess cooking progress (see chart below). When the meat is cooked, remove the thermometer and place it on a plate to cool.

BEEF

Rare	–	60°C/140°F
Medium	–	70°C/158°F
Well Done	–	80°C/176°F

LAMB

Medium	–	70-75°C/158-167°F
Well Done	–	75-80°C/167-176°F

PORK

Medium	–	75-80°C/158-176°F
Well Done	–	80-85°C/176-185°F

VEAL

Well Done	–	80-85°C/176-185°F

ROAST RIBS OF BEEF WITH YORKSHIRE PUDDING

This impressive joint is also known as a standing rib roast. Ask the butcher to trim the thin ends of the bones so that the joint will stand upright. The recipe below, as in Mrs Beeton's day, uses clarified dripping for cooking, but the roast may be cooked without any additional fat, if preferred. There will be sufficient fat from the meat for basting.

2.5 kg/5½ lb forerib of beef
50-75 g/2-3 oz beef dripping
salt and pepper
vegetable stock or water (see method)

YORKSHIRE PUDDING
100 g/4 oz plain flour
1 egg, beaten
150 ml/¼ pint milk

Set the oven at 230°C/450°F/gas 8. Wipe the meat but do not salt it. Melt 50 g/2 oz of the dripping in a roasting tin, add the meat and quickly spoon some of the hot fat over it. Roast for 10 minutes.

Lower the oven temperature to 180°C/350°F/gas 4. Baste the meat thoroughly, then continue to roast for a further 1¾ hours for rare meat; 2¼ hours for well-done meat. Baste frequently during cooking.

Meanwhile make the Yorkshire pudding batter. Sift the flour into a bowl and add a pinch of salt. Make a well in the centre of the flour and add the beaten egg. Stir in the milk, gradually working in the flour. Beat vigorously until the mixture is smooth and bubbly, then stir in 150 ml/¼ pint water.

About 30 minutes before the end of the cooking time, spoon off 30 ml/2 tbsp of the dripping and divide it between six 7.5 cm/3 inch Yorkshire pudding tins. Place the tins in the oven for 5 minutes or until the fat is very hot, then carefully divide the batter between them. Bake above the meat for 15-20 minutes.

When the beef is cooked, salt it lightly, transfer it to a warmed serving platter and keep hot. Pour off almost all the water in the roasting tin, leaving the sediment. Pour in enough vegetable stock or water to make a thin gravy, then heat to boiling point, stirring all the time. Season with salt and pepper and serve in a heated gravyboat, with the roast and Yorkshire puddings.

SERVES 6 TO 8

> **MRS BEETON'S TIP** Yorkshire pudding is traditionally cooked in a large tin below the joint, so that some of the cooking juices from the meat fall into the pudding to give it an excellent flavour. In a modern oven, this means using a rotisserie or resting the meat directly on the oven shelf. The pudding should be cooked in a large roasting tin, then cut into portions and served as a course on its own before the meat course. Gravy should be poured over the portions of pudding.

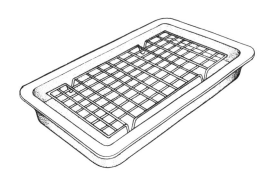

BEEF WELLINGTON

Illustrated on page 141

This classic Beef Wellington differs from beef en croûte in that the meat is covered with fine pâté – preferably pâté de foie gras – before it is wrapped.

800 g-1 kg/1¾-2¼ lb fillet of beef
freshly ground black pepper
25 g/1 oz butter
15 ml/1 tbsp oil
100 g/4 oz button mushrooms, sliced
5 ml/1 tsp chopped fresh mixed herbs
5 ml/1 tsp chopped parsley
75 g/3 oz fine liver pâté

PUFF PASTRY
   225 g/8 oz plain flour
   2.5 ml/½ tsp salt
   225 g/8 oz butter
   3.75 ml/¾ tsp lemon juice
   beaten egg for glazing

Make the pastry. Sift the flour and salt into a mixing bowl and rub in 50 g/2 oz of the butter. Add the lemon juice and mix to a smooth dough with cold water. Shape the remaining butter into a rectangle on greaseproof paper. Roll out the dough on a lightly floured surface to a strip a little wider than the butter and rather more than twice its length. Place the butter on one half of the pastry, fold the other half over it, and press the edges together with the rolling pin. Leave in a cool place for 15 minutes to allow the butter to harden.

Roll out the pastry into a long strip. Fold the bottom third up and the top third down, press the edges together with the rolling pin and turn the pastry so that the folded edges are on the right and left. Roll and fold again, cover and leave in a cool place for 15 minutes. Repeat this process until the pastry has been rolled out six times. Chill the pastry well between each rolling, wrapping it in cling film to prevent it drying on the surface. After the final rolling, leave the wrapped pastry in the refrigerator until required.

Set the oven at 230°C/450°F/gas 8. Wipe, trim and tie the meat into a neat shape. Season with pepper. Melt the butter in the oil in a large frying pan, add the fillet and brown it quickly all over. Carefully transfer the fillet to a roasting tin, reserving the fat in the pan, and roast it for 10-20 minutes (for rare to medium result). Remove and cool. Leave the oven on.

Heat the fat remaining in the frying pan, add the mushrooms and fry over moderate heat for 2-3 minutes. Remove from the heat, add the herbs and leave to cool.

Roll out the pastry on a lightly floured surface to a rectangle large enough to enclose the fillet. Using a slotted spoon, transfer the mushroom mixture to one half of the pastry. Lay the beef on top and spread the pâté over the meat. Wrap the pastry around the beef to form a neat parcel, sealing the edges well. Place on a baking sheet with the join underneath. Garnish with leaves and/or a lattice of strips cut from the pastry trimmings, glaze with the beaten egg and bake for about 30 minutes. Serve hot or cold.

SERVES 6

VARIATION

To make individual beef wellingtons, use six portions of raw fillet. Wrap individually, including mushrooms and pâté, bringing up the pastry sides to make neat parcels, glaze and bake, allowing 15-20 minutes for rare beef; 25-30 minutes for medium-cooked beef.

GRILLING STEAKS AND SMALL CUTS

Providing firm guidelines for grilling is difficult as the performance of individual appliances varies enormously. Equally, the exact thickness and shape of the food, its position under the heat and personal preferences all determine the cooking time. The following timings are intended as a guide only. They are based upon initial cooking under a grill preheated to the hottest setting, the temperature being reduced partway through cooking once the outside of the meat is sealed.

Meat	Thickness	Time for Each Side
Beef Steak, rare	2 cm/¾ inch	2½ minutes
Beef Steak, medium	as above	4 minutes
Beef Steak, well done	as above	6 minutes
Minute Steak	5 mm/¼ inch	1 minute
Pork Chop	2.5 cm/1 inch	10 minutes
Lamb Chop	2.5 cm/1 inch	5-8 minutes
Lamb Cutlet	2.5 cm/1 inch	4-5 minutes

CHATEAUBRIAND STEAK

Châteaubriand is a luxury cut, from the thickest part of the beef fillet. It may be served simply, with maître d'hôtel butter, or with Béarnaise Sauce (page 352).

a double fillet steak, not less than 4 cm/ 1½ inches thick, trimmed
melted butter
freshly ground black pepper
maître d'hôtel butter (see Mrs Beeton's Tip) to serve

Brush the steak generously all over with melted butter, season with pepper and place on a rack in a grill pan. Cook under a very hot grill for 2-3 minutes until browned and sealed. Turn the steak over, using a palette knife or spoons, and grill until browned. Lower the heat slightly and continue grilling, turning the steak once or twice, until cooked to taste. Rare meat will require a total cooking time of about 20 minutes; for medium-rare add an extra 5 minutes.

Cut the meat downwards at a slight angle into 4 even slices. Put 2 slices on each of 2 heated plates, top with maître d'hôtel butter and serve at once.

SERVES 2

> 🍯 **MRS BEETON'S TIP** Maître d'hôtel butter is easy to make. Cream 50 g/2 oz butter in a small bowl. Finely chop 2-3 parsley sprigs and add them to the butter a little at a time. Beat until well combined. Season the mixture with salt and a small pinch of pepper and add a few drops of lemon juice to intensify the flavour. Use at once, press into small pots or shape into a roll, wrap in freezer paper and freeze in a polythene bag. Convenient slices can then be cut off with a warm knife when required.

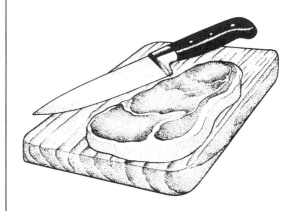

STEAKS WITH MUSTARD SAUCE

4 (150-175 g/5-6 oz) fillet or sirloin
    steaks, trimmed
freshly ground black pepper
25 g/1 oz unsalted butter
30 ml/2 tbsp oil
150 ml/¼ pint soured cream
5 ml/1 tsp lemon juice
10 ml/2 tsp French mustard
salt
watercress to garnish

Beat each steak lightly on both sides with a cutlet bat or rolling pin. Season with pepper (see Mrs Beeton's Tip). Melt the butter in the oil in a heavy-bottomed frying pan. When hot, add the steaks to the pan and fry quickly on both sides, allowing 2-3 minutes a side for rare steak; 3½-4 minutes for medium-rare and 5-6 minutes a side for well done.

Lift out the steaks, transfer them to a warmed serving dish and keep hot. Stir the soured cream into the juices remaining in the pan and heat through gently, without boiling. Stir in the lemon juice, mustard and salt to taste.

Pour the mustard sauce over the steak, garnish with watercress and serve at once.

SERVES 4

🥣 **MRS BEETON'S TIP** Do not salt the steaks before frying as this draws out the juices.

STEAK AU POIVRE

Illustrated on page 142

20 ml/4 tsp whole black and white
    peppercorns, mixed
4 (150-200 g/5-7 oz) steaks (fillet, sirloin
    or entrecôte), wiped and trimmed
1 garlic clove, cut in half
60 ml/4 tbsp olive oil
50 g/2 oz butter

PARSLEY BUTTER
50 ml/2 oz butter, softened
30 ml/2 tbsp chopped parsley
salt and pepper

Make the parsley butter. Beat the butter until creamy in a small bowl. Add the parsley, beating until well combined, then season the mixture with salt and a small pinch of pepper. Form into a roll, wrap in greaseproof paper, and refrigerate until required.

Crush the peppercorns in a mortar with a pestle. Set aside. Rub the steaks on both sides with the cut clove of garlic, then brush both sides generously with olive oil. With the heel of your hand, press the crushed peppercorns into the surface of the meat on each side.

Melt the butter with any remaining olive oil in a heavy bottomed frying pan. When hot, add the steaks to the pan and fry quickly on both sides, allowing 2-3 minutes a side for rare steak; 3½-4 minutes for medium-rare and 5-6 minutes a side for well done.

Using a palette knife or two spoons, transfer the steaks to a warmed serving dish. Slice the parsley butter into rounds and place one on top of each steak. Serve at once.

SERVES 4

TOURNEDOS ROSSINI

Tournedos is a slice from the fillet, usually about 2 cm/³⁄₄ inch thick and a neat round shape. In the classic version of this recipe, foie gras and truffles are used instead of liver pâté and mushrooms, and the dish is served with a brown sauce enriched with Madeira.

4 (175 g/6 oz) tournedos steaks, trimmed
4 slices white bread
100 g/4 oz butter
15 ml/1 tbsp cooking oil
salt and pepper

GARNISH
    4 rounds good quality liver pâté, 5 mm/
       ¼ inch thick
    4 small flat mushrooms
    20 ml/4 tsp chilled butter
    watercress sprigs

Tie the tournedos to a neat shape. Cut the bread slices into 4 rounds, each large enough to accommodate one of the steaks. Melt half the butter in the oil in a large, deep frying pan and fry the bread rounds over moderate heat until pale gold and crisp on both sides. Transfer to a warmed serving dish, cover with buttered grease-proof paper and keep warm.

Add half the remaining butter to the pan. When hot, add the steaks to the pan and fry quickly for 2-3 minutes on each side, or until well seared and browned all over, but rare inside. Remove them from the pan, using a palette knife or two spoons, and place one on each fried bread round. Keep hot.

Heat the remaining butter in a small frying pan, add the pâté slices and mushrooms and turn over high heat until the mushrooms are soft and the pâté is lightly browned but still holds its shape.

Place a slice of pâté on each tournedos and cap it with a mushroom, gill side down. Top each mushroom with 5 ml/1 tsp chilled butter. Garnish with watercress and serve at once, with freshly ground black pepper.

SERVES 4

STEAK CHASSEUR

75 g/3 oz butter
30 ml/2 tablespoons finely chopped
    shallots or spring onions
100 g/4 oz mushrooms, sliced
125 ml/4 fl oz dry white wine
4 (150 g/5 oz) fillet steaks
125 ml/4 fl oz good quality beef stock
15 ml/1 tbsp tomato purée
15 ml/1 tbsp finely chopped parsley

Melt 25 g/1 oz of the butter in a small saucepan. Add the shallots or spring onions and cook gently until softened but not browned. Add the mushrooms and shake over high heat for 2-3 minutes. Pour in the wine. Boil it rapidly, uncovered, until reduced to about half. Set aside while cooking the steaks.

Melt the remaining butter in a frying pan. When hot, add the steaks to the pan and fry quickly on both sides, allowing 2-3 minutes a side for rare steak; 3½-4 minutes for medium-rare and 5-6 minutes a side for well done. Arrange on a heated dish.

Pour off most of the fat from the pan and add the beef stock and tomato purée. Boil rapidly, stirring to incorporate any sediment on the base of the pan, until reduced to about half. Stir in the mushroom mixture and parsley, pour over the steaks and serve.

SERVES 4

STEAK AND ONIONS

Illustrated on page 142

Serve creamy mashed potatoes, fine potato chips or French fries, or plain boiled potatoes sprinkled with a little parsley with this traditional dish of fried steak with onions.

beef dripping for cooking
2 large onions, thinly sliced
1 bay leaf
1 fresh thyme sprig
4 (225-350 g/8-12 oz) slices rump steak
salt and pepper
60 ml/4 tbsp plain flour
15 ml/1 tbsp tomato purée
300 ml/½ pint beef stock
dash of Worcestershire sauce

GARNISH (OPTIONAL)
4 small tomatoes, halved or quartered
fresh herb sprigs

Melt a knob of dripping in a large frying pan. Add the onions, bay leaf and thyme, and cook the onions over moderate heat, stirring occasionally, until they are evenly browned. This takes up to 25 minutes – do not increase the heat to hurry the browning; the secret of a good flavour is the long cooking.

Meanwhile, trim any gristle and excess fat from the steak, then beat the pieces with a meat mallet or rolling pin to tenderize them. Avoid beating the meat in such a way that the steaks are thinned. Place the steaks on a plate. Add plenty of seasoning to the flour, then sprinkle half over the steaks, dusting them evenly. Turn the meat over and sprinkle the remaining flour over the second sides.

Use a slotted spoon to remove the onions from the pan. Drain them on absorbent kitchen paper and transfer to a heated serving dish or individual plates. Keep hot. Leave the bay and thyme in the pan and add a little extra dripping if necessary. When the fat is hot, add the steaks and brown them quickly on both sides. Allow about 3 minutes on each side for rare steaks. For medium or well done steaks, lower the heat slightly once the meat is sealed and continue to cook for 4-7 minutes on each side. The exact time depends on the thickness of the meat.

Transfer the steaks to the dish or plates, cover loosely and keep hot. Stir any remaining flour into the juices in the pan, then stir in the tomato purée and the stock. Bring to the boil, stirring, and boil rapidly to reduce the sauce by about a third. Add a little Worcestershire sauce and taste for seasoning.

Spoon the sauce and onions over the steaks. Garnish with tomatoes and herbs, if liked. Serve at once.

SERVES 4

MRS BEETON'S BOEUF A LA MODE

2 rindless back bacon rashers
1 kg/2¼ lb thick flank of beef (see Mrs
    Beeton's Tip)
25 g/1 oz butter
1 onion, sliced
2 celery sticks, sliced
1 carrot, chopped
½ turnip, chopped
100 ml/3½ fl oz red wine vinegar
75 ml/5 tbsp port
salt and pepper

SEASONING MIXTURE
1 clove
4 black peppercorns
3 allspice berries
3 parsley sprigs, finely chopped
1 fresh thyme sprig, leaves finely chopped
    or 1.25 ml/¼ tsp dried thyme
1 bay leaf, finely crumbled

Cut the bacon crossways into 2 cm/¾ inch strips, including fat and lean in each strip. Trim the meat and, using a sharp knife, make sufficient deep slits in the flesh to accommodate all the bacon strips.

Make the seasoning mixture. Pound the clove, peppercorns and allspice in a mortar with a pestle. Add the remaining ingredients and mix well.

Pour the vinegar into a shallow bowl. Dip the bacon strips into the vinegar and then into the spice mixture. Insert a bacon strip into each slit in the meat. Rub any remaining spice mixture over the surface of the meat, then tie the beef into a neat shape.

Melt the butter in a flameproof casserole large enough to hold the piece of beef. Add the onion and fry gently until golden brown, then stir in the celery, carrot and turnip. Place the meat on the vegetables. Gently pour in the vinegar, with 250 ml/8 fl oz water, and cover the pan closely. Heat to boiling point, lower the heat and simmer very gently for about 1¾ hours, turning the meat over after 40 minutes' cooking time, and again after a further 30 minutes.

When cooked, transfer the meat to a warmed serving dish and keep hot. Strain the cooking liquid into a pan, skim off the fat, and add the port. Bring to the boil over gentle heat. Add salt and pepper if required. Remove the strings from the meat and pour a little of the sauce over. Serve the remaining sauce in a warmed sauceboat.

SERVES 4 TO 6

> **MRS BEETON'S TIP** Thick flank or top rump, as it is often called, is usually sold with extra fat tied around it. The quantity of meat stipulated above is without the added fat.

BRAISED BRISKET

1.25-1.5 kg/2¾-3¼ lb brisket of beef,
    trimmed
25 g/1 oz dripping or 30 ml/2 tbsp oil
25 g/1 oz rindless streaky bacon rashers,
    chopped
1 large carrot, thickly sliced
1 small turnip, thickly sliced
1 large onion, chopped, or 15 button
    onions
2 celery sticks, thickly sliced
1 bouquet garni
salt and pepper
250-300 ml/8-10 fl oz beef stock

GRAVY
    30 ml/2 tbsp dripping or oil
    10 ml/2 tsp plain flour
    450 ml/¾ pint beef stock
    10 ml/2 tsp tomato purée

Tie the meat into a neat shape if necessary. Heat the dripping or oil in a large flameproof casserole, add the meat and brown it on all sides. Remove the meat and set it aside.

Add the bacon and vegetables, and fry gently until beginning to soften. Tuck in the bouquet garni and add salt and pepper to taste. Place the meat on top of the vegetables and pour the stock over. Cover with a tight fitting lid and cook over gentle heat for 2 hours or until the meat is tender. Baste occasionally and add more stock if required. Alternatively, cook in a preheated 160°C/325°F/gas 3 oven for about 2 hours.

To make the gravy, heat the dripping or oil in a saucepan. Stir in the flour and cook gently until pale brown. Gradually add the stock, stirring constantly, then add the tomato purée. Bring to the boil, stirring all the time, then lower the heat and simmer uncovered for 15-20 minutes.

When the meat is cooked, transfer it to a heated serving dish, remove the string, if used, and keep hot. Strain any stock remaining in the casserole into the gravy. Garnish the meat with the vegetables and serve the gravy separately.

SERVES 10 TO 12

VARIATION

If liked, slivers of garlic may be inserted into the meat, and red wine used in place of part or all of the beef stock. For a rich and tasty gravy made from the pan juices, combine 30 ml/2 tbsp tomato purée, 15 ml/1 tbsp soy sauce, 5 ml/1 tsp German prepared mustard, 5 ml/1 tsp Worcestershire sauce and a pinch of brown sugar in a bowl. Mix well and spread over the surface of the meat about 45 minutes before it is cooked. Leave for 15 minutes, then remove the pan lid and baste the meat with the stock so that the spicy mixture combines with it. Serve as suggested above, but use the pan gravy as an accompaniment, skimming any fat from the surface before serving.

BRAISED BEEF WITH PEPPERS

1 kg/2¼ lb topside or brisket of beef
25 g/1 oz dripping or 30 ml/2 tbsp oil
2 rindless streaky bacon rashers, chopped
1 large carrot, sliced
1 small turnip, sliced
12 button onions, peeled but left whole
100 g/4 oz button mushrooms
2 celery sticks, thickly sliced
2 leeks, trimmed, sliced and washed
1 bouquet garni
salt
6 black peppercorns
250 ml/8 fl oz beef stock

GRAVY
15 ml/1 tbsp dripping or oil
30 ml/2 tbsp plain flour
250 ml/8 fl oz beef stock
5 ml/1 tsp tomato purée

GARNISH
3 red peppers, seeded and sliced into
1 cm/½ inch wide strips
12 black olives (optional)

Tie the meat into a neat shape if necessary. Heat the dripping or oil in a large flameproof casserole or heavy-bottomed saucepan, add the meat and brown it on all sides. Remove the meat and set it aside.

Add the bacon and vegetables to the fat remaining in the casserole or pan. Fry gently until beginning to soften. Tuck in the bouquet garni and add salt to taste. Stir in the peppercorns. Place the meat on top of the vegetables and pour the stock over. Cover with a tight fitting lid and cook over gentle heat for 2½-3 hours or until the meat is tender. Baste occasionally and add more stock if required. Alternatively, cook in a preheated 160°C/325°F/gas 3 oven for about 2½ hours.

Meanwhile make the gravy. Heat the dripping or oil in a saucepan. Stir in the flour and cook gently until pale brown. Gradually add the stock, stirring constantly, then add the tomato purée. Bring to the boil, stirring all the time, then lower the heat and simmer uncovered for 15-20 minutes.

Lift out the meat from the casserole or pan. Add the pepper strips to the remaining stock and simmer for 10 minutes. Meanwhile remove the string from the meat, carve it into neat slices and arrange on a heated serving dish. Use a slotted spoon to arrange the pepper strips and vegetables around the meat slices. Complete the garnish with the black olives, if liked. Pour the cooking juices from the meat into the gravy and spoon a little over the meat. Serve at once, offering the remaining gravy separately.

SERVES 6

> 🥄 **MRS BEETON'S TIP** It is hard to believe that the sweet bell peppers, used here, come from the same family as the fiery chillies that enliven Mexican and Indian cooking. Sweet peppers come in a variety of shapes, sizes and colours. Raw fresh peppers contain significant amounts of vitamin C.

BEEF OLIVES

Illustrated on page 143

This makes an excellent main course for a casual dinner party and has the advantage that the meat is prepared in individual portions and needs very little last-minute attention.

450 g/1 lb rump or chuck steak, trimmed
45 ml/3 tbsp dripping or oil
1 large onion, sliced
45 ml/3 tbsp plain flour
600 ml/1 pint beef stock
1 tomato, peeled and sliced
1 carrot, sliced
15 ml/1 tbsp Worcestershire sauce
salt and pepper
30 ml/2 tbsp chopped parsley
fresh herb sprigs to garnish

STUFFING
50 g/2 oz margarine
100 g/4 oz fresh white breadcrumbs
pinch of grated nutmeg
15 ml/1 tbsp chopped parsley
5 ml/1 tsp chopped fresh mixed herbs
grated rind of ½ lemon
1 egg, beaten

Make the stuffing. Melt the margarine in a small saucepan. Add the breadcrumbs, nutmeg, herbs and lemon rind, with salt and pepper to taste. Add enough beaten egg to bind the mixture.

Cut the meat into four slices and flatten each with a cutlet bat or rolling pin. Divide the stuffing between the meat slices, spreading it out evenly. Roll each piece of meat up tightly and tie securely with fine string or cotton.

Heat the dripping or oil in a large saucepan and fry the beef olives, turning them frequently until browned. Using a slotted spoon, transfer them to a plate.

Add the onion slices to the fat remaining in the pan and fry until golden brown. Using a slotted spoon, transfer to the plate with the beef olives. Add the flour to the pan and cook until golden brown, stirring constantly. Gradually add the stock, stirring until the mixture boils, then lower the heat and simmer for 5 minutes.

Return the beef olives and onion slices to the pan. Add the tomato, carrot and Worcestershire sauce, with salt and pepper to taste. Cover the pan with a tight-fitting lid and simmer for 1½-2 hours.

Having removed the strings from the beef olives, serve them on a bed of mashed potato or rice. Strain the sauce and pour it over the beef olives. Sprinkle with chopped parsley and garnish with fresh herbs (as used in the stuffing). Serve at once.

SERVES 4

VARIATIONS

HANOVER ROULADEN: Omit the stuffing. Instead lay a strip of gherkin on each portion of beef, with 15 ml/1 tbsp finely chopped onion, 15 ml/1 tbsp chopped ham and 5 ml/1 tsp capers. Proceed as in the recipe above but cook for 1½ hours only.

MUSHROOM PAUPIETTES: Use a mushroom stuffing instead of herb. Chop 1 rindless bacon rasher and fry without additional fat for 2 minutes. Add 100 g/4 oz finely chopped mushrooms and fry over gentle heat for 5 minutes, stirring. Stir in 100 g/4 oz fresh white breadcrumbs, a knob of butter and pinch of grated nutmeg. Add salt and pepper to taste. Bind with beaten egg. Prepare and cook the paupiettes as for the beef olives in the recipe above, but stir 250 ml/8 fl oz soured cream into the sauce just before serving.

CARBONNADE OF BEEF

Illustrated on page 143

50 g/2 oz butter or margarine
675 g/1½ lb stewing steak, trimmed and
    cut into 4 cm/1½ inch cubes
2 large onions, sliced
1 garlic clove, crushed
15 ml/1 tbsp plain flour
250 ml/8 fl oz beef stock
375 ml/13 fl oz brown ale
salt and pepper
1 bouquet garni
pinch of grated nutmeg
pinch of soft light brown sugar
5 ml/1 tsp red wine vinegar
6 thin slices of French bread
15 ml/1 tbsp French mustard

Set the oven at 160°C/325°F/gas 3. Melt the butter or margarine in a heavy-bottomed frying pan, add the beef and fry quickly until browned on all sides. Using a slotted spoon, transfer the beef to a casserole and keep hot. Add the onions to the fat remaining in the pan and fry until lightly browned, then stir in the garlic and fry over gentle heat for 1 minute.

Pour off any excess fat from the pan to leave about 15 ml/1 tbsp. Add the flour and cook, stirring constantly, until lightly browned. Gradually stir in the stock and ale, with salt and pepper to taste. Add the bouquet garni, nutmeg, brown sugar and vinegar. Bring to the boil, then pour the liquid over the beef in the casserole. Cover and bake for 1½-2 hours or until the beef is tender. Remove the bouquet garni.

Spread the French bread slices with mustard. Arrange them, mustard side up, on top of the carbonnade, pressing them down so that they absorb the gravy. Return the casserole, uncovered, to the oven for about 15 minutes or until the bread browns slightly. Alternatively, place under a hot grill for a few minutes. Serve immediately, straight from the casserole.

SERVES 6

BEEF AND POTATO PIE

675 g/1½ lb stewing steak, trimmed and
    cut into 2 cm/¾ inch cubes
3 onions, sliced
3 large carrots, sliced
1 kg/2¼ lb potatoes, sliced
salt and pepper
hot beef stock, see method

Set the oven at 160°C/325°F/gas 3. Layer the meat with the onion, carrot and potato slices in an ovenproof casserole, finishing with a neat layer of potatoes. Season with salt and pepper.

Pour in enough hot stock to three quarters cover the contents of the casserole, reserving some stock for adding if the dish begins to dry out during cooking. Cover with a tight fitting lid or foil and bake for 3-3½ hours, or until the beef is very tender.

About 30-40 minutes before the end of the cooking time, remove the casserole lid to allow the top layer of potato to brown. Serve straight from the casserole.

SERVES 6

> **MRS BEETON'S TIP** If liked, the top layer of potato may be sprinkled with paprika before browning. Use a sweet Hungarian rose paprika if possible.

SCOTCH COLLOPS

Collop is said to be derived from escalope, meaning slice. It was also used as an everyday term for veal, so sliced veal could equally well have been used in this old-fashioned dish. Minced collops, a less extravagant variation on this recipe, used hand-minced, or diced steak in place of sliced meat.

50 g/2 oz dripping, lard or butter
675 g/1½ lb rump steak, beaten and cut
    into thin slices, about 7.5 cm/3 inches
    long
25 g/1 oz plain flour
salt and pepper
½ small onion or 1 shallot, finely chopped
250 ml/8 fl oz good beef stock
5 ml/1 tsp chopped capers
1 pickled walnut, chopped

Heat the fat in a deep frying pan. In a bowl or stout polythere bag, toss the meat with the flour and seasoning, then add the slices to the hot fat and fry until browned on all sides. With a slotted spoon, remove the meat from the pan. Add the onion or shallot to the fat remaining in the pan and fry gently until softened but not browned. Stir in any flour left from dusting the meat and cook for about 5 minutes, stirring all the time, until the flour begins to bown.

Gradually add the stock, stirring constantly, then add the capers, pickled walnut and salt and pepper to taste. Bring to the boil, stirring constantly, then lower the heat and replace the meat. Simmer very gently for 10 minutes and serve piping hot.

SERVES 4 TO 6

> 🥣 **MRS BEETON'S TIP** To make sippets, toast white or granary bread. Cut into triangles or cubes.

MOCK HARE

30 ml/2 tbsp plain flour
salt and pepper
675 g/1½ lb chuck steak or shin of beef,
    trimmed and cut into 2 cm/¾ inch
    cubes
100 g/4 oz rindless fat bacon, diced
1 onion
3 cloves
400 ml/14 fl oz well-flavoured stock
1 bouquet garni
15 ml/1 tbsp redcurrant jelly
125 ml/4 fl oz port
10 ml/2 tsp chopped gherkins

GARNISH
Mrs Beeton's Forcemeat Balls (page 349)
parsley sprigs

Mix the flour, salt and pepper in a sturdy polythene bag. Add the beef cubes and toss until well coated. Shake off excess flour. Put the bacon in a large flameproof casserole and heat gently until the fat runs. Add the floured meat cubes, a few at a time, turning them until evenly browned. As the cubes brown push them to the sides of the casserole, or use a slotted spoon to transfer them to a plate, replacing them when all the cubes have been browned.

Peel the onion and press the cloves into it. Add it to the casserole with the stock and bouquet garni. Bring to the boil, lower the heat, cover and cook gently for 1½-2 hours for chuck steak, 2-2½ hours for shin. Remove the onion and bouquet garni.

Add the redcurrant jelly, port and gherkins to the casserole, stirring until the jelly melts. Serve the meat from the casserole, garnished with forcemeat balls and parsley.

SERVES 6

BEEF AND BEAN STEW

Stews and casseroles improve if cooked a day ahead. Cool the cooked stew as quickly as possible, cover and store in the refrigerator. Next day, remove any fat from the surface of the stew and reheat on top of the stove or in the oven set at 180°C/350°F/gas 4.

675 g/1½ lb leg of beef, trimmed and cut
   in neat 1 cm/½ inch thick pieces
seasoned flour
60 ml/4 tbsp oil
1 large onion, chopped
2 carrots, chopped
1 small turnip, chopped
750 ml/1¼ pints beef stock
30 ml/2 tbsp tomato purée
salt and pepper
75 g/3 oz haricot beans, soaked in water
   overnight
100 g/4 oz mushrooms, sliced

Toss the beef cubes in seasoned flour until well coated. The easiest way to do this is in a tightly closed stout polythene or paper bag. Tip the contents of the bag into a sieve and shake off excess flour.

Heat the oil in a flameproof casserole and fry the onion, carrots and turnip until golden. With a slotted spoon, transfer the vegetables to a bowl and set aside. Add the floured beef cubes to the fat remaining in the pan and cook until browned on all sides. Pour off any excess fat and return the partially cooked vegetables to the pan. Gradually stir in the stock and tomato purée, with salt and pepper to taste. Heat gently until just simmering.

Drain the beans and place them in a separate saucepan with cold water to cover. Bring to the boil, boil vigorously for 10 minutes, then drain. Add the beans to the stew and simmer gently for about 2-2½ hours or until the meat and beans are tender. Stir occasionally during cooking, never allowing the liquid to boil as this will toughen the meat.

Add the mushrooms and cook for 20-30 minutes more. Serve at once, or transfer to a suitable covered container to cool, chill and refrigerate for serving the next day.

SERVES 6

PRESSURE COOKER TIP Follow the recipe above, but add only 600 ml/1 pint beef stock. After adding the beans, close the cooker, bring to 15 lb pressure and cook for 20 minutes. Reduce the pressure quickly. Stir the stew, taking care to incorporate any sediment on the bottom of the pan, then add the mushrooms, if time permits. Cook in the open pan for 15-20 minutes over gentle heat. Proceed as above.

———————— ◆ ————————

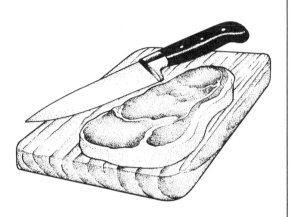

STEW WITH SAVOURY PARSLEY DUMPLINGS

30 ml/2 tbsp dripping or oil
675 g/1½ lb chuck or blade steak,
    trimmed and cut into 5 cm/2 inch
    cubes
3 onions, chopped
45 ml/3 tbsp plain flour
600 ml/1 pint beef stock
5 ml/1 tsp vinegar
salt and pepper

PARSLEY DUMPLINGS
    175 g/6 oz self-raising flour
    2.5 ml/½ tsp salt
    75 g/3 oz shredded beef suet
    15 ml/1 tbsp finely chopped parsley

Heat the dripping or oil in a large heavy-bottomed saucepan. Add the meat and fry until browned on all sides, then remove with a slotted spoon and set aside. Add the onions to the fat remaining in the pan and fry gently until golden brown. Stir in the flour and cook until lightly browned.

Gradually stir in the stock. Bring to the boil, stirring, then lower the heat to simmering point. Stir in the vinegar, with salt and pepper to taste. Return the beef cubes, cover the pan and simmer gently for 1½ hours, or until the meat is tender.

To make the parsley dumplings, sift the flour and salt into a mixing bowl and stir in the suet and parsley. Add about 90 ml/6 tbsp water amd mix lightly to make a firm elastic dough. Divide the dough into 12 equal pieces, shaping each into a ball.

Bring the stew to boiling point and drop in the parsley dumplings. Lower the heat, half cover the pan and simmer for a further 20 minutes or until the dumplings are cooked. To serve, arrange the dumplings around a heated serving dish, then ladle the meat in the centre.

SERVES 6

PRESSURE COOKER TIP The stew can be made very successfully in a pressure cooker. Follow the recipe above, removing the pan from the heat before adding the stock. The pan should not be more than half full. Close the cooker, bring to 15 lb pressure and cook for 20 minutes. Reduce the pressure quickly. Return the cooker – without the lid – to the heat and bring to the boil. Add the dumplings and lower the heat. Place the lid lightly on top to serve as a cover, but do not close or add weights. Simmer gently until the dumplings are cooked. Serve as suggested above.

Fillets of Duck Bigarade (page 73) and Roast Quail in a Vine-leaf Coat (page 107)

Raised Pheasant Pie (page 104)

Pheasant Veronique (page 103) and Pigeons in Red Wine (page 106)

Casserole of Rabbit (page 107) and Quick Curried Rabbit (page 307) with spiced basmati rice

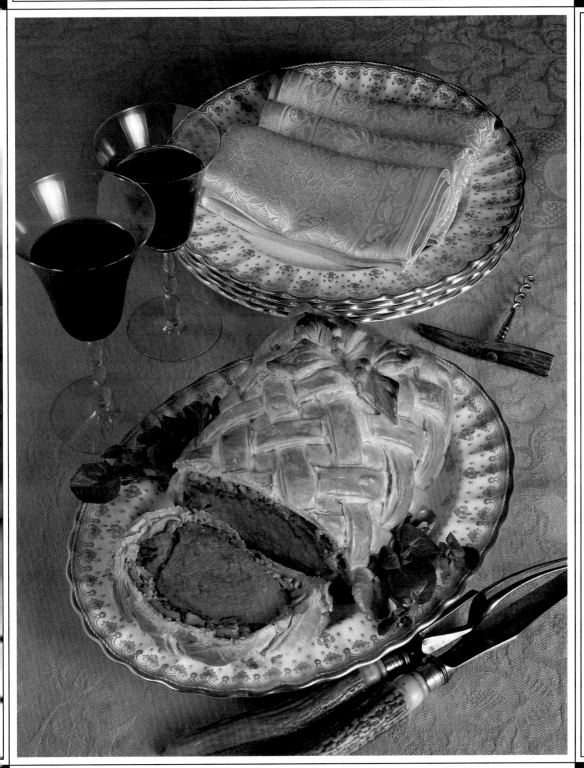

Beef Wellington (page 124)

Steak and Onions (page 128) and Steak au Poivre (page 126)

Carbonnade of Beef (page 133) and Beef Olives (page 132)

Boiled Beef and Dumplings (page 146)

BEEF CREOLE

4 rindless streaky bacon rashers
1 kg/2¼ lb rump steak, trimmed
salt and pepper
2 small red chillies, seeded and very
    finely chopped
2 garlic cloves, crushed
575 g/1¼ lb onions, sliced
1 each red and green peppers, seeded
    and sliced
575 g/1¼ lb tomatoes, sliced
225 g/8 oz long-grain rice

Set the oven at 160°C/325°F/gas 3. Lay the bacon rashers on the base of a casserole large enough to hold the meat snugly. Place the meat on top and season well. Sprinkle the chillies and garlic on top.

Smother the meat with onions, then top with a layer of peppers and tomato slices. Cover with foil or a tight fitting lid. Bake for 3-3½ hours, until the beef is tender.

About 20 minutes before the beef is cooked, place the rice in a saucepan and pour in 600 ml/1 pint water. Add a little salt, then bring just to the boil. Stir once, cover and turn the heat to the lowest setting, leave the rice to cook for 20 minutes. Turn the heat off but leave the rice with the lid on the pan for a further 5-10 minutes.

Fork up the rice and turn it out on a large heated platter or shallow dish. Use a slotted spoon to transfer the onions, peppers and tomatoes to the bed of rice. Slice or cut up the meat and arrange it over the vegetables. Cut up the bacon and sprinkle over the meat. Cover and keep hot. Boil the cooking juices until reduced by half. Season; pour over beef and serve at once.

SERVES 4 TO 6

BEEF STROGANOFF

675 g/1½ lb thinly sliced rump steak,
    trimmed
45 ml/3 tbsp plain flour
salt and pepper
50 g/2 oz butter
225 g/8 oz onions, thinly sliced
225 g/8 oz mushrooms, thinly sliced
250 ml/8 fl oz soured cream

Beat the steak slices with a cutlet bat or rolling pin, then cut them into thin strips. Put the flour in a shallow bowl, season with plenty of salt and pepper and coat the beef strips.

Melt half the butter in a large heavy-bottomed saucepan, add the onion slices and fry for about 10 minutes until golden. Stir in the mushrooms and continue cooking for a further 2-3 minutes. Using a slotted spoon, transfer the vegetables to a dish. Set aside.

Melt the remaining butter to the pan, add the meat and fry rapidly for 2-3 minutes, turning frequently. Return the vegetables to the pan and heat through for 1 minute. Pour in the soured cream, stir once or twice, and heat for 1-2 minutes until all the ingredients are heated through (see Mrs Beeton's Tip). Serve at once, with noodles, boiled new potatoes or rice.

SERVES 4

> **MRS BEETON'S TIP** Do not allow the sauce to approach boiling point after the soured cream has been added, or it will curdle.

BOILED BEEF AND DUMPLINGS

Illustrated on page 144

1-1.25 kg/2¼-2¾ lb beef brisket or
    silverside, trimmed
5 ml/1 tsp salt
3 cloves
10 peppercorns
1 bouquet garni
3 onions, quartered
4 potatoes, halved or quartered
4 large carrots, cut lengthways in
    quarters, then in thick sticks
4 small turnips, halved
1 small swede, cut in chunks

DUMPLINGS
    225 g/8 oz self-raising flour
    2.5 ml/½ tsp salt
    100 g/4 oz shredded beef suet

Weigh the meat and calculate the cooking time, allowing 25 minutes per 450 g/1 lb plus 20 minutes over. Tie the meat to a neat shape with string, if necessary. Put it into a large heavy-bottomed sancepan, cover with boiling water and add the salt. Bring to the boil again and boil for 5 minutes to seal the surface of the meat. Lower the heat to simmering point, skim, then add the cloves, peppercorns and bouquet garni. Cover and simmer for the rest of the calculated cooking time.

About 45 minutes before the end of the cooking time, add the onions; 15 minutes later add the potatoes and carrots. Make the dumplings by sifting the flour and salt into a mixing bowl. Stir in the suet and add enough cold water to make a firm elastic dough. Divide the dough into walnut-sized pieces, shaping each into a ball.

Twenty minutes before the end of the cooking time, add the turnips and swede, and bring the stock around the beef to boiling point. Drop in the dumplings (see Mrs Beeton's Tip). Lower the heat, half cover the pan and simmer until the dumplings are cooked, turning them over once with a slotted spoon during this time.

To serve, remove the dumplings from the pan and arrange them as a border on a large heated serving dish. Remove and discard the bouquet garni, then lift out the vegetables with a slotted spoon and arrange them with the dumplings, placing excess vegetables in a separate dish. Remove any strings from the meat, skewer it if necessary to retain the shape, and set it in the centre of the dish. Serve some of the cooking liquid separately in a sauceboat.

SERVES 8 TO 10

BOILED BRISKET

15 ml/1 tbsp red wine vinegar
5 ml/1 tsp salt
1.25-1.5 kg/2¾-3¼ lb boned and rolled
    beef brisket
150 g/5 oz rindless streaky bacon rashers
2 carrots, thickly sliced
2 onions, thickly sliced
1 turnip, chopped
1-2 celery sticks, sliced
1 blade of mace
10 black peppercorns
1 bouquet garni
25 g/1 oz butter
25 g/1 oz plain flour
salt and pepper

Mix the vinegar with half the salt in a small bowl. Rub the mixture over the surface of the meat. Set aside in a cool place, covered, for 2-3 hours.

Cover the base of a heavy-bottomed saucepan with half the bacon rashers. Place the meat on top and lay the remaining rashers over the meat. Add the vegetables, mace, peppercorns and bouquet garni to the pan and pour in enough water to cover. Bring to the boil, skim well, then lower the heat, cover the pan tightly, and cook very gently for 2½ hours (see Mrs Beeton's Tip), checking the level of water occasionally. The liquid should always two-thirds to three-quarters cover the meat.

When cooked, remove the meat from the pan and place it on a warmed serving dish. Remove any strings and keep the meat hot. Using a slotted spoon, remove the vegetables and arrange them around the meat on the dish.

Make the sauce. Strain the stock remaining in the pan, skim off excess fat from the surface and measure 350 ml/12 fl oz. Melt the butter in a small saucepan, stir in the flour and cook for 1 minute. Gradually stir in the stock, then bring to the boil, stirring constantly, and cook until thickened. Add salt and pepper to taste. Serve the vegetables with the meat, and offer the sauce in a sauceboat.

SERVES 10 TO 12

MRS BEETON'S TIP Check the dish occasionally during cooking. If the quantity of liquid seems to be getting low, top it up with additional boiling water or stock.

GOULASH

It is the paprika that gives this hearty Hungarian stew its delicious flavour. Serve simply, with crusty bread.

50 g/2 oz dripping or lard
675 g/1½ lb chuck or blade steak, trimmed and cut into 2 cm/¾ inch cubes
2 onions, sliced
30 ml/2 tbsp plain flour
125 ml/4 fl oz beef stock
125 ml/4 fl oz red wine
450 g/1 lb tomatoes, peeled and diced or 1 (397 g/14 oz) can chopped tomatoes
2.5 ml/½ tsp salt
15 ml/1 tbsp paprika
1 bouquet garni
450 g/1 lb potatoes
150 ml/¼ pint soured cream

Heat the dripping in a flameproof casserole and fry the meat until browned on all sides. Using a slotted spoon, remove the meat and set aside. Add the onions to the fat remaining in the casserole and fry gently until just beginning to brown. Add the flour and cook, stirring until browned. Gradually add the stock and wine, with the tomatoes, salt, paprika and bouquet garni. Bring to the boil, stirring, then lower the heat and simmer for 1½-2 hours or until the meat is tender. Alternatively, transfer the goulash to a casserole and bake at 160°C/325°F/gas 3 for 1½-2 hours.

Thirty minutes before the end of the cooking time, peel the potatoes, cut them into cubes and add them to the goulash. When cooked they should be tender but not broken. Just before serving, remove the bouquet garni and stir in the soured cream.

SERVES 6

MRS BEETON'S STEAK PIE

575 g/1¼ lb chuck or blade steak,
    trimmed and cut into 1 cm/½ inch
    cubes
45 ml/3 tbsp seasoned flour
2 onions, chopped
about 250 ml/8 fl oz beef stock

ROUGH PUFF PASTRY
    200 g/7 oz plain flour
    1.25 ml/¼ tsp salt
    150 g/5 oz butter or half butter, half lard,
      well chilled
    2.5 ml/½ tsp lemon juice
    flour for rolling out
    beaten egg or milk to glaze

Make the pastry. Sift the flour and salt into a bowl. If butter and lard are used, blend them together evenly with a round-bladed knife and chill. Cut the fat into pieces the size of walnuts and add to the flour. Make a well in the centre, mix in the lemon juice, then gradually add enough cold water to make an elastic dough. On a lightly floured surface, roll into a long strip, keeping the edges square.

Fold the bottom third over the centre third, then fold the top third over. With the rolling pin, press to seal the edges. Turn the pastry so that the folded edges are on the left and right. Repeat the rolling and folding three more times, allowing the pastry to rest in a cool place for 10 minutes between the second and third rollings. Finally, wrap the pastry in foil and store in the refrigerator until required.

In a stout polythene or paper bag, toss the beef cubes in seasoned flour until well coated. Shake off excess flour, then transfer the cubes to a 1 litre/1¾ pint pie dish, piling them higher in the centre than at the sides and sprinkling chopped onion between the layers. Pour in enough of the stock to quarter-fill the dish. Reserve the remaining stock.

Set the oven at 230°C/450°F/gas 8. Roll out the pastry on a lightly floured surface. Cut a strip of pastry from around the outside of the piece. Dampen the rim of the pie dish and press the pastry strip on it, trimming off any extra length. Use the remaining pastry to cover the dish. Trim the edge, knock up with the back of a knife and flute the edge. Make a small hole in the centre of the lid and garnish around it with pastry leaves made from the trimmings. Make a pastry tassel or rose to cover the hole after baking, if liked. Brush the pastry with the beaten egg or milk.

Place the pie on a baking sheet, with the pastry tassel, if made, next to it. Bake for about 10 minutes until the pastry is risen and golden brown. Lower the oven temperature of 180°C/350°F/gas 4 and, if necessary, place the pie on a lower shelf. Cover loosely with foil to prevent over-browning and continue to cook for about 2 hours or until the meat is tender when tested through the crust with a skewer.

Heat the reserved beef stock in a small saucepan. Pour it into the pie through a funnel inserted in the hole in the crust. Cover the hole with the pastry tassel or rose, if made, and serve at once.

SERVES 6

VARIATIONS

STEAK AND KIDNEY PIE As above, but add 2 sheep's or 150 g/5 oz ox kidneys. Skin, core and slice the kidneys before mixing with the steak and onion.
STEAK AND MUSHROOM PIE As above, but add 100 g/4 oz sliced mushrooms to the meat in the pie dish.

STEAK AND KIDNEY PUDDING

fat for greasing
150 g/5 oz lamb, pig or ox kidney
575 g/1¼ lb stewing steak, trimmed and
    cut into 1 cm/½ inch cubes
1 onion, chopped
45 ml/3 tbsp plain flour
5 ml/1 tsp salt
1.25 ml/¼ tsp freshly ground black
    pepper
45 ml/3 tbsp beef stock or water

SUET CRUST PASTRY
    225 g/8 oz self-raising flour
    2.5 ml/½ tsp salt
    100 g/4 oz shredded beef suet

Grease a 1.1 litre/2 pint pudding basin. Make the pastry. Sift the flour and salt into a mixing bowl. Stir in the suet and add enough cold water (about 150 ml/¼ pint) to make a firm dough.

Wash the kidney and remove the membrane and white core. Cut into 2.5 cm/1 inch chunks. In a bowl, mix the beef cubes, kidney and onion with the flour, salt and pepper.

Set aside one quarter of the pastry for the lid. Roll out the remaining pastry on a lightly floured surface to a round 1 cm/½ inch larger than the rim of the prepared basin. The pastry should be about 5 mm/¼ inch thick. Press the round well into the basin to remove any creases.

Half fill the lined basin with the steak mixture, add the stock, then spoon in the rest of the meat. Roll out the reserved pastry to make a lid. Put the lid on the pudding, tucking its edges down around the meat. Dampen the top edge of the lid, then fold the top of the lining pastry over it.

Cut a large piece of greaseproof paper, fold a pleat in it and grease it. Cover the pudding with the pleated paper, top with pleated foil and tie down securely.

Prepare a steamer or half-fill a large saucepan with water and bring to the boil. Put the pudding in the perforated part of the steamer, or stand it on an old saucer or plate in the saucepan of boiling water. The water should come halfway up the sides of the basin. Cover the pan tightly and steam the pudding over boiling water for about 5 hours, topping up the steamer or pan with boiling water frequently to prevent it boiling dry.

Serve the pudding from the basin. Fold a clean tea-towel or large table napkin in half or thirds, then wrap it neatly around the side and up to the rim of the basin. Beef gravy may be served with the pudding.

SERVES 6

PRESSURE COOKER TIP To save time, the steak and kidney mixture may be precooked with 300 ml/½ pint beef stock. Cook in a pressure cooker, allowing 15 minutes at 15 lb pressure. Cool the mixture, then fill the pastry-lined pudding basin, using only enough of the gravy to half cover the meat. Steam gently without weights for 10 minutes, then bring to 5 lb pressure and cook for 35 minutes. Reduce the pressure slowly. Reheat the remaining gravy, add more salt and pepper if required, then pour it into the pudding through a hole cut in the crust.

BEEF GALANTINE

The raspings and aspic improve the appearance
of the galantine but they are not essential.

margarine or lard for greasing
200 g/7 oz lean rindless back bacon,
   minced
450 g/1 lb chuck or blade steak, minced
150 g/5 oz fresh white or brown
   breadcrumbs
salt and pepper
1 egg, beaten
75 ml/3 fl oz beef stock
60 ml/4 tbsp raspings (see Mrs Beeton's
   Tip)
125 ml/4 fl oz chopped aspic jelly to
   garnish (optional)

The galantine may either be steamed or
boiled in stock, If the former, prepare a
steamer. Alternatively, half fill a large
saucepan with stock and bring to the boil.

Combine the bacon, meat and breadcrumbs in a bowl. Add salt and pepper to
taste and mix together well. Mix the egg
and measured stock together and combine
this thoroughly with the meat mixture.
Shape into a short, thick roll, then wrap
in greased greaseproof paper. Wrap in
a scalded pudding cloth, tying the ends
securely.

Put the roll on the perforated part of the
steamer, curving it round, and steam for
2½-3 hours, or lower it gently into the fast-
boiling stock, lower the heat and simmer
for 2 hours. Check the volume of water
frequently if using a steamer, and top it
up with boiling water from a kettle as
necessary.

When cooked, lift out the roll, unwrap it,
and then roll up tightly in a clean dry
pudding cloth. Press the roll between two
plates until just cold. Then remove the
cloth, roll the meat in the raspings and chill
until ready to serve. Place on a plate and
garnish with aspic jelly, if liked.

SERVES 6 TO 8

> **MRS BEETON'S TIP** Raspings,
> otherwise known as brown
> breadcrumbs, are an ideal way of using up
> bread crusts or pieces of stale bread.
> Spread them on a baking sheet and bake in
> a preheated 180°C/350°F/gas 4 oven until
> golden brown and crisp. Crush with a
> rolling pin or in a blender or food
> processor. These are not suitable for use in
> stuffings, but are ideal for coating
> croquettes, fish cakes and rissoles, or for
> topping gratins.

CHILLI CON CARNE

225 g/8 oz red kidney beans, soaked
   overnight in water to cover
salt and pepper
225 g/8 oz rindless smoked streaky bacon
   rashers, chopped
1 Spanish onion, chopped
2 garlic cloves, crushed
30 ml/2 tbsp ground coriander
15 ml/1 tbsp ground cumin
15 ml/1 tbsp chilli powder or to taste
450 g/1 lb minced beef
1 beef stock cube
30 ml/2 tbsp tomato purée
30 ml/2 tbsp chopped fresh coriander or
   parsley

Drain the beans and put them in a large
saucepan. Add plenty of water and bring to
the boil. Boil vigorously for 10 minutes,
then lower the heat, cover the pan and
simmer gently for 30 minutes.

Put the bacon in a large heavy-bottomed saucepan. Heat gently until the fat runs. Add the onion and fry, stirring frequently for about 5 minutes until the onion is soft but not browned. Stir in the garlic, ground coriander, cumin and chilli powder. Cook for 1 minute, stirring, then add the meat and cook until lightly browned. Crumble in the stock cube and pour in 600 ml/1 pint water. Stir in the tomato purée and add salt and pepper to taste. Bring to the boil.

Drain the beans. Add them to the saucepan and bring the stock back to the boil. Cover the pan, lower the heat and simmer gently for about 1 hour or until the beans are tender and the liquid has been absorbed. Stir in the coriander or parsley. Serve at once, with rice, crusty bread or as a filling for Baked Jacket Potatoes (page 308-9).

SERVES 4

*L*AMB PROVENCALE

butter for greasing
4 canned anchovy fillets
1 (2.5-3 kg/5½-6½ lb) leg of lamb
lardons of fat bacon (see Mrs Beeton's Tip)
4 parsley sprigs
2 garlic cloves, halved lengthways

MARINADE
1 small onion, chopped
3 parsley sprigs
3 thyme sprigs
2-3 bay leaves
salt and pepper
250 ml/8 fl oz olive oil
30 ml/2 tbsp vinegar

Cut the anchovy fillets in half lengthways, then across into four thin strips.

Weigh the meat and calculate the cooking time. Allow 25 minutes per 450 g/1 lb plus 25 minutes over; slightly less time if you like your lamb 'pink'. Carefully use a pointed knife to make four cuts under the skin, taking care not to damage the meat underneath. Tuck the lardons, anchovy strips, parsley and garlic under the skin.

Make the marinade by combining all the ingredients in a bowl large enough to hold the lamb. Mix well, then add the lamb, cover and marinate for 2-3 hours, turning frequently.

Set the oven at 180°C/350°F/gas 4. Line a roasting tin with a large sheet of foil, making sure that there is enough foil to enclose the leg of lamb. Remove the lamb from the marinade and put it in the tin, cover with the onion and herbs from the marinade and bring up the sides of the foil to make a neat parcel. Roast for the calculated cooking time, opening the parcel for the final 20 minutes to brown the meat. Serve on a heated platter.

SERVES 6 TO 10

> **MRS BEETON'S TIP** Lardons are strips of bacon fat, cured pork fat or fat from belly pork. They are threaded through lean areas of meat to keep it moist during cooking and/or to add flavour. The lardons are usually threaded into the joint across the grain of the meat. The technique is illustrated on page 98.

*H*ERBED SHOULDER OF LAMB

Illustrated on page 177

This recipe may be used for leg as well as for shoulder of lamb.

1 shoulder of lamb, boned
4 garlic cloves, peeled and quartered
   lengthways
about 6 each small fresh rosemary and
   thyme sprigs
4 bay leaves
2 oranges
60 ml/4 tbsp olive oil
salt and pepper
300 ml/½ pint red wine

GARNISH
   orange slices
   fresh herbs

Trim any lumps of fat from the lamb, then tie it in a neat shape if the butcher has not already done this, weigh the joint and calculate the cooking time at 30 minutes per 450 g/1 lb plus 30 minutes (see guide to cooking times, page 122). Use a small pointed knife to make short cuts into the lamb, at an angle running under the skin, all over the joint. Insert pieces of garlic and the rosemary and thyme sprigs into the cuts. Place the joint in a deep dish, with 2 bay leaves underneath and 2 on top.

Pare 2 long strips of rind off 1 orange and add them to the dish, next to or on top of the lamb. Squeeze the juice from the oranges, then mix it with the olive oil, salt and pepper. Pour this mixture over the lamb, cover and marinate for several hours or overnight. Turn the joint at least once during marinating.

Set the oven at 180°C/350°F/gas 4. Transfer the joint to a roasting tin, adding the bay leaves and orange rind but reserving the marinade. Cook for half the calculated time, brushing occasionally with the reserved marinade and basting with cooking juices from the tin. Pour the remaining marinade and the wine over the joint and continue roasting. Baste the lamb occasionally and add a little water to the juices in the tin if they begin to dry up – if the roasting tin is large they will evaporate more speedily.

Transfer the cooked joint to a serving dish, cover with foil and set aside. Pour 300 ml/½ pint boiling water or vegetable cooking water into the roasting tin. Boil the cooking juices rapidly, stirring and scraping the sediment off the base and sides of the pan, until they are reduced by half. Taste for seasoning, then strain the sauce into a heated sauceboat.

Garnish the lamb with orange slices and fresh herbs and serve at once, carving it into thick slices. Offer the sauce separately.

MRS BEETON'S TIP Once it has been reduced, the sauce may be thickened by whisking in small knobs of beurre manié, then boiling for 2 minutes, whisking all the time. To make beurre manié cream 25 g/1 oz butter with 30-45 ml/2-3 tbsp plain flour.

LOIN OF LAMB WITH LEMON AND PARSLEY STUFFING

Adapted from one of Mrs Beeton's first edition recipes for a loin of mutton, this lightly spiced roast joint was originally part baked and part stewed. It was justifiably described as 'very excellent'. The same combination of ingredients and stuffing will complement a leg or shoulder joint.

1 (1.4-1.6 kg/3-3½ lb) boned and rolled
    double loin of lamb, bones reserved,
    trimmed
salt and pepper
1.25 ml/¼ tsp each ground allspice and
    mace, and grated nutmeg
6 cloves
600 ml/1 pint lamb, chicken or vegetable
    stock
30 ml/2 tbsp plain flour
25 g/1 oz butter
125 ml/4 fl oz port
30 ml/2 tbsp mushroom ketchup
100 g/4 oz button mushrooms, sliced

STUFFING
50 g/2 oz shredded beef suet
50 g/2 oz cooked ham, chopped
15 ml/1 tbsp finely chopped parsley
5 ml/1 tsp chopped fresh thyme
grated rind of ½ lemon
175 g/6 oz fresh white breadcrumbs
2.5 ml/½ tsp grated nutmeg or ground
    mace
pinch of cayenne pepper
1 egg, beaten
a little milk

Open out the lamb and sprinkle the inside lightly with salt and pepper. Mix the allspice, mace and nutmeg, then rub the spices all over the meat, outside and on the cut surface. Cover and allow to marinate for at least 1 hour, or up to 24 hours.

Make the stuffing. Combine the suet, ham, parsley, thyme, lemon rind, bread-crumbs and nutmeg or mace in a bowl. Add salt and pepper to taste, and the cayenne. Stir in the egg and add enough milk to bind the mixture lightly together. Spread the stuffing evenly over the inside of the lamb, carefully roll it up again and tie it neatly. Stick the cloves into the joint, piercing it first with the point of a knife.

Set the oven at 180°C/350°F/gas 4. Put the lamb bones in the bottom of a roasting tin and pour over just enough stock to cover them. Weigh the meat and calculate the cooking time. Allow 30 minutes per 450 g/ 1 lb plus 30 minutes over. Place the stuffed lamb on top of the bones in the tin. Cook for the calculated time, adding extra stock or water during cooking to maintain the level of liquid just below the top of the bones and joint. Baste the joint occasionally with the cooking juices.

When the lamb is cooked, transfer it to a heated serving platter and allow to rest under tented foil. Remove the bones and skim off most of the fat from the liquid in the roasting tin. Beat the flour and butter to a smooth paste. Place the roasting liquid over medium heat, stir in the port and mushroom ketchup, then bring the mixture to simmering point. Whisking all the time, gradually add small lumps of the butter and flour mixture. Continue whisking well after each addition, then until the sauce boils and thickens. Stir in the mushrooms and simmer for 3 minutes.

Taste the sauce for seasoning before serving it with the lamb, carved into thick slices. Redcurrant jelly, new potatoes and fresh peas are excellent accompaniments.

SERVES 6

◇

CROWN ROAST OF LAMB

2 best ends of neck of lamb, chined and
    trimmed
salt and pepper
Wild Rice Stuffing (page 350) or
    Sausagemeat Stuffing (page 350)
grated rind and juice of 1 orange
50 g/2 oz walnuts, chopped
15 ml/1 tbsp chopped fresh rosemary
30 ml/2 tbsp chopped parsley
4 bay leaves
a little oil
45 ml/3 tbsp plain flour
300 ml/½ pint red wine
15 ml/1 tbsp tomato purée

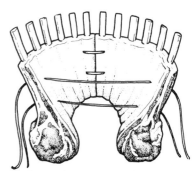

The butcher will prepare the lamb: the
racks of lamb should have the back bones
sawn through (chined) and the end of the
cutlets should be trimmed of all fat so that
the bones are clean. Trim off any thick areas
of fat. Slice the meat two-thirds of the way
in between the bones, so that the cutlets
remain attached.

Use a trussing needle to sew the racks
together in one long joint. Pull the un-
attached ends of the racks together to form
a complete circle, with the fleshy part on
the inside. Sew the joints together.

Set the oven at 190°C/375°F/gas 5.
Stand the crown of meat in a roasting tin
and season it well, particularly on the
outside. Have the chosen stuffing in a
bowl. Mix in the orange rind and juice,
then add the walnuts, rosemary and
parsley. Spoon the stuffing into the middle
of the crown of meat. Place any excess
stuffing in a greased ovenproof dish to bake.

Place the bay leaves on top of the stuffing
and trickle a little oil over them. Brush the
outside of the joint with oil and cover each
of the bone ends with a piece of foil to
prevent them burning. If using the rice
stuffing, cover it with a small piece of foil
to prevent it drying out. Roast the joint
for 1¼-1½ hours for the rice stuffing;
1¾-2 hours for the sausagemeat stuffing,
lowering the temperature to 160°C/325°F/
gas 3 after 1½ hours.

Use a large fish slice to transfer the joint
to a serving plate, remove the foil from the
bone ends and tent the whole joint with
foil, then keep hot. Drain off any excess fat
from the roasting tin, leaving the juices
and a little fat. Add the bay leaves to the
roasting tin. Place over moderate heat and
stir in the flour. Cook for a minute, stirring
to scrape all the sediment off the pan, then
pour in 450 ml/¾ pint water or vegetable
stock. Bring to the boil, stirring. Stir in the
wine and bring to the boil again, then
add the tomato purée, stirring until it is
combined with the sauce.

Boil the sauce – not too rapidly – for
about 5 minutes, until it is reduced and
well flavoured. Stir it often to incorporate
all sediment from the sides and base of the
tin. Taste for seasoning.

Top each of the bone ends with a cutlet
frill, if liked. To serve, slice between the
cutlets. Allow 2 per person, with some of
the stuffing from the middle of the joint.
Ladle a little of the sauce over and offer the
rest separately.

SERVES 6 TO 8

GUARD OF HONOUR

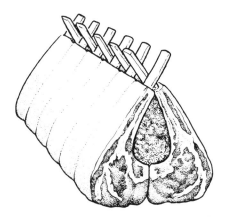

2 best ends of neck of lamb, chined and
    trimmed
salt and pepper
30 ml/2 tbsp oil
1 small onion, chopped
1 garlic clove, crushed
100 g/4 oz button or closed cup
    mushrooms, roughly chopped
grated rind of 1 lemon
30 ml/2 tbsp raisins
100 g/4 oz fresh white breadcrumbs
60 ml/4 tbsp chopped parsley
60 ml/4 tbsp sherry
30 ml/2 tbsp plain flour
600 ml/1 pint vegetable stock or water
dash of Worcestershire sauce

GARNISH
    50 g/2 oz butter
    225 g/8 oz oyster or button mushrooms
    a little chopped parsley

The joints should be prepared by the
butcher as for the crown roast opposite.
Season them all over, particularly the fat.
Set the oven at 190°C/375°F/gas 5.

Make the stuffing. Heat the oil, then add
the onion and garlic, and cook, stirring, for
5 minutes. Stir in the mushrooms, lemon
rind and raisins. Cook over moderate heat,
stirring until the mushrooms give up their
juices, then continue cooking, stirring
occasionally, until all the liquid has evaporated. The mushrooms shrink significantly; they should be just moist when
cooked.

Off the heat, stir in the breadcrumbs and
parsley. Add salt and pepper to taste and
bind the stuffing with the sherry. Holding
one rack of lamb, meat down, tilt it so that
the curve of the bone is at a good angle
to hold the stuffing. Spoon some of the
stuffing along the curve of the bone and
press it in well. Do the same with the
second joint.

Bring the racks of lamb together in a
roasting tin, spooning any remaining
stuffing between them. Then press the
joints firmly together with the bones
interlocking. Cover the top of the bones
with foil and roast the joint for 1¼-1½
hours, or until browned and cooked
through to taste.

Transfer the joint to a heated serving
platter and keep hot. Pour away excess
fat from the roasting tin, then stir in the
flour. Cook over moderate heat, stirring,
for 1 minute, then pour in the stock or
water, stirring all the time, and bring to the
boil. Lower the heat slightly so the sauce
just boils. Cook for 5 minutes. Add the
Worcestershire sauce, with salt and pepper
to taste before serving.

For the garnish, melt the butter in a
frying pan and toss the mushrooms in it for
2 minutes, until just hot. Sprinkle with the
parsley.

Remove the foil from the lamb and
arrange the mushrooms around the joint.
Cut between the cutlets to serve them and
offer the sauce separately.

SERVES 4

*L*AMB CUTLETS EN PAPILLOTES

oil for greasing
4-6 slices cooked ham
6 lamb cutlets, trimmed
15 ml/1 tbsp oil
1 onion, finely chopped
25 g/1 oz button mushrooms, finely
    chopped
10 ml/2 teaspoons finely chopped parsley
grated rind of ½ lemon
salt and pepper

Set the oven at 190°C/375°F/gas 5. Cut out 12 small rounds of ham, each large enough to cover the round part of a cutlet. Heat the oil in a small saucepan and fry the onion for 4-6 minutes until tender and lightly browned. Remove from the heat and stir in the mushrooms, parsley and lemon rind, with salt and pepper to taste. Leave to cool.

Cut out six heart-shaped pieces of double thickness greaseproof paper or foil large enough to hold the cutlets. Grease the paper generously with oil. Centre one of the ham rounds on the right half of one of the prepared paper hearts, spread with a little of the mushroom mixture and lay the cutlet on top. Spread the cutlet with a little more of the mushroom mixture and add another round of ham so that the round part of the cutlet is neatly sandwiched. Fold over the paper and twist the edges well together.

Lay the wrapped cutlets on a greased baking sheet and bake for 30 minutes. Transfer, still in their wrappings, to a warmed platter and serve at once.

SERVES 6

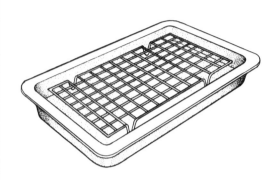

*L*AMB SHASHLIK

50 g/2 oz butter
450 g/1 lb boned leg of lamb, cut into
    2 cm/¾ inch cubes
200 g/7 oz lean bacon, cut into 1 cm/
    ½ inch cubes
8 button onions
8 bay leaves
salt and pepper

Heat 25 g/1 oz of the butter in a large frying pan, add the lamb cubes and brown on all sides. Bring a small saucepan of water to the boil, add the onions and cook for 3 minutes; drain thoroughly.

Divide the meat, bacon, onions and bay leaves into 4 portions. Thread each portion on to a long skewer. Season with salt and pepper. Melt the remaining butter in a small pan and brush the meat and vegetables generously all over.

Cook the shashlik under a hot grill or over medium coals for 8-10 minutes, turning the skewers occasionally until the meat is well browned. Serve with rice and Cucumber in Yogurt (page 341).

SERVES 4

LAMB SHISH KEBAB

Illustrated on page 178

1 kg/2¼ 1b boned lean lamb, preferably from the leg, trimmed and cut into 2.5 cm/1 inch cubes
18 cherry tomatoes
3 small green peppers, seeded and cut into chunks

MARINADE
1 large onion, thinly sliced
45 ml/3 tbsp olive oil
45 ml/3 tbsp lemon juice
15 ml/1 tbsp salt
2.5 ml/½ tsp freshly ground black pepper

Make the marinade by combining all the ingredients in a shallow dish large enough to hold all the meat cubes in a single layer. Add the cubes and stir well to coat them thoroughly. Cover the dish and leave the meat to marinate for several hours, stirring occasionally.

Drain the lamb cubes, reserving the marinade. Thread the tomatoes, meat cubes and pepper chunks alternately on to 6 kebab skewers.

Grill the shish kebabs under high heat or over medium coals, turning occasionally, until the vegetables are well browned and the lamb is done to taste. Baste occasionally with the reserved marinade. For pink lamb, allow about 10 minutes; for well-done lamb, allow about 15 minutes.

SERVES 6

NOISETTES JARDINIERE

Illustrated on page 178

1 kg/2¼ lb boned best end of neck of lamb
30 ml/2 tbsp oil
salt and pepper
450 g/1 lb potatoes, halved and cooked
25 g/1 oz butter
15-30 ml/2-3 tbsp single cream
Gravy to serve (page 352)

GARNISH
50 g/2 oz green beans, diced
1 carrot, diced
1 small turnip, diced
2 celery sticks, diced

Wipe the meat. Roll it up and tie with fine string at 2.5 cm/1 inch intervals. Cut through the roll between the string.

Brush the noisettes with oil, season generously with salt and pepper and cook for 6-7 minutes under a moderate grill until cooked through and browned on both sides. Meanwhile make the garnish. Cook each vegetable separately in boiling salted water until just tender. Drain and mix.

Mash the potatoes until smooth. Beat in the butter and single cream. Spoon the creamed potato into a piping bag fitted with a large star nozzle and pipe a border of mashed potato around the edge of a heated serving dish. Arrange the noisettes and vegetables on the dish. Serve at once with hot gravy made using the cooking juices.

SERVES 6

> **MRS BEETON'S TIP** If preferred, the noisettes may be cooked in a frying pan. Heat the oil, add the noisettes and fry for about 3 minutes on each side.

*E*PIGRAMS OF LAMB

1 breast of lamb, about 450 g/1 lb
1 onion, thickly sliced
½ turnip, thickly sliced
1 carrot, thickly sliced
1 bouquet garni
salt and pepper
15 g/½ oz gelatine
500 ml/17 fl oz Béchamel Sauce (see Mrs
    Beeton's Tip, page 47)
1 egg, lightly beaten
90 ml/6 tbsp fresh white breadcrumbs
oil for deep frying

ONION SAUCE
1 onion, chopped
20 g/¾ oz butter
45 ml/3 tbsp plain flour
150 ml/¼ pint milk
salt and pepper
few drops of lemon juice

Put 1 litre/1¾ pints water in a large saucepan. Bring to the boil, add the meat and boil for 5 minutes. Add the onion, turnip and carrot with the bouquet garni. Season with salt and pepper. Lower the heat, cover the pan and simmer gently for about 1 hour or until the meat is tender. When cooked, take the meat out of the pan. Remove the skin, bones and gristle, and press the meat between two plates until cold and firm.

Place 30 ml/2 tbsp water in a small bowl. Sprinkle the gelatine on to the liquid. Stand the bowl over a saucepan of hot water and stir the gelatine until it has dissolved completely. Mix it with the hot Béchamel sauce, then set the sauce aside until cold and beginning to thicken.

Cut the cold meat into neat pieces for serving. Season the meat well with salt and pepper, then coat it completely with the Béchamel sauce. Repeat the coating if necessary to give a thick covering of sauce. Chill these epigrams until the sauce is set.

Meanwhile make the onion sauce. Put the onion in a small saucepan with 250 ml/8 fl oz water. Bring to the boil, lower the heat and simmer for 10-15 minutes until softened. Drain thoroughly, reserving the onion and 150 ml/¼ pint of the cooking liquid. Melt the butter in a saucepan and add the flour. Cook for 1 minute, stirring, then gradually add the reserved onion liquid and milk, stirring until the mixture boils and thickens. Add salt and pepper to taste. Stir in the reserved onion and sharpen the flavour with the lemon juice. Set aside until required.

Put the beaten egg in a shallow dish. Spread out the breadcrumbs on a sheet of foil. When the sauce-coated lamb epigrams are set and firm, dip them into beaten egg and then into breadcrumbs.

Put the oil for frying into a deep wide saucepan to a depth of at least 7.5 cm/3 inches. Heat the oil to 180-190°C/350-375°F or until a cube of bread added to the oil browns in 30 seconds. If using a deep-fat fryer, follow the manufacturer's instructions. Fry the epigrams quickly until golden brown. Drain on absorbent kitchen paper. Reheat the sauce.

Serve the epigrams in a circle around the edge of a heated serving dish, with the onion sauce in a sauceboat in the centre.

SERVES 4 TO 6

BRAISED LEG OF LAMB

fat for greasing
25 g/1 oz dripping or 30 ml/2 tbsp oil
2 onions, thickly sliced
1 turnip, thickly sliced
2 carrots, thickly sliced
vegetable stock (see method)
1 bouquet garni
10 black peppercorns
1.8-2.25 kg/4-5 lb leg of lamb
30 ml/2 tbsp butter
2 shallots, finely chopped
45 ml/3 tbsp plain flour
salt and pepper

Heat the dripping or oil in a large flameproof casserole, add the vegetables, cover the pan and sweat them gently for 5-10 minutes. Add enough stock to almost cover the vegetables, tuck the bouquet garni among them and sprinkle in the peppercorns. Put the meat on top and cover with a piece of greased greaseproof paper, greased side down. Cover the pan with a tight-fitting lid. Cook over low heat for 2½-3 hours or until the lamb is cooked. Baste the lamb occasionally with the stock, and add more stock as necessary.

When the meat is cooked, transfer it to a warmed serving dish and keep hot. Strain the stock into a measuring jug and make up to 500 ml/17 fl oz with water if necessary.

Melt the butter in a small saucepan, add the shallots and fry gently for about 4 minutes until softened. Stir in the flour and cook until well browned. Gradually add the reserved stock, stirring until the mixture boils and thickens. Add salt and pepper to taste. Pour a little of the sauce over the meat and serve the rest in a sauceboat.

SERVES 6 TO 10

OXFORD JOHN

575 g/1¼ lb boned leg of lamb, trimmed
salt and pepper
15 ml/1 tbsp finely chopped ham
5 ml/1 tsp finely chopped onion
5 ml/1 tsp chopped parsley
2.5 ml/½ tsp dried mixed herbs
50 g/2 oz butter or margerine
25 g/1 oz plain flour
250 ml/8 fl oz lamb or beef stock
5 ml/1 tsp lemon juice

Cut the meat into neat, thin round slices, about 10 cm/4 inches in diameter. Season with salt and pepper. Put the ham in a bowl and add the onion, herbs and a little salt and pepper. Use this filling to sandwich the rounds of meat together in pairs. Place them on a baking sheet, cover and leave for 1 hour to absorb the flavours.

Melt the butter in a large frying pan and fry the meat 'sandwiches', a few at a time, until browned and cooked. As they cook, transfer the 'sandwiches' to a heated dish; keep hot.

Stir the flour into the fat remaining in the pan and cook until it is well browned. Gradually add the stock, stirring until the mixture boils and thickens. Add the lemon juice and return the meat. Simmer for 10 minutes. Serve hot.

SERVES 6

STUFFED BREAST OF LAMB WITH PILAF

1 breast of lamb, about 675 g/1½ lb
salt and pepper
350 g/12 oz pork sausagemeat
15 ml/1 tbsp oil
2 rindless streaky bacon rashers, chopped
1 large carrot, chopped
1 large onion, chopped
1 bouquet garni
250 ml/8 fl oz lamb or chicken stock

PILAF
30 ml/2 tbsp oil (preferably olive oil)
1 large onion, chopped
1 bay leaf
1 cinnamon stick
1 garlic clove, crushed
225 g/8 oz long-grain rice
750 ml/1¼ pints vegetable stock
50 g/2 oz sultanas
50 g/2 oz blanched almonds, cut into
    slivers and toasted
250 ml/8 fl oz Fresh Tomato Sauce
    (page 352)

Set the oven at 180°C/350°F/gas 4. Remove all the bones from the meat and trim off any excess fat. Flatten it, if necessary, with a cutlet bat or rolling pin, season with salt and pepper and spread the sausagemeat over the surface. Roll up tightly and tie the meat neatly.

Heat the oil in a frying pan, add the bacon and cook until the fat runs. Add the vegetables and fry quickly until lightly browned, then place them in a large casserole. Add the bouquet garni, sprinkle with salt and pepper, and pour in just enough stock to cover the vegetables. Put the rolled breast of lamb on top of the vegetables and cover the casserole with a tight-fitting lid. Bake for 2-2½ hours, until tender.

Prepare the pilaf about 30 minutes before the lamb is ready. Heat the oil in a saucepan, add the onion, bay leaf, cinnamon stick and garlic, then fry gently for about 10 minutes until the onion is slightly softened but not browned. Add the rice, stir well, then pour in the stock. Add salt and pepper to taste, bring the stock to the boil and stir once. Cover, lower the heat and simmer for 15 minutes. Sprinkle the sultanas and almonds over the rice, replace the lid (without stirring) and cook for a further 5 minutes. Turn the heat off and leave for 5 minutes. Heat the tomato sauce.

Turn out the pilaf on a warmed serving dish. Cut the lamb into thick slices and lay them on the pilaf, then pour the tomato sauce over the meat. Serve at once.

SERVES 6

COLLARED LAMB

2 breasts of lamb, total weight about
    1.5 kg/3¼ lb
30-45 ml/2-3 tbsp oil
10 ml/2 tsp grated lemon rind
salt and pepper
pinch of ground allspice
10 ml/2 tsp anchovy essence
50 g/2 oz gherkins, chopped
30 ml/2 tbsp chopped parsley
5 ml/1 tsp dried thyme
5 ml/1 tsp snipped chives
100 g/4 oz fresh white breadcrumbs
750 ml/1¼ pints well-flavoured lamb or
    chicken stock

Set the oven at 160°C/325°F/gas 3. Remove the bones from the meat without piercing through the flesh. Set the bones aside. Brush the boned sides of the lamb with the oil, and sprinkle with the lemon rind, seasoning, spice and anchovy essence.

In a bowl, mix the gherkins with the herbs and breadcrumbs. Use a little of the stock to bind the mixture, then spread it over the seasoned sides of the lamb.

Place the breasts end to end, overlapping slightly, and roll up together like a Swiss roll. Tie with string at regular intervals. Cover the meat tightly with muslin and secure with string.

Put the collared lamb into a large casserole, add the reserved lamb bones and the remaining stock. Cover the casserole with foil or a lid and cook for 3 hours, until the lamb is tender and cooked through. Serve thickly sliced.

SERVES 6 TO 10

IRISH STEW

1 kg/2¼ lb middle neck or scrag end of
    neck of lamb
2 large onions, thinly sliced
1 kg/2¼ lb potatoes, thinly sliced
salt and pepper
well-flavoured lamb or chicken stock
30 ml/2 tbsp chopped parsley to serve

Set the oven at 190°C/375°F/gas 5. Cut the meat into neat cutlets or pieces, trimming off any excess fat. Layer the meat, onions and potatoes in a casserole, sprinkling each layer with salt and pepper, and ending with potatoes.

Add enough stock to half fill the casserole. Cover with a lid and bake for 2-2½ hours, removing the lid for the last 30 minutes of the cooking time, to allow the potato topping to brown. Sprinkle with chopped parsley to serve.

SERVES 4 TO 6

LANCASHIRE HOT POT

fat for greasing
1 kg/2¼ lb potatoes
1 kg/2¼ lb middle neck of lamb or
    mutton, trimmed and cut into neat
    cutlets
3 lambs' kidneys, skinned, cored and
    sliced
2 large onions, sliced
salt and pepper
250 ml/8 fl oz hot lamb or vegetable stock
25 g/1 oz lard or dripping

Set the oven at 180°C/350°F/gas 4. Slice half the potatoes and cut the rest into chunks. Arrange half the sliced potatoes in the bottom of a large deep casserole. Layer the meat, kidneys, onion slices and potato chunks on top, seasoning each layer lightly with salt and pepper. Finish with the remaining potato slices.

Pour in the hot stock. Melt the lard or dripping and brush it over the top layer of potatoes. Cover the casserole with a tight-fitting lid and bake for about 2 hours or until the meat and potatoes are tender.

Remove the lid, increase the oven temperature to 220°C/425°F/gas 7 and cook for 20 minutes more or until the top layer of potatoes is brown and crisp. Serve from the casserole.

SERVES 6

VARIATION

LAMB AND OYSTER HOT POT Add a central layer, consisting of 8 sliced flat mushrooms and 18 shelled fresh oysters. Proceed as in the recipe above.

FRICASSEE OF LAMB

1 breast of lamb, about 675 g/1¼ lb, boned
25 g/1 oz dripping or 30 ml/2 tbsp oil
1 onion, sliced
2 bay leaves ● 2 cloves
1 blade of mace
6 white peppercorns
salt and pepper
600 ml/1 pint lamb or chicken stock
1 kg/2¼ lb potatoes, halved
50 g/2 oz butter
25 g/1 oz plain flour
15 ml/1 tbsp milk
10 ml/2 tsp roughly chopped capers

Cut the meat into 5 cm/2 inch squares, trimming off any excess fat. Melt the dripping or heat the oil in a heavy-bottomed saucepan. Add the meat, onion, bay leaves, cloves, mace and peppercorns, with salt to taste. Half cover the pan and cook the mixture very gently for about 30 minutes, stirring frequently. Add the stock or water and bring just to the boil. Lower the heat, partly cover the pan and continue simmering the mixture for about 1½ hours more, until the meat is tender.

About 30 minutes before the end of the cooking time, cook the potatoes in a saucepan of salted boiling water. When the meat is tender, strain the stock into a clean saucepan and place over medium heat. Set the meat aside. In a small bowl, blend 25 g/1 oz of the butter with the flour. Gradually add small pieces of the mixture to the simmering stock, whisking in each addition. Continue whisking until the sauce boils. Add the meat and heat through.

Meanwhile drain and mash the potatoes. Beat in the remaining butter and the milk to make a creamy piping consistency. Spoon the creamed potato into a piping bag fitted with a large star nozzle and pipe a border of mashed potato around the rim of a heated serving dish. Spoon the meat mixture into the middle and sprinkle with capers. Serve at once.

SERVES 4 TO 6

COLLOPS WITH ASPARAGUS

450 g/1 lb cold pink-cooked roast lamb
30 ml/2 tbsp plain flour
salt and pepper
2.5 ml/½ tsp grated lemon rind
1.25 ml/¼ tsp dried mixed herbs
1 (340 g/12 oz) can asparagus tips
30 ml/2 tbsp butter
250 ml/8 fl oz well-flavoured lamb or
   chicken stock

Cut the meat into 7.5 cm/3 inch slices, about 1 cm/½ inch thick. Mix half the flour with the salt and pepper, lemon rind and herbs in a small bowl. Sprinkle the mixture over the collops and stand for 1 hour.

Heat the asparagus tips in their liquid in a small saucepan. Melt the butter in a large frying pan, add the collops and cook them quickly over moderate heat until lightly browned on both sides. Remove them with a fish slice and arrange in a close circle on a heated serving dish. Keep hot.

Stir the remaining flour into the fat remaining in the pan and cook until browned. Gradually add the stock, stirring until the mixture boils and thickens. Add salt and pepper to taste.

Drain the asparagus tips and place them in the centre of the ring of collops. Spoon the sauce over the collops and serve.

SERVES 4

BLANQUETTE OF LAMB

1 kg/2¼ lb best end of neck of lamb
salt and pepper
1 onion, sliced
1 bouquet garni
6 black peppercorns
pinch of grated nutmeg
30 ml/2 tbsp butter
30 ml/2 tbsp plain flour
100 g/4 oz small button mushrooms
90 ml/6 tbsp single cream
1 egg yolk

Bone the meat and cut it into pieces about 5 cm/2 inches square. Put it into a heavy-bottomed saucepan with salt to taste. Add water to cover and bring to the boil. Add the bouquet garni, peppercorns and nutmeg. Lower the heat, cover the pan tightly and simmer for 1½-2 hours until tender. Keep meat hot. Strain 250 ml/8 fl oz stock.

Melt the butter in a saucepan, stir in the flour and cook for 1 minute. Gradually add the reserved stock, stirring the mixture until it boils and thickens. Lower the heat and simmer for 2-3 minutes.

Meanwhile prepare the garnish by heating the button mushrooms in a small saucepan with 60 ml/4 tbsp of the single cream. Add salt and pepper to taste. Cook gently, without allowing the cream to boil.

Beat the egg yolk and remaining cream in a small bowl. Stir in a little of the hot sauce and mix well. Add the contents of the bowl to the sauce mixture and heat gently, stirring. Do not allow the sauce to boil. Add salt and pepper to taste. Strain the liquid from the mushrooms into the sauce, then pour it over the meat. Garnish with the poached mushrooms and serve at once.

SERVES 4 TO 6

BOILED LAMB WITH CAPER SAUCE

1 (2 kg/4½ lb) leg of lamb, trimmed
5 ml/1 tsp salt
1 bay leaf
10 black peppercorns
2 onions, quartered
4 carrots, cut into large chunks
2 turnips or 1 large parsnip, cut into chunks
1-2 leeks, trimmed, sliced and washed

CAPER SAUCE
25 g/1 oz butter
25 g/1 oz plain flour
150 ml/¼ pint lamb stock
150 ml/¼ pint milk
15 ml/1 tbsp chopped capers
15 ml/1 tbsp pickling vinegar from the jar
   of capers

Put the lamb into a large heavy-bottomed saucepan with the salt, bay leaf and peppercorns. Pour in enough cold water to cover. Bring to the boil. Skim, lower the heat, cover the pan with a tight-fitting lid and simmer for 2½-3 hours or until the meat is tender, adding the vegetables about 45 minutes before the end of the cooking time.

When the lamb is almost cooked, make the caper sauce. Melt the butter in a saucepan, stir in the flour and cook for 1-2 minutes. Gradually add the lamb stock, stirring constantly, then add the milk in the same way. Bring the sauce to the boil, stirring until it thickens. Add the capers and vinegar; stir well.

Drain the meat and vegetables from the cooking liquid. Place the meat on a heated serving dish, coat with the caper sauce, and surround with the vegetables. Serve.

SERVES 8 TO 10

SAVOURY LOIN OF PORK

1-1.5 kg/2¼-3¼ lb loin of pork on the
    bone
15 ml/1 tbsp finely chopped onion
2.5 ml/½ tsp dried sage
2.5 ml/½ tsp salt
1.25 ml/¼ tsp freshly ground pepper
pinch of dry mustard
30 ml/2 tbsp sieved apricot jam, melted
125 ml/4 fl oz Apple Sauce (page 351)

Set the oven at 220°C/425°F/gas 7.
Weigh the meat and calculate the cooking
time at 30 minutes per 450 g/1 lb plus
30 minutes over. Mix the onion, sage, salt,
pepper and mustard in a small bowl. Rub
the mixture well into the surface of the
meat.

Put the meat in a roasting tin and roast
for 10 minutes, then lower the oven
temperature to 180°C/350°F/gas 4 and
roast for the remainder of the calculated
cooking time. About 30 minutes before
serving, remove the pork from the oven
and brush with melted apricot jam. Continue cooking to crisp the crackling.

Serve the pork on a heated serving dish,
offering the apple sauce separately. Serve
with roast potatoes, Broad Beans with
Cream Sauce (page 210) and Celeriac Purée
(page 215).

SERVES 6

> **MRS BEETON'S TIP** If a savoury
> glaze is preferred for the crackling,
> brush with oil and sprinkle with salt. Raise
> the oven temperature to 220°C/435°F/gas
> 7, return the pork to the oven and
> continue cooking for 15-20 minutes.

ROAST PORK WITH MUSHROOM AND CORN STUFFING

Illustrated on page 179

*If the whole joint is taken to the table, you may
like to add a garnish of baby sweetcorn cobs
(cook them in boiling water for 3-5 minutes)
and button mushrooms tossed in hot butter.*

1.5 kg/3¼ lb boned bladebone of pork,
    scored (see Mrs Beeton's Tip)
45 ml/3 tbsp oil
15 ml/1 tbsp cooking salt

STUFFING
25 g/1 oz butter or margarine
1 onion, finely chopped
1 celery stick, finely chopped
100 g/4 oz mushrooms, finely chopped
50 g/2 oz thawed frozen sweetcorn
50 g/2 oz fresh white breadcrumbs
15 ml/1 tbsp chopped parsley
2.5 ml/½ tsp ground mace
5 ml/1 tsp lemon juice
salt and pepper

Set the oven at 230°C/450°F/gas 8. Make
the stuffing. Melt the butter or margarine
in a small saucepan. Add the onion and
celery and fry for 4-6 minutes until soft but
not browned. Remove from the heat and
add the remaining ingredients.

Spoon the stuffing evenly into the
'pocket' left when the meat was boned. Roll
up the joint and tie with thin string at
regular intervals. Generously brush 15 ml/
1 tbsp of the oil over the rind and sprinkle
with the cooking salt, rubbing it well in.

Heat the remaining oil in a roasting tin,
add the meat, turning it in the hot fat, and
roast for 20-30 minutes until the crackling
crisps. Do not cover the meat or the

crackling will soften again. Lower the heat to 180°C/350°F/gas 4 and cook for about 1½ hours more or until the pork is cooked.

Transfer the meat to a warmed serving dish, remove the string and keep hot. If liked, pour off the fat from the roasting tin, using the sediment for gravy (see page 352).

SERVES 6

> 🪣 **MRS BEETON'S TIP** If the butcher has not already scored the pork rind, do this yourself, using a very sharp knife and making the cuts about 3 mm/⅛ inch deep and 1 cm/½ inch apart.

LOIN OF PORK STUFFED WITH PRUNES

1.25-1.5 kg/2¾-3¼ lb boned loin of
    pork
200 g/7 oz ready-to-eat prunes
juice of 1 lemon
salt and pepper

Set the oven at 180°C/350°F/gas 4. Weigh the meat and calculate the cooking time at 30 minutes per 450 g/1 lb plus 30 minutes over. Spread the prunes over the pork flesh, roll up the meat and tie it securely. Pour the lemon juice all over the meat, rubbing it well in.

Put the meat in a roasting tin, season with salt and pepper and roast for the calculated cooking time, basting occasionally. Serve on a heated platter, accompanied with a thickened gravy made from the sediment in the roasting tin (se page 352).

SERVES 6

MRS BEETON'S ROAST GRISKIN OF PORK

fat for greasing
1 kg/2¼ lb neck end of chine of pork or
    griskin (see Mrs Beeton's Tip)
flour for dredging
50 g/2 oz lard
15 ml/1 tbsp dried sage
20 ml/4 tsp plain flour
salt and pepper

Set the oven at 220°C/425°F/gas 7. Dredge the meat lightly with flour. Melt the lard in a roasting tin. When it is hot, add the meat and spoon the melted fat over the top. Roast for 20 minutes, baste well, then cover the meat loosely with greased greaseproof paper.

Reduce the oven temperature to 180°C/350°F/gas 4. Roast the meat for a further 1¼-1½ hours, basting often. Ten minutes before the end of the cooking time, remove from the oven, sprinkle with the sage, and return to the oven, uncovered.

Pour off all but 15 ml/1 tbsp of the fat from the roasting tin. Sprinkle in the flour. Cook, stirring, for 3-4 minutes until lightly browned. Gradually add 300 ml/½ pint water, stirring until the mixture boils. Season, simmer for 1 minute, then strain and serve the pork.

SERVES 4

> 🪣 **MRS BEETON'S TIP** The griskin is the backbone, spine or chine of a pig, cut away when preparing a side for bacon. The term is also used for a shoulder of pork, stripped of fat. As it is sold without rind or fat, it needs frequent basting.

CIDERED PORK CHOPS

4 pork loin chops, trimmed
60 ml/4 tbsp dry cider
1 bouquet garni
2 cooking apples
2 onions, chopped
pinch of ground cinnamon
salt and pepper
100 g/4 oz flat mushrooms, thickly sliced
200 g/7 oz fresh peas
25 g/1 oz butter
200 g/7 oz cooked small whole beetroot
225 g/8 oz tagliatelle, cooked

Set the oven at 160°C/325°F/gas 3. Heat a frying pan. Brown the chops on both sides. Remove the chops and place them in a casserole. Pour the cider over the chops and add the bouquet garni. Cover the casserole and start cooking it in the oven.

Peel, core and chop the apples. Add them with the onions to the fat remaining in the frying pan and fry gently for 5 minutes. Stir in the cinnamon, with just enough water to cover the onion mixture. Cover the pan and simmer for about 15 minutes, until the onions and apples are soft. Rub the mixture through a sieve into a bowl, add salt and pepper to taste, then spoon the mixture over the chops in the casserole. Return to the oven for 45 minutes.

Add the mushrooms and peas to the casserole and cook for 30 minutes more. Towards the end of the cooking time, melt the butter in a small saucepan, add the beetroot and heat gently, turning often. Arrange the tagliatelle and chops on a heated serving dish with the chops on top. Arrange the mushrooms, peas and beetroot around them.

SERVES 4

PORK AND APPLE HOT POT

Illustrated on page 180

fat for greasing
1 cooking apple
45 ml/3 tbsp oil
1 onion, thinly sliced
100 g/4 oz mushrooms, thinly sliced
4 pork loin chops, trimmed
2.5 ml/½ tsp dried sage or savory
450 g/1 lb potatoes, cut into 2 cm/¾ inch
    cubes
salt and pepper

GARNISH (OPTIONAL)
1-2 slices eating apple, cored and halved
parsley sprigs

Set the oven at 180°C/350°F/gas 4. Peel, core and slice the apple. Heat the oil in a large frying pan, add the apple and onion and fry over moderate heat until golden brown.

Put the mushrooms on the base of a large shallow greased casserole. Add the chops and cover with the apple and onion. Sprinkle the herbs over the top. Cover with the potatoes, brushing them with the fat remaining in the pan. Pour in enough water to come halfway up the meat and vegetables.

Cover the casserole with foil or a tight-fitting lid. Bake for 1½ hours, removing the covering 30 minutes before the end of the cooking time to allow the potatoes to brown. Garnish with apple and parsley (if used), then serve from the casserole. Carrots with Cider (page 214) may be served as an accompaniment, if liked.

SERVES 4

BARBECUED SPARE RIBS

Illustrated on page 180

2 kg/4½ lb pork spare ribs
1 lemon, cut in wedges
herb sprigs to garnish (optional)

BARBECUE SPICE MIXTURE
90 ml/6 tbsp soft light brown sugar
15 ml/1 tbsp grated lemon rind
15 ml/1 tbsp paprika ● salt and pepper

BASTING SAUCE
200 ml/7 fl oz tomato juice
45 ml/3 tbsp tomato ketchup
15-30 ml/1-2 tbsp Worcestershire sauce
30 ml/2 tbsp soft light brown sugar
5 ml/1 tsp mustard powder
1.25 ml/¼ tsp chilli powder

Cut the ribs into individual portions, if necessary, trimming any loose ends. Mix all the ingredients for the barbecue spice mixture together in a small bowl. Rub the mixture thoroughly into the ribs, especially the bony side.

Meanwhile make the basting sauce. Combine all the ingredients in a small saucepan. Add 100 ml/3½ fl oz water, bring to the boil, then lower the heat and simmer for 15 minutes. Spread out the ribs in a large shallow dish or roasting tin and brush generously with the basting sauce. Cover and set aside for 30 minutes at cool room temperature. Brush again and leave for 30 minutes more.

Cook the ribs on a grid placed high over medium coals for 1-1¼ hours, turning frequently and basting with the sauce. Alternatively, bake in a preheated 150°C/300°F/gas 2 oven for about 1 hour or until nearly cooked. Baste frequently. Finish by cooking under a hot grill – or over the fire.

Serve with lemon wedges, so that their juice may be squeezed over the meat, and garnish with fresh herb sprigs, if used.

SERVES 6 TO 8

BRAISED PORK

1 pork spare rib joint, about 2 kg/4½ lb, trimmed
45 ml/3 tbsp oil
1 large onion, sliced
2 large carrots, sliced
1 garlic clove, crushed
125 ml/4 fl oz dry cider
125 ml/4 fl oz well-flavoured chicken or vegetable stock
1 bouquet garni
salt and pepper

Weigh the pork and calculate the cooking time at 30-35 minutes per 450 g/1 lb. Heat the oil in a large, flameproof casserole and fry the joint, turning frequently, until browned on all sides. Remove the meat and set aside.

Add the vegetables and garlic to the fat remaining in the casserole. Fry gently for 5 minutes. Pour in the cider and stock, and add the bouquet garni. Return the meat to the pan and season it with plenty of salt and pepper. Bring the liquid to the boil, lower the heat, cover the casserole and simmer gently for the calculated cooking time. Turn the meat occasionally.

When cooked, transfer the meat to a heated serving dish. Strain the liquid from the casserole into a clean saucepan. Skim off the excess fat from the surface, then boil the liquid until reduced to a thin gravy. Serve in a heated gravyboat.

SERVES 8 TO 10

HOT WATER CRUST PASTRY

This pastry is used for pork, veal and ham, and raised game pies. It must be moulded while still warm.

200 g/7 oz plain flour
2.5 ml/½ tsp salt
75 g/3 oz lard
100 ml/3½ fl oz milk or water

Sift the flour and salt into a warm bowl and make a well in the centre. Keep the bowl in a warm place.

Meanwhile, heat the lard and milk or water until boiling. Add the hot mixture to the flour, mixing well with a wooden spoon until the pastry is cool enough to knead with the hands. Knead thoroughly and mould as required.

Bake at 220°C/425°F/gas 7 until the pastry is set, then lower the oven temperature to 180°C/350°F/gas 4 until fully baked.

MAKES 350 G/12 OZ

TO MOULD A RAISED PIE

Hot Water Crust Pastry (above)
fat for greasing
flour

Use a jar, round cake tin or similar container, as a mould: grease and flour the sides and base of the mould and invert it.

Reserve one-quarter of the warm pastry for the lid and leave in the bowl in a warm place, covered with greased polythene.

Roll out the remainder to about 5 mm/¼ inch thick, in a round or oval shape. Lay the pastry over the mould, then ease the pastry round the sides. Take care not to pull the pastry and make sure that the sides and base are of an even thickness. Leave to cool.

When cold, remove the pastry case from the mould and put in the filling. Roll out the pastry reserved for the lid, dampen the rim of the case, put on the lid, pressing the edges firmly together. Tie 3 or 4 folds of greaseproof paper round the pie to hold it in shape during baking and to prevent it from becoming too brown.

MAKES ONE 13 CM/5 INCH PIE

USING A RAISED PIE MOULD
Decorative pie moulds may be purchased from cookshops. Usually oval in shape, they range in size from those which provide up to 6 servings to others which make pies large enough to feed 40 people.

The two sides of the mould fit into a base and they are secured with clips. The sides should be secured and the inside of the mould should be well greased. The pastry should be rolled out to about two-thirds of the required size.

Lift the pastry into the mould and secure its edge just below the rim of the mould. Use your fingers to press the pastry into the mould, easing it upwards at the same time so that it comes above the rim of the mould when the lining is complete. The pie may be filled at once.

The sides of the mould should be removed about 15-30 minutes before the end of the cooking time. Brush the pastry with beaten egg immediately and return the pie to the oven promptly to prevent the sides from collapsing.

RAISED VEAL PIE

If preferred, these ingredients can be made into
6 individual pies. The eggs should be sliced and
divided between the smaller pies.

Hot Water Crust Pastry (opposite), using
    400 g/14 oz flour
400 g/14 oz pie veal
400 g/14 oz lean pork
25 g/1 oz plain flour
7.5 ml/1½ tsp salt
1.25 ml/¼ tsp ground pepper
3 hard-boiled eggs
beaten egg for glazing
about 125 ml/4 fl oz well-flavoured,
    cooled and jellied stock or canned
    consommé

Set the oven at 230°C/450°F/gas 8. Line a 20 cm/8 inch round pie mould with three-quarters of the pastry, or use a round cake tin to mould the pie as described opposite. Use the remaining quarter for the lid.

Cut the meat into small pieces, removing any gristle or fat. Season the flour with the salt and pepper, then toss the pieces of meat in it. Put half the meat into the pastry case and put in the whole eggs. Add the rest of the meat and 30 ml/2 tbsp water. Put on the lid and brush with beaten egg. Make a hole in the centre to allow steam to escape. Bake for 15 minutes, then reduce the oven temperature to 140°C/275°F/gas 1. Continue baking for 2½ hours. Remove the greaseproof paper or mould for the last 30 minutes of the cooking time and brush the top and sides of the pastry with beaten egg.

Heat the stock or consommé until melted. When the pie is cooked, pour it through the hole in the lid using a funnel until the pie is full. Leave to cool.

SERVES 6

RAISED PORK PIES

about 400 g/14 oz pork bones
1 small onion, finely chopped
salt and pepper
300 ml/½ pint stock or cold water
Hot Water Crust Pastry (opposite), using
    400 g/14 oz flour
500 g/18 oz lean pork, minced
1.25 ml/¼ tsp dried sage
beaten egg for glazing

Simmer the pork bones, onion, salt, pepper and stock or water, covered, for 2 hours. Strain and cool. Make one 15 cm/6 inch pie (as left) or divide three-quarters of the pastry into 6 portions. Mould each piece using a jam jar, as described opposite, keeping the crust about 5 mm/¼ inch thick. Use the remaining pastry for the lids. Set the oven at 220°C/425°F/gas 7.

Season the pork with salt, pepper and sage. Divide between the prepared pie crusts and add 10 ml/2 tsp of the jellied stock to each. Put on the lids, brush with beaten egg, and make holes in the centres.

Bake for 15 minutes, then lower the oven temperature to 180°C/350°F/gas 4. Continue baking for 45 minutes (1 hour for a large pie). Remove the greaseproof paper for the last 30 minutes and brush the top and sides of the pastry with egg.

When cooked, remove from the oven and leave to cool. Warm the remainder of the jellied stock and pour through the hole in the pastry lids using a funnel until the pies are full. Leave to cool.

SERVES 6

SAUSAGES

You may be able to buy skins from a family butcher who makes his own sausages, but this may mean buying in bulk. Natural sausage skins will keep in an airtight container in the bottom of the refrigerator for 2-3 months – and the filled sausages may be frozen – but it may be simplest to forego skins altogether, and simply shape the sausagemeat into patties, dip these in flour, and fry or grill them.

Some of the larger food mixers have sausage-filling attachments, which are easy to use. If you do not own one of these, try the following method, which is quite successful. Cut the sausage skin into manageable lengths – each no longer than 0.9 m/1 yd – and soak in cold water for at least 30 minutes, preferably overnight. Drain, rinse and drain again, repeating this process until all the salt has been removed. Finally put the lengths of skin in a bowl and cover with fresh water.

Have the sausagemeat ready. Fit a large piping bag with a large (1-2.5 cm/½-1 inch) nozzle. Put some of the sausagement into the bag and press down to fill the nozzle. Carefully open the end of one of the sausage skins. With the filled bag resting on the work surface, carefully push the sausage skin as far up the nozzle and the outside of the piping bag as possible. When most of the skin is on the nozzle, start squeezing out the mixture. When a little of the skin has been filled, tie a neat knot in the end.

Continue to fill the sausage skin, keeping up a low steady pressure on the piping bag, at the same time allowing the skin to flow off the end of the nozzle, so that the skin fills evenly without bursting. The length of sausage may either be twisted at regular lengths to make conventional sausages, or looped round, pinwheel fashion, to make a single large sausage.

When cooking home-made sausages, do not prick the skins. Bake them slowly in the oven until the centres are cooked and the skins crisp. Alternatively, fry or grill them, using moderate heat so that the skins do not burst. Drain on absorbent kitchen paper before serving.

PORK SAUSAGES WITH CABBAGE

1 large hard white cabbage, about 1 kg/
    2¼ lb
75 g/3 oz butter
1 small onion, finely chopped
6 juniper berries, crushed
salt and pepper
50 ml/2 fl oz vegetable or chicken stock
450 g/1 lb pork sausages

Trim the cabbage and cut it into quarters. Shred it finely lengthways. Melt the butter in a large saucepan, add the onion and fry over gentle heat for about 5 minutes until transparent. Add the cabbage and juniper berries, with salt and pepper to taste. Pour in the stock, cover with a tight-fitting lid and cook gently for 1 hour. Stir occasionally and top up the liquid if it threatens to evaporate, leaving the cabbage dry.

Meanwhile grill, bake or fry the sausages until cooked through. Pile the cooked cabbage in a heated serving dish. Arrange the hot sausages on top and serve at once.

SERVES 4

*O*XFORD SAUSAGES

Illustrated on page 182

1.5 kg/3¼ lb pork, minced
450 g/1 lb fresh white breadcrumbs
5 ml/1 tsp freshly ground black pepper
grated rind of ½ lemon
2.5 ml/½ tsp grated nutmeg
6 sage leaves, chopped
2.5 ml/½ tsp chopped winter savory
2.5 ml/½ tsp dried marjoram

Mix the pork with the other ingredients in a large bowl. Add enough water to make a mixture with a soft piping consistency. Fill sausage skins, following the instructions above, or shape into small patties. If possible, allow the sausages to mature overnight in refrigerator, then cook.

MAKES 36 SAUSAGES

*B*OILED DRESSED HAM

Illustrated on page 181

1 leg of ham
250 ml/8 fl oz cider or white wine (optional)
1 large onion, roughly chopped
3-4 celery sticks, roughly chopped
1 large turnip, roughly chopped
1 large carrot, roughly chopped
1 bouquet garni

GARNISH
raspings (see Mrs Beeton's Tip, page 150)
demerara sugar • cloves
small bunches of watercress

Weigh the ham. Depending on how salty the ham is, it may be necessary to soak it in cold water for up to 12 hours. Soaking is not usually necessary with modern curing, however, since less salt is used. Check with your butcher.

Drain the ham if necessary. Place it in a large saucepan, cover with fresh water and bring to the boil. Skim off any scum that rises to the surface, lower the heat and simmer for 20 minutes per 450 g/1 lb, or until the bone at the knuckle end sticks out about 2.5 cm/1 inch and starts to feel loose.

Pour off the water from the pan and add the cider or wine, if used. Add fresh tepid water to cover, together with the prepared vegetables and bouquet garni. Bring the liquid to simmering point, halt cover the pan and simmer gently for 10 minutes per 450 g/1 lb.

When the ham is cooked, lift it out of the pan. Remove the rind and score the fat into a diamond pattern, using a sharp knife and making the cuts about 5 mm/¼ inch deep.

Cover the fat with equal quantities of raspings and demerara sugar. Press a clove into the centre of each diamond pattern. Place small bunches of watercress at either end of the ham and cover the knuckle with a pie frill. Serve hot or cold.

> **MRS BEETON'S TIP** Whole hams vary considerably in size and in the relation of meat to bone. It is therefore difficult to give exact servings. As a general guide, a 4.5 kg/10 lb ham should feed 30 people.

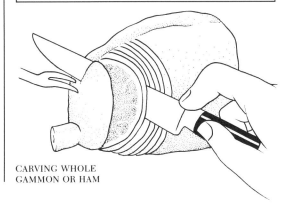

CARVING WHOLE
GAMMON OR HAM

HAM WITH RAISIN AND ORANGE SAUCE

Illustrated on page 182

1.5-2 kg/3¼-4½ lb ham, parboiled
   (see page 171)
225 g/8 oz soft dark brown sugar
cloves
100 ml/3½ fl oz white wine vinegar

RAISIN SAUCE
   50 g/2 oz soft dark brown sugar
   2.5 ml/½ tsp prepared mustard
   15 ml/1 tbsp cornflour
   75 g/3 oz seedless raisins
   15 ml/1 tbsp grated orange rind
   100 ml/3½ fl oz fresh orange juice

Set the oven at 160°C/325°F/gas 3. Drain and weigh the ham. Put it in a shallow baking tin. Bake for 10 minutes per 450 g/ 1 lb. Thirty minutes before the end of the calculated cooking time, lift the ham out of the pan, reserving the juices in a measuring jug. Remove the rind and score the fat into a diamond pattern. Cover with brown sugar and garnish with cloves.

Return the ham to the pan and trickle the vinegar over the top, taking care not to wash off the sugar. Continue baking, basting once or twice with the juices, until the ham is fully cooked.

Meanwhile make the sauce. Mix the brown sugar, mustard and cornflour in a small saucepan. Stir in the remaining ingredients with 200 ml/7 fl oz water. Cook over very gentle heat for about 10 minutes or until syrupy.

When the ham is cooked, transfer it to a heated platter. Serve the sauce separately.

SERVES 8 TO 10

PORK BRAWN

Although the idea of cooking a pig's head may be anathema to modern cooks, the butcher prepares the 'joint' beyond immediate recognition and it is worth the effort of cooking brawn to experience the full flavour of long-cooked meat jellied in a stock rich with aromatics. The beef in the recipe that follows is an optional extra, mainly for bulk; the flavour is excellent without it. You will need a large saucepan for this, or a stainless steel preserving pan with a makeshift foil cover. The meat must be kept covered with plenty of water during cooking.

½ pig's head, ears, brain and snout
   removed
1 pig's trotter, split
350 g/12 oz shin of beef (optional)
15 ml/1 tbsp salt
6 black peppercorns
6 cloves
5 ml/1 tsp dried marjoram or oregano
5 ml/1 tsp ground mace or 2 blades of
   mace
2 bay leaves
large sage sprig
2 thyme sprigs
1 rosemary sprig
1 savory sprig (optional)
4 parsley sprigs, with long stalks
2 onions, cut into chunks
2 large carrots, sliced
1 small turnip, cubed

Pig's heads are sold as part of the carcass, so any good butcher or supermarket which butchers its own meat (rather than taking prepacked deliveries) will be able to supply a head within a few days of ordering. Ask for the ears, snout and brain to be removed, and for the half head to be chopped into two pieces so that it fits easily into a large saucepan. Have the trotter split in half.

Wash the head well in salted cold water,

then rinse it under clear water and place the pieces in a large pan. Add the shin of beef, if used, the trotter, salt, peppercorns, cloves, marjoram and mace. Tie the bay leaves and herb sprigs into a neat bouquet garni and add them to the pan. A dried bouquet garni is no replacement for fresh herbs as their flavour is important.

Add the onions, carrots and turnip to the pan, then pour in cold water to cover the meat amply. Bring to the boil, then use a slotted spoon to skim the surface of the liquid for the first 5-10 minutes cooking, or until the scum has stopped forming. Take care to avoid removing any onion or too much of the dried herb and mace. Lower the heat so that the liquid is just boiling and cover the pan. Cook for 3 hours.

Have a very large bowl or saucepan, metal colander and two large meat plates ready, then lift the head and shin (if used) from the pan on to one plate. A large fish slice and barbecue forks are ideal for this. Strain the cooking liquid through a colander into the bowl or pan. Replace the trotters in the bowl or pan but discard the vegetables and herbs. If the stock has been strained into a bowl, pour it back into the clean pan. Bring it just to the boil.

Transfer a piece of meat to the clean plate for preparation. Use a sharp pointed knife to cut off the rind, leaving a thin layer of fat over the meat. Cut all the meat off the bones, using the point of the knife to scrape the crevices – this is an easy task as the meat literally falls away from the carcass.

Do not discard all the fat as it contributes flavour and moistens the finished brawn; however, remove all blood vessels and any small, dark and hard portions that are offal-like in appearance and texture. The meat is easy to distinguish as it is quite stringy and plentiful. Cut the meat into small pieces,

across the grain, and chop the fat. Return any bones to the pan of stock for further boiling. Continue until all the carcass is cleaned. Trim any fat and gristle from the beef, if used, and chop the meat. Mix it with the pork.

Cook the stock with the bones in the open pan until well reduced to less than half its original volume, then strain it again. You should aim to reduce the stock to 1.1-1.25 litres/2-2½ pints as this concentrates the flavour and gives a firm brawn. Although further reduction will intensify the flavour, the resultant brawn would set more firmly than is desirable. Lastly, strain the stock through a sieve lined with scalded muslin.

Mix the pork and fat well with the beef if used and place it in a 1.1 litre/2 pint basin. Stir in about 450 ml/¾ pint of the strained stock, mixing well at first, until all the meat is evenly distributed and the top just covered with stock (see Mrs Beeton's Tip). Cover and cool, then chill for at least 3 hours, or until set.

To serve, slide the point of a knife around the rim of the brawn, between it and the basin. Cover with a plate and invert both the basin and the plate, giving them a firm jerk to release the jellied meat. Cut into slices and serve the brawn with ripe tomatoes or salad and baked or fried potatoes. Alternatively, offer it with plain chunks of bread. Any leftover brawn makes a delicious sandwich filling.

SERVES 4 TO 6

MRS BEETON'S TIP The leftover stock makes delicious soup or it may be used in casseroles: cool, then freeze it in usable quantities.

FAGGOTS

fat for greasing
800 g/1¾ lb pig's liver
2 onions, quartered
2.5 ml/½ tsp dried thyme
10 ml/2 tsp dried sage
generous pinch of grated nutmeg
2.5 ml/½ tsp ground mace
salt and pepper
1 egg, lightly beaten
100 g/4 oz fresh white breadcrumbs
caul fat, pork dripping, lard or butter

Remove the skin and any tubes from the liver and slice it thinly. Put it in a saucepan with the onions. Add just enough water to cover. Bring to the boil, lower the heat, cover and simmer for 30 minutes. Drain.

Mince the liver and onions finely or process in a food processor. Add the herbs, spices, seasoning, egg and enough breadcrumbs to make a firm mixture.

Divide the mixture into 8 equal portions and shape into balls. Wrap in caul fat, if used. Lay the faggots side by side in a greased baking tin and dot with fat if caul is not used. Cover the tin loosely with foil. Bake for 25 minutes, then remove the foil and bake for 10-15 minutes more to brown the tops of the faggots. Serve hot, with a thickened gravy.

SERVES 4 TO 6

> **MRS BEETON'S TIP** Caul fat is a tough membrane laced with fat. Salted caul is seldom available; however should it be obtained, it must be soaked in cold water for 30 minutes, then thoroughly rinsed and soaked in fresh water with a little vinegar added. Finally, it should be rinsed and spread out on a perfectly clean tea-towel ready for use.

LIVER HOT POT

fat for greasing
450 g/1 lb lamb's liver, sliced
45 ml/3 tbsp flour
salt and pepper
2 large onions, thinly sliced
800 g/1¾ lb potatoes, thinly sliced
500 ml/18 fl oz beef stock
6-8 rindless streaky bacon rashers

Set the oven at 180°C/350°F/gas 4. Remove the skin and any tubes from the liver. Mix the flour with salt and pepper in a shallow bowl. Coat the liver slices in the seasoned flour. Shake off excess flour.

Arrange layers of liver, onion and potatoes in a greased casserole, ending with a layer of potatoes. Heat the stock in a small saucepan and pour in just enough to cover the potatoes. Cover the casserole with a lid or foil and bake for 1 hour or until the liver is tender.

Remove the lid and arrange the bacon rashers on top of the potatoes. Return the casserole to the oven for about 15 minutes or until the bacon is browned. Serve immediately, straight from the casserole.

SERVES 6

KIDNEYS IN ITALIAN SAUCE

Illustrated on page 183

450 g/1 lb lambs' kidneys
45 ml/3 tbsp flour
salt and pepper
8 young fresh sage leaves (optional)
1 small onion, finely chopped
30 ml/2 tbsp beef dripping
25 g/1 oz butter or margarine
375 ml/13 fl oz beef stock
100 g/4 oz mushrooms, sliced
15-30 ml/1-2 tbsp sherry
75 g/3 oz mange tout, lightly cooked

Wash the kidneys, halve and remove the membrane and white core from each. Cut into slices. Mix the flour with salt and pepper in a shallow bowl. Coat the kidneys in seasoned flour, shake off excess flour and reserve.

Heat the dripping in a frying pan, add the kidney slices and sage, if using, and fry quickly, stirring, until firm. Add the onion, lower the heat, cover and fry gently for 20 minutes.

Meanwhile, melt the butter or margarine in a saucepan, stir in the reserved flour and cook until nut brown in colour. Gradually add the stock, stirring constantly, and bring to the boil. Lower the heat and simmer for 5 minutes.

With a slotted spoon, transfer the kidney slices and onions to the sauce. Half cover the pan and simmer the mixture for 45 minutes, then add the mushrooms and sherry, with extra salt and pepper if liked. Simmer for 15 minutes more. Serve at once, garnished with mange tout.

SERVES 4

DEVILLED KIDNEYS

8 lambs' kidneys
30 ml/2 tbsp oil
15 ml/1 tbsp chopped onion
2.5 ml/½ tsp salt
1.25 ml/¼ tsp cayenne pepper
5 ml/1 tsp Worcestershire sauce
10 ml/2 tsp lemon juice
2.5 ml/½ tsp prepared mustard
125 ml/4 fl oz beef stock
2 egg yolks
fresh white breadcrumbs
buttered wholemeal toast to serve

Skin, halve and core the kidneys, then chop them into small pieces. Heat the dripping or oil in a small saucepan, add the onion and cook gently for 4-6 minutes until softened but not browned. Add the kidneys, salt, cayenne, Worcestershire sauce, lemon juice, mustard and stock. Bring to the boil, lower the heat and simmer for 15-20 minutes, until the kidneys are cooked. Cool slightly.

Beat the egg yolks lightly and stir them quickly into the kidney mixture. Sprinkle in enough of the breadcrumbs to give the mixture a soft consistency. Add more salt and pepper if required. Serve on buttered wholemeal toast.

SERVES 4

KIDNEYS TURBIGO

15 ml/1 tbsp oil
225 g/8 oz cocktail sausages
1 small onion, finely chopped
450 g/1 lb lambs' kidneys, halved and
    cored
salt and pepper
100 g/4 oz small button mushrooms
15 ml/1 tbsp plain flour
30 ml/2 tbsp tomato purée
150 ml/¼ pint dry white wine
150 ml/¼ pint vegetable or chicken stock
45 ml/3 tbsp chopped parsley

Heat the oil in a large frying pan, add the sausages and cook them over moderate heat until evenly golden. Using a slotted spoon, transfer them to a dish and set aside.

Pour off any excess fat from the pan, leaving enough to cook the remaining ingredients. Add the onion and cook, stirring, for 10 minutes, until softened. Add the kidneys, with salt and pepper to taste. Cook them, turning often, until browned all over and just cooked.

Add the mushrooms to the pan and continue cooking for about 5 minutes, so that the mushrooms are lightly cooked. Use a slotted spoon to transfer the kidneys and mushrooms to the dish with the sausages.

Stir the flour into the fat remaining in the pan. Stir in the tomato purée, then gradually stir in the wine and stock. Bring to the boil, stirring all the time, then lower the heat and return the sausages, mushrooms and kidneys to the pan. Simmer gently for 5 minutes.

Add the parsley and seasoning to taste before serving with cooked pasta or rice.

SERVES 4

STUFFED HEARTS

butter for greasing
4 lambs' hearts (see Mrs Beeton's Tip)
50 g/2 oz dripping or 60 ml/4 tbsp oil
250 ml/8 fl oz strong lamb or beef stock
15 ml/1 tbsp plain flour ● salt and pepper

STUFFING
50 g/2 oz margarine
100 g/4 oz fresh white breadcrumbs
30 ml/2 tbsp chopped parsley
2.5 ml/½ tsp chopped fresh thyme
grated rind of ½ lemon

Set the oven at 180°C/350°F/gas 4. Melt the margarine and stir in the remaining stuffing ingredients, with seasoning. Divide between the hearts. Skewer or sew together the flaps at the top to seal.

Heat the dripping or oil in a small baking tin. Put in the hearts and baste well. Bake for 45 minutes, basting several times. Transfer to a serving dish, remove the skewers if necessary, and keep hot.

Drain off most of the fat from the baking tin, retaining any meat juices. Tranfer the tin to the top of the stove and stir in the flour over low heat. Cook for 1 minute, then gradually add the stock, stirring until the mixture boils. Add seasoning and serve with the hearts.

SERVES 4

MRS BEETON'S TIP Wash lambs' hearts under running water. Cut off the lobes, flaps and gristle. Cut away membranes which separate the cavities inside. Soak in cold water for 30 minutes, then dry on kitchen paper.

Herbed Shoulder of Lamb (page 152)

Noisettes Jardinière and Lamb Shish Kebab (both on page 157) with rice

Roast Pork with Mushroom and Corn Stuffing (page 164) with Courgettes with Almonds (page 225) and Red Cabbage with Apples (page 213)

Barbecued Spare Ribs (page 167) and Pork and Apple Hot Pot (page 166)

Boiled Dressed Ham (page 171) with Strawberry and Tomato Salad (page 347) and new potatoes

Ham with Raisin and Orange Sauce (page 172) and Oxford Sausages (page 171)

Calf's Liver with Savoury Rice (page 188) and Kidneys in Italian Sauce (page 175)

Osso Buco (page 190) with Risotto Milanese (page 246)

TONGUE WITH RAISIN SAUCE

1 fresh ox tongue, about 2 kg/4½ lb, or
   6 lambs' tongues
1 onion, chopped
1 carrot, diced
1 turnip, diced
1 celery stick, sliced
1 bouquet garni
6 whole allspice
4 whole cloves
6 black peppercorns
chopped parsley to garnish

RAISIN SAUCE
50 g/2 oz butter
25 g/1 oz plain flour
600 ml/1 pint cider
100 g/4 oz seedless raisins
5 ml/1 tsp grated lemon rind
2.5 ml/½ tsp French mustard

Weigh the tongue, then wash it thoroughly. Soak in cold water for 2 hours. Drain and put in a large saucepan. Cover with fresh cold water, bring to the boil, then drain again. Repeat the process with fresh cold water.

Return the tongue to the pan again, cover with cold water once more and add the vegetables, bouquet garni and spices. Bring to the boil, cover with a tight-fitting lid, lower the heat and simmer gently until tender. An ox tongue will take about 3 hours; lambs' tongues 1-1½ hours (see Mrs Beeton's Tip).

When cooked, lift out the tongue(s) and plunge into cold water. Drain. Remove the skin carefully and take out the small bones at the root of the tongue, together with any excess fat, glands and gristle. Carve the tongue in slices and arrange on a large platter. Keep hot while making the sauce.

Melt the butter in a saucepan, stir in the flour and cook for 1 minute. Add the cider and raisins, stirring until the mixture boils and thickens. Lower the heat and simmer for 5 minutes, then stir in the lemon rind and mustard. Spoon the sauce over the tongue slices and serve at once.

SERVES 9 TO 12

VARIATION

PRESSED TONGUE To serve an ox tongue cold, cook, skin and trim as above. While it is still hot, curl the tongue into an 18 cm/7 inch straight-sided dish or tin. Spoon over a little of the stock in which the tongue was cooked, to fill up the crevices. Put a flat plate, just large enough to fit inside the dish, on top of the tongue, and add a heavy weight. Chill overnight to set, then run a knife around the edge of the tongue and turn it out. Cut in thin slices and serve with salad.

> **MRS BEETON'S TIP** To test whether the tongue is cooked, attempt to pull out one of the small bones near the root. If it comes away easily, the tongue is ready.

TRIPE AND ONIONS

Tripe is the muscular lining of the four stomachs of cattle or sheep. It varies in consistency and appearance, depending on the source. Honeycomb tripe is the most delicate type. It is usually sold blanched and parboiled. It is highly perishable and should always be cooked as soon as possible after purchase.

450 g/1 lb dressed tripe
600 ml/1 pint milk
salt and pepper
3 onions, chopped
25 g/1 oz butter
25 g/1 oz plain flour

GARNISH
15 ml/1 tbsp chopped parsley
toast triangles

Wash the tripe and cut it into 5 cm/2 inch squares. Put it in a heavy-bottomed saucepan. Add the milk, with salt and pepper to taste. Stir in the onions. Bring the milk to the boil, lower the heat, cover with a tight-fitting lid and simmer for about 2 hours (see Mrs Beeton's Tip) or until the tripe is tender.

Knead the butter and flour together until evenly blended. Add it in small pieces to the contents of the pan. Stir until smooth, then continue cooking for a further 30 minutes. Serve on a heated dish, garnished with parsley and toast triangles.

SERVES 4

MRS BEETON'S TIP Cooking time for tripe varies, depending on type and preliminary preparation. Ask the butcher's advice.

FRIED SWEETBREADS

3 pairs lambs' sweetbreads, total weight about 675 g/1½ lb
chicken or lamb stock (see method)
40 g/1½ oz butter
2.5 ml/½ tsp lemon juice
30 ml/2 tbsp plain flour
salt and pepper
1 egg, lightly beaten
fresh white breadcrumbs for coating

CUCUMBER SAUCE
15 g/½ oz butter
½ cucumber, chopped
15 ml/1 tbsp chicken or lamb stock
125 ml/4 fl oz Béchamel sauce (see Mrs Beeton's Tip, page 47)
salt and pepper
pinch of sugar
grated nutmeg
lemon juice
30 ml/2 tbsp single cream

Soak the sweetbreads in cold water to cover for 1-2 hours to remove blood.

Meanwhile, make the sauce. Melt the butter in a saucepan, add the cucumber and cook gently for 10 minutes. Add the stock and continue cooking until the cucumber is very soft. Rub it through a fine sieve into a clean pan, then simmer until slightly reduced. Stir in the Béchamel sauce and heat through if necessary. Add salt, pepper, sugar and nutmeg to taste; sharpen the flavour with lemon juice. Cover the surface of the sauce closely with buttered grease-proof paper and set aside.

Drain the sweetbreads. Put them in a saucepan with fresh water to cover. Bring to the boil, then pour off the liquid. Rinse the sweetbreads under cold water; remove the black veins and as much as possible of the membranes which cover them.

Put the sweetbreads in a saucepan with just enough stock to cover them; add 5 ml/ 1 tsp of the butter and the lemon juice. Bring the stock to the boil, lower the heat, cover the pan and simmer for 15-20 minutes. Leave the sweetbreads to cool in the stock, then drain.

Spread out the flour in a shallow bowl and season with salt and pepper. Put the egg into a second bowl and the bread-crumbs on a sheet of foil. Dip the sweet-breads in flour, then in egg and finally in breadcrumbs. Heat the remaining butter in a frying pan, add the crumbed sweet-breads and fry for about 8 minutes until golden brown on all sides. Remove with a slotted spoon and drain on absorbent kitchen paper. Arrange on a serving dish. Reheat the sauce; off the heat, stir in the cream. Serve with the sweetbreads.

SERVES 6

OXTAIL HOT POT

1 kg/2¼ lb oxtail, jointed
30 ml/2 tbsp plain flour
salt and pepper
2 large onions, thinly sliced
800 g/1¾ lb potatoes, sliced
5 ml/1 tsp dried mixed herbs
beef stock (see method)
6 rindless streaky bacon rashers, cut in
    small squares

Set the oven at 180°C/350°F/gas 4. Wash the oxtail, dry it thoroughly and trim off any excess fat. Mix the flour with salt and pepper, and use to coat the oxtail.

Place alternate layers of onions, oxtail and potatoes in a pie dish or casserole, sprinkling each layer with salt, pepper and dried mixed herbs, and ending with a layer of potatoes. Pour in just enough beef stock

to cover the meat. Cover the casserole and bake for 2½-3 hours, or until the meat is tender. Check the hot pot from time to time, and add more stock if necessary.

Remove the lid from the casserole, lay the bacon rashers over the top and bake for 30 minutes more. Serve.

SERVES 4

WIENER SCHNITZEL

plain flour
salt and pepper
1 egg
2-3 drops of oil
dried white breadcrumbs for coating
6 thin escalopes of veal, each measuring
    about 13 × 7.5 cm/5 × 3 inches
oil and butter for shallow frying

GARNISH
6 lemon slices
15 ml/1 tbsp chopped parsley

Spread out the flour in a shallow bowl and season with salt and pepper. Put the egg in a second bowl, add the oil and beat lightly. Spread out the breadcrumbs on a sheet of foil. Coat the escalopes in flour, then in egg and finally in breadcrumbs, pressing them on well.

Heat the oil and butter in a large frying pan. Put in the escalopes and fry over gentle to moderate heat for 7-10 minutes, turning them over once only.

Remove the escalopes and place them, overlapping slightly, on a heated flat serving dish. Garnish the middle of each escalope with a slice of lemon sprinkled with parsley.

SERVES 6

CALF'S LIVER WITH SAVOURY RICE

Illustrated on page 183

butter or oil for frying
450 g/1 lb calf's liver, sliced
40 g/1½ oz butter or margarine
1 onion, finely chopped
2 garlic cloves, crushed
150 g/5 oz long-grain rice
375 ml/13 fl oz well-flavoured chicken or
    vegetable stock
salt and pepper
1.25-2.5 ml/¼-½ tsp powdered saffron
plain flour for coating
bacon rolls (see Mrs Beeton's Tip, page
    49) to garnish

SAUCE
    15 ml/1 tbsp dripping or lard
    1 carrot, thinly sliced
    1 small onion, thinly sliced
    30 ml/2 tbsp plain flour
    300 ml/½ pint lamb or vegetable stock
    30 ml/2 tbsp tomato purée
    15 ml/1 tbsp shredded fresh sage or 1.25
        ml/¼ tsp dried sage

Remove the skin and any tubes from the liver. Melt 25 g/1 oz of the butter or margarine in a frying pan, add the onion and garlic and sauté without colouring for 2-3 minutes. Stir in the rice and cook over gentle heat for 3 minutes. Add the stock, with salt and pepper to taste, then sprinkle in the saffron. Cover the pan and cook for about 20 minutes until the rice is soft and has absorbed all the stock. Add the remaining butter or margarine, mix well, then press into a ring mould. Put on one side until set.

Set the oven at 160°C/325°F/gas 3. Make the sauce. Melt the dripping or lard in a saucepan. Add the carrot and onion and fry over gentle heat until the onion is golden brown. Stir in the flour, lower the heat and cook for 1 minute. Gradually add the stock, tomato purée and sage, stirring constantly. Bring to the boil, stirring all the time, then lower the heat, cover and simmer for 15 minutes. Strain into a clean pan and add salt and pepper to taste. Cover the surface of the sauce with dampened greaseproof paper and set aside.

Place the flour in a shallow bowl, add salt and pepper and coat the slices of liver on both sides. Heat the fat for frying in a large frying pan, add the liver and fry quickly for about 4 minutes, turning once, until browned and crisp on the outside but still pink in the centre. Drain the liver, then cut the slices into strips.

Turn the rice ring on to a heated serving dish, cover lightly with buttered greaseproof paper and heat through in the oven for 10-12 minutes. Meanwhile reheat the sauce until just below boiling point. Stir in the liver, lower the heat and simmer for 2-3 minutes until heated through. Spoon the liver mixture into the centre of the rice ring, garnish with the bacon rolls and serve at once.

SERVES 6

FRIED FILLETS OF VEAL WITH LEMON SAUCE

300 g/10 oz fillet of veal, trimmed and cut
    into 4 slices
1 egg, lightly beaten
2.5 ml/½ tsp chopped parsley
1.25 ml/¼ tsp chopped fresh thyme
5 ml/1 tsp grated lemon rind
5 ml/1 tsp lemon juice
dried white breadcrumbs for coating
50 g/2 oz butter
bacon rolls (see Mrs Beeton's Tip, page
    49) to garnish

LEMON SAUCE
    15 ml/1 tbsp plain flour
    250 ml/8 fl oz chicken stock
    2.5 ml/½ tsp lemon juice
    salt and pepper
    15-30 ml/1-2 tbsp single cream

Place the veal slices between greaseproof paper and flatten them with a cutlet bat or rolling pin. Put the egg in a shallow bowl with the herbs, lemon rind and juice. Add the veal slices, turn them in the egg, then cover and marinate in the refrigerator for 30 minutes. Spread out the breadcrumbs on a sheet of foil and use to coat the veal slices, pressing the crumbs in well.

Heat the butter in a large frying pan and fry the veal slices over moderate heat until golden brown on both sides, then lower the heat and cook more slowly for 7-10 minutes in all. Remove the fillets with a fish slice, drain on absorbent kitchen paper and place in a heated dish. Keep hot.

Make the lemon sauce. Stir the flour into the fat remaining in the frying pan. Cook gently for about 2 minutes. Gradually add the stock, stirring the mixture until it boils and thickens. Add the lemon juice with salt and pepper to taste. Simmer the sauce for 3 minutes, then remove from the heat.

Pour some of the lemon sauce over the veal and serve the rest in a heated sauceboat.

SERVES 3 TO 4

ESCALOPES WITH HAM AND CHEESE

6 thin escalopes of veal
plain flour
salt and pepper
1 egg
2-3 drops of oil
dried white breadcrumbs for coating
butter and oil for shallow frying
6 thin slices of lean cooked ham
6 thin slices of Gruyère cheese

Set the oven at 200°C/400°F/gas 6. Wipe the escalopes, place them between greaseproof paper and flatten them with a cutlet bat or rolling pin. Coat them in seasoned flour, egg and breadcrumbs as for Wiener Schnitzel (page 187).

Heat the oil and butter in a large frying pan. Put in the escalopes and fry over gentle to moderate heat for about 3 minutes on each side.

Remove the escalopes and lay them in a flat ovenproof dish. Cover each escalope with a slice of ham and top with a slice of cheese. Spoon a little of the pan juices over the top of each escalope, put the dish in the oven and bake until the cheese melts – about 20 minutes. Serve at once.

SERVES 6

OSSO BUCO

Illustrated on page 184

450 g/1 lb tomatoes, peeled, seeded and
    chopped or 1 (397 g/14 oz) can chopped
    tomatoes
30 ml/2 tbsp tomato purée
200 ml/7 fl oz beef stock
salt and pepper
50 g/2 oz plain flour
4 veal knuckles or 4 veal shank slices,
    about 2 cm/¾ inch thick
60 ml/4 tbsp oil
1 onion, finely chopped
2 garlic cloves, crushed
2 carrots, finely chopped
2 celery sticks, sliced
juice of 1 lemon
150 ml/¼ pint dry white wine
2 bay leaves
2 thyme sprigs

GREMOLADA
    45 ml/3 tbsp chopped parsley
    1 garlic clove, chopped
    grated rind of ½ lemon

Set the oven at 180°C/350°F/gas 4. Put
the tomatoes, with any juices, into a bowl.
Stir in the tomato purée and stock, with salt
and pepper to taste. Set the mixture aside.

Put the flour in a stout polythene or
paper bag. Season with salt and pepper.
Add the veal knuckles or shank slices and
toss until well coated. Shake off excess
flour. Heat the oil in a large flameproof
casserole, add the meat and fry for about
8 minutes, turning once or twice, until
browned all over. With tongs, transfer the
meat to a plate and set aside.

Add the onion, garlic, carrots and celery
to the fat remaining in the casserole.
Fry over gentle heat for 6-8 minutes or
until the onion is golden brown. Add the
reserved tomato mixture and bring to the
boil, scraping in any sediment on the base
of the pan. Remove from the heat and add
the lemon juice and wine, with the bay
leaves and thyme.

Return the veal to the casserole, pushing
the pieces well down so that they are
completely covered by the sauce. Cover
the dish tightly with foil and a lid and bake
for 1½-2 hours or until the meat is very
tender. Remove the bay leaves and thyme
sprigs. If necessary, place the casserole
over moderate heat for 5-10 minutes,
stirring occasionally, to reduce the sauce.

Make the *gremolada* by mixing all the
ingredients together in a small bowl.
Sprinkle over the osso buco just before
serving. Serve with Risotto Milanese (page
246) and Italian Spinach (page 234) if liked.

SERVES 4

FRICADELLES OF VEAL

275 g/10 oz fresh white breadcrumbs
60 ml/4 tbsp milk
450 g/1 lb lean pie veal, trimmed (see Mrs
    Beeton's Tip) or minced veal
100 g/4 oz shredded beef suet
grated rind of 1 lemon
generous pinch of grated nutmeg
salt and pepper
3 eggs
750 ml/1¼ pints veal or chicken stock
oil for deep frying
400 ml/14 fl oz Fresh Tomato Sauce
    (page 352)

GARNISH
    lemon slices
    black olives

Put 175 g/6 oz of the breadcrumbs in a
shallow bowl, sprinkle the milk over and

leave to stand for 5 minutes. Squeeze out as much milk as possible; rub out any lumps. Mince the pie veal or process it roughly in a food processor. Scrape it into a bowl and add the soaked bread, suet, lemon rind and nutmeg, with plenty of salt and pepper. Beat 2 of the eggs lightly and stir into the mixture. Shape into balls about the size of large walnuts.

Bring the stock to the boil in a large saucepan, add the veal balls and cook for 6 minutes, until firm and cooked. Remove with a slotted spoon and drain well. Cool slightly before coating with egg and bread-crumbs. Beat the remaining egg lightly in a shallow bowl. Spread out the remaining breadcrumbs on a sheet of foil. Coat the fricadelles in egg and breadcrumbs.

Heat the oil for deep frying to 180-190°C/350-375°F or until a cube of bread added to the oil browns in 30 seconds. Fry the fricadelles until golden brown.

Meanwhile, reheat the tomato sauce to simmering point in a large saucepan. As the fricadelles cook, remove them with a slotted spoon and drain them on absorbent kitchen paper. Serve piping hot, with the tomato sauce, garnished with lemon and black olives. Offer cooked rice or pasta with the fricadelles.

SERVES 6

MRS BEETON'S TIP If the veal is boned by the butcher, ask him for the bones. These may be used for stock.

MRS BEETON'S BAKED VEAL OR HAM LOAF

Leftover roast veal would have been commonplace in Mrs Beeton's day but the recipe will work equally well if cooked ham or other cold cooked meat or poultry is used.

fat for greasing
200 g/7 oz cold roast veal or cooked ham
4 rindless streaky bacon rashers
175 g/6 oz fresh white breadcrumbs
250 ml/8 fl oz veal or chicken stock
2.5 ml/½ tsp grated lemon rind
2.5 ml/½ tsp ground mace
1.25 ml/¼ tsp cayenne pepper
30 ml/2 tbsp chopped parsley
salt
2 eggs, lightly beaten

Thoroughly grease a 450 g/1 lb loaf tin or 750 ml/1¼ pint ovenproof dish. Set the oven at 160°C/325°F/gas 3. Mince the veal or ham and bacon together finely or process in a food processor. Scrape into a bowl and add the breadcrumbs, stock, lemon rind, mace, cayenne and parsley with salt to taste. Mix in the eggs.

Spoon the mixture into the prepared tin or dish and bake for 1 hour, or until the mixture is firm and lightly browned. Serve hot, with gravy or tomato sauce, if liked.

SERVES 3 TO 4

MRS BEETON'S TIP If the loaf tin has a tendency to stick, line the base with baking parchment or greaseproof paper so that the loaf will turn out easily.

VEGETABLES

Variety and quality are all-important in the selection and use
of vegetables. This chapter offers traditional and
contemporary ideas to ensure that, whatever their role, the
vegetables will complement the rest of the menu.

BUYING VEGETABLES

Although most vegetables are on sale all
year, it is still worth taking advantage of
locally grown produce in season, both for
flavour and economy. Look out for home
grown produce in supermarkets and take
advantage of any local market gardens and
farms. Remember, too, that markets are an
excellent place to shop for value – in some
rural areas they can be the best place to buy
really fresh produce.

Whatever – and wherever you buy,
always look for good-quality produce.
Vegetables should look fresh – firm, crisp
and bright. Avoid limp, yellowing and
wrinkled produce; onions that are soft or
sprouting; and items that have been ex-
cessively trimmed. Do not buy green
potatoes as they are inedible; this should be
brought to the attention of the seller.

The fact that vegetables have been
cleaned is not necessarily an indication of
their quality – for example, vegetables that
have a certain amount of earth on them or
retain their leaves are often better quality
than thoroughly washed, trimmed and
prepacked items.

When buying packs of vegetables always
check that they are not sweating, with
moisture inside the bag causing rapid
deterioration in quality. Turn items over,
feel them and inspect them for soft spots
or bad patches.

STORING

Vegetables should be used as fresh as
possible. The majority of vegetables should
be stored in the refrigerator: salad vegetables should be polythene-wrapped or
stored in the salad drawer. Carrots,
parsnips and similar vegetables soon
deteriorate if they are stored in polythene
bags, so thick paper bags are the best
wrapping in the salad drawer. Similarly,
mushrooms go off quickly if they are stored
in polythene. Green vegetables and cauliflower should be stored in polythene bags.

Potatoes should be stored only if suitable
conditions are available, that is a cool, dry
place where the tubers may be kept in a
thick brown paper bag to exclude all light.
They should not be stored in warm, light,
moist conditions for any length of time. So
only buy large polythene bags of potatoes if
you use them within a few days.

As a general rule, buy little and often for
best quality and food value.

FROZEN VEGETABLES

Frozen vegetables are excellent quality, in
terms of food value as well as flavour. They
are also easy to prepare at home. Take
advantage of pick-your-own farms or farm
shops if you do not grow your own vegetables, and freeze only good quality
produce which is freshly picked and processed as quickly as possible.

COOKING METHODS

British cooking is given a bad name by the
characteristic overboiling of vegetables,
rendering high-quality produce unpalatable

and lacking in nutrients. Happily, attitudes are changing and a broader range of cooking methods are now commonly used, with shorter cooking times and greater appreciation of the value of raw vegetables, for their texture and flavour as well as for their food value. Flavourings have become more adventurous and salt, once added automatically to every pan of boiling vegetables, is now very much a matter of personal choice.

Boiling This is an easy and practical cooking method for many vegetables, including potatoes, carrots, swedes, parsnips, beans, cauliflower and cabbage. However, it is important that the boiling process is only long enough to make the vegetables tender.

There are two methods of boiling. The first involves covering vegetables with water, which is then brought to the boil. The heat is then lowered and the pan covered so that the water just boils. For the second method, a comparatively small amount of water is brought to the boil, the vegetables are added and are cooked more fiercely with or without a lid on the pan. This takes less time.

The first method is used for potatoes, swedes and similar vegetables which require to be covered with liquid to make them tender in the shortest possible time. The liquid from cooking may be used for sauces, such as gravy, or soups.

The second method is suitable for quick-cooking vegetables such as cabbage, green beans, Brussels sprouts and cauliflower. Once the vegetables are added to the pan, the liquid should be brought back to the boil quickly, then the heat controlled so that the cooking is fairly rapid. Cooking times will vary, depending on the vegetables.

Salt may be added to the cooking water. This is a matter for personal choice but the water should not be heavily salted.

Never add bicarbonate of soda to the cooking water for green vegetables. In the days when vegetables were regularly overcooked, this was regarded as a good way of preserving the colour; however it destroys the vitamin C content of the food and should be avoided.

Stewing and Braising Ratatouille is one of the best-known, classic vegetable stews. Stewing and braising are used for vegetables which require moderate to lengthy cooking, or which benefit from a moist cooking method. They are also used to combine vegetable flavours and create a mixed vegetable dish.

Celery, fennel, cucumber and carrots are typical examples of vegetables that respond well to braising, with the addition of a little onion, some stock or wine and herbs. The braising process should be fairly slow so that the vegetables are tender throughout. The cooking juices are either reduced or thickened, then poured over the vegetables to serve.

Steaming This is a good, plain method which gives results similar to boiling. Nutrients are lost from the vegetables by seepage via the steam into the water below. To conserve as much food value as possible steam vegetables over a main dish, such as a stew so that the nutrients are retained.

Although a perforated container is usually used, vegetables that require light cooking, such as courgettes, may be steamed in a dish, on a plate over a saucepan of water or wrapped in foil.

The flavour of some vegetables is heightened by steaming rather than boiling. Cauliflower, broccoli and cabbage are all examples.

Frying Shallow frying, under the guise of sautéing, is a popular method for vegetables that require little cooking. Courgettes are often cooked by this method. The thinly cut vegetables are tossed in a little butter or oil over moderate to high heat.

Deep frying is not a practical way of cooking many vegetables but it is used for potato chips and for making fritters or vegetable croquettes. In the latter case, the portions of vegetable are protected by a coating, such as batter.

Stir Frying A comparatively modern method for Western cooks, this is suitable for most vegetables. The results are crisp, flavoursome and colourful. Many stir-fried vegetables are ideal for grilled dishes but are not the best accompaniment for casseroles or roasts.

Grilling This method is not often used for vegetables other than mushrooms or tomatoes. However, courgettes, auber-gines and peppers may be grilled.

Microwave Cooking Microwave cooking is excellent for the majority of vegetables, particularly when small to medium quantities are cooked. Remember:
■ Check the manufacturer's handbook and timings – most give comprehensive information on cooking vegetables.
■ Never add salt before cooking.
■ Cook vegetables with a small amount of water or liquid.
■ Use a covered microwave-proof container or roasting bag, closed loosely to allow steam to escape.
■ Arrange tougher areas, such as stalks, towards the outside of a dish, where they receive most energy.
■ Turn and rearrange vegetables at least once during cooking.
■ Spinach, peas, French beans, cauli-flower florets, new potatoes, Jerusalem and globe artichokes are just a few examples which cook very well in the microwave.
■ Less successful vegetables include celery (unless as part of a dish), old carrots in chunks, large quantities of 'boiled' potatoes – particularly for mashing – and larger quantities of green cabbage.

A GUIDE TO VEGETABLES

ARTICHOKES

Globe At their best and least expensive during late summer, these are the flower buds of a large thistle. They should be thoroughly washed and drained. Trim off loose leaves around the base of the head. Snip off the ends of the leaves and the top of the head. Place in acidulated water to prevent discoloration and cook promptly in boiling salted water with lemon juice added. Allow 25-45 minutes, depending on size. To check if the artichokes are cooked, pull off one of the base leaves: it should come away easily. Drain well until cool enough to handle.

Separate the leaves slightly to reveal the group of leaves that form the central part of the artichoke. Pull these out to reveal the 'choke', a cushion of fine hairs seated in the centre of the vegetable. Use a teaspoon to carefully scrape the choke away, leaving a pad of pale, tender flesh known as the bottom, base or *fond*. Trim off the stalk so that the artichoke sits neatly and fill the centre with an oil and vinegar dressing or a stuffing.

Like asparagus, artichokes are eaten with the fingers. Each leaf is pulled off individually and the small portion of pale flesh at the base dipped in dressing before being eaten. The rest of the tough leaf is discarded.

Artichoke bottoms (or *fonds*) are re-garded as a delicacy and frequently form the basis of more sophisticated dishes. If only the artichoke bottoms are required, the leaves, chokes and stalks may be removed and the artichoke bottoms care-fully peeled before being cooked in boiling water until tender.

Jerusalem These look like small, knobbly new potatoes, but have a delicate nutty flavour. They should be scrubbed and peeled or cooked with the peel left on. Jerusalem artichokes discolour quickly, so should be placed in acidulated water. Boil them for 10-15 minutes until tender or cook by steaming.

They may be served gratinéed, with a crumb topping, mashed, coated in sauce, tossed in melted butter or sliced and topped with cheese, then grilled. They also make good soup.

ASPARAGUS

Although greengrocers have supplies throughout the year, home-grown asparagus is a summer vegetable, ready in May and June. Look for bright, firm but slim spears that are not woody. On larger spears, make sure that there is a good length of tender green stalk once the tougher end is trimmed. Allow 6-8 spears per portion.

Trim off the woody ends and scrape or peel any remaining tough spear ends. Tie the asparagus in bundles. Cook them in a special asparagus pan or stand them in a saucepan of boiling water, with the tender tips exposed. Tent with foil and simmer for about 15 minutes, or until tender. The tips will steam while the stalks cook in the simmering water.

Alternatively, asparagus may be steamed over boiling water on a rack in a wok or on a wire rack over boiling water in a roasting tin, with the tips towards the outside of the wok or tin so that they do not overcook.

Serve with melted butter poured over. The trimmings may be used to flavour soups or sauces.

AUBERGINES

Also known as eggplants (in America) and brinjals (in India), these vegetables have pale, tender but firm flesh. The shiny skins are usually purple, although white varieties are also available. They should be firm and shiny outside, with a bright green calyx.

Aubergines are cooked in a wide variety of ways: they may be stewed in ratatouille; cubed and grilled on skewers; braised with meat or poultry; roasted and mashed to make a dip; stuffed and baked; sliced, fried and layered with meat in moussaka; or spiced in Indian or Mediterranean dishes.

Since the flesh can be rather bitter, aubergines should be salted and allowed to stand in a colander or sieve over a bowl for 15-30 minutes before use. This process is known as *degorging*.

BEANS

Broad Available from early spring through to autumn, broad beans are best when young and small. Allow about 225 g/8 oz pods per person, selecting firm plump pods with a good green colour. Shrivelled, blackened or largely empty pods are not a good buy. Equally, very large hard pods yield tough old beans.

Shell the beans and cook them in boiling water for 5-15 minutes, depending on their age and your personal taste. Add a sprig of summer savory to the cooking water if liked.

Serve the beans with butter and pepper. They are excellent with diced cooked ham or crisp grilled bacon, or they may be sauced with Hollandaise sauce or soured cream.

French These require little preparation. Buy bright, firm beans which are not damaged or shrivelled. Trim off their ends and wash them well. Add to a pan of boiling water and cook for 2-10 minutes, depending on size and use. A crunchy result can quickly be achieved if the beans are very slim.

Serve French beans topped with butter or fried breadcrumbs. Chopped hard-boiled egg and chopped parsley are another popular topping.

Lightly cooked and cooled, these beans are good in salads. They may be stir fried.

Runner These are best freshly picked. It is usually necessary to remove the strings, or trim these beans down both sides, before cooking. Some varieties do not need stringing. Avoid very large beans or any that have shrivelled.

Slice the beans at an angle into long thin pieces, add these to a saucepan of boiling water and cook for 3-10 minutes, depending on taste. About 5 minutes is average; any longer and the beans become soft. Toss with butter and serve freshly cooked.

BEAN SPROUTS

These are usually mung beans, although a variety of dried beans may be sprouted. Bean sprouts provide a useful amount of protein and are therefore ideal for adding to vegetable stir fries which contain little meat or fish.

The bean sprouts should be rinsed and drained, then cooked very briefly – stir frying for 3 minutes or less is the best method. The bean sprouts may be added to sauced mixtures and braised for 1-2 minutes, but avoid overcooking them or they will become limp and unpleasant.

BEETROOT

Do not peel raw beetroot before boiling. Simply wash away dirt and twist off the leaves above stalk level. Put the beetroot in a large saucepan with water to cover. Add some salt, if liked. Bring to the boil, lower the heat and simmer, covered, for 45-60 minutes for small to medium young beetroot. Larger, older vegetables can take up to 1½-2 hours to cook but these are not often sold. Beetroot is cooked when it feels tender and the skin rubs off easily.

Drain off the cooking water and replace it with cold water to cover the beetroot. Working under water while the beetroot is still hot, rub off the skins. These should slip off easily with their stalks. Place the peeled beetroot in a dish, cover and leave until cool.

Beetroot may be served hot with fried breadcrumbs and chopped onion. It combines well with other vegetables in hot bakes, or it may be allowed to cool before being used in salads or served simply with soured cream or fromage frais.

Beetroot may be sliced or preserved whole in vinegar. It is a traditional accompaniment for cold roast meats. The uncooked vegetable is also used to make a delicious soup, known as *bortsch*.

BROCCOLI

The two main types are sprouting broccoli, with long stalks, a few leaves and small heads in purple or pale green, and calabrese with larger heads and shorter stalks. The stalks on young sprouting broccoli are tender when cooked and may be included as part of the vegetable; slightly older stalks will have to be discarded.

Broccoli should be washed and trimmed, then broken if the heads are large. Cook in a saucepan of boiling water. Tender young sprouting broccoli cooks quite quickly and it will be tender after 3-5 minutes but larger heads may require 10-15 minutes. Broccoli may also be steamed or stir fried, and makes an excellent soup.

Serve plain with butter or coated with a sauce, such as cheese sauce. Broken into small florets, broccoli may be cooked in a little olive oil with garlic and onion for tossing with pasta and serving with grated Parmesan cheese.

Broccoli is useful as a filling for pies, with chicken or fish, and it also makes a first class pancake filling.

BRUSSELS SPROUTS

This winter vegetable is one of the traditional accompaniments to roast turkey. Look for small firm sprouts which are slightly shiny and green. Avoid very loose, yellowing or insect-nibbled sprouts.

Wash the vegetables thoroughly. Cut a cross in the stalk of larger ones so that they cook evenly. Add to a saucepan of boiling water and cook for 5-10 minutes.

Small, young sprouts may be steamed; halved sprouts may be stir fried. Cooked sprouts may be served plain or tossed with cooked chestnuts (see page 52) or browned blanched almonds.

CABBAGE

There are many varieties, the key differences being that they may be hard or loose-packed. The following are some of the varieties most commonly sold in Britain:

White Cabbage A hard creamy-white to pale green cabbage with tightly packed leaves.

Red Cabbage Resembles white cabbage but has dark red leaves.

Savoy Cabbage A large cabbage with a neat firm heart and slightly crinkly leaves.

Winter Cabbage A term used for cabbage with a firm heart and looser outer leaves, similar to Savoy but without the characteristic crinkly, deeply veined leaves.

Spring Greens The new growth of loose leaves which do not have a heart.

There are many cooking methods for cabbage; all types may also be eaten raw. For salads, white and red cabbage are the most popular; they are also ideal for stir frying or braising. Red cabbage is also suitable for pickling in vinegar and white cabbage is traditonally salted to make sauerkraut.

Green cabbages may be boiled, steamed or stir fried. Individual leaves may be blanched until soft, then stuffed and braised. Shredded green cabbage may be blanched, drained, then deep fried and tossed in sugar and soy sauce to be served Chinese style as 'seaweed'.

Wedges of cabbage heart may be steamed or braised. Shredded cabbage may be combined with rice in risottos or added to soups.

To boil cabbage, add the trimmed leaves to the minimum of boiling water, pressing them down well. Cover the pan tightly and cook quickly for 3-7 minutes, according to taste. Drain and roughly chop the cabbage before tossing it with butter and pepper.

Steaming times vary according to the method of preparation: if the cabbage is cut in chunks allow up to 15 minutes. Braised cabbage may be cooked for anything from 15 minutes to 1½ hours (for red cabbage cooked with onions and apples).

CARROTS

Young, or baby, carrots have the best flavour. Look out for firm, unblemished carrots preferably sold in bundles with leaves. If you do buy carrots prepacked in polythene, check that they are not wet from condensation; in damp conditions, they deteriorate very rapidly.

Young carrots do not require peeling; a good scrub or scrape is sufficient. Whether older carrots are peeled or scrubbed is a matter of taste. Small carrots are best cooked whole by boiling or steaming briefly. Medium and large carrots may be halved, quartered, cut in sticks or slices. Boil, steam or stir fry them. To glaze carrots, cut them into fine strips and cook them in a little water with a small amount of salt and pepper and a knob of butter. By the time the carrots are just tender the water should have evaporated, leaving the vegetables coated in a glossy glaze. A little sugar may be added when cooking old carrots. The carrots should be stirred or the pan shaken often to prevent them burning.

Small new carrots take about 5-7 minutes to boil until tender; older carrots take 10-15 minutes, depending on size.

Carrots may be cooked for slightly longer, then mashed with swede or potatoes. Well cooked carrots may also be rubbed through a sieve or puréed in a food processor, then enriched with a little butter and cream.

Carrots are an essential flavouring vegetable for soups, stocks and stews. They are also valuable in mince dishes and they make delicious soup. Grated carrot is a useful salad ingredient and this versatile vegetable may also be used in preserves and sweet dishes, such as carrot cake or a lightly spiced Indian dessert. Carrot marmalade was a clever war-time invention as a substitute for orange preserve: the finely cut carrots were flavoured with orange rind and juice and cooked in syrup.

CAULIFLOWER

Green and purple cauliflowers are now available in addition to the more familiar white-headed vegetables, and very small cauliflowers are cultivated as individual portions.

Look for firm, white unblemished vegetables that are neatly packed with a small amount of green leaves. Avoid soft, rubbery cauliflowers or any that have very long stalks and loose heads. Cauliflowers that are not perfectly white are not necessarily inferior in flavour, provided that they are good quality in other respects. It is as well, however, to avoid any that have softening brown patches or have been trimmed.

Cauliflowers may be cooked whole or divided into florets. Boiling, steaming or stir frying are the most common cooking methods. Used raw or briefly blanched, cauliflower florets make very good additions to salads, and they may be coated in cheese-flavoured choux pastry, then deep fried to make delicious fritters.

Overcooked cauliflower is soft, watery and tasteless. About 5-7 minutes is sufficient boiling time for florets and a whole cauliflower should not be boiled for more than 10-15 minutes. Steaming is a particularly good cooking method for cauliflower. For florets allow the same time as for boiling; when steaming a whole cauliflower increase the cooking time to 20-30 minutes, depending on size.

Serve cauliflower plain, with a little butter; coated with a cheese sauce; or topped with fried breadcrumbs. Cauliflower is excellent in vegetable curry, it makes good soup (particularly topped with cheese) or it may be puréed and enriched with cream or fromage frais.

CELERIAC

This is a cream-coloured root vegetable, about the same size as a swede and with a similarly thick skin. It has a delicate flavour reminiscent of celery. To prepare celeriac, peel and trim it, then plunge it straight into a bowl of acidulated water as it discolours quickly.

Cut celeriac into neat cubes or sticks and cook in a saucepan of boiling water until tender – about 8-10 minutes for small pieces. If preferred, the vegetable may be cut into large chunks and boiled for 15-20 minutes, then mashed with butter and pepper. Boiling is a better option than steaming, although finely cut celeriac may be steamed in packets of mixed vegetables or as a flavouring for fish and poultry.

Celeriac may also be served raw, usually coarsely grated or finely shredded. If adding it to long-cooked soups and stews, put it in towards the end of the cooking time or it may become very soft. It also makes good soup. Plain cooked celeriac (in chunks or slices) is delicious coated with cheese sauce.

CELERY

A versatile vegetable for serving raw or cooked, or using as a flavouring ingredient. Look for firm, unblemished heads of celery with leaves that are bright and crisp. Stalks with large ribs may be stringy. Trimmed celery hearts are also available for braising whole. Canned celery hearts are a useful storecupboard standby for wrapping in cooked ham and coating in cheese sauce as a supper dish.

The top of the head and stalk ends should be cut off but not discarded. The leaves and stalk tops may be used as part of a bouquet garni or they may be reserved for garnish. Cut up small, they are perfectly good in salads, soups and stews.

Remove stalks from the celery as required, scrub them well and cut off any blemished parts. Slice the celery or cut it into lengths for cooking. If a recipe calls for diced or chopped celery, cut the stalks into thin strips lengthways before slicing them across into small pieces. Cut into very thin strips, about 5 cm/2 inches long, then soaked for about 30 minutes in iced water, celery is excellent in salads.

Serve lengths of raw celery with dips or cheese. Braise lengths or hearts with a small amount of sautéed onion and diced carrot in a little stock or wine. Cook for about 40-60 minutes, depending on size and age, until the celery is tender. The cooking juices may be thickened with beurre manié to serve as an accompanying sauce.

Stir frying is a good cooking method for celery. The sticks should be sliced thinly or cut into fine strips. Slicing at an angle is an Oriental technique popular for stir fries.

Celery may also be cooked by boiling and steaming. Boil for 10-20 minutes, depending on size and age; or allow up to 30 minutes' steaming time. Celery is delicious in soups, sauces and stews.

CHICORY

Small oval heads of pale, closely packed leaves tipped with yellow, chicory has a slightly bitter flavour. It may be used raw in salads or braised until tender.

Trim off the stalk end of each head and wash well. Cut the head across into slices for mixing into salads or separate the leaves and use them as a base for serving a variety of dishes. The whole leaves may also be served with dips.

Chicory may be boiled in a saucepan of acidulated water until tender – about 15-20 minutes but the preferred cooking method is braising. Cook a small amount of finely chopped onion in butter or oil, then turn the chicory heads in the fat. Pour in stock or wine to come about a third to halfway up the heads. Cover and braise for 30-60 minutes depending on the size of the chicory heads, until tender throughout. Turn once or twice. The cooking juices may be thickened and poured over the chicory.

The American name for chicory is endive.

CHINESE LEAVES

Also known as Chinese cabbage. A tall, fairly loosely packed vegetable consisting mainly of tender crunchy stalks edged by pale green-yellow leaves. The vegetable has a mild, cabbage-like flavour. It may be shredded for use in salads or stir fries. Thicker slices may be added to sauced dishes, usually well-seasoned Chinese braised mixtures, and cooked very briefly.

Overcooking gives limp, tasteless results.

COURGETTES

Both green and yellow varieties are available. Look for firm, unblemished vegetables. Trim off the ends and peel the courgettes if liked, although they may be cooked with the peel on. Cut courgettes into slices, chunks or sticks, or grate them. They may be halved and baked with a topping, or their middles scooped out and a stuffing added.

Basic cooking methods include steaming, braising, baking, sautéing, stir frying and shallow frying. Although courgettes may be boiled, this cooking method does not do them justice as even brief boiling tends to oversoften the delicate flesh. Coated in batter or breadcrumbs, courgettes are also delicious deep fried. In Italy and America, where the vegetable is known as *zucchini*, the flowers are regarded as a delicacy and are frequently coated in light batter and deep fried.

For steaming, wrap sliced courgettes in foil; cook for about 10 minutes. Sautéing and stir frying are excellent methods. Thinly cut vegetables will require 2-5 minutes. Baking is a practical method when the courgettes are served with a baked dish; simply dot them with butter, sprinkle them with salt and pepper and cook in a covered dish for 15-30 minutes at 180°C/350°F/gas 4. Braise courgettes with onions and tomatoes or other vegetables, allowing about 20 minutes' cooking, or up to 45 minutes depending on the way in which the vegetables are cut and the other ingredients.

CUCUMBER

Although they are usually eaten raw in salads, cucumbers are also good braised. But firm, bright medium-sized cucumbers. Avoid any with very dark, thick-looking skins, as these may have large seeds, poor texture and a strong flavour.

Cucumbers may be peeled, partially peeled or served with the peel on for salads. The classic preparation is to slice the cucumber very thinly, sprinkle it with a little salt and allow it to drain in a colander for 10 minutes before use. This extracts excess liquid from the vegetable. Having been prepared in this way, the cucumber slices may be dried on absorbent kitchen paper and used to make delicious sandwiches. It may also be topped with a little chopped mint or snipped chives for serving as a plain salad. An oil and vinegar dressing, or cider vinegar, are classic additions.

Grated or diced cucumber may be mixed with plain yogurt to make a dip or side dish for spicy food. Add garlic and a little chopped onion to make *tzatziki*, a Greek starter served with plenty of crusty bread.

Peel cucumber before cooking, then cut it into 5 cm/2 inch lengths. The seeds are usually scooped out. Braise trimmed cucumber in stock for about 20 minutes. Sticks of cucumber may be stir fried briefly with other vegetables.

ENDIVE

This resembles a curly lettuce. It has firm leaves which are usually pale yellow-green with darker green tips. To prepare endive, trim off the stalk, wash well and use in salads.

The American term for endive is chicory.

FENNEL

Florence fennel is a bulbous vegetable with a texture like that of celery and an aniseed flavour. There are usually a few fronds of feathery leaves attached to the trimmed stalks at the top of the bulbs – these may be reserved for garnishing or used in cooking.

Trim away tough stalk ends, then thoroughly wash and slice fennel for use in salads. The bulbs may be braised as for celery, either whole or as halves and will take about 1-1¼ hours to cook.

KOHLRABI

This is the swollen stem of a member of the cabbage family. It has a flavour slightly similar to swede. Either purple or green skinned, and ranging in size from that of a large potato to a small swede, kohlrabi may be served raw or cooked.

Peel the vegetable and place it in a bowl of acidulated water. For serving raw, kohlrabi should be grated or cut into small pieces. Small kohlrabi may be boiled whole; larger vegetables should be sliced or cut into chunks. Cook in boiling water for

15-45 minutes or until tender. Follow the longer time if cooking whole vegetables.

Sticks of kohlrabi may be stir fried with other vegetables, such as leeks or onions. Diced or cubed kohlrabi may be added to soups and stews.

LEEKS

These vary considerably in size. Look for firm, well-formed vegetables with a good ratio of white to green. Trim off the ends and slice, then wash in a colander, separating the slices into rings. Alternatively, slit the leeks three-quarters through down their length, then open each one out and hold it under cold running water to wash away all the grit.

Leeks may be boiled, steamed, fried, stewed, braised or baked. Allow 10-20 minutes for boiling or steaming, the longer time for large lengths or small whole vegetables. Drain well and serve coated with cheese sauce. Alternatively, top with grated cheese and breadcrumbs and grill until brown.

Fry sliced leeks in butter until tender but not soft – about 15 minutes – or stir fry them with other vegetables. Add leeks to soups and stews or use them to flavour stocks.

LETTUCE

There are a wide variety of lettuces on offer all year. These are the most common types:

Round The traditional British salad leaf; a loosely packed bright vegetable with a small heart. Flavour and texture are not particularly interesting.

Cos Lettuce A tall, dark-leafed lettuce with crisp firm leaves and a good flavour.

Webb's Wonderful A round lettuce with slightly wrinkled, crisp dark leaves, and a firm heart.

Iceberg A tightly packed, pale green lettuce with very crisp leaves and a good flavour.

Lamb's Lettuce Small oval-leafed plants, resembling immature round lettuce but darker.

Lollo Rosso/Lollo Biondo A frilly, firm-textured lettuce which is loosely packed. The lollo rosso variety has dark leaves fringed with deep red, whereas the biondo type has pale-edged leaves.

Wash all lettuce well and discard any tough or damaged stalks. It is traditional to shred lettuce by hand rather than to cut it with a knife, but this is a matter for personal taste. Never prepare lettuce a long time before serving.

Although lettuce is usually served raw, it is also delicious when braised with a little finely chopped onion in stock or wine. Fresh peas braised with lettuce is a classic French dish. Allow about 30 minutes' gentle cooking in a small amount of liquid and a covered pan or dish.

MARROW

From the same family as courgettes and pumpkin, marrow has a tough skin and soft, fibrous centre with lots of seeds surounded by firm flesh. Cut the vegetable in half or slice it into rings, then remove the soft flesh and seeds before peeling thickly.

Marrow may be baked, braised, steamed, stir fried or boiled, the latter being the least interesting cooking method. Overcooked marrow is watery and mushy, particularly when boiled. Baking or braising with onions and herbs are the best methods. Chunks of marrow (about 5 cm/2 inches in size) take about 40 minutes to bake at 180°C/350°F/gas 4, depending on the other ingredients added. They may also be braised for about 30 minutes with onions and herbs, either in their own juice or with the addition of tomatoes or a little wine or cider.

Stuffings for marrow range from meat

mixtures to rice or breadcrumb stuffings. Rings or halves may be stuffed, or the vegetable may be laid on its side and a thick slice removed from the top as a lid. The hollowed-out marrow may then be stuffed and the 'lid' replaced. Bake the stuffed marrow, until tender, then remove the 'lid' to allow the stuffing to brown. At 180°C/350°F/gas 4, a medium-sized whole marrow will require 1¼-1¾ hours to bake, whereas rings cook in 45 minutes-1¼ hours, depending on size and filling.

Marrow may also be used as a key ingredient for making chutney. It is usually combined with fruit, such as apples, and lots of onions for flavour. It may also be cooked with ginger to add bulk to jam.

MUSHROOMS

Most of the mushrooms available in green-grocers and supermarkets are the same variety – they differ only in the stage of development at which they have been harvested. Fully open or flat mushrooms traditionally known as field mushrooms are the most mature. They may be re-cognized by their dark gills and large heads. Flat mushrooms have good flavour but tend to discolour dishes to which they are added, so are usually used for grilling and stuffing.

Cup mushrooms or open mushrooms are slightly paler in colour and they have a lip around the edge. Useful for stuffing.

Button mushrooms may be fully closed or partially closed, with little of the gill area showing. They vary in size; very small buttons are perfect for adding whole to casseroles and sauces. Button mushrooms are ideal for sauces and pale dishes which require a delicate colour and flavour.

In addition to the grades of cultivated mushroom described above, at least three other types of fresh mushroom are commonly available.

Chestnut mushrooms have a darker skin than ordinary mushrooms and a more pronounced flavour. They are usually sold as large buttons.

Oyster mushrooms are flat and pale creamy-yellow in colour with a soft texture and delicate flavour. They break easily and require very little cooking.

Shiitake are strongly flavoured mushrooms from China and Japan. They are popular in Oriental cooking. They are usually sold dried in delicatessens and Oriental super-markets, when their flavour is very pro-nounced, but are also available fresh. The fresh mushrooms are darker than cultivated British field mushrooms and they have a firmer, slightly more rubbery texture.

Wild mushrooms are a separate issue from cultivated varieties. Before they are gathered, a specialist source of information should be consulted to avoid any danger of consuming a poisonous species. Some specialist stores sell wild mushrooms but they are most commonly available dried from delicatessens.

Cultivated mushrooms do not require peeling. Trim tough stalks from shiitake or oyster mushrooms. Rinse mushrooms, gills down under slowly running cold water, rubbing them gently. Alternatively, simply wipe them with dampened absorbent kitchen paper. Never leave mushrooms to soak as they will absorb water, ruining both texture and flavour.

Mushrooms may be brushed with a little fat and grilled, flat or on skewers. They may also be poached in a little milk, stock or wine for a few minutes. Alternatively, whole or cut-up mushrooms may be shallow fried or stir fried in oil or butter, either whole or cut up. Coated with egg and breadcrumbs, dipped in choux pastry or batter, button mushrooms are delicious deep fried. They are also excellent baked particularly when topped with breadcrumbs and cheese.

For frying or poaching, allow about 5-15 minutes' cooking time. Allow 15-30 minutes for baking, depending on the topping or stuffing. Grill mushrooms briefly for about 5 minutes, gills uppermost.

Pale mushrooms may be added to sauces and soups; all types are suitable for flavouring stews, the choice depending on the colour of the stew.

OKRA

Also known as ladies' fingers, these pale green ridged pods vary in size, the smaller ones being the most tender. Look for unblemished whole vegetables with the stalks intact. Trim off the stalk ends and wash well. The okra pods may be cooked whole or sliced before cooking. Do not prepare the vegetable too far in advance of cooking as slices may discolour.

Okra contains a gum-like substance that seeps out of the pods during long cooking to thicken stews and braised dishes. Typical dishes with okra include *gumbo*, a classic Creole stew, and spiced okra with onions, which is often served as a side dish in Indian restaurants. Okra may also be stuffed and braised or baked.

Cooking times for okra should either be brief, using fierce heat, or long enough to tenderize the pods. Sliced okra may be coated in flour and seasonings or spices, then shallow or deep fried for a few minutes until browned. Sliced okra may be braised briefly or added to casseroles and stews towards the end of cooking; however, the vegetable quickly becomes slimy when sliced and long-cooked by moist methods. Whole pods may be braised with onions, tomatoes and garlic until tender – about 15-30 minutes, depending on the size and age of pods.

ONIONS

Large Spanish onions are the mildest variety. These are ideal for boiling whole and serving with butter or a sauce, or for stuffing. The medium-sized common onions, most often used in cooking, are stronger in flavour. Small, pickling or button onions have a strong flavour. They may be boiled and coated with sauce or peeled and added whole to casseroles. Cocktail, or silverskin, onions are tiny. They are sometimes available fresh but are most often sold pickled in vinegar. Spring – or salad – onions have not formed bulbs. They have a dense white base leading to hollow green ends. Once trimmed, the whole of the onion may be used raw or in cooking. Shallots and Welsh onions are small onions. Each shallot consists of two or three cloves, similar in shape to garlic cloves, clumped together inside the papery skin. They are mild in flavour and may be peeled and chopped or used whole. The tops from fresh young shallots may also be used in cooking.

Onions are often fried briefly as a preliminary cooking stage in more complicated dishes. The aim is to soften the onion but not brown it, and the cooking process will only be completed when the onion has been incorporated with other ingredients and cooked until tender. Browning onions by frying requires significantly longer cooking, depending on the number cooked. Onions shrink significantly when fried until brown, and this should be done over moderate heat, turning occasionally, for about 20-30 minutes until the onions are golden and evenly cooked. If fried by this method they will be tender and flavoursome. Onions that are browned quickly over too high a heat, will not be cooked through, but simply scorched outside.

Onions may also be boiled or steamed. Allow 30 minutes for small vegetables or up to 1¼ hours for large onions. Large onions may be baked whole, washed but unpeeled, until very tender, then split and filled or topped with butter.

PARSNIPS

Look for firm, unblemished parsnips. To prepare them, peel, then cut them in half, in chunks or slices. They may be boiled, steamed or roasted.

Chunks of parsnip will be tender when boiled for 10 minutes; larger pieces require about 20 minutes. When tender, drain well and serve with a soured cream sauce, or mash with butter and pepper.

To roast parsnips arrange them around a joint of meat or in a separate dish and brush with fat. Allow about 45 minutes-1¼ hours at 180-190°C/350-375°F/gas 4-5, until tender and golden.

Parsnips are delicious in mixed vegetable curry and may also be added to soups and stews. Parsnip fritters may be made by coating par-boiled vegetables in batter and deep frying them until golden.

PEAS

Fresh peas are in season from May to September. Look for bright, fresh plump pods. The peas inside should not be bullet-hard or very large as they can become very dry in texture and flavour. Allow about 350-400 g/12-14 oz per person as a good deal of weight is lost to the pods.

Split the pods over a colander and slide the peas out using a fingertip. Wash well, then add to a small amount of just boiling water. Cook for 7-10 minutes, until the peas are tender. Alternatively, peas may be steamed for 15-20 minutes. It is traditional to add a sprig of mint to the water when cooking peas.

Mange Tout The name means 'eat all', a fitting description. Mange tout are flat pea pods with tiny peas just forming inside. The entire pod is edible, excluding the stalk, which is trimmed. Mange tout may be cooked in boiling water for 2-3 minutes, or steamed for up to 5 minutes, but are at their best when stir fried for 3-5 minutes.

Sugar Snaps These are small peas enclosed in edible pods. They have an excellent flavour. Everything is edible except the stalk, which should be trimmed. Cook sugar snaps in a saucepan of boiling water for 3-5 minutes, or by steaming for about 5 minutes. They are more substantial and flavoursome than mange tout.

PEPPERS

Large sweet or bell peppers come from the capsicum family. They are also known as pimento (or pimientos when bottled). The most common type is the green pepper, which changes colour as it ripens, first to yellow and then to red. A variety of other colours is also available, including white and purple-black.

To prepare a pepper, remove the stalk end and cut out the core from the inside. Discard the ribs, pith and seeds. The pepper shell may then be washed clean and drained.

Peppers are used in a variety of ways: they may be eaten raw in salads or crudités; lightly cooked in stir fries; stuffed and baked or braised; grilled on skewers; or long stewed with meat, poultry or other vegetables.

When raw they have a crunchy texture and fresh flavour, but when cooked they soften and their flavour mellows.

POTATOES

These may loosely be divided into new and old, the former being the thin-skinned, spring crop for immediate consumption and the latter being the second crop of thicker-skinned potatoes grown for winter storage. The choice is always changing, with imported varieties and new strains constantly being developed.

Avoid buying or eating potatoes that have turned green. Cut out any eyes and sprouting areas from potatoes in preparation. Store potatoes in a cool, dry place in thick brown paper bags that exclude all light.

Although new potatoes are now available all year, Jerseys are the traditional 'first' new potatoes in the shops. Imported early in the year, from Christmas or even before, these have a fine flavour but are expensive. Small, waxy and firm, they are ideal for steaming or boiling. Small, waxy 'salad' potatoes are also available all year at a price.

The following are good all round, old potatoes for boiling, mashing, baking and frying: King Edward, Redskin, Maris Piper, Pentland Hawk, Pentland Ivory and Desirée. Majestic tend to break up easily when boiled, so they are better for baking and frying. Pentland Squire are floury and good for baking, as are Cara, because they are large and even in size and shape.

Boiling Peel the potatoes, if liked, or scrub them well. Remove all eyes and blemishes and any green areas. Cut large potatoes in half or into quarters and place in a saucepan. Cover with cold water, add salt if wished, and bring to the boil. Reduce the heat, partly cover the pan and cook for about 20 minutes. Small chunks cook in 10-15 minutes (useful for mashing); larger, unpeeled, potatoes take somewhat longer. New potatoes cook more quickly, in 10-15 minutes.

Baking An easy cooking method, this is discussed, with serving suggestions, on page 308. Floury potatoes – the sort that do not boil well – give best results for baking. Scrub the potatoes well and prick them all over to prevent them from bursting. Potatoes may be brushed with oil if wished.

Roasting Peeled potatoes, cut in halves or quarters, may either be roasted from raw or par-boiled for 5-10 minutes, dusted with plain flour, and then added to the hot fat in the roasting tin. They should be coated in hot fat and turned once or twice during cooking. For crisp results, raw potatoes will take 1-1½ hours, depending on the size of the potatoes and the oven temperature. Par-boiled potatoes require about 1 hour at 190°C/375°F/gas 5.

Chipped Potatoes Cut the thoroughly scrubbed, or washed and peeled, potatoes into thick fingers and deep fry in oil at 190°C/375°F until just beginning to brown. Lift the chips out of the oil and drain them well. Bring the oil back to the original cooking temperature. Lower the chips into the oil again and cook for a couple of minutes more, until crisp and golden. Drain well on absorbent kitchen paper and serve at once.

PUMPKIN

Pumpkin belongs to the same family as marrow. Pumpkins vary enormously in size. Small ones may be sold whole, but you are more likely to encounter wedges cut from a large vegetable.

The central soft core of seeds should be removed and the orange-coloured flesh thickly peeled. The flesh is firmer than marrow and is delicious roasted, baked or braised with onions, herbs and bacon and a cheese topping for about an hour. Pumpkin may also be boiled and mashed or steamed for 30-45 minutes and puréed for use in savoury and sweet dishes, particularly the American sweet and spicy pumpkin pie. Pumpkin also makes good soup.

RADISHES

These are usually eaten raw in salads or as crudités; however, large white radishes are also combined with other ingredients in stir fries and steamed Oriental-style dishes.

Small round red radishes are the most common, but the long white radish known as mooli or daikon (in Japanese cooking) is becoming increasingly popular. Red radishes require no preparation other than washing, topping and tailing. Large white radishes must be peeled. Very large, old white radishes can be fibrous, stringy and unpleasant to eat even when cut fine.

SALSIFY AND SCORZONERA

These root vegetables are in season from October to May. Salsify is a creamy colour and scorzonera is black. Although both have a delicate flavour, scorzonera is considered salsify's superior.

Do not use a carbon steel knife to prepare these vegetables and cook them as soon as possible after preparation, or they may discolour. The moment the vegetables have been trimmed and peeled, put them into acidulated water. To cook, cut into lengths or fingers and add to a saucepan of salted boiling water to which a little lemon juice has been added. Cook for 20-30 minutes, or until tender. Drain and serve with butter or with a coating sauce such as Béchamel or Hollandaise.

Salsify or scorzonera which is three-quarters cooked by boiling, may be drained and fried in butter before serving or coated in a light batter and deep fried to make fritters.

SEAKALE

Resembling celery stalks surrounded by dark green, tough, frilly leaves, seakale grows wild on the beaches of South East England between December and May and is also and found in Western Europe. Although it is also cultivated, it is seldom available in the shops. To prepare seakale, wash it thoroughly and trim off the thick, tough stalk. It should be freshly cooked in a small amount of boiling water for about 15 minutes, or until tender, then thoroughly drained and used like spinach.

SORREL

Sorrel is used both as a vegetable and a herb. There are many varieties, some quite bitter. It should be treated as spinach, with a little sugar added to taste during cooking to counteract the natural acidity.

SPINACH

There are winter and summer varieties of this versatile, easy-to-cook vegetable. Since it shrinks considerably on cooking, allow about 225 g/8 oz fresh spinach per portion.

Wash the leaves well and trim off any tough stalk ends. Pack the wet leaves into a large saucepan and cover with a tight-fitting lid. Place over moderate to high heat and cook for about 3 minutes, shaking the pan often, until the spinach has wilted. Lower the heat slightly, if necessary, and cook for 3-5 minutes more, or until the spinach is tender. Drain well in a sieve, squeezing out all the liquid if the vegetable is to be chopped.

Serve spinach tossed with butter and pepper or a little nutmeg. It may be used in a variety of pasta dishes, pies, quiches, soufflés and soups. Spinach is delicious topped with scrambled or poached eggs, poached fish or grilled chicken.

SQUASHES

Squash is an American term applied to marrow and a wide variety of vegetables of the same family. Availability in Britain and Europe is somewhat unpredictable; however these are a few of the main types:

Butternut Squash A small vegetable with pale, beige-peach coloured skin and deep orange-coloured flesh. The halved vegetable has a small central hollow for seeds, so that it resembles a large avocado. The whole or halved squash is usually baked.

Crookneck This is a large, rough-skinned, long-bodied yellow squash. As its name suggests it has a long, narrow, curved neck. The flesh may be treated as marrow.

Hubbard Squash A melon-shaped gourd with rough green skin, this may be treated as marrow once peeled.

Custard Marrow A pale, flat, fluted squash.

Spaghetti Squash Oval, yellow-skinned squash about the size of a large yellow melon. It gets its name from the flesh, which resembles spaghetti when cooked. The squash should be boiled or steamed whole, or halved and wrapped in foil, for 20-50 minutes, depending on size. When cooked, halve the squash if necessary, discard the seeds from the middle and use a fork to scoop out the strands of flesh. These are at their best when still slightly crunchy. They have plenty of flavour and are delicious topped with butter and cheese or any sauce suitable for pasta.

SWEDES

Large, inexpensive root vegetables with thick skin and pale orange flesh. Wash, trim and peel thickly, then cut into chunks for cooking. Boil for 20-30 minutes, or until tender, then drain thoroughly and mash with butter and pepper. This is the traditional accompaniment for haggis. Swedes may also be mashed with carrots or potatoes.

The diced vegetable is excellent in soups and stews. Puréed cooked swede may be used in soufflé mixtures.

SWEETCORN

Corn cobs are surrounded by silky threads and an outer covering of leafy husks, which must be removed before cooking unless the corn is to be cooked on a barbecue. The kernels are pale when raw, becoming more yellow in colour on cooking.

Place the corn cobs in a pan with water to cover and bring to the boil. Do not add salt as this toughens the kernels. Simmer for about 10 minutes, or until the corn kernels are tender and come away easily from the cob. Drain well and serve topped with a little butter. Corn holders – pronged utensils inserted at either end of the cob – make it possible to eat these tasty vegetables without burning your fingers.

For using in salads or other dishes, the cooked kernels may be scraped off the cobs using a kitchen knife. It is usually simpler, however, to use frozen or canned sweetcorn kernels, both of which are of excellent quality.

Whole cobs may be baked in their husks or barbecued. Carefully fold back the husks and remove the silky threads, then wash well and drain. Fold the husks back over the corn. Cook over medium coals or roast in the oven at 190°C/375°F/gas 5 for about 40 minutes, or until the kernels are tender.

SWISS CHARD

The leaves of this vegetable may be cooked exactly as for spinach, giving very similar results. The tender stalks, which resemble thin, wide celery sticks, are delicious when lightly cooked in boiling water and served with butter. Allow about 5 minutes to cook tender stalks. Serve them as a separate vegetable or starter, perhaps with Hollandaise or with some grated Parmesan cheese.

SWEET POTATOES

In spite of their name, these are not potatoes at all, but are red-skinned, large vegetables with pale orange flesh and a slightly sweet flavour. Sweet potatoes may be baked or boiled in their skins. To boil, allow about 30-40 minutes, depending on size. Bake as for ordinary potatoes (page 308). Once cooked, peel and cut into cubes, then toss with butter and a little nutmeg. Alternatively, mash with butter and nutmeg or mace.

Sweet potatoes are used in a variety of sweet and savoury dishes.

TOMATOES

Although tomatoes are technically fruit, they are used as a vegetable. Of the many varieties available, all may be used raw and many are ideal for cooking. Freshly picked sun-ripened tomatoes are delicious, but it is worth investigating some of the other varieties.

Cherry Tomatoes Very small tomatoes, these can have an excellent sweet flavour when ripe. However, some purchased tomatoes can be sharp and lacking in flavour. Ideal for salads or for skewering with other ingredients for kebabs.

Marmande, Beef or Beefsteak Tomatoes Very large tomatoes that are ideal for stuffing. They should be a good deep red when ripe. Sun-ripened large tomatoes have an outstanding flavour. Sadly this is seldom found in purchased fruit, which is usually picked well before it is ripe.

Cooking methods for tomatoes include grilling and frying. They are usually cut in half – or in slices for speed – are traditionally served with grilled meat or fish, mixed grill or as part of a traditional cooked breakfast. Grilled or fried tomatoes on toast make a good snack or light meal.

Baked tomatoes are usually scooped out and filled with a rice- or breadcrumb-based stuffing or a minced meat mixture.

Plum Tomatoes Deep red, oval, small to medium-sized fruit. Plum tomatoes have a good flavour and are valued for cooking and as the prime ingredient in tomato purée. They are also good in salads.

Yellow Tomatoes Large or cherry-sized, these tomatoes are sweet when ripe but can lack flavour when picked too early. They should be a rich yellow colour. Used mainly raw, yellow tomatoes may be cooked with yellow peppers, yellow courgettes and white aubergines in a pale version of ratatouille.

TURNIPS

Small, round summer turnips have delicate flavour. They are ideal for cooking whole and serving as a vegetable accompaniment. Larger main crop turnips are better suited to dicing or cutting into chunks and using in soups and stews.

To prepare turnips, trim off the ends and remove the peel; small young vegetables require thin peeling. Cook small whole turnips in a saucepan of boiling acidulated water for about 15 minutes, or until tender. Drain well and toss with butter and parsley or serve coated with cheese, Béchamel or Hollandaise sauce.

Larger turnips may be boiled, drained and mashed or puréed. Matchstick strips of turnip are suitable for stir frying or baking in foil with parsnips and carrots cut to a similar size. Small, young turnips may also be parboiled, then glazed with the minimum of liquid and a little butter as for carrots.

The leaves of fresh young turnips may be trimmed from their stalks and cooked as for cabbage.

YAMS

These tubers resemble large potatoes, with white, floury flesh. Scrub and boil yams in their skin.

There are a number of vegetables available which belong to the yam and cassava family, including small dark and hairy eddoes. These vegetables must not be eaten raw as they contain natural toxins: in fact, prepared cassava should be soaked in water for about 30 minutes before cooking.

Note More information and cooking methods, including microwave instructions are listed, where appropriate, under individual recipes.

GARLANDED ASPARAGUS

30 asparagus spears
75 g/3 oz butter
salt and pepper
50 g/2 oz Parmesan cheese, grated
4 egg yolks, unbroken
butter for frying

Set the oven at 200°C/400°F/gas 6. Prepare and cook the asparagus (see page 195). Drain thoroughly and place in an ovenproof dish. Melt half the butter in a small frying pan and spoon it over the top. Sprinkle with salt and pepper to taste and top with the Parmesan cheese. Bake for 15 minutes or until the cheese topping is golden brown.

Meanwhile, add the remaining butter to the frying pan and melt over gentle heat. Add the egg yolks, taking care not to break them, and cook gently until just set outside, basting often. Using an egg slice, carefully lift them out of the pan, draining off excess fat, and arrange them around the asparagus. Serve at once.

SERVES 4

ARTICHOKES AU GRATIN

675 g/1½ lb Jerusalem artichokes
50 g/2 oz Cheddar cheese, grated
25 g/1 oz fresh white breadcrumbs

CHEESE SAUCE
40 g/1½ oz butter
40 g/1½ oz plain flour
450 ml/¾ pint milk
salt and pepper
40 g/1½ oz Cheddar cheese, grated

Prepare the artichokes (see Mrs Beeton's Tip) and cook them in a saucepan of boiling water for 10-15 minutes until tender.

Meanwhile, make the sauce. Melt the butter in a saucepan. Stir in the flour and cook over low heat for 2-3 minutes, without allowing the mixture to colour. Gradually add the milk, stirring constantly until the mixture boils and thickens. Stir in the grated cheese.

Drain the artichokes, tip them into a flameproof dish and pour the cheese sauce over the top. Mix lightly. Combine the cheese and breadcrumbs in a small bowl, sprinkle the mixture over the artichokes and place under a moderate grill until golden brown. Alternatively, brown the topping in a preheated 220°C/425°F/gas 7 oven for about 10 minutes.

SERVES 4

MRS BEETON'S TIP Wash the artichokes and peel them thinly. Artichokes discolour readily, so put them into acidulated water (water to which lemon juice has been added) as soon as they are peeled. It is a good idea to cook them in salted acidulated water too. Large artichokes may be cut into smaller pieces, or knobbles may be broken off, before cooking. They may be sliced or cooked, in which case they cook quite quickly – about 10 minutes. As with potatoes, it is not essential to peel artichokes before cooking; however they should be thoroughly scrubbed with a stiff brush.

FRIED AUBERGINES WITH ONION

2 aubergines
salt and pepper
50 g/2 oz plain flour
cayenne pepper
oil for frying
1 onion, finely chopped
30 ml/2 tbsp chopped parsley to serve

Cut the ends off the aubergines, slice them thinly and put them in a colander. Sprinkle generously with salt. Set aside for 30 minutes, then rinse, drain and dry thoroughly on absorbent kitchen paper.

Mix the flour with a pinch each of salt and cayenne. Add the aubergine slices, toss until lightly coated, then shake off excess flour.

Heat a little oil in a large frying pan, add the onion and cook over moderate heat for about 10 minutes until golden. Using a slotted spoon, transfer to a small bowl and keep hot. Add the aubergine slices, a few at a time, to the hot oil in the pan. Fry until soft and lightly browned, turning once during cooking. As the slices brown, remove them from the pan with a fish slice, arrange on a heated serving dish and keep hot. Add extra oil and heat it as necessary between batches of aubergine slices.

When all the aubergine slices have been fried, sprinkle them with the fried onion and the chopped parsley. Serve at once.

SERVES 6

BROAD BEANS WITH CREAM SAUCE

250 ml/8 fl oz chicken stock
15 ml/1 tbsp chopped fresh herbs
   (parsley, thyme, sage, savory)
1 kg/2¼ lb broad beans, shelled
1 egg yolk
150 ml/¼ pint single cream
salt and pepper

Combine the stock and herbs in a saucepan. Bring to the boil, add the beans and cook for 5-15 minutes until tender. Lower the heat to a bare simmer.

Beat the egg yolk with the cream in a small bowl. Add 30 ml/2 tbsp of the hot stock and mix well, then pour the contents of the bowl into the saucepan. Heat gently, stirring all the time, until the sauce thickens slightly. Do not allow the mixture to boil or it will curdle. Add salt and pepper to taste and serve.

SERVES 4

BEANS WITH SOURED CREAM

fat for greasing
450 g/1 lb runner beans
150 ml/¼ pint soured cream
1.25 ml/¼ tsp grated nutmeg
1.25 ml/¼ tsp caraway seeds
salt and pepper
50 g/2 oz butter
50 g/2 oz fresh white breadcrumbs

Set the oven at 200°C/400°F/gas 6. Grease a 1 litre/1¾ pint baking dish. Wash the beans, string them if necessary and slice them thinly. Cook in boiling water for 3-7 minutes until cooked to taste. Alternatively, cook in a steamer over boiling water. Drain thoroughly.

Combine the soured cream, nutmeg and caraway seeds in a bowl. Stir in salt and pepper to taste. Add the beans and toss well together. Spoon the mixture into the prepared baking dish.

Melt the butter in a small frying pan, add the breadcrumbs and fry over gentle heat for 2-3 minutes. Sprinkle the mixture over the beans. Bake for 20-30 minutes or until the topping is crisp and golden.

SERVES 3 TO 4

☀ **MICROWAVE TIP** The first stage of this recipe – cooking the runner beans – may be done in the microwave. Put the beans in a dish with 60 ml/4 tbsp water. Cover loosely and cook on High for 10-12 minutes, stirring once or twice. Take care when removing the cover to avoid being scalded by the steam.

STIR-FRIED BEANS WITH SAVORY

450 g/1 lb French beans, trimmed
salt and pepper
15 ml/1 tbsp butter
15 ml/1 tbsp oil
15 ml/1 tbsp finely chopped summer
    savory
4 spring onions, thinly sliced

Cook the beans in boiling salted water for 2 minutes, then drain, refresh under cold running water and drain again.

Melt the butter in the oil in a large frying pan or wok. Add the beans and half the savory. Stir fry for 3 minutes. Add the spring onions, with salt and pepper to taste, and stir fry for 2-3 minutes more. The beans should be tender but still crisp. Sprinkle with the remaining savory and serve at once.

SERVES 4

VARIATION

Use only 225 g/8 oz beans and add 225 g/8 oz sliced button mushrooms with the onions. Substitute 10 ml/2 tsp fennel seeds for the savory, if liked. A few water chestnuts, thinly sliced, may be added for extra crunch.

POLISH BEETROOT

30 ml/2 tbsp butter
1 small onion, finely chopped
30 ml/2 tbsp plain flour
250 ml/8 fl oz plain yogurt
675 g/1½ lb cooked beetroot, peeled and
    grated
30 ml/2 tbsp finely grated horseradish
salt and pepper
sugar (optional)
15 ml/1 tbsp chopped parsley to garnish

Melt the butter in a saucepan, add the onion and fry for 4-6 minutes until soft but not coloured. Stir in the flour and cook for 1 minute, then lower the heat and gradually stir in the yogurt.

Bring to the boil, stirring constantly until the sauce thickens. Add the beetroot and horseradish and heat thoroughly. Season to taste with salt and pepper, and add a little sugar, if liked. Serve hot, garnished with the parsley.

SERVES 6

BRUSSELS SPROUTS WITH CHESTNUTS

This is a classic accompaniment to the Christmas turkey. The slightly sweet flavour of the chestnuts is the perfect foil for the Brussels sprouts.

225 g/8 oz chestnuts, shelled (see Mrs
  Beeton's Tip, page 52)
1 kg/2¼ lb Brussels sprouts
75 g/3 oz cooked ham, finely chopped
60 ml/4 tbsp single cream
salt and pepper

Set the oven at 180°C/350°F/gas 4. Place the cleaned nuts in a saucepan, just cover with water and bring to the boil. Cover the pan, lower the heat, and simmer for about 20 minutes or until the nuts are tender. Drain thoroughly, then cut each chestnut into quarters.

Trim the sprouts, pulling off any damaged leaves. Using a sharp knife, cut a cross in the base of each. Cook the sprouts in a saucepan of salted boiling water for 5-10 minutes until just tender. Drain well.

Combine the sprouts, chestnuts and ham in a small casserole. Stir in the cream and season with salt and pepper. Cover and bake for 15 minutes.

SERVES 6

☀ **MICROWAVE TIP** Shelling chestnuts is made a lot easier by using the microwave. Make a slit in the shell of each nut, then rinse them thoroughly but do not dry them. Put the damp nuts in a bowl, cover loosely and cook on High for 5 minutes. When cool enough to handle, remove the shells.

BAVARIAN CABBAGE

75 g/3 oz butter
1 onion, finely chopped
1.1 kg/2½ lb white cabbage, washed,
  quartered and shredded
1 cooking apple
salt and pepper
10 ml/2 tsp sugar
125 ml/4 fl oz vegetable stock or water
1.25 ml/¼ tsp caraway seeds
15 ml/1 tbsp cornflour
60 ml/4 tbsp white wine

Melt the butter in a heavy-bottomed saucepan. Add the onion and fry gently for 10 minutes until soft but not coloured. Stir in the cabbage, tossing it lightly in the fat.

Peel and core the apple, chop it finely and stir it into the pan. Add salt and pepper to taste, then stir in the sugar, stock or water, and caraway seeds. Cover the pan with a tight-fitting lid and simmer very gently for 1 hour.

Meanwhile mix the cornflour and wine together in a small bowl. Stir the mixture into the pan. Bring to the boil, stirring the mixture constantly until it thickens Cook for 2-3 minutes, still stirring. Serve at once.

SERVES 6

VARIATION

For a slightly more fruity flavour, increase the number of apples to 2 and substitute cider for the stock and white wine. Omit the caraway seeds.

RED CABBAGE WITH APPLES

Illustrated on page 179

45 ml/3 tbsp oil
1 onion, finely chopped
1 garlic clove, crushed
900 g/2 lb red cabbage, finely shredded
2 large cooking apples
15 ml/1 tbsp soft light brown sugar or
    golden syrup
juice of ½ lemon
30 ml/2 tbsp red wine vinegar
salt and pepper
15 ml/1 tbsp caraway seeds (optional)

Heat the oil in a large saucepan, add the onion and garlic and fry gently for 5 minutes. Add the cabbage. Peel, core and slice the apples and add them to the pan with the sugar or syrup. Cook over very gentle heat for 10 minutes, shaking the pan frequently.

Add the lemon juice and vinegar, with salt and pepper to taste. Stir in the caraway seeds, if used. Cover and simmer gently for 1-1½ hours, stirring occasionally and adding a little water if the mixture appears dry. Check the seasoning before serving.

SERVES 6

⭐ **FREEZER TIP** The cooked cabbage freezes very successfully. Cool it quickly, tip it into a rigid container, cover, seal and freeze for up to 3 months.

SAUERKRAUT WITH JUNIPER BERRIES

One of the oldest forms of preserved food, sauerkraut is simply fermented cabbage. It is sometimes possible to buy it loose from a large barrel in a delicatessen, but is more generally sold in cans or jars.

400 g/14 oz sauerkraut
50 g/2 oz butter
4 rindless streaky bacon rashers, chopped
1 large onion, chopped
1 garlic clove, crushed
6 juniper berries, crushed
2 bay leaves
5 ml/1 tsp caraway seeds
250 ml/8 fl oz chicken stock

Put the sauerkraut in a large bowl, add cold water to cover and soak for 15 minutes. Drain thoroughly, then squeeze dry.

Melt the butter in a saucepan, add the bacon and onion and fry over gentle heat for about 10 minutes. Add all the remaining ingredients, cover the pan and simmer for 1 hour. Add more salt and pepper, if required, before serving.

SERVES 4

MRS BEETON'S TIP For a richer, creamier flavour, stir in 150 ml/¼ pint plain yogurt or soured cream just before serving the sauerkraut. Do not allow the mixture to approach boiling point after adding the yogurt or cream.

CARROTS WITH CIDER

This traditional way of cooking carrots was originally known as the 'conservation method' because it preserved as many of the nutrients as possible.

75 g/3 oz butter
625 g/1½ lb young carrots, trimmed and
    scraped
salt
60 ml/4 tbsp double cream
125 ml/4 fl oz dry cider
few drops of lemon juice
pepper

Melt 25 g/1 oz of the butter in a heavy-bottomed pan. Add the carrots and cook over very gentle heat for 10 minutes, shaking the pan frequently so that the carrots do not stick to the base. Pour over 100 ml/3½ fl oz boiling water, with salt to taste. Cover the pan and simmer the carrots for about 10 minutes more or until tender. Drain, reserving the liquid for use in soup or stock.

Melt the remaining butter in the clean pan. Gradually stir in the cream and cider. Add the lemon juice and salt and pepper to taste. Stir in the carrots, cover the pan and cook gently for 10 minutes more. Serve at once.

SERVES 6

☀ **MICROWAVE TIP** Another way of preserving as many nutrients as possible is to cook the carrots in the microwave, but the results will be more satisfactory if smaller quantities are used. Combine 225 g/8 oz young carrots with 30 ml/2 tbsp butter in a dish. Cover loosely and cook on High for 5-7 minutes, stirring once. Before serving, add salt and pepper to taste.

GLAZED CARROTS

50 g/2 oz butter
575 g/1¼ lb young carrots, scraped but
    left whole
3 sugar cubes
1.25 ml/¼ tsp salt
beef stock (see method)
15 ml/1 tbsp chopped parsley to garnish

Melt the butter in a saucepan. Add the carrots, sugar and salt. Pour in enough stock to half cover the carrots. Cook over gentle heat, without covering the pan, for 15-20 minutes or until the carrots are tender. Shake the pan occcasionally to prevent sticking.

Using a slotted spoon, transfer the carrots to a bowl and keep hot. Boil the stock rapidly in the pan until it is reduced to a rich glaze. Return the carrots to the pan, 2 or 3 at a time, turning them in the glaze until thoroughly coated. Place on a heated serving dish, garnish with parsley and serve at once.

SERVES 6

CAULIFLOWER POLONAISE

1 large cauliflower, trimmed
salt
50 g/2 oz butter
50 g/2 oz fresh white breadcrumbs
2 hard-boiled eggs
15 ml/1 tbsp chopped parsley

Put the cauliflower, stem down, in a saucepan. Pour over boiling water, add salt to taste and cook for 10-15 minutes or until the stalk is just tender. Drain thoroughly.

Meanwhile, melt the butter in a frying pan, add the breadcrumbs and fry until crisp and golden. Chop the egg whites finely. Sieve the yolks and mix them with the parsley in a small bowl.

Drain the cauliflower thoroughly and place it on a heated serving dish. Sprinkle first with the breadcrumbs and then with the egg yolk mixture. Arrange the chopped egg white around the edge of the dish. Serve at once.

SERVES 4

CAULIFLOWER WITH BEANS

Illustrated on page 220

45 ml/3 tbsp oil
knob of butter (optional)
1 small onion, chopped
1 small cauliflower, broken in florets
225 g/8 oz French beans, trimmed and
    cut in pieces or thawed if frozen
salt and pepper
15-45 ml/1-3 tbsp chopped fresh herbs

Heat the oil and butter (if used) in a large frying pan or wok. Stir fry the onion for 5 minutes, until slightly softened. Add the cauliflower and cook, stirring, for 5 minutes, until the florets are translucent and lightly cooked.

Add the beans and continue stir frying for a further 3-4 minutes or until all the vegetables are just cooked but still crunchy. Add salt and pepper to taste and stir in the herbs. Serve at once.

SERVES 4 TO 6

CELERIAC PUREE

15 ml/1 tbsp lemon juice
1 large celeriac root, about 1 kg/2¼ lb
salt and white pepper
90 ml/6 tbsp single cream
15 ml/1 tbsp butter
60 ml/4 tbsp pine nuts

Have ready a large saucepan of water to which the lemon juice has been added. Peel the celeriac root fairly thickly so that the creamy white flesh is exposed. Cut it into 1 cm/½ inch cubes. Add the cubes to the acidulated water and bring to the boil over moderate heat. Add salt to taste, if desired, and cook for 8-10 minutes or until the celeriac is tender.

Drain the celeriac and purée it with the cream and butter in a blender or food processor. Alternatively, mash until smooth, then press through a sieve into a bowl. Reheat the purée if necessary, adjust the seasoning, stir in the nuts and serve at once.

SERVES 4

VARIATION

CELERIAC AND POTATO PUREE Substitute potato for half the celeriac. Cook and purée as suggested above.

MICROWAVE TIP The celeriac can be cooked in the microwave. Toss the celeriac cubes in acidulated water, drain off all but 60 ml/4 tbsp, and put the mixture in a roasting bag. Close the bag lightly with an elastic band and cook on High for 15 minutes. Shake the bag once during cooking. It will be very hot, so protect your hand in an oven glove. Drain by snipping an end off the bag and holding it over the sink. Purée as above.

BRAISED CELERY

The celery is cooked on a bed of vegetables or mirepoix, which adds flavour, keeps the celery moist and prevents scorching.

15 ml/1 tbsp dripping or margarine
2 rindless bacon rashers, chopped
2 onions, finely chopped
1 carrot, finely chopped
½ turnip, finely chopped
chicken stock (see method)
4 celery hearts, washed but left whole
15 ml/1 tbsp chopped coriander or
    parsley

Melt the dripping or margarine in a large heavy-bottomed saucepan. Add the bacon and fry for 2 minutes, then stir in the onions, carrot and turnip. Cook over gentle heat, stirring occasionally, for 10 minutes.

Pour over enough chicken stock to half cover the vegetables. Place the celery on top and spoon over some of the stock. Cover the pan tightly with foil and a lid and cook over very gentle heat for 1½ hours or until the celery is very tender. Baste the celery occasionally with the stock.

Using a slotted spoon, transfer the celery to a heated serving dish. Drain the cooking liquid into a small saucepan, reserving the mirepoix in a small heated serving dish.

Boil the cooking liquid rapidly until it is reduced to a thin glaze, then pour it over the celery. Sprinkle the mirepoix with the chopped coriander or parsley and serve it as a separate vegetable dish.

SERVES 4

BRAISED CHESTNUTS WITH ONION AND CELERY

600 ml/1 pint beef stock
1 kg/2¼ lb chestnuts, peeled (see Mrs
    Beeton's Tip, page 52)
1 small onion stuck with 2 cloves
1 celery stick, roughly chopped
1 bay leaf
1 blade of mace
pinch of cayenne pepper
salt
pastry fleurons (see Mrs Beeton's Tip) to
    garnish

Bring the stock to the boil in a saucepan. Add the chestnuts, onion, celery, bay leaf, mace and cayenne, with a little salt. Cover and simmer for about 30 minutes or until the chestnuts are tender.

Drain the chestnuts, reserving the cooking liquid, and keep them hot in a serving dish. Chop the onion, discarding the cloves, and add it to the chestnuts. Discard the bay leaf and mace. Return the cooking liquid to the clean pan. Boil the liquid rapidly until it is reduced to a thin glaze. Pour the glaze over the chestnuts and garnish with the pastry fleurons.

SERVES 6

MRS BEETON'S TIP To make pastry fleurons, roll out 215 g/7½ oz puff pastry on a floured board. Cut into rounds, using a 5 cm/2 inch cutter. Move the cutter halfway across each round and cut in half again, making a half moon and an almond shape. Arrange the half moons on a baking sheet, brush with beaten egg and bake in a preheated 200°C/400°F/ gas 6 oven for 8-10 minutes. The almond shapes may either be baked as biscuits or rerolled and cut into more fleurons.

Potatoes Lyonnaise (page 232) and Anna Potatoes (page 231)

Tofu and Spring Onion Stir Fry (page 243) and Tofu Parcels (page 242)

Curried Eggs and Eggs Florentine (both on page 244)

Boston Roast (page 249) with Cauliflower with Beans (page 215)

Chick Pea Casserole (page 253) with Italian Spinach (page 234)

Vegetable Chilli (page 255) with Cucumber in Yogurt (page 341)

Mixed Grill (page 266)

Scrambled Eggs (page 258) with Grilled Bacon (page 259) and Eggs Benedict (page 261)

COURGETTES IN TOMATO SAUCE

30 ml/2 tbsp olive or sunflower oil
450 g/1 lb courgettes, trimmed and sliced
6 spring onions, chopped
1 garlic clove, crushed
225 g/8 oz tomatoes, peeled, halved and
    seeded or 1 (227 g/8 oz) can chopped
    tomatoes, drained
15 ml/1 tbsp tomato purée
1 bay leaf
15 ml/1 tbsp dried basil
30 ml/2 tbsp dry white wine
salt and pepper

Heat the oil in a saucepan, add the courgettes, spring onions and garlic and cook over gentle heat for 5 minutes. Stir in the tomatoes, tomato purée, bay leaf, basil and wine, with salt and pepper to taste. Boil, lower the heat, cover and simmer for 15 minutes. Remove the bay and serve.

SERVES 4

COURGETTES WITH ALMONDS

Illustrated on page 179

*The cooked courgettes should be firm and full
flavoured not overcooked and watery.*

25 g/1 oz butter
25 g/1 oz blanched almonds, split in half
450 g/1 lb courgettes, trimmed and thinly
    sliced
salt and pepper
30 ml/2 tbsp snipped chives or chopped
    parsley

Melt the butter in a large frying pan. Add the almonds and fry over moderate heat,

stirring, until lightly browned. Tip the courgettes into the pan and cook, gently stirring and turning the slices all the time, for 3-5 minutes.

Tip the courgettes into a heated serving dish, add salt and pepper to taste and sprinkle the chives or parsley over them. Serve at once.

SERVES 4 TO 6

FENNEL WITH LEEKS

4 fennel bulbs, trimmed and halved
juice of ½ lemon
knob of butter or 30 ml/2 tbsp olive oil
4 leeks, sliced
1 bay leaf
2 fresh thyme sprigs
salt and pepper
150 ml/¼ pint chicken or vegetable stock
45 ml/3 tbsp dry sherry (optional)

Set the oven at 180°C/350°F/gas 4. As soon as the fennel is prepared, sprinkle the lemon juice over the cut bulbs. Heat the butter or oil in a frying pan and sauté the leeks for 2 minutes to soften them slightly. Add the pieces of fennel to the pan, pushing the leeks to one side. Turn the pieces of fennel in the fat for a minute or so, then tip the contents of the pan into an ovenproof casserole.

Add the bay leaf and thyme to the vegetables and sprinkle in salt and pepper to taste. Pour the stock and sherry (if used) over the fennel and cover the dish. Bake for 1-1¼ hours, turning the fennel mixture over twice, until tender. Taste for seasoning, remove the bay leaf and serve.

SERVES 4

LETTUCE WITH HERB SAUCE

salt and pepper
6 small heads of lettuce, trimmed
25 g/1 oz butter
25 g/1 oz plain flour
250 ml/8 fl oz chicken or vegetable stock
10 ml/2 tsp snipped chives
1 bay leaf
10 ml/2 tsp chopped parsley

Bring a large saucepan of salted water to the boil, add the lettuces and blanch for 2 minutes. Drain thoroughly, blotting off excess water with absorbent kitchen paper.

Melt the butter in a small saucepan, stir in the flour and cook for 1 minute. Gradually add the stock, stirring all the time until the mixture boils and thickens. Stir in the herbs, with salt and pepper to taste. Add the lettuces.

Cover the pan and cook the lettuces in the sauce for 20-30 minutes, stirring occasionally, but taking care not to break up the heads. Remove the bay leaf, add more salt and pepper if required, and serve.

SERVES 6

SHERRIED MUSHROOMS

25 g/1 oz butter
30 ml/2 tbsp plain flour
250 ml/8 fl oz milk
45 ml/3 tbsp dry sherry
350 g/12 oz mushrooms, sliced
salt and pepper
toast triangles to serve

Melt the butter in a saucepan, add the flour and cook for 1 minute. Gradually add the milk, stirring all the time until the mixture boils and thickens.

Stir in the sherry, then add the mushrooms, with salt and pepper to taste. Cook over gentle heat, stirring frequently, for about 5 minutes or until the mushrooms are just cooked.

Spoon on to a heated serving dish and serve at once, with toast triangles.

SERVES 4 TO 6

☀ **MICROWAVE TIP** The microwave makes short work of this dish. Simply combine the butter and flour in a bowl, whisk in the milk and sherry and cook on High for 6 minutes, stirring once or twice. Whisk thoroughly when cooking is complete, then stir in the mushrooms. Cook for 2 minutes more on High, stir thoroughly and serve as suggested above.

MUSHROOMS WITH BACON AND WINE

6 rindless streaky bacon rashers, chopped
400 g/14 oz button mushrooms, halved or
    quartered if large
5 ml/1 tsp snipped chives
5 ml/1 tsp chopped parsley
10 ml/2 tsp plain flour
75 ml/5 tbsp white wine or cider
salt and pepper

Cook the bacon gently in a heavy-bottomed saucepan until the fat begins to run, then increase the heat to moderate and fry for 10 minutes. Add the mushrooms and herbs, tossing them in the bacon fat.

Sprinkle the flour over the mushrooms,

cook for 1 minute, stirring gently, then add the wine or cider. Simmer for 10 minutes, stirring occasionally. Season and serve.

SERVES 6

> 🍶 **MRS BEETON'S TIP** Store mushrooms in a paper bag inside a polythene bag. The paper absorbs condensation and the mushrooms keep for three days in the refrigerator.

MUSHROOMS IN CREAM SAUCE

50 g/2 oz butter
450 g/1 lb small button mushrooms
10 ml/2 tsp arrowroot
125 ml/4 fl oz chicken or vegetable stock
15 ml/1 tbsp lemon juice
30 ml/2 tbsp double cream
salt and pepper
30 ml/2 tbsp chopped parsley

Melt the butter in large frying pan, add the mushrooms and fry over gentle heat without browning for 10 minutes.

Put the arrowroot in a small bowl. Stir in 30 ml/2 tbsp of the stock until smooth. Add the remaining stock to the mushrooms and bring to the boil. Lower the heat and simmer gently for 15 minutes, stirring occasionally. Stir in the arrowroot, bring to the boil, stirring, then remove the pan from the heat.

Stir in the lemon juice and cream, with salt and pepper to taste. Serve sprinkled with parsley.

SERVES 4 TO 6

OKRA AND AUBERGINE BAKE

1 aubergine
salt and pepper
400 g/14 oz okra
60 ml/4 tbsp olive oil
1 onion, finely chopped
2 garlic cloves, crushed
10 ml/2 tsp fennel seeds
3 tomatoes, peeled and sliced
10 ml/2 tsp chopped marjoram
60 ml/4 tbsp wholemeal breadcrumbs
15 ml/1 tbsp butter

Set the oven at 190°C/375°F/gas 5. Trim the ends off the aubergine and cut it into cubes. Put the cubes in a colander and sprinkle generously with salt. Set aside for 30 minutes.

Meanwhile wash the okra in cold water. Pat dry on absorbent kitchen paper. Trim but do not completely remove the stems. Rinse the aubergines thoroughly, drain and pat dry.

Heat the oil in a flameproof casserole, add the onion, garlic, fennel seeds and aubergine and cook over gentle heat for about 20 minutes until the onion is soft but not coloured and the aubergine is tender. Stir in the okra, tomatoes and marjoram.

Sprinkle the breadcrumbs over the top of the casserole, dot with the butter and bake for 15-20 minutes. Serve at once.

SERVES 6

> 🍶 **MRS BEETON'S TIP** When preparing the okra, take care not to split the pods or the sticky juices inside will be lost and the okra will lose their shape during cooking.

GLAZED ONIONS

Glazed onions make a tasty accompaniment to grilled steak, baked ham or bacon chops. They are often used as a garnish.

400 g/14 oz button onions
chicken stock (see method)
salt and pepper
15 ml/1 tbsp light soft brown sugar
25 g/1 oz butter
pinch of grated nutmeg

Skin the onions and put them in a single layer in a large saucepan. Add just enough stock to cover. Bring to the simmering point and cook for 15-20 minutes until the onions are just tender, adding a small amount of extra stock if necessary.

By the time the onions are cooked, the stock should have reduced almost to a glaze. Remove from the heat and stir in the remaining ingredients. Turn the onions over with a spoon so that the added ingredients mix well and the onions are coated in the mixture.

Return the pan to the heat until the onions become golden and glazed. Serve at once, with the remaining syrupy glaze.

SERVE 4

VARIATION

CITRUS GLAZED ONIONS Melt 25 g/1 oz butter in a frying pan. Add 400 g/ 14 oz button onions. Sprinkle with 15 ml/ 1 tbsp soft light brown sugar. Add salt and pepper to taste and fry, turning the onions occasionally until golden brown. Stir in 150 ml/¼ pint orange juice and 10 ml/2 tsp lemon juice. Cover and simmer for 15 minutes.

ONIONS ITALIAN-STYLE

675 g/1½ lb button onions
30 ml/2 tbsp olive oil
2 bay leaves
2 cloves
4 white peppercorns
30 ml/2 tbsp white wine vinegar
5 ml/1 tsp caster sugar

Cook the onions in their skins in a saucepan of boiling water for 15-20 minutes, until just tender. Drain. When cool enough to handle, slip off the skins.

Heat the oil in a saucepan. Put in the bay leaves, cloves and peppercorns and shake the pan over moderate heat for 2-3 minutes. Add the onions to the pan and cook very gently for 5 minutes. Stir in the vinegar and sugar. Continue cooking until the liquid is reduced to a syrup. Serve hot.

SERVES 6

MRS BEETON'S TIP Try to find silverskin or small white onions for this recipe. Slices of the deep reddish-purple Italian onions may also be used, in which case substitute red wine vinegar for the white.

PANFRIED ONION AND APPLE

40 g/1½ oz butter
350 g/12 oz onions, sliced in rings
450 g/1 lb cooking apples
10 ml/2 tsp caster sugar
salt and pepper

Melt the butter in a heavy-bottomed frying pan. Add the onions and fry gently.

Peel, core and slice the apples into the pan. Mix lightly to coat the apples in the melted butter. Sprinkle the sugar over the top, cover and simmer for 30 minutes or until the onions and apples are tender. Add salt and pepper to taste before serving.

SERVES 4

ONIONS AND TOMATOES IN CIDER

6 large onions, peeled but left whole
50 g/2 oz butter or margarine
225 g/8 oz tomatoes, peeled and sliced
2 bay leaves
2 cloves
150 ml/¼ pint medium cider
125 ml/4 fl oz vegetable stock
salt and pepper

Bring a saucepan of water to the boil. Add the onions and cook for 2 minutes, then drain thoroughly. Cool, cut into rings and dry on absorbent kitchen paper.

Melt the butter or margarine in a deep frying pan. Add the onion rings. Fry over gentle heat until golden. Add the tomatoes, bay leaves, cloves, cider and stock. Cover and simmer for 45 minutes. Remove the bay and cloves, season and serve.

SERVES 6

MRS BEETON'S TIP For home-made vegetable stock, fry 2 chopped onions, 2 diced potatoes and 2 celery sticks. Stir in 1 sliced parsnip or swede and 1 small sliced turnip, and add 1.1 litres/2 pints water. Add a bouquet garni. Simmer for 1-1¼ hours and strain.

CREAMED ONIONS

fat for greasing
1 kg/2¼ lb small onions, peeled but left whole
100 ml/3½ fl oz double cream
Béchamel sauce (see Mrs Beeton's Tip, page 47), made using 300 ml/½ pint milk
grated nutmeg
salt and pepper
25 g/1 oz butter
50 g/2 oz dried white breadcrumbs
30 ml/2 tbsp chopped parsley

Grease a 2 litre/1¾ pint casserole. Set the oven at 160°C/325°F/gas 3. Bring a saucepan of water to the boil. Add the onions and cook for 10-15 minutes until just tender. Drain well.

Add the double cream to the Béchamel sauce and reheat gently without boiling. Stir in the nutmeg with salt and pepper to taste, add the onions and mix lightly.

Spoon the mixture into the prepared casserole. Top with the breadcrumbs and dot with the butter. Bake for 20 minutes. Serve hot, sprinkled with the parsley.

SERVES 6 TO 8

MRS BEETON'S TIP To make about 100 g/4 oz dried breadcrumbs, cut the crusts off six slices (175 g/6 oz) of bread, then spread the bread out on baking sheets. Bake in a preheated 150°C/300°F/gas 2 oven for about 30 minutes until dry but not browned. Cool, then crumb in a food processor or blender. Alternatively, put the dried bread between sheets of greaseproof paper and crush with a rolling pin.

SWEET PARSNIP BAKE

fat for greasing
450 g/1 lb parsnips, sliced
250 ml/8 fl oz apple purée
75 g/3 oz soft light brown sugar
salt
2.5 ml/½ tsp grated nutmeg
15 ml/1 tbsp lemon juice
75 g/3 oz butter
75 g/3 oz fresh white breadcrumbs
1.25 ml/¼ tsp paprika

Grease an ovenproof dish. Set the oven at 190°C/375°F/gas 5. Put the parsnips in a saucepan of cold water, bring to the boil and cook for 15-20 minutes or until tender. Drain thoroughly, then mash the parsnips by hand or purée in a blender or food processor.

Arrange alternate layers of parsnip purée and apple purée in the prepared dish, sprinkling each layer with brown sugar, salt, nutmeg, lemon juice and flakes of butter. Top with the breadcrumbs and a dusting of paprika. Bake for 30 minutes.

SERVES 6

PETITS POIS A LA FRANCAISE

50 g/2 oz butter
1 lettuce heart, shredded
1 bunch of spring onions, finely chopped
675 g/1½ lb fresh shelled garden peas or frozen petits pois
pinch of sugar • salt and pepper

Melt the butter in a heavy-bottomed saucepan and add the lettuce, spring onions, peas and sugar, with salt and pepper to taste. Cover and simmer very gently until the peas are tender. Frozen petits pois may be ready in less than 10 minutes, but fresh garden peas could take 25 minutes.

SERVES 6

PEASE PUDDING

575 g/1¼ lb split peas, soaked overnight in cold water to cover
1 small onion, peeled but left whole
1 bouquet garni • salt and pepper
50 g/2 oz butter, cut into small pieces
2 eggs, beaten

Drain the peas, put them in a saucepan and add cold water to cover. Add the onion, the bouquet garni and salt and pepper to taste. Bring to the boil, skim off any scum on the surface of the liquid, then reduce the heat to very low and simmer the peas for 2-2½ hours or until tender.

Drain the peas thoroughly. Press them through a sieve or purée in a blender or food processor. Add the pieces of butter or margarine with the beaten eggs. Beat well.

Spoon the mixture into a floured pudding cloth and tie tightly. Suspend the bag in a large saucepan of boiling salted water and simmer gently for 1 hour. Remove from the pan, take the pudding out of the cloth and serve very hot.

SERVES 6

MRS BEETON'S TIP Modern cooks, unfamiliar with pudding cloths, can bake this nutritious pudding in a greased casserole. It will need about 30 minutes to cook in a preheated 180°C/350°F/gas 4 oven.

POTATOES SAVOYARDE

1 small garlic clove, cut in half
75 g/3 oz Gruyère cheese, grated
1 kg/2¼ lb potatoes, thinly sliced
salt and pepper
freshly grated nutmeg
40 g/1½ oz butter
about 375 ml/13 fl oz chicken or vegetable
    stock

Set the oven at 190°C/375°F/gas 5. Rub the cut garlic all over the inside of a 2 litre/3½ pint baking dish. Set aside 30 ml/2 tbsp of the grated cheese.

Put the potatoes into a mixing bowl. Add salt, pepper and a little nutmeg to taste, then mix in the remaining cheese. Use a little of the butter to grease the baking dish generously, add the potato mixture and pour in enough stock to just cover.

Dot the remaining butter over the potatoes and sprinkle with the reserved grated cheese. Bake for 1¼ hours or until golden brown and the potatoes are tender.

SERVES 6

DUCHESSE POTATOES

These attractive potatoes make a popular garnish to dinner party fish and meat dishes.

butter or margarine for greasing
450 g/1 lb old potatoes
salt and pepper
25 g/1 oz butter or margarine
1 egg or 2 egg yolks
grated nutmeg (optional)
beaten egg for brushing

Butter a baking sheet. Cut the potatoes into pieces and cook in a saucepan of salted water for 15-20 minutes. Drain thoroughly, then press the potatoes through a sieve into a large bowl.

Set the oven at 200°C/400°F/gas 6. Beat the butter or margarine and egg or egg yolks into the potatoes. Add salt and pepper to taste and the nutmeg, if used. Spoon the mixture into a piping bag fitted with a large rose nozzle. Pipe rounds of potato on to the prepared baking sheet. Brush with a little beaten egg. Bake for about 15 minutes, until the potatoes are golden brown.

SERVES 6

ANNA POTATOES

Illustrated on page 217

fat for greasing
1 kg/2¼ lb even-sized potatoes
salt and pepper
melted clarified butter (see Mrs Beeton's
    Tip, page 313)

Grease a 20 cm/8 inch round cake tin and line the base with greased greaseproof paper. Set the oven at 190°C/375°F/gas 5.

Trim the potatoes so that they will give equal-sized slices. Slice them very thinly using either a sharp knife or a mandoline. Arrange a layer of potatoes, slightly overlapping, in the base of the tin. Add salt and pepper to taste, then spoon a little clarified butter over them. Make a second layer of potatoes and spoon some more butter over them. Complete these layers until all the potatoes have been used. Cover the tin with greased greaseproof paper and foil.

Bake for 1 hour. Check the potatoes several times during cooking and add a little more clarified butter if they become too dry. Invert the tin on to a warm serving dish to remove the potatoes. Serve at once.

SERVES 6

POTATOES LYONNAISE

Illustrated on page 217

This is a very good way of using up leftover boiled new potatoes. A crushed garlic clove may be added to the onion, if liked.

1 kg/2¼ lb potatoes, scrubbed but not
    peeled
75 g/3 oz butter or margarine
225 g/8 oz onions, thickly sliced
salt and pepper
15 ml/1 tbsp chopped parsley

Boil or steam the potatoes in their jackets until tender. When cool enough to handle, peel and cut into slices 5 mm/¼ inch thick.

Melt the butter or margarine in a large frying pan. Add the onions and fry over moderate heat until just golden. Using a slotted spoon, transfer the onions to a plate; keep warm. Add the potatoes to the fat remaining in the pan and fry on both sides until crisp and golden.

Return the onions to the pan and mix with the potatoes. Season to taste with salt and pepper, turn into a serving dish and sprinkle with the parsley.

SERVES 6

MRS BEETON'S TIP Use an electric frying pan, if you have one, for this recipe. The size and depth means that the onions and potatoes will be easy to cook, and the readily-controlled temperature will be an asset when frying the potatoes.

POTATO CROQUETTES

450 g/1 lb potatoes, halved or quartered
25 g/1 oz butter or margarine
2 whole eggs plus 2 egg yolks
salt and pepper
15 ml/1 tbsp chopped parsley
flour for dusting
dried white breadcrumbs for coating
oil for deep frying

Cook the potatoes in boiling water for about 20 minutes until tender. Drain throughly and press through a sieve into a mixing bowl. Beat in the butter or margarine with the egg yolks and add salt and pepper to taste. Add the parsley.

Spread out the flour for dusting in a shallow bowl. Put the whole eggs in a second bowl and beat them lightly with a fork. Spread the breadcrumbs on a plate or sheet of foil.

Form the potato mixture into balls or cylindrical rolls. Coat them first in flour, then in egg and finally in breadcrumbs. Repeat the operation so that they have a double coating, then place them on a baking sheet and chill for 1 hour to firm the mixture.

Heat the oil for deep frying to 180-190°C/350-375°F or until a cube of bread added to the oil browns in 30 seconds. Fry the potato croquettes, a few at a time, until golden brown. Drain on absorbent kitchen paper and keep hot while cooking successive batches.

MAKES 12 TO 15

*P*OTATOES DAUPHINE

575 g/1¼ lb potatoes
salt and pepper
oil for deep frying

CHOUX PASTRY
100 g/4 oz plain flour
pinch of salt
50 g/2 oz butter or margarine
2 whole eggs plus 1 yolk

Scrub the potatoes, but do not peel them. Steam them or cook in a large saucepan of boiling water for 20-30 minutes, or until tender. Drain, peel and press through a sieve into a mixing bowl. Beat in salt and pepper to taste. Set aside.

Make the choux pastry. Sift the flour and salt on to a sheet of greaseproof paper. Put 250 ml/8 fl oz water in a saucepan and add the butter or margarine. Heat gently until the fat melts. When the fat has melted, bring the liquid rapidly to the boil and add all the flour at once. Immediately remove the pan from the heat and stir the flour into the liquid to make a smooth paste which leaves the sides of the pan clean. Set aside to cool slightly.

Add the egg yolk and beat well. Add the whole eggs, one at a time, beating well after each addition. Continue beating until the paste is very glossy. Add the potato purée to the choux pastry mixture and beat well.

Put the oil for frying into a deep wide saucepan to a depth of at least 7.5 cm/ 3 inches. Heat the oil to 180-190°C/ 350-375°F or until a cube of bread added to the oil browns in 30 seconds. If using a deep-fat fryer, follow the manufacturer's instructions.

Drop small spoonfuls of the potato mixture, a few at a time, into the hot fat, and cook until they are puffed up and golden brown. Remove from the pan and drain on absorbent kitchen paper and keep hot while cooking successive batches. Serve freshly cooked.

SERVES 6

> **MRS BEETON'S TIP** Although Potatoes Dauphine are traditionally deep fried, they may also be baked. Using 2 teaspoons, place rounds of the mixture on to greased baking sheets. Bake in a preheated 220°C/425°F/gas 7 oven for 10 minutes, then lower the heat to 180°C/350°F/gas 4 and bake for 20 minutes.

*S*CALLOPED POTATOES WITH ONIONS

fat for greasing
675 g/1½ lb potatoes, peeled and cut into
    5 mm/¼ inch slices
450 g/1 lb onions, sliced in rings
salt and pepper
125 ml/4 fl oz milk or cream
20 ml/4 tsp butter

Grease a baking dish. Set the oven at 190°C/375°F/gas 5. Layer the potatoes and onions in the prepared dish, sprinkling salt and pepper between the layers and ending with potatoes. Pour the milk or cream over the top. Dot the surface with butter and cover with foil or a lid. Bake for 1½ hours, removing the cover for the last 20-30 minutes of the cooking time to allow the potatoes on the top to brown.

SERVES 4 TO 6

MRS BEETON'S POTATO RISSOLES

Mrs Beeton suggests that these rissoles may be made very simply, without the onion, or that their flavour may be improved by adding a little chopped cooked tongue or ham.

50 g/2 oz butter
1 large onion, finely chopped
350 g/12 oz hot mashed potato
salt and pepper
10 ml/2 tsp chopped parsley
2 eggs, beaten
75 g/3 oz dried white breadcrumbs
oil for shallow frying

Meet half the butter in a frying pan. Cook the onion, stirring often, until soft but not browned. Season the mashed potato generously, then stir in the parsley and onion with all the butter from the pan. Allow the mixture to cool completely. When cold, shape into small balls.

Put the beaten egg in a shallow bowl and the breadcrumbs on a plate or sheet of foil. Dip the potato rissoles in the egg, then coat them thoroughly in breadcrumbs. Place them on a baking sheet and chill for 15 minutes to firm the mixture.

Heat the remaining butter with the oil for shallow frying in a deep frying pan. Put in the rissoles and turn them in the hot fat for 6-9 minutes until golden brown all over. Drain on absorbent kitchen paper and serve hot.

MAKES ABOUT 10

ITALIAN SPINACH

Illustrated on page 221

25 g/1 oz sultanas
1 kg/2¼ lb spinach
30 ml/2 tbsp oil
1 garlic clove, crushed
salt and pepper
25 g/1 oz pine nuts

Put the sultanas in a small bowl or mug, pour on boiling water to cover and set aside for 2-3 minutes until plumped. Drain well and set aside.

Wash the fresh spinach several times and remove any coarse stalks. Put into a saucepan with just the water that clings to the leaves, then cover the pan. Put the pan over high heat for 2-3 minutes, shaking it frequently. Reduce the heat, stir the spinach and cook for a further 5 minutes, turning the spinach occasionally, until cooked to your liking. Drain thoroughly, then chop the spinach coarsely.

Heat the oil in a large frying pan. Add the spinach and garlic, with salt and pepper to taste. Turn the spinach over and over in the pan with a wide spatula to heat it thoroughly without frying. Turn into a heated serving bowl, add the sultanas and nuts and mix lightly. Serve at once.

SERVES 4

> **MRS BEETON'S TIP** Pine nuts – or pine kernels as they are sometimes known – are produced inside the cones of a pine tree that grows in North America and in the southern Mediterranean. White and waxy in appearance, they are used extensively in the cooking of the Middle East and are also an important ingredient in the Italian sauce, *pesto*.

RATATOUILLE

Traditionally, the vegetable mixture is cooked long and slow – for about 45-60 minutes – and it is richer, and more intensely flavoured if prepared ahead, cooled and thoroughly reheated. This recipe suggests cooking for slightly less time, so that the courgettes and aubergines still retain a bit of bite; the final simmering time may be shortened, if liked, to give a mixture in which the courgettes contribute a slightly crunchy texture.

2 aubergines
salt and pepper
125-150 ml/4-5 fl oz olive oil
2 large onions, finely chopped
2 garlic cloves, crushed
2 peppers, seeded and cut into thin strips
30 ml/2 tbsp chopped fresh marjoram or
   10 ml/2 tsp dried marjoram
450 g/1 lb tomatoes, peeled and chopped
4 courgettes, thinly sliced
30 ml/2 tbsp finely chopped parsley or
   mint

Trim the ends of the aubergines and cut them into cubes. Put the cubes in a colander and sprinkle generously with salt. Set aside for 30 minutes, then rinse thoroughly, drain and pat dry on absorbent kitchen paper.

Heat some of the oil in a large saucepan or flameproof casserole, add some of the aubergine cubes and cook over moderate heat, stirring frequently, for 10 minutes. Using a slotted spoon, transfer the aubergine to a bowl; repeat until all the cubes are cooked, adding more oil as necessary. Add the onions to the oil remaining in the pan and fry for 5 minutes, until slightly softened. Stir in the garlic, peppers and marjoram, with salt and pepper to taste. Cook, stirring occasionally for 15-20 minutes, or until the onions are thoroughly softened.

Stir the tomatoes and courgettes into the vegetable mixture. Replace the aubergines, heat until bubbling, then cover and simmer for a further 15-20 minutes, stirring occasionally. Serve hot, sprinkled with parsley, or cold, sprinkled with mint.

SERVES 4 TO 6

PEPERONATA

A delicious starter from Italy, peperonata is perfect for serving with prosciutto or salami.

45 ml/3 tbsp olive oil
1 large onion, sliced
2 garlic cloves, crushed
350 g/12 oz tomatoes, peeled, seeded and
   cut in quarters
2 large red peppers, seeded and cut in
   thin strips
1 large green pepper, seeded and cut in
   thin strips
1 large yellow pepper, seeded and cut in
   thin strips
2.5 ml/½ tsp coriander seeds, lightly
   crushed (optional)
salt and pepper
15 ml/1 tbsp red wine vinegar (optional)

Heat the oil in a large frying pan, add the onion and garlic and fry over gentle heat for 10 minutes. Add the tomatoes, peppers and coriander seeds, if using, with salt and pepper to taste. Cover and cook gently for 1 hour, stirring from time to time. Add more salt and pepper before serving if necessary. To sharpen the flavour, stir in the red wine vinegar, if liked.

SERVES 4

MARROW WITH TOMATOES

30 ml/2 tbsp olive or sunflower oil
1 onion, finely chopped
1-2 garlic cloves, crushed
450 g/1 lb ripe tomatoes, peeled and
    chopped
10 ml/2 tsp paprika
15 ml/1 tbsp tomato purée
1 (1 kg/2¼ lb) marrow, peeled, seeded
    and cubed
salt and pepper
45 ml/3 tbsp chopped parsley

Heat the oil in a flameproof casserole. Add the onion and garlic, and fry gently for about 15 minutes until soft but not coloured. Stir in the tomatoes, paprika and tomato purée and cook, stirring occasionally, for 10 minutes.

Add the marrow cubes, with salt and pepper to taste, stir well until simmering, then cover and cook gently for about 25 minutes. Stir occasionally during cooking. The marrow should be tender but not watery. Add the parsley and taste for seasoning before serving.

SERVES 6

VARIATION

MARROW MONTGOMERY Set the oven at 190°C/375°F/gas 5. Add the marrow as above, then stir in 40 g/1½ oz cubed dark rye bread. Buy an unsliced rye loaf for this recipe as the pre-sliced bread sold in packets is cut too thin. Bake the mixture, uncovered, for 30-40 minutes, sprinkle with parsley and serve.

MIXED VEGETABLE CASSEROLE

45 ml/3 tbsp oil
2 onions, finely chopped
2 garlic cloves, crushed
4 rindless streaky bacon rashers, diced
2 celery sticks, chopped
1 green pepper, seeded and diced
1 small red pepper, seeded and diced
45 ml/3 tbsp tomato purée
750 ml/1¼ pints chicken stock
salt and pepper
1 kg/2¼ lb potatoes, quartered
225 g/8 oz tomatoes, seeded and roughly
    chopped
15 ml/1 tbsp chopped mixed herbs
150 g/5 oz Parmesan cheese, grated

Heat the oil in a flameproof casserole, add the onion and garlic and fry over gentle heat for 4-6 minutes until soft but not coloured. Add the celery and peppers and cook, stirring occasionally, for 5 minutes more.

Stir the tomato purée and stock into the pan, with salt and pepper to taste. Bring to the boil and add the potatoes, tomatoes and herbs. Mix well. Lower the heat and cover the casserole.

Cook gently for 20-30 minutes, or until the potatoes are tender but not mushy. Sprinkle the cheese on top and brown under a preheated grill. Serve at once.

SERVES 6

VEGETARIAN SPECIALITIES

You don't have to be a vegetarian to enjoy vegetarian meals.
This style of eating is becoming increasingly popular, not
only for ethical reasons, but also for considerations of health,
economy and variety, and many people now include some
vegetarian dishes in their diet every week. This chapter
offers a selection of interesting recipes to inspire meat-eaters
and vegetarians alike.

Following a vegetarian diet means excluding all fish, poultry and meat, along with any other products that necessitate the killing of an animal for food. Dairy produce, such as milk, yogurt and eggs, are generally eaten and many vegetarians eat ordinary cheese; however, because rennet – an enzyme from the stomach of a calf – is used in cheese-making many vegetarians prefer vegetarian cheese, which is made with an alternative clotting agent.

Although eggs are not excluded, many vegetarians of long standing prefer to avoid eating them in recognizable form – poached, boiled, fried or even scrambled – although they will accept them in quiches, cakes and other composite dishes.

Since the most important protein foods are excluded from a standard vegetarian diet, it is important to consider the balance of nutrients. Including dairy produce means that the lack of meat and fish is not a problem. Regularly substituting a large proportion of cheese and other foods with a high fat content does not make for balanced eating, however, so a large proportion of the protein in a vegetarian diet should come from eating a wide variety of vegetables, grains and pulses. It is the variety that is important to the diet, since this ensures a plentiful supply of the components that make up the essential protein.

Pulses, nuts (with the exception of chestnuts) and seeds are rich sources of protein. When they are combined with dairy produce and a regular, varied, supply of vegetables and fruit, the diet is likely to be well balanced. It is worth remembering that soya beans are a rich and complete source of protein.

Other useful sources of protein include bean sprouts, tofu and myco protein. Tofu is a soya bean product, available in many forms, plain, smoked, marinated or flavoured. It is a versatile ingredient in both savoury and sweet dishes, since it is flavourless when plain and readily absorbs the flavours of ingredients with which it is cooked.

MENU PLANNING

Planning a vegetarian menu is neither more nor less difficult than organizing a meat-based meal.

The main dish may not be the only source of protein but it should provide a useful supply. For example, it may contain nuts, pulses or dairy produce. If the main dish is based on mixed vegetables, however, a side dish of pulses may balance the food value. Alternatively, the first course may include beans or pulses, tofu or dairy foods and the dessert may also be rich in protein, as when tofu is used in a sweet recipe, such as a cheesecake. Since portions are small for the first and final courses, remember to include some other protein in the meal.

Contrasts in colour and texture are all-important when planning a vegetarian menu. The problem with texture is frequently not a lack of it but a jaw-aching excess of chewy foods in one meal.

There should be some source of moisture in the main course, whether this is a braised main dish, a sauce-coated side dish of vegetables or a sauce as an accompaniment. If the rest of the meal is well balanced, do not be tempted to add confusing salads or vegetable accompaniments – again, a common mistake by cooks eager to fit as much food value as possible into every dish. Plain salads and simple steamed, boiled or sautéed vegetables in a classic dressing are often more appropriate accompaniments than mixed salads topped with nuts, seeds and toasted crumbs or a medley of half a dozen mixed vegetables with toasted nuts and seeds.

Barbecues, buffets and dinner parties can pose a problem for the non-vegetarian cook entertaining guests of mixed dietary habits. The well-planned meal will include the vegetarian courses as part of the overall menu. There is nothing worse than providing a meat dish, with two plain cooked vegetables and gravy for the majority of diners while offering a miserable nut cutlet or bean roast as compensation for the vegetarians. Instead, select a mixed vegetable dish, such as ratatouille, and a rice or bean dish, a plain pilaf or some lightly spiced chick peas as an integral part of the main course, offering meat, fish or poultry which is grilled, baked or roasted with herbs. A vegetable gratin with a crunchy breadcrumb and cheese topping goes well with grilled meats and fish and also makes a tempting vegetarian dish. Make sure that the first course suits all your guests – garlic mushrooms, spinach-stuffed cannelloni, stuffed tomatoes, peppers or mushrooms with a non-meat filling, avocados or fruit in some form are all appropriate.

For a barbecue, opt for vegetable kebabs with aubergines, mushrooms, peppers and parboiled new potatoes accompanied by a flavoursome sauce. Other options include roasted halved peppers, which may be filled with a rice or grain mixture just before serving, or roasted halved aubergines topped with a creamy avocado and cheese dressing. Remember that most vegetarians find even the possibility of meat juices falling on their food quite unacceptable, so keep a distinct area clear on the barbecue or invest in a small disposable barbecue pack if space is short.

The key point to remember about special meals is that nobody expects them to be perfect examples of a nutritionally balanced diet. If they lack certain nutrients or are too rich in others, this is unlikely to pose problems as they are eaten occasionally.

PULSES

Whether you prepare them yourself, or save time by using a quality canned product, dried beans, peas and lentils make a valuable, inexpensive contribution to a balanced diet.

As a general rule, dried beans should be soaked for several hours or overnight before cooking. Never serve raw, soaked beans, and always start the cooking process by boiling the beans vigorously for at least 10 minutes before simmering until tender. This destroys natural toxins. Cooking time varies from about 40 minutes for small beans to 1½ hours for some of the larger thicker-skinned varieties. The cooking medium may be boiling water or salt-free stock; salt is excluded because it toughens the beans. Season dishes once the beans are thoroughly cooked.

Dried peas are treated in much the same way as beans. Soaked whole green peas and chick-peas should be simmered slowly until tender; about 1½ hours. Split peas take less time, but also benefit from long slow cooking. Lentils differ in that they do not need to be soaked, and cook in 20-50 minutes, depending on type.

Some of the most popular pulses are described below:

Aduki Small, round red beans with a nutty flavour.

Black-eyed Beans Small kidney-shaped whole beans with a prominent black spot.

Borlotti Beans Mottled pink beans, often used in Italian cooking.

Brown Beans Medium, oval beans, often used in Mediterranean cuisines.

Butter Beans Large white beans which cook comparitively quickly when soaked and become mushy if overcooked.

Chick-peas Also known as *garbanzos*. They resemble small, light brown nuts and have an affinity for spices.

Flageolet Beans Small, oval, pale green beans with a delicate flavour.

Haricot Beans There are many varieties and sizes, but the name is generally used for small, oval white beans.

Lentils Several different varieties are available. Unlike most other pulses, lentils do not need to soaked before being cooked. For more information, see Boiled Lentils, page 250.

Peas Dried green peas are not as popular as they once were, but make a tasty soup or purée, especially when flavoured with onion and bacon or ham.

Pinto Beans Mottled, pink beans often confused with borlotti beans from the same family.

Processed Peas The familiar 'mushy peas' are processed marrowfat peas. Bright green in colour and slightly sweet, they are usually sold in cans.

Red Kidney Beans Dark red, oval beans, an essential ingredient of Chilli con Carne. Also delicious when cooked with Indian spices, onions and tomatoes.

Soya Beans Creamy-beige small beans, rounded in shape. They require long soaked and cooking. Highly nutritious.

Split Peas The basis of pea soup and pease pudding. They require less cooking time than whole dried peas. Although both yellow and green varieties are available, the former are most widely used. Like split lentils, they lose their shape when cooked.

FREEZE-DRIED PRODUCE

Freeze-drying is a commercial method of preserving food by using the drying properties of freezing. You may have noticed the drying properties of freezing on poorly packed produce, notably meat which displays a dry surface known as freezer burn. The commercial process turns this disadvantage into a boon by accelerating the drying to produce dried foods with a good flavour and excellent reconstituting properties. Freeze-dried vegetables – peas, beans and mixed vegetables – do not require lengthy soaking. Their flavour comes close to that of fresh produce. Always follow manufacturer's instructions for use.

BROAD BEANS WITH SPANISH SAUCE

Serve these with wholemeal pasta, buckwheat, brown or wild rice for a satisfying lunch or supper.

1 small onion, finely chopped
400 ml/14 fl oz vegetable stock
2-3 thyme sprigs
1 bay leaf
1 kg/2¼ lb broad beans, shelled
25 g/1 oz butter
30 ml/2 tbsp oil
100 g/4 oz mushrooms, sliced
25 g/1 oz plain flour
5 ml/1 tsp chopped parsley
5 ml/1 tsp lemon juice
salt and pepper

TO SERVE

75 g/3 oz Gruyère cheese, grated
2 spring onions, finely chopped

Put the onion in a saucepan with the stock, thyme and bay leaf. Bring to the boil, add the beans and cook for 10-15 minutes or until tender. Drain, reserving the stock but discarding the herbs. Put the beans in a bowl.

Melt the butter in the oil in a saucepan. Add the mushrooms and fry over fairly high heat for about 10 minutes, stirring constantly. Using a slotted spoon, add the mushrooms to the bowl containing the beans.

Stir the flour into the butter and oil mixture remaining in the pan. Cook for 1 minute, stirring constantly, then gradually add the reserved stock from the beans. Bring to the boil, stirring the sauce until it thickens. Add the bean and mushroom mixture with the parsley and lemon juice.

Stir in salt and pepper to taste. Simmer until the beans and mushrooms are heated through, then spoon the mixture into a heated serving dish.

To serve, mix the grated Gruyère and spring onions in a small bowl. Sprinkle a little of the mixture on top of the beans and mushrooms and serve the rest separately.

SERVES 4

MRS BEETON'S TIP To prevent shelled broad beans from drying out when prepared, cover them with a thick layer of pods. Rinse in cold water before cooking.

STUFFED AUBERGINES

2 large aubergines
salt
30 ml/2 tbsp oil
15 ml/1 tbsp grated Parmesan cheese
15 ml/1 tbsp olive oil

STUFFING
30 ml/2 tbsp oil
1 onion, finely chopped
100 g/4 oz mushrooms, finely chopped
1 large tomato, peeled and chopped
50 g/2 oz fresh white breadcrumbs
15 ml/1 tbsp chopped parsley
pepper

Cut the aubergines in half lengthways, score the flesh with a knife, sprinkle with salt and set aside for 30 minutes. Rinse and dry on absorbent kitchen paper.

Set the oven at 200°C/400°F/gas 6. Brush the aubergines with oil and cook under a low grill for about 20 minutes or until tender. Remove the aubergine pulp, taking care to keep the shells intact. Chop the pulp finely. Set the skins aside.

Make the stuffing. Heat the oil in a saucepan, add the chopped onion and mushrooms and cook over gentle heat for 5 minutes. Add the chopped aubergines and cook, stirring occasionally, for 5 minutes more, then stir in the tomato, all but 15 ml/1 tbsp of the breadcrumbs and the parsley. Season with plenty of salt and pepper.

Pile the mixture back into the aubergine shells and place in an ovenproof dish. Mix the remaining breadcrumbs with the Parmesan cheese and sprinkle over the stuffing. Drizzle olive oil over each stuffed aubergine shell. Bake for 20 minutes.

SERVES 4

VARIATIONS

SOFT CHEESE Stir 50 g/2 oz low fat soft cheese into the stuffing. Use cream cheese with garlic, or cream cheese with herbs for variety.

TOMATO Omit the mushrooms, increase the number of tomatoes to 3 (or use 225 g/8 oz chopped canned tomatoes) and add 15 ml/1 tbsp tomato purée. Use wholemeal breadcrumbs instead of white and increase the quantity if necessary to absorb the extra liquid generated by the tomatoes. Chopped olives or capers may be added for extra flavour.

*P*EPPERS WITH COURGETTE FILLING

4 large red or yellow peppers
25 g/1 oz butter
1 large onion, finely chopped
25 g/1 oz plain flour
250 ml/8 fl oz milk
salt and pepper
1 eating apple, peeled, cored and
  chopped
100 g/4 oz Gruyère cheese, grated
225 g/8 oz courgettes, trimmed, thinly
  peeled and diced

Set the oven at 180°C/350°F/gas 4. Cut the stalk ends off the peppers and reserve these as lids. Scoop out all the seeds and pith from inside, being careful to keep the shells intact. Wash them thoroughly and then add them to a large pan of boiling water. Bring back to the boil, cook for 2 minutes and drain upside down on absorbent kitchen paper.

Melt the butter in a saucepan, add the onion and cook, stirring, for 10 minutes, until softened. Stir in the flour. Gradually add the milk, stirring constantly, then cook until the sauce boils and becomes smooth and thick. Add salt and pepper to taste. Remove from the heat.

Stir the apple, cheese and courgettes into the sauce. Stand the peppers upright in a casserole dish into which they will fit snugly. Fill the centres with the apple mixture and replace the pepper lids. Cover with foil and bake for 40 minutes. Serve with rice and grilled tomatoes sprinkled with olive oil and fresh basil or oregano, if liked.

SERVES 4

CELERY, SPINACH AND NUT FRICASSEE

45 ml/3 tbsp olive oil
1 onion, finely chopped
1 garlic clove, crushed
1 head celery, thinly sliced
30 ml/2 tbsp plain flour
150 ml/¼ pint vegetable stock
150 ml/¼ pint white wine or medium
    cider
1 bay leaf
salt and pepper
1 kg/2¼ lb fresh spinach
30 ml/2 tbsp butter
75 g/3 oz cashew nuts
30 ml/2 tbsp chopped parsley
5 ml/1 tsp celery seed
30 ml/2 tbsp single cream

Heat the oil in a saucepan, add the onion and garlic and cook over gentle heat for 5 minutes. Add the celery and cook for 3-4 minutes, then stir in the flour. Cook for 1 minute, then gradually add the stock and wine, stirring until the sauce boils and thickens. Add the bay leaf and stir in salt and pepper to taste. Lower the heat and simmer the mixture for 20 minutes.

Wash the spinach several times and remove any coarse stalks. Put into a saucepan with just the water that clings to the leaves, then cover the pan with a tight-fitting lid. Place over moderate heat for about 3 minutes, shaking the pan often, until the spinach has wilted. Lower the heat slightly and cook for 3-5 minutes more.

When the spinach is tender, drain thoroughly in a colander. Cut through several times with a knife to chop roughly. Melt half the butter in the clean pan, add the spinach with salt and pepper to taste, and heat through gently.

Melt the remaining butter in a small frying pan, add the nuts, parsley and celery seed and fry lightly for 2-3 minutes. Arrange the spinach in a ring on a heated serving platter. Pile the celery mixture in the middle and sprinkle with the nut mixture. Serve at once.

SERVES 4

 MRS BEETON'S TIP Frozen spinach may be used instead of fresh. Use 2 (225 g/8 oz) packets frozen leaf spinach, and cook according to packet directions.

TOFU PARCELS

Illustrated on page 218

fat for greasing
1 carrot, diced
100 g/4 oz fine French beans, thinly sliced
salt and pepper
2 spring onions, chopped
30 ml/2 tbsp chopped parsley
4 large sheets filo pastry
50 g/2 oz butter, melted or 60 ml/4 tbsp
    olive oil
100 g/4 oz low-fat soft cheese with garlic
    and herbs
275 g/10 oz smoked tofu, quartered

WATERCRESS CREAM
    1 bunch watercress, trimmed and
        chopped
    5 ml/1 tsp grated lemon rind
    150 ml/¼ pint soured cream, fromage
        frais or Greek-style yogurt

Blanch the carrot and French beans in a saucepan of boiling salted water for 2 minutes, then drain and mix with the spring onions and parsley. Set the oven at 200°C/400°F/gas 6. Grease a baking sheet.

Work on 1 sheet of filo at a time, keeping the others covered. Brush the pastry with butter or olive oil and fold it in half. Place a quarter of the soft cheese in the middle, spreading it slightly but taking care not to tear the pastry. Divide the vegetable mixture into quarters. Use a teaspoon to sprinkle half of one portion over the cheese. Top with a quarter of the tofu, then sprinkle the remainder of the vegetable portion over.

Fold one side of the filo over the filling, brush lightly with butter or oil, then fold the opposite side over, pressing the pastry together. Brush with more fat and fold the two remaining sides over as before to make a neat parcel. Brush the top with a little oil or butter, then invert the parcel on the prepared baking sheet, so that the thicker layers of pastry are underneath. Brush the top with more fat. Repeat with the remaining pastry and filling.

Bake the parcels for about 30 minutes, until golden and crisp. Meanwhile, mix the watercress, lemon rind and soured cream, fromage frais or yogurt in a bowl. Add a little salt and pepper. Use a metal slice to transfer the parcels to serving plates and serve at once, with the watercress cream.

SERVES 4

> 🥣**MRS BEETON'S TIP** Tofu is another name for bean curd. It is white and set, with a texture which varies from very soft and rather jelly-like to firm with a hint of resistance to the bite. For stir frying buy a firm variety. Plain tofu is flavourless but it readily absorbs flavours from other ingredients. Tofu is also available smoked or flavoured with seasonings.

TOFU AND SPRING ONION STIR FRY

Illustrated on page 218
This tasty stir fry goes well with cooked rice or Oriental noodles.

350 g/12 oz firm tofu (see Mrs Beeton's Tip), cut into 2.5 cm/1 inch cubes
1 garlic clove, crushed
45 ml/3 tbsp soy sauce
5 cm/2 inch fresh root ginger, peeled and chopped
5 ml/1 tsp sesame oil
5 ml/1 tsp cornflour
30 ml/2 tbsp dry sherry
60 ml/4 tbsp vegetable stock
30 ml/2 tbsp oil
1 red pepper, seeded and diced
1 bunch of spring onions, trimmed and sliced diagonally
100 g/4 oz button mushrooms, sliced
salt and pepper

Place the tofu in a large, shallow dish. Mix the garlic, soy sauce, ginger and sesame oil in a bowl, then sprinkle the mixture evenly over the tofu. Cover and leave to marinate for 1 hour. In a jug, blend the cornflour to a paste with the sherry, then stir in the stock and set aside.

Heat the oil in a wok or large frying pan. Add the tofu and stir fry until lightly browned. Add the pepper and continue cooking for 2-3 minutes before stirring in the spring onions. Once the onions are combined with the tofu, make a space in the middle of the pan and stir fry the mushrooms for 2 minutes. Pour in the cornflour mixture and stir all the ingredients together. Bring the juice to the boil, stirring all the time, then lower the heat and simmer for 2 minutes. Taste the mixture, for seasoning, then serve.

SERVES 4

EGGS FLORENTINE

Illustrated on page 219

butter for greasing
1 kg/2¼ lb fresh spinach or 2 (225 g/8 oz)
    packets frozen leaf spinach
15 ml/1 tbsp butter
salt and pepper
4 eggs
100 g/4 oz Fontina or Cheddar cheese,
    finely grated

Set the oven at 190°C/375°F/gas 5. Wash the fresh spinach several times and remove any coarse stalks. Put into a saucepan with just the water that clings to the leaves, then cover the pan with a tight-fitting lid. Place over moderate heat for about 3 minutes, shaking the pan often until the spinach has wilted. Lower the heat slightly and cook for 3-5 minutes more. (Cook frozen spinach according to the directions on the packet.)

When the spinach is tender, drain it thoroughly in a colander. Cut through the leaves several times with a knife to chop them roughly. Melt the butter in the clean pan, add the spinach with salt and pepper to taste, and heat through gently.

Spoon into a greased ovenproof dish and, using the back of a spoon, make 4 small hollows in the surface. Break an egg into each hollow, add salt and pepper to taste, then sprinkle the grated cheese over the eggs. Bake for 12-15 minutes until the eggs are lightly set. Serve at once.

SERVES 4

CURRIED EGGS

Illustrated on page 219

60 ml/4 tbsp oil
2 onions, finely chopped
1 cooking apple
15-30 ml/1-2 tbsp mild curry powder
30 ml/2 tbsp plain flour
10 ml/2 tsp tomato purée
500 ml/17 fl oz vegetable stock
30 ml/2 tbsp mango chutney
15 ml/1 tbsp soft light brown sugar
30 ml/2 tbsp lemon juice
salt
6 eggs, hard boiled, shelled and cut into
    quarters
30 ml/2 tbsp plain yogurt

Heat the oil in a saucepan, add the onions and sauté for 4-6 minutes until soft but not coloured. Peel, core and chop the apple. Add it to the onions and continue cooking for 5 minutes.

Stir in the curry powder and flour and fry for 2-3 minutes, then add the tomato purée, vegetable stock, chutney, sugar, lemon juice and a pinch of salt. Bring to the boil, stirring constantly, then lower the heat, cover and simmer for 30 minutes, stirring occasionally.

Add the hard-boiled eggs and warm through over gentle heat. To serve, remove from the heat and gently stir in the yogurt, taking care not to break up the curried eggs.

SERVES 4

🥄 **MRS BEETON'S TIP** Cook some Basmati rice according to the instructions on page 355, adding a few frozen peas halfway through cooking. Serve the rice and peas with the eggs.

SPINACH GNOCCHI

butter for greasing
450 g/1 lb fresh spinach or 1 (225 g/8 oz)
   packet frozen spinach
100 g/4 oz butter
salt and pepper
150 g/5 oz ricotta
1 egg, beaten
30 ml/2 tbsp double cream
40 g/1½ oz plain flour
25 g/1 oz semolina
75 g/3 oz Parmesan cheese, grated
1.25 ml/¼ tsp grated nutmeg

Wash the fresh spinach several times and remove any coarse stalks. Put into a saucepan with just the water that clings to the leaves, then cover the pan and cook over moderately high heat, shaking the pan, until wilted. Lower the heat and cook for 3-5 minutes more. (Cook frozen spinach according to the directions on the packet.)

When the spinach is tender, drain thoroughly in a colander. Cut through several times with a knife to chop roughly. Melt 50 g/2 oz of the butter in the clean pan, add the spinach with salt and pepper to taste, and cook over moderate heat until it is quite dry, stirring constantly. Rub the ricotta through a sieve, add to the spinach and cook for 2-3 minutes. Remove the pan from the heat.

Beat the egg into the spinach mixture with the cream, flour, 15 g/½ oz semolina and 25 g/1 oz Parmesan cheese. Add more salt and pepper, if needed, and stir in the nutmeg. Put the mixture on a flat dish and chill for 1-2 hours.

Grease an ovenproof dish. Bring a large saucepan of water to the boil. Use two dessertspoons to shape the semolina mixture into small ovals and drop them into the water, a few at a time. Remove the gnocchi with a slotted spoon as soon as they rise to the surface, and place them in the dish.

Melt the remaining butter in a small pan and pour it over the gnocchi. Sprinkle with the rest of the Parmesan cheese and remaining semolina. Place under a hot grill for a few minutes until the cheese has melted and the topping is golden brown.

SERVES 4 TO 6

POLENTA WITH CHEESE

Polenta is also known as maize flour and cornmeal.

5 ml/1 tsp salt
200 g/7 oz polenta
50 g/2 oz butter
50 g/2 oz Parmesan cheese, grated

Bring 500 ml/17 fl oz water to the boil in a saucepan with the salt. Add the polenta and stir well with a wooden spoon. Cook for 20-30 minutes, stirring all the time. When the mixture leaves the sides of the saucepan cleanly, stir in the butter and Parmesan quickly and thoroughly.

Put the mixture on a dish which has been sprinkled with cold water. Serve in slices.

SERVES 3 TO 4

VARIATION

Cut cold polenta into pieces, 1 cm/½ inch thick. Place in a pie dish and cover with a thick layer of grated cheese. Continue layering the polenta and cheese until all the polenta has been used up. Top with a thick layer of cheese and dot with butter. Bake in a preheated 190°C/375°F/gas 5 oven for 20-25 minutes.

CHEESE PUDDING

butter for greasing
100-150 g/4-5 oz Cheddar or Gruyère
  cheese, grated
2 eggs, beaten
250 ml/8 fl oz whole or skimmed milk
100 g/4 oz fresh white breadcrumbs
salt (optional)

Butter a 600 ml/1 pint ovenproof dish. Set the oven at 180°C/350°F/gas 4.

Combine the cheese, eggs and milk in a bowl. Add the breadcrumbs with a little salt, if needed. Mix thoroughly, then pour into the prepared dish.

Bake for 25-30 minutes, until set in the centre and browned on top. Serve hot.

SERVES 4

CORN PUDDING

fat for greasing
100 g/4 oz plain flour
5 ml/1 tsp salt
2.5 ml/½ tsp black pepper
2 eggs, beaten
500 ml/17 fl oz milk
400 g/14 oz fresh or frozen sweetcorn
  kernels

Grease a 1.5 litre/2¾ pint pie or ovenproof dish. Set the oven at 180°C/350°F/ gas 4.

Sift the flour, salt and pepper into a bowl. Add the beaten eggs, stirring well. Beat together with the milk and then the corn to form a batter. Turn into the prepared dish. Bake for 1 hour. Serve hot.

SERVES 6

RISOTTO MILANESE

Illustrated on page 184

75 g/3 oz butter
30 ml/2 tbsp olive oil
1 onion, finely chopped
350 g/12 oz risotto rice
600 ml/1 pint vegetable stock
300 ml/½ pint dry white wine
2.5 ml/½ tsp saffron threads
salt and pepper
150 g/5 oz Parmesan cheese, grated

Heat 25 g/1 oz of the butter with the olive oil in a large saucepan. Add the onion and fry gently, stirring occasionally for 10 minutes. Add the rice and cook for a few minutes, stirring gently until all the rice grains are coated in fat. Meanwhile heat the stock to simmering point in a separate pan.

Put the saffron threads in a mortar and pound them with a pestle. Stir in a little of the hot stock to dissolve the saffron, then set aside.

Add the wine and half the remaining stock to the rice, with salt and pepper to taste. Bring to the boil. Stir once, lower the heat and cover the pan tightly. Leave over low heat for 10 minutes. Pour in half the remaining hot stock, do not stir, then cover and cook for 5 minutes, shaking the pan occasionally to prevent sticking. Finally, add the remaining stock and saffron liquid. Stir once or twice, cover and cook for about 10 minutes, until the rice is cooked, creamy and moist.

Stir in the remaining butter and the cheese. Taste the risotto, adding more salt and pepper if required. Cover tightly and leave to stand for 5 minutes before serving.

SERVES 4

MUSHROOM OVEN OMELETTE

Although any mushrooms can be used for this omelette, button or closed cup mushrooms yield less liquid and give a better colour than dark open or flat mushrooms.

butter for greasing
50 g/2 oz unsalted butter or margarine
225 g/8 oz mushrooms, sliced
salt and pepper
15 ml/1 tbsp plain flour
250 ml/8 fl oz milk
30 ml/2 tbsp double cream
15 ml/1 tbsp dry sherry
4 eggs, beaten

Grease a 23 cm/9 inch flan dish. Set the oven at 180°C/350°F/gas 4. Heat the butter in a frying pan, add the mushrooms and fry over moderate to high heat for about 3 minutes until tender. Add salt and pepper to taste, then add the flour. Cook, stirring, for 1 minute. Gradually add half the milk, stirring constantly until the mixture boils and thickens. Cook for 1-2 minutes, stirring constantly.

Remove the mushroom mixture from the heat, allow it to cool slightly, then stir in the sherry. Spoon into the prepared dish. Spread the mixture out evenly.

Beat the eggs and remaining milk together, add salt and pepper to taste and pour this over the mushroom mixture. Bake for 30 minutes until golden brown. Serve at once.

SERVES 2

CREAM CHEESE FLAN

175 g/6 oz plan flour
salt and pepper
75 g/3 oz margarine
7.5 ml/1½ tsp gelatine
1 egg yolk
60 ml/4 tbsp milk, warmed
100 g/4 oz full-fat soft cheese
30 ml/2 tbsp snipped chives
150 ml/¼ pint soured cream
60 ml/4 tbsp grated Parmesan cheese
6 tomatoes, roughly chopped

Set the oven at 200°C/400°F/gas 6. Mix the flour and salt in a bowl, then rub in the margarine until the mixture resembles fine breadcrumbs. Bind with cold water.

Roll out the pastry on a lightly floured surface and use to line a 20 cm/8 inch flan tin. Line the pastry with greaseproof paper and fill with baking beans. Bake for 15 minutes. Remove the paper and beans; cook for a further 10-15 minutes.

Place 30 ml/2 tbsp water in a small bowl and sprinkle the gelatine on to the liquid. Set aside for 15 minutes, until the gelatine is spongy. Stand the bowl over a saucepan of hot water and stir until dissolved.

Whisk the egg yolk, with the milk, salt and pepper to taste in a bowl. Stir in the dissolved gelatine. In a separate, larger, bowl, beat the cheese until creamy. Gradually add the milk mixture, then chill until on the point of setting. Stir in the chives, soured cream and Parmesan cheese. Turn the mixture into the prepared flan case and chill for at least 2 hours.

Arrange concentric circles of chopped tomato on top of the cheese mixture to fill the flan case. Serve soon after topping.

SERVES 6

CURRIED BEANS

Most dried beans can be curried to provide a tasty, nourishing and inexpensive main meal. Simply adjust the cooking time after soaking and boiling for 10 minutes. Borlotti beans require 30 minutes; black-eyed beans 30-40 minutes; black beans 30-60 minutes (depending on type and size) and pinto or haricot beans 1-1¼ hours. Red kidney beans take 50-60 minutes to cook and chick-peas require 1 hour. Soya beans are particularly nutritious and have a good flavour; however, they must be soaked for a full 24 hours and boiled rapidly for 45 minutes, then simmered until tender – which can take up to 2 hours. Top up the water during cooking.

225 g/8 oz dried beans, soaked overnight
    in water (see note above)
30 ml/2 tbsp oil
1 onion, chopped
2 celery sticks, sliced
1 carrot, diced
2 garlic cloves, crushed
5 cm/2 inch fresh root ginger, peeled and
    chooped
30 ml/2 tbsp ground coriander
15 ml/1 tbsp ground cumin
5 ml/1 tsp turmeric
2 (397 g/14 oz) cans chopped tomatoes
1 bay leaf
salt and pepper

Drain the beans. Put them in a saucepan with fresh water to cover. Bring to the boil, boil vigorously for 10 minutes, then lower the heat, cover the pan and simmer until the beans are tender.

Heat the oil in a saucepan and add the onion, celery, carrot, garlic and ginger. Fry over gentle heat for about 10 minutes until the onion is soft. Add the spices and cook for 2-3 minutes more, stirring all the time.

Stir in the tomatoes, with their juices. Drain the beans, reserving the cooking liquid, and add them to the pan, with the bay leaf. Turn the mixture lightly, then add 300 ml/½ pint of the reserved cooking liquid, with salt and pepper to taste. Cover and cook over low heat for 1 hour. Transfer to a heated serving dish, top with a *baghar* (see Mrs Beeton's Tip) and serve with Nan bread and plain cooked spinach with yogurt.

SERVES 4 TO 6

> **MRS BEETON'S TIP** To make a *baghar*, melt 30 ml/2 tbsp ghee or butter in a small frying pan. Add 1 very thinly sliced onion, 30 ml/2 tbsp cumin seeds and 15 ml/1 tbsp mustard seeds. Cover the pan and fry the mixture until the seeds pop. Pour over the curry when serving.

HARICOT BEANS WITH PARSLEY SAUCE

200 g/7 oz haricot beans, soaked
    overnight in water to cover
30 ml/2 tbsp butter
1 onion, finely chopped
100 g/4 oz mushrooms, thinly sliced
15 ml/1 tbsp lemon juice
Pesto Sauce (see Mrs Beeton's Tip) to
    serve

PARSLEY SAUCE
    25 g/1 oz butter
    25 g/1 oz plain flour
    300 ml/½ pint milk
    salt and pepper
    60 ml/4 tbsp chopped parsley

Drain the beans. Put them in a saucepan with fresh water to cover. Bring to the boil, boil vigorously for 10 minutes, then lower the heat, cover the pan and simmer for about 1 hour or until the beans are tender.

When the beans are almost cooked, melt the butter in a small frying pan, add the onion and fry over gentle heat for 10 minutes until the onion is soft and transparent. Add the mushrooms and cook for a further 5 minutes. Set the pan aside.

Make the parsley sauce. Melt the butter in a saucepan, stir in the flour and cook for 1 minute. Gradually add the milk, stirring constantly, and cook until the mixture boils and thickens. Add salt and pepper to taste, then stir in the parsley.

Drain the haricot beans. Add them to the parsley sauce with the lemon juice. Toss together lightly. Stir in the reserved mushroom mixture, with salt and pepper to taste. Place over moderate heat for a few minutes until the beans are heated through.

Serve in individual bowls, topping each portion with a dollop of pesto sauce.

SERVES 6

MRS BEETON'S TIP Pesto sauce can be bought in jars from most supermarkets and delicatessens. To make your own, grind 30 ml/2 tbsp pine nuts with 2 crushed garlic cloves. Use a blender, food processor or mortar and pestle. Chop a large handful of fresh basil (use thin stalks as well as leaves). Add the basil to the nuts with 60 ml/4 tbsp Parmesan cheese; blend the mixture to a purée. Gradually work in 150 ml/¼ pint olive oil to make a thick mayonnaise-like mixture. Add salt and pepper to taste. If not using at once, pour into a clean jar, cover with a thin layer of olive oil and store in the refrigerator.

BOSTON ROAST

Illustrated on page 220

fat for greasing
300 g/11 oz haricot beans, soaked
    overnight in water to cover
salt and pepper
15 ml/1 tbsp oil
1 onion, chopped
150 g/5 oz Cheddar cheese, grated
60 ml/4 tbsp vegetable stock
1 egg, beaten
100 g/4 oz fresh white breadcrumbs
5 ml/1 tsp dried thyme
2.5 ml/½ tsp grated nutmeg

Drain the beans, put them in a saucepan and add fresh water to cover. Do not add salt. Bring to the boil, cook for 10 minutes, then lower the heat and simmer for about 1 hour or until tender. Drain the beans. Mash them finely with salt to taste, or purée in a blender or food processor.

Set the oven at 180°C/350°F/gas 4. Heat the oil in a frying pan, add the onion and fry for about 10 minutes, or until softened. Tip the onion into a large bowl and add the mashed or puréed beans with the rest of the ingredients.

Spoon the mixture into a well greased 900 g/2 lb loaf tin. Cover the surface with greased greaseproof paper. Bake for 45 minutes, until firm and slightly shrunk. Serve with Fresh Tomato Sauce (page 352).

SERVES 6

FREEZER TIP Boston Roast freezes very well. Cool quickly, then slice. Separate individual slices with freezer film and wrap in an airtight polythene bag. Remove individual slices as required.

SOYA BEAN BAKE

fat for greasing
450 g/1 lb soya beans, soaked for 24 hours
   in water to cover
2 onions, finely chopped
1 green pepper, seeded and chopped
1 carrot, coarsely grated
1 celery stick, sliced
45 ml/3 tbsp molasses
45 ml/3 tbsp chopped parsley
5 ml/1 tsp dried thyme
5 ml/1 tsp dried savory or marjoram
salt and pepper
2 (397 g/14 oz) cans chopped tomatoes
175 g/6 oz medium oatmeal
50 g/2 oz Lancashire or Caerphilly
   cheese, finely crumbled or grated
45 ml/3 tbsp snipped chives
50 ml/2 fl oz olive oil

Grease a large ovenproof dish – a lasagne dish is ideal. Set the oven at 180°C/350° F/ gas 4. Drain the beans. Put them in a saucepan with fresh water to cover. Bring to the boil, boil vigorously for 45 minutes, then lower the heat, add more boiling water if necessary, cover the pan and simmer for 1½-2 hours or until tender. Top up the water as necessary.

Drain the beans and put them in a mixing bowl with the onions, green pepper, carrot and celery. Warm the molasses in a small saucepan and pour it over the bean mixture. Stir in the herbs, with salt and pepper. Mix in the canned tomatoes.

Spoon the mixture into the prepared dish. Mix the oatmeal, cheese and chives. Spoon the oatmeal mixture over the beans, then drizzle the olive oil over the top. Cover the dish with foil or a lid and bake for 45 minutes. Remove the lid and bake for a further 15 minutes. Serve hot.

SERVES 6

BOILED LENTILS

Red lentils are readily available. This type needs no presoaking and quickly cooks to a pale gold mass. It does not retain its shape when cooking, a characteristic which makes it ideal for purées, vegetarian pâtés, soups and layer bakes. Continental lentils (green or brown lentils) take slightly longer to cook. They do not lose their shape and are useful for adding texture to dishes. The black *lentilles de Puy* from the Auvergne in France have the finest flavour.

Measure the liquid for red lentils as it should all be absorbed at the end of cooking, leaving the pulses soft and moist – rather like mashed potato when stirred. Allow 600 ml/1 pint liquid to 225 g/8 oz red lentils, checking two-thirds of the way through cooking and adding a little extra liquid if necessary. It is important that the lentils do not dry before they are tender. Bring to the boil, lower the heat, cover and simmer until tender. Red lentils will take about 20 minutes. Green and brown lentils take 30-45 minutes and Puy lentils 40-50 minutes.

Allow 50 g/2 oz per person as a side dish; 75 g/3 oz with vegetables; 100 g/4 oz served simply as a main course.

1 onion stuck with 2 cloves
450 g/1 lb split red lentils
1 bouquet garni
25 g/1 oz butter • salt and pepper

Put the onion into a saucepan with the lentils and bouquet garni. Add 1.1 litres/ 2 pints water and bring to the boil. Lower the heat, cover tightly and simmer for 20 minutes or until the lentils are soft. Check that the water is not absorbed completely before the lentils are tender. Discard the onion and bouquet garni. Stir in the butter with salt and pepper. Serve at once.

SERVES 4 TO 6

SPICED LENTILS

Illustrated on page 292

450 g/1 lb red lentils
2 whole cardamoms, lightly crushed to
    split the pods
2.5 ml/½ tsp sea salt
45 ml/3 tbsp oil
1 onion, chopped
5 ml/1 tsp turmeric
15 ml/1 tbsp grated fresh root ginger or
    5 ml/1 tsp ground ginger
3 tomatoes, chopped
1 garlic clove, crushed
5 ml/1 tsp ground coriander
pinch of chilli powder

GARNISH (optional)
    chopped fresh coriander leaves
    finely chopped onion

Put the lentils and cardamoms in a large pan. Add 1 litre/1¾ pints water and stir in the salt. Bring to the boil, lower the heat and cover the pan. Simmer for 20 minutes, checking after 15 minutes to ensure the lentils have not dried up. The cooked lentils should have absorbed all the water, and they should be very soft. Set aside.

Heat the oil in a large deep frying pan, add the onion, turmeric and ginger, and fry gently until the onion is soft and lightly browned. Add the remaining ingredients. Fry for 3-4 minutes, stirring all the time. Remove from the heat.

Add the lentils to the pan. Mix thoroughly to coat them with the spicy mixture. Replace over moderate heat and cook, stirring occasionally, until heated through and quite mushy. Serve very hot, sprinkled with the coriander and onion, if liked.

SERVES 4 TO 6

LENTIL PASTIES

100 g/4 oz split red lentils
300 ml/½ pint vegetable stock
25 g/1 oz butter
salt and pepper
pinch of grated nutmeg
4 button mushrooms, sliced
15 ml/1 tbsp double cream
beaten egg or milk to glaze

SHORT CRUST PASTRY
225 g/8 oz plain flour
2.5 ml/½ tsp salt
100 g/4 oz margarine
flour for rolling out

Make the pastry. Sift the flour and salt into a bowl, then rub in the margarine until the mixture resembles fine breadcrumbs. Add enough cold water to make a stiff dough. Press the dough together with your fingertips. Wrap in greaseproof paper and chill until required.

Put the lentils in a saucepan with the vegetable stock. Bring to the boil, lower the heat and cover the pan. Simmer for 20 minutes or until the lentils are soft and all the liquid is absorbed. Beat in the butter and season with salt, pepper and nutmeg. Stir in the mushrooms and cream. Set aside. Set the oven at 200°C/400°F/gas 6.

Roll out the pastry very thinly on a floured surface, and cut into 8 × 13 cm/ 5 inch rounds. Divide the lentil filling between the rounds, dampen the edges and fold over to form half circles. Press the edges together and seal firmly, then brush with a little beaten egg or milk. Place on baking sheets and bake for about 15 minutes, or until the pastry is cooked and browned.

MAKES 8

LENTIL AND STILTON LASAGNE

225 g/8 oz green lentils
8 sheets of lasagne
salt and pepper
30 ml/2 tbsp olive oil
1 large onion, chopped
1 garlic clove, crushed
5 ml/1 tsp dried marjoram
225 g/8 oz mushrooms, sliced
2 (397 g/14 oz) cans chopped tomatoes
225 g/8 oz ripe blue Stilton cheese
    (without rind)
30 ml/2 tbsp plain flour
300 ml/½ pint milk

Cook the lentils in plenty of boiling water for 35 minutes, until just tender. Cook the lasagne in boiling salted water with a little oil added for 12-15 minutes, or until just tender. Drain both and set the lentils aside; lay the lasagne out to dry on absorbent kitchen paper.

Heat the remaining oil in a large saucepan. Add the onion, garlic and marjoram, and cook for 10 minutes, or until slightly softened. Stir in the mushrooms and cook for 5 minutes before adding the tomatoes. Stir in the cooked lentils with plenty of salt and pepper and bring to the boil. Reduce the heat and cover the pan, then simmer for 5 minutes.

Set the oven at 180°C/350°F/gas 4. Grease a lasagne dish or large ovenproof dish. Pour half the lentil mixture in the base of the dish and top it with half the lasagne. Pour the remaining lentil mixture over the pasta, then end with the remaining pasta.

Mash the Stilton in a bowl with a sturdy fork or process it in a food processor. Sprinkle a little of the flour over the cheese and work it in, then add the remaining flour in the same way to make the mixture crumbly. Gradually work in the milk, a little at a time, pounding the cheese at first, then beating it as it softens. When the mixture is soft and creamy, the remaining milk may be incorporated more quickly. Add some pepper and just a little salt. Pour the mixture over the lasagne, scraping the bowl clean. Bake for 40-45 minutes, or until the top of the lasagne is well browned and bubbling.

SERVES 6

LENTIL AND BROCCOLI GRATIN

225 g/8 oz green or brown lentils
2 onions, chopped
1 bay leaf
750 ml/1¼ pints vegetable stock
450 g/1 lb broccoli, broken into small
    florets
30 ml/2 tbsp oil
6 tomatoes, peeled and quartered
150 ml/¼ pint medium cider
salt and pepper
225 g/8 oz mozzarella cheese, diced

Place the lentils in a saucepan with 1 onion, the bay leaf and the stock. Bring to the boil, then lower the heat and cover the pan. Simmer the lentils for 40-50 minutes, until they are tender and most of the stock has been absorbed. Check that they do not become dry during cooking. Replace the cover and leave to stand off the heat.

Meanwhile, cook the broccoli in a saucepan of boiling water for 2-3 minutes, until just tender. Drain. Heat the oil in a large flameproof casserole and add the remaining onion. Cook, stirring, for 10-15 minutes, or until softened. Stir in the broccoli, tomatoes and cider with salt and pepper. Cook, stirring occasionally, for 15 minutes.

Discard the bay leaf from the lentils, then tip them into the pan with the broccoli mixture. Stir to combine all the ingredients. Taste and add more salt and pepper if required. Top with the mozzarella cheese and grill until the cheese is bubbling, crisp and golden. Serve piping hot.

SERVES 4 TO 6

SPICY SPINACH AND CHICK-PEAS

The use of canned chick-peas makes this delicious dish a quick-cook option.

25 g/1 oz butter
30 ml/2 tbsp cumin seeds
15 ml/1 tbsp coriander seeds, crushed
15 ml/1 tbsp mustard seeds
1 large onion, chopped
2 garlic cloves, crushed
2 (425 g/15 oz) can chick-peas, drained
5 ml/1 tsp turmeric
1 kg/2¼ lb fresh spinach, cooked
salt and pepper

Melt the butter in a saucepan, add the cumin, coriander and mustard seeds and cook gently, stirring, for about 3 minutes, or until the seeds are aromatic. Keep the heat low to avoid burning the butter.

Add the onion and garlic to the pan and continue to cook for about 15 minutes, until the onion is softened. Stir in the chick-peas and turmeric and cook for 5 minutes, until thoroughly hot. Tip the spinach into the pan and stir it over moderate heat until heated through. Season and serve.

SERVES 4 TO 6

CHICK-PEA CASSEROLE

Illustrated on page 221

A few fresh herb sprigs used as a garnish improve the appearance of individual portions.

300 g/11 oz chick-peas, soaked overnight
    in water to cover
30 ml/2 tbsp olive oil
1 onion, chopped
1 garlic clove, crushed
1 bay leaf
1 green pepper, seeded and sliced
200 g/7 oz white cabbage, shredded
100 g/4 oz mushrooms, sliced
1 (397 g/14 oz) can chopped tomatoes
2.5 ml/½ tsp ground ginger
pinch of ground cloves
salt and pepper
30 ml/2 tbsp chopped mint
60 ml/4 tbsp chopped parsley

Drain the chick-peas, put them in a saucepan and add fresh water to cover. Do not add salt. Bring to the boil, cook for 10 minutes, then lower the heat and simmer for 1-1½ hours or until tender. Drain the chick-peas, reserving the cooking liquor.

Heat the olive oil in a large saucepan, add the onion, garlic, bay leaf, green pepper and cabbage and fry over moderate heat for 10 minutes. Add the mushrooms, chick-peas and tomatoes. Stir in 100 ml/4 fl oz of the reserved cooking liquor, with the ginger and ground cloves. Add salt and pepper to taste. Bring to the boil, lower the heat and cook very gently for 1 hour, adding more liquid, if required, during cooking. The cooked casserole should be moist, but there should not be too much liquid. Before serving, stir in the mint, parsley and more seasoning if necessary.

SERVES 4

BLACK-EYED BEAN AND TOMATO GOULASH

225 g/8 oz black-eyed beans, soaked
    overnight
1 large aubergine, trimmed and diced
salt and pepper
45 ml/3 tbsp oil
2 large onions, chopped
1 garlic clove, crushed
4 celery sticks, diced
1 large red pepper, seeded and diced
1 bay leaf
2 thyme sprigs
15 ml/1 tbsp paprika
15 ml/1 tbsp suger
2 (397 g/14 oz) cans chopped tomatoes
150 ml/¼ pint plain yogurt

Drain the soaked beans. Put them in a saucepan with plenty of fresh water. Bring to the boil, boil vigorously for 10 minutes, then lower the heat and cover the pan. Simmer for 30-40 minutes, or until tender.

Meanwhile, place the aubergine in a colander. Sprinkle with salt, then leave over a bowl or in the sink for 30 minutes. Rinse and drain well.

Heat the oil in a saucepan. Add the chopped onion, garlic, celery, pepper, bay leaf and thyme. Cook, stirring often, for 15-20 minutes, or until the onion is soft but not brown. Add the aubergine. Cook, stirring often, for 15 minutes, until tender.

Add salt and pepper to taste, stir in the paprika and sugar, then pour in the tomatoes and bring the mixture to the boil. Drain the black-eyed beans and add them to the pan. Mix well and simmer for 5 minutes, then taste for seasoning. Top each portion with a little yogurt.

SERVES 4 TO 6

TAGLIATELLE WITH BORLOTTI BEANS

350 g/12 oz tagliatelle
salt and pepper
25 g/1 oz butter
30 ml/2 tbsp olive oil
1 garlic clove, crushed
1 onion, chopped
100 g/4 oz button mushrooms, sliced
2 (425 g/15 oz) cans borlotti beans,
    drained
225 g/8 oz tomatoes, peeled and chopped
5 ml/1 tsp dried oregano
45 ml/3 tbsp chopped parsley
grated Parmesan cheese to serve

Bring a large saucepan of salted water to the boil and cook the pasta. Allow 3 minutes for fresh pasta or about 12 minutes for the dried type. Drain well and set aside.

Heat the butter, oil and garlic in a large frying pan. Add the onion and fry it over gentle heat, stirring, for about 15 minutes or until softened. Add the mushrooms and cook for 5 minutes before stirring in the beans and tomatoes with the herbs. Add salt and pepper to taste and cook for 10 minutes.

Tip the tagliatelle into the pan and toss it with the bean mixture until piping hot – about 5 minutes. Divide between 4 large bowls and serve with freshly grated Parmesan cheese.

SERVES 4

VEGETABLE CHILLI

Illustrated on page 222

1 large aubergine, trimmed and cut into
    2.5 cm/1 inch cubes
salt and pepper
60 ml/4 tbsp oil
1 large onion, chopped
4 celery sticks, sliced
1 green pepper, seeded and chopped
2 garlic cloves, crushed
1 large potato, cut into 2.5 cm/1 inch
    cubes
1 large carrot, diced
5-10 ml/1-2 tsp chilli powder
15 ml/1 tbsp ground coriander
15 ml/1 tbsp ground cumin
100 g/4 oz mushrooms, sliced
2 (397 g/14 oz) cans chopped tomatoes
2 (425 g/15 oz) cans red kidney beans,
    drained
2 courgettes, halved lengthways and cut
    in chunks
100 g/4 oz frozen cut green beans or peas

Place the aubergine cubes in a colander, sprinkling each layer with salt. Stand the colander over a bowl or in the sink and leave for 30 minutes. Rinse the aubergine and dry the cubes on absorbent kitchen paper.

Heat the oil and fry the onion, celery, pepper and garlic until the onion is slightly softened. Stir in the aubergine and cook, stirring, until the outside of the cubes are lightly cooked. Stir in the potato, carrot, chilli, coriander and cumin. Stir for a few minutes to coat all the vegetables in the spices, then lightly mix in the mushrooms and tomatoes. Bring to the boil, lower the heat so that the mixture simmers and cover. Cook, stirring occasionally, for 30 minutes.

Add the kidney beans, courgettes, beans or peas, with salt and pepper to taste. Cover and continue to cook for a further 30 minutes, stirring occasionally, or until all the vegetables are tender. The juice from the vegetables, combined with the canned tomatoes, should be sufficient to keep the mixture moist. If the mixture cooks too quickly the liquid will evaporate and the vegetables may stick to the pan.

SERVES 4

FLAGEOLET AND FENNEL STIR FRY

30 ml/2 tbsp oil
1 large onion, halved and sliced
1 bay leaf
2 fennel bulbs, thinly sliced
2 (425 g/15 oz) cans flageolet beans,
    drained
salt and pepper
2 avocados
juice of ½ lemon
30 ml/2 tbsp chopped mint

Heat the oil in a wok or large frying pan. Add the onion, bay leaf and fennel. Stir fry the vegetables for about 20 minutes, or until they are slightly tender.

Add the flageolets with salt and pepper to taste. Stir well, then lower the heat and leave to cook gently for 5 minutes, or until the beans are hot. Meanwhile, halve, stone and peel the avocados. Dice the flesh, put it into a bowl, add the lemon juice and toss lightly.

Stir the avocado into the bean mixture, add the mint and cook for 1 minute. Serve at once, with a plain risotto or warmed crusty bread and a crisp green salad, if liked.

SERVES 4

ADUKI PILAF

45 ml/3 tbsp olive oil
1 garlic clove, crushed
1 cinnamon stick
4 cloves
1 bay leaf
2 onions, sliced
225 g/8 oz brown rice
600 ml/1 pint vegetable stock
300 ml/½ pint dry white wine
salt and pepper
100 g/4 oz aduki beans, soaked, drained
   and cooked
100 g/4 oz blanched almonds, split
2 celery sticks, diced
1 eating apple, peeled, cored and diced
100 g/4 oz ready-to-eat dried apricots,
   diced
grated rind of 1 lemon
30 ml/2 tbsp chopped mint

Heat 30 ml/2 tbsp of the oil in a heavy-bottomed saucepan. Add the garlic, cinnamon, cloves, bay leaf and half the onion slices. Cook for 5 minutes, stirring, then add the rice.

Stir in the stock. Pour in the wine and add salt and pepper. Bring to the boil, lower the heat and cover the pan. Cook for 15 minutes.

Drain the beans if necessary. Tip them into the pan but do not mix them into the rice. Replace the lid quickly and continue cooking for a further 15 minutes over low heat. Turn the heat off and leave the pan covered.

Meanwhile, heat the remaining oil in a frying pan. Add the almonds and brown them all over, then using a slotted spoon, transfer them to a plate. Add the remaining onion and the celery to the oil remaining in the pan and cook until the onion is browned – about 20-30 minutes. Stir occasionally to prevent the onion from burning.

Stir the apple and apricots into the onion, with a little salt and pepper. Cook for 5 minutes more. Lastly stir in the browned almonds, lemon rind and mint.

Fork the beans into the rice, then turn it into a large serving dish. Sprinkle the onion mixture over the pilaf and serve at once.

SERVES 4

THREE-BEAN SAUTE

A quick and easy dish for a light meal, this sauté tastes delicious when served on a base of mixed green salad – crunchy Iceberg lettuce, some thinly sliced green pepper and sliced cucumber.

100 g/4 oz shelled broad beans
juice of 2 oranges
2 carrots, cut into matchstick strips
225 g/8 oz fine French beans
salt and pepper
30 ml/2 tbsp oil
1 onion, halved and thinly sliced
2 (425 g/15 oz) cans butter beans, drained
30 ml/2 tbsp chopped parsley
4 tomatoes, peeled, seeded and cut into
   eighths

Place the broad beans in a saucepan with the orange juice. Add just enough water to cover the beans, then bring to the boil. Lower the heat slightly so that the beans simmer steadily. Cook for 5 minutes.

Add the carrots and French beans, mix well and sprinkle in a little salt and pepper. Continue to cook, stirring often, until the carrots are just tender and the liquid has evaporated to leave the vegetables juicy. Set aside.

Heat the oil in a clean sancepan and cook the onion until softened but not browned – about 10 minutes. Stir in the butter beans and parsley, and cook for 5 minutes, stirring until the beans are hot. Tip the carrot mixture into the pan, add the tomatoes and mix well. Cook for 1-2 minutes before serving.

SERVES 4

FLAGEOLET BEAN SALAD

The fresh green colour and tender flavour of flageolets makes them an ideal candidate for a light summer salad. For non-vegetarians, add a little crumbled grilled bacon or drained flaked tuna. Serve with French bread.

225 g/8 oz dried flageolet beans, soaked
    overnight in water to cover
1 bouquet garni
150 ml/¼ pint mayonnaise
1 onion, finely chopped
15 ml/1 tbsp finely chopped parsley
salt

Drain the beans, put them in a clean saucepan with the bouquet garni and add fresh water to cover. Bring the water to the boil, boil briskly for 10 minutes, then lower the heat and simmer the beans for 1¼-1½ hours until tender.

Drain the beans thoroughly, remove the bouquet garni and tip into a bowl. While the beans are still warm, stir in the mayonnaise, onion and parsley, with salt to taste. Toss lightly.

Allow the salad to stand for at least 3 hours before serving to allow the flavours to blend.

SERVES 4 TO 6

LENTIL SALAD

225 g/8 oz brown or green lentils
1 bouquet garni
2 garlic cloves, crushed
30 ml/2 tbsp olive oil
salt and pepper
½ cucumber, diced
3 spring onions, finely chopped
4 tomatoes, peeled and diced
30 ml/2 tbsp shredded fresh basil or
    chopped parsley
1 avocado
15 ml/1 tbsp lemon juice
200 g/7 oz feta cheese, diced

Put the lentils into a saucepan with the bouquet garni. Add water to cover generously. Bring to the boil, lower the heat and simmer for 30-45 minutes until the lentils are tender. Green lentils should be cooked in 30-35 minutes, brown ones take slightly longer. Drain the lentils, discarding the bouquet garni.

Tip the lentils into a bowl and toss with the garlic and olive oil. Add salt and pepper to taste and set aside to cool. Add the cucumber, spring onions, tomatoes and basil or parsley.

Just before serving, peel the avocado and dice it into a bowl. Add the lemon juice. Mix lightly into the salad, with the feta.

SERVES 4 TO 6

MRS BEETON'S TIP Feta has a slightly sharp and salty flavour and a white, moist appearance. The cheese originated in Greece, but has become so popular that it is widely produced. Made from ewes', goats' or cows' milk and matured in brine, it is generally sold in vacuum packs which seal in the moisture.

BREAKFASTS AND BRUNCHES

Although everyday breakfasts have become quick and practical light meals, weekends, holidays and festive occasions still provide ideal opportunities for relaxing over traditional morning fare.

Before the days of central heating, cars and quick modes of transport, a hearty hot breakfast was a winter necessity. From thick porridge or 'pobs' – bread soaked in sweetened milk or hot tea – to splendid country-house feasts, breakfasts were designed to fuel the body for the day ahead or permit the fortunate few to linger over their morning mail and newspapers.

Breakfast cereals and porridge, toast or quick-cooked eggs – with bacon as an occasional treat – are still very popular, but many people prefer to start the day with fruit, a continental pastry or a yogurt. This chapter concentrates on a few traditional cooked dishes to serve as the main course of a breakfast or brunch menu. If you are planning a special meal, offer fruit juice, fresh fruit, cereals, toast, muffins or croissants and marmalade or honey. Coffee or tea are the traditional beverages, but Buck's Fizz, a mixture of fresh orange juice and champagne, may be served to add a bit of sparkle to the proceedings, if liked.

COOKING EGGS

Boiling Bring the eggs to room temperature before cooking to avoid cracking the shell if it is very cold. If an egg does crack, add 15 ml/1 tbsp vinegar or lemon juice to the cooking water to set the white quickly as it escapes.

Bring a small saucepan of water to the boil, allowing enough water to cover the eggs. Place an egg on a spoon and lower it into the water. Begin timing the cooking as soon as the egg is in the water. Regulate the heat so that the water is just boiling. Timing for boiled eggs is very personal but the following provides a guide when cooking average-sized eggs (sizes 3-4):

Soft boiled (soft set white) 3¼ minutes
Medium (soft yolk, firm white) 4-4¾ minutes
Hard (firm white, just firm yolk) 10 minutes

Poaching Pour about 5 cm/2 inches water into a pan – a frying pan is ideal. Add 15 ml/1 tbsp cider vinegar and bring just to simmering point. Crack a fresh egg on to a saucer. Use a draining spoon to swirl the water in the pan, then slide the egg into the middle of the gentle swirl. (The swirling water gives the egg a good shape.) Simmer for about 3 minutes, or until the egg is set. Spoon the simmering water over the egg to set it evenly. Up to 4 eggs may be cooked at the same time in a frying pan. Use a slotted spoon to drain the eggs as they are cooked. Trim the edges of the whites and serve at once.

Scrambled Eggs Allow 2 eggs per person. Put the requisite number of eggs in a bowl. Add 15-30 ml/1-2 tbsp milk for each pair of eggs. Sprinkle in salt and pepper to taste and beat lightly.

Melt a little butter in a small saucepan. There should be just enough butter to cover the bottom of the pan; do not allow it become too hot. Pour in the egg. Cook gently, stirring or whisking all the time, until the eggs are lightly set and creamy. Remove from the heat and serve at once. If the eggs are allowed to stand in the hot pan or left on the heat, they set firmly and separate into curds and a thin liquid.

A variety of flavourings may be stirred into the cooked eggs. They may be enriched by using single cream instead of milk or by stirring in a little extra cream as the eggs begin to thicken. Diced smoked salmon or a little grated cheese may be added just before serving.

Fried Eggs Heat a thin layer of oil or half oil and half butter in a frying pan. Bacon fat may be used instead or this may be combined with oil. Crack an egg into a saucer, then slide it into the hot fat. Cook over moderate heat, spooning fat over the egg, until the white is set and the yolk is covered with a lightly set white film. For a firmer set, use a fish slice to turn the eggs over as soon as the white is set firmly underneath. Cook for a further 30-60 seconds before serving – this gives a yolk which is partially set. A soft fried egg is usually ready in 2-3 minutes, slightly sooner if basted often.

COOKING BACON

Bacon may be fried or grilled. Remove any rind and snip the fat to prevent the rashers curling up during cooking. Lay the bacon in a heavy-bottomed frying pan and place over moderate heat. Cook until the fat begins to run, then turn the rashers over and cook for 1-2 minutes on each side, until lightly browned. Drain well and serve at once on heated plates.

To grill bacon, lay the rashers on a rack in the grill pan, then place them under a hot grill for 2-3 minutes on each side, turning once, until lightly browned. Bacon may be cooked until crisp if preferred.

EGGS IN COCOTTES

25 g/1 oz butter
4 eggs
salt and pepper
60 ml/4 tbsp milk or single cream

Butter 4 ramekins or cocottes at least 3.5 cm/1¼ inches deep. Stand them in a baking tin and add enough warm water to come half-way up their sides. Set the oven at 180°C/350°F/gas 4.

Break an egg into each warm dish and add salt and pepper to taste. Top with any remaining butter, cut into flakes. Spoon 15 ml/1 tbsp milk or cream over each egg.

Bake for 6-10 minutes, depending on the thickness of the dishes. The whites of the eggs should be just set. Wipe the outsides of the dishes and serve at once.

SERVES 4

VARIATIONS

■ Shake ground nutmeg or cayenne pepper over the eggs before cooking.
■ Sprinkle the eggs with very finely grated cheese before cooking.
■ Put sliced, fried mushrooms, chopped ham, cooked diced chicken or lightly sautéed, diced Italian sausage in the bottom of each dish before adding the eggs.
■ Put 15-30 ml/1-2 tbsp spinach purée in the dishes before adding the eggs.

———————— ◆ ————————

MOULDED EGGS

50 g/2 oz butter
30 ml/2 tbsp finely chopped parsley
4 eggs
4 slices of white bread

Butter 4 dariole moulds generously, reserving the remaining butter. Set the oven at 180°C/350°F/gas 4.

Coat the insides of the moulds lightly with the parsley. Break an egg into each, then put the moulds in a baking tin. Pour in enough warm water to come half-way up the sides of the moulds. Bake for 10-12 minutes, until the whites are just firm.

Meanwhile, cut a circle 7.5 cm/3 inches in diameter from each slice of bread. Melt the remaining butter in a frying pan. Fry the bread rounds until golden brown on each side. Loosen the cooked eggs in the moulds, turn out on to the fried bread, and serve immediately.

SERVES 4

VARIATIONS

■ Use 15 ml/1 tbsp finely snipped chives instead of the parsley.
■ Use 25 g/1 oz mushrooms, finely chopped, cooked in butter and drained, instead of the parsley.
■ Use 25 g/1 oz minced ham mixed with 10 ml/2 tsp chopped parsley instead of the parsley alone.
■ The bread can be toasted and buttered instead of fried.
■ The eggs can be turned out on to rounds of cooked pastry or into pastry cases.
■ Large flat mushrooms, lightly cooked in butter, can be used instead of the bread.
■ Tomatoes, peeled, cut in half and seeded, can be used instead of the bread.

SHIRRED EGGS

butter for greasing
4 eggs
salt
1.25 ml/¼ tsp paprika
10 ml/2 tsp snipped chives or chopped
    parsley

Grease a shallow ovenproof dish, about 30 cm/12 inches across. Set the oven at 180°C/350°F/gas 4. Separate the eggs, keeping each yolk intact and separate.

Put the egg whites into a clean, dry bowl. Add 2.5 ml/½ tsp salt and whisk to very stiff peaks. Spread the whites lightly over the prepared dish – they should form a layer about 5 cm/2 inches deep.

Using the back of a spoon, make 4 hollows in the egg white. Space the hollows as evenly as possible and do not make them too near the edge. Slip 1 egg yolk into each hollow.

Bake for about 10 minutes or until the eggs are just set. Sprinkle with paprika and chopped chives and serve.

SERVES 4

VARIATION

SHIRRED EGGS ON TOAST Use 4 egg yolks but only 2 whites. Whisk the whites with 1.25 ml/¼ tsp salt until very stiff and fold in 50 g/2 oz finely grated Cheddar cheese. Lightly toast 4 slices of bread. Pile the cheesy meringue mixture on the toast, make a depression in each and slip in an egg yolk. Sprinkle about 15 ml/1 tbsp grated cheese over each egg yolk and cook under a low grill until the meringue is golden and the egg yolks are cooked. Serve at once.

ANCHOVY EGGS

4 slices of white bread
75 g/3 oz butter
anchovy paste (see method)
4 eggs
10 ml/2 tsp tarragon vinegar
20 ml/4 tsp chopped parsley

Toast the bread on both sides and cut off the crusts. Spread each slice with butter and a little anchovy paste.

Melt the remaining butter in a frying pan and fry the eggs until set. Put one egg on each slice of toast and keep hot.

Continue heating the butter with the vinegar until the mixture browns. Pour it over the eggs, top with parsley and serve.

SERVES 4

FRAMED EGGS

4 thick slices of white bread
oil for shallow frying ● 4 eggs

Cut each slice of bread into a 10 cm/ 4 inch round, then cut a second 6 cm/2½ inch round from the centres, so that four bread rings are left.

Heat the oil in a large frying pan and fry the bread rings until brown and crisp on one side. Turn them over, lower the heat and break an egg into the centre of each ring. Fry gently, spooning the oil over the top from time to time, until the eggs are set. Using a fish slice, remove the framed eggs from the pan, draining excess oil.

SERVES 4

EGGS BENEDICT

Illustrated on page 224

2 muffins, split or 4 slices white bread
30 ml/2 tbsp butter
4 slices of ham
4 eggs

HOLLANDAISE SAUCE
45 ml/3 tbsp white wine vinegar
6 peppercorns
½ bay leaf
1 blade of mace
3 egg yolks
100 g/4 oz butter, softened
salt and pepper

Make the Hollandaise sauce. Combine the vinegar, peppercorns, bay leaf and mace in a small saucepan. Boil rapidly until the liquid is reduced to 15 ml/1 tbsp. Strain into a heatproof bowl and leave to cool. Add the egg yolks and a nut of butter to the vinegar and place over a saucepan of gently simmering water. Heat the mixture gently, beating constantly until thick. Do not allow it to approach boiling point. Add the remaining butter, a little at a time, beating well after each addition. When all the butter has been added the sauce should be thick and glossy. Season lightly.

Toast the muffins or bread slices, then butter them. Trim the ham slices to fit the bread. Put the trimmings on the hot muffins or toast and cover with the ham slices. Put on a large heated platter or individual plates and keep hot.

Poach the eggs and drain well. Put an egg on each piece of ham, cover with about 15 ml/1 tbsp of the Hollandaise sauce and serve the remaining sauce separately.

SERVES 4

OMELETTES

The secret of a light omelette is to add water, not milk, to the mixture, beating it only sufficiently to mix the yolks and whites. The mixture must be cooked quickly until evenly and lightly set, then served when still moist. Have everything ready before you start to cook, including the diner, so that the omelette can be taken to the table as soon as it is ready.

2 eggs
salt and pepper
15 ml/1 tbsp unsalted butter or margarine

Break the eggs into a bowl, add 15 ml/ 1 tbsp cold water and season with salt and pepper. Beat lightly with a fork. Thoroughly heat a frying pan or omelette pan. When it is hot, add the butter or margarine, tilting the pan so that the whole surface is lightly greased. Without drawing the pan off the heat, add the egg mixture. Leave to stand for 10 seconds.

Using a spatula, gently draw the egg mixture from the sides to the centre as it sets, allowing the uncooked egg mixture to run in to fill the gap. Do not stir or the mixture will scramble.

When the omelette is golden and set underneath, but still slightly moist on top, remove it from the heat. Loosen the edges by shaking the pan, using a round-bladed knife or the edge of a spatula, then flip one-third of the omelette towards the centre. Flip the opposite third over towards the centre. Tip the omelette on to a hot plate, folded sides underneath. Alternatively, the cooked omelette may be rolled out of the pan after the first folding, so that it is served folded in three. A simpler method is to fold the omelette in half in the pan, then slide it out on to the plate.

SERVES 1

FILLINGS

CHEESE Add 40 g/1½ oz grated cheese to the beaten eggs. Sprinkle a further 15 g/½ oz over the omelette.

FINES HERBES Add 2.5 ml/½ tsp chopped tarragon, 2.5 ml/½ tsp chopped chervil, 5 ml/1 tsp chopped parsley and a few snipped chives to the beaten eggs.

HAM Add 50 g/2 oz chopped ham to the egg mixture.

FISH Add 50 g/2 oz flaked cooked fish to the omelette just before folding.

BACON Grill 2 rindless bacon rashers until crisp; crumble into the centre of the omelette just before folding.

MUSHROOM Fry 50 g/2 oz sliced mushrooms in butter. Spoon into the centre of the omelette just before folding.

SHRIMP OR PRAWN Sauté 50 g/2 oz shrimps or prawns in a little butter in a saucepan. Add a squeeze of lemon juice and spoon into the omelette before folding.

CHICKEN Chop 25 g/1 oz cooked chicken. Mix with 60 ml/4 tbsp white sauce. Heat gently in a small saucepan. Spoon into the omelette before folding.

> **MRS BEETON'S TIP** In Mrs Beeton's day, most households would have a special omelette pan. When new, this would be 'seasoned' by melting a little butter in the pan, sprinkling it with salt, and rubbing vigorously with a soft cloth. This process helped to prevent the egg mixture from sticking. The omelette pan would not be washed after use; instead it would be rubbed all over with a soft cloth. Salt would be used, if necessary, to remove any egg still sticking to the pan. Today's cooks are less likely to keep a frying pan specifically for omelettes (and more likely to have a non-stick pan which should be washed after every use) but an uncoated pan should still be seasoned using oil and absorbent kitchen paper instead of a cloth, each time it is used.

CHEESE AND ASPARAGUS CUSTARD

It is important to cook asparagus upright, so that the stalks are poached while the delicate tips are gently steamed. If the asparagus is too tall for the saucepan, cover it with a dome of foil, crumpled around the pan's rim, instead of using the lid. You can buy asparagus pans from specialist kitchen shops.

butter for greasing
1 bundle small or sprue asparagus,
    trimmed, or 225 g/8 oz canned or
    frozen asparagus
100 g/4 oz cheese, grated
4 eggs
salt and pepper
500 ml/17 floz milk

Butter a 750 ml/1¼ pint ovenproof dish. Tie fresh asparagus in small bundles. Add enough salted water to a deep saucepan to come three-quarters of the way up the stalks. Bring to the boil. Wedge the bundles of asparagus upright in the pan, or stand them in a heatproof container in the pan. Cover and cook gently for 10-15 minutes, depending on the thickness of the stalks. Drain carefully. Drain canned asparagus or cook frozen asparagus according to the directions on the packet.

Set the oven at 150°C/300°F/gas 2. Cut the asparagus into short lengths and put into the prepared dish, with the tips arranged on the top. Sprinkle the grated cheese over the asparagus. Beat the eggs, salt and pepper together lightly and stir in the milk. Strain the custard into the dish.

Stand the dish in a shallow tin containing enough warm water to come half-way up the sides of the dish. Bake for 1½ hours, until the custard is set in the centre.

SERVES 4

HOT STUFFED AVOCADOS

2 large avocados
100 g/4 oz cooked smoked haddock or cod
50 g/2 oz ricotta cheese
lemon juice
salt and pepper
chopped parsley
about 25 g/1 oz fresh white breadcrumbs
butter
lemon rind to garnish

Set the oven at 200°C/400°F/gas 6. Cut the avocados in half lengthways and remove the stones.

Flake the fish into a bowl and mix with the ricotta. Fill the hollows of the avocados with the fish mixture. Sprinkle the surface of the avocado and fish with lemon juice, and season the avocado only with a sprinkling of salt and pepper. Stir some parsley into the breadcrumbs, then spoon over the avocados. Dot with a very small amount of butter.

Place the avocados in a baking dish. Bake for 15-20 minutes. Garnish with lemon rind. Serve at once, with toast if liked.

SERVES 4

MRS BEETON'S TIP This is a good way to use avocados which are past their best. It does not matter if they are slightly discoloured, but they should not be mushy.

KEDGEREE

No Victorian country-house breakfast would have been complete without kedgeree. Hard-boiled egg and parsley are the traditional garnish, sometimes arranged in the shape of the cross of St. Andrew.

salt and pepper
150 g/5 oz long-grain rice
125 ml/4 fl oz milk
450 g/1 lb smoked haddock
50 g/2 oz butter
15 ml/1 tbsp curry powder
2 hard-boiled eggs, roughly chopped
cayenne pepper

GARNISH
15 g/½ oz butter
15 ml/1 tbsp chopped parsley
1 hard-boiled egg, white and yolk sieved
    separately

Bring a saucepan of salted water to the boil. Add the rice and cook for 12 minutes. Drain thoroughly, rinse under cold water and drain again. Place the strainer over a saucepan of simmering water to keep the rice warm.

Put the milk in a large shallow saucepan or frying pan with 125 ml/4 fl oz water. Bring to simmering point, add the fish and poach gently for 4 minutes. Using a slotted spoon and a fish slice, transfer the haddock to a board. Discard the cooking liquid.

Remove the skin and any bones from the haddock and break up the flesh into fairly large flakes. Melt half the butter in a large saucepan. Blend in the curry powder and cook for 1 minute, then add the flaked fish. Warm the mixture through. Remove from the heat, lightly stir in the chopped eggs and season with salt, pepper and cayenne.

Melt the remaining butter in a second pan, add the rice and toss until well coated. Season with salt, pepper and cayenne. Add the rice to the haddock mixture and mix well. Pile the kedgeree on to a warmed dish.

Dot the kedgeree with the butter, garnish with parsley, sieved hard-boiled egg yolk and egg white. Serve at once.

SERVES 4

SHRIMP AND RICE STIR

salt and pepper
200 g/7 oz long-grain rice
100 g/4 oz butter
100 g/4 oz mushrooms, sliced
100 g/4 oz cooked ham, cut in thin strips
225 g/8 oz peeled cooked shrimps

Bring a saucepan of salted water to the boil. Add the rice and cook for 15 minutes. Drain thoroughly, rinse under cold water and drain again. Place the strainer over a saucepan of simmering water to keep the rice warm.

Melt the butter in a frying pan, add the mushrooms and fry for 3-4 minutes until golden. Stir in the rice and fry for 4 minutes, then add the ham and shrimps. Lower the heat and simmer for 2-3 minutes. Add salt and pepper to taste, pile on to a warmed serving dish and serve at once.

SERVES 4

KOULIBIAC

Koulibiac is a large oblong pastry filled with a mixture of cooked rice and salmon. Smoked salmon offcuts or canned salmon may be used instead of fresh salmon. This is good either hot or cold and is therefore ideal for formal meals, buffets or picnics.

fat for greasing
450 g/1 lb salmon fillet or steaks
salt and pepper
juice of ½ lemon
175 g/6 oz long-grain rice
50 g/2 oz butter
1 onion, chopped
60 ml/4 tbsp chopped parsley
4 hard-boiled eggs, roughly chopped
15 ml/1 tbsp chopped fresh tarragon
    (optional)
450 g/1 lb puff pastry
1 egg, beaten, to glaze
150 ml/¼ pint soured cream to serve

Lay the salmon on a piece of greased foil large enough to enclose it completely. Sprinkle with salt, pepper and a little of the lemon juice, then wrap the foil around the fish, sealing the edges firmly.

Place the rice in a large saucepan and add 450 ml/¾ pint water. Bring to the boil, lower the heat and cover the pan. Simmer the rice for 10 minutes, then place the foil-wrapped fish on top of the rice. Cover the pan again and cook for about 10 minutes more or until the grains of rice are tender and all the water has been absorbed.

At the end of the cooking time, remove the foil-packed salmon from the pan. Transfer the fish to a board, reserving all the cooking juices, then discard the skin and any bones. Coarsely flake the flesh and set the fish aside. Tip the cooked rice into a bowl.

Melt half the butter in a small saucepan. Add the onion and cook over low heat for about 15 minutes until it is soft but not browned. Mix the cooked onion with the rice and add the salmon and parsley, with salt and pepper to taste. Put the chopped hard-boiled eggs in a bowl. Add the tarragon, if used. Melt the remaining butter and trickle it over the eggs.

Set the oven at 220°C/425°F/gas 7. Cut a large sheet of foil, at least 30 cm/12 inches long. On a floured board, roll out the pastry to a rectangle measuring about 50 × 25 cm/20 × 10 inches. Trim the pastry to 43 × 25 cm/17×10 inches. Cut the trimmings into long narrow strips. Set aside.

Lay the pastry on the foil. Spoon half the rice mixture lengthways down the middle of the pastry. Top with the egg mixture in an even layer, then mound the remaining rice mixture over the top. Fold one long side of pastry over the filling and brush the edge with beaten egg. Fold the other side over and press the long edges together firmly. Brush the inside of the pastry at the ends with egg and seal them firmly.

Use the foil to turn the koulibiac over so that the pastry seam is underneath, then lift it on to a baking sheet or roasting tin. Brush all over with beaten egg and arrange the reserved strips of pastry in a lattice pattern over the top. Brush these with egg too.

Bake the koulibiac for 30-40 minutes, until the pastry is well puffed and golden. Check after 25 minutes and if the pastry looks well browned tent a piece of foil over the top to prevent it from overcooking.

Serve a small dish of soured cream with the koulibiac, which should be cut into thick slices.

SERVES 8

MIXED GRILL

Illustrated on page 223

4 pork sausages
4 lamb cutlets
4 lambs' kidneys, skinned, cored and
  halved
a little oil
2 gammon rashers, rind removed and
  halved or 8 rindless bacon rashers
salt and pepper
8 flat mushrooms
4 tomatoes

GARNISH (optional)
  fried bread (see Mrs Beeton's Tip)
  parsley sprigs

Trim excess fat from the cutlets. Place the sausages on the rack in the grill pan. Cook for 5 minutes, turning once, before adding the cutlets and lambs' kidneys to the rack. Brush with a little oil. If serving gammon, lay the steaks on the rack at the same time and brush with a little oil.

Continue cooking, turning the sausages often and turning the cutlets, kidneys and gammon when browned on one side. Allow about 5 minutes on each side for the cutlets, depending on thickness. Brush occasionally with juices from the pan and rearrange the food so that it all cooks at the same rate, pushing the sausages to a cooler part of the grill when they are browned. Have a heated serving dish ready and transfer cooked items to it promptly.

Lastly, brush the mushrooms and tomatoes with cooking juices and sprinkle them with a little salt and pepper. Place them on the grill rack when the meats are almost cooked. Grill the mushrooms for 1-2 minutes on each side, so that they are very lightly cooked, and grill the tomatoes cut sides uppermost for 2 minutes.

Arrange the grilled foods on a serving plate, adding fried bread and parsley sprigs if liked. Serve freshly cooked.

SERVES 4

> **MRS BEETON'S TIP** For fried bread, cut medium thick slices of bread. Trim off the crusts, if preferred, then cut the slices crossways in half or into quarters in the shape of triangles. Heat some dripping (ideally from bacon or gammon) or a mixture of oil and butter, add the bread and turn the slices almost immediately. This allows both sides to absorb a little fat and reduces the overall quantity of fat required to cook the bread. Cook until crisp and golden, then turn and cook the second side. Serve immediately.

HAM AND EGGS

4 gammon steaks
4 eggs

Trim the rind from the gammon steaks. Put it in a large cold frying pan. Heat, gently at first, until the fat runs, pressing the rind to extract the fat. Tilt the pan to grease it thoroughly, then discard the rind.

Snip the fat around the gammon steaks at intervals, add them to the pan and cook for about 20 minutes, turning several times.

Using tongs, transfer the gammon to a heated platter. Fry the eggs in the fat remaining in the pan, spooning the fat over the top from time to time until the whites are firm and the yolks set. Alternatively, poach the eggs. Serve on top of the ham.

SERVES 4

LUNCHES
AND SUPPERS

Lunches and suppers can be the most enjoyable of meals, especially when shared with friends. By their nature they are relaxing, lighter and simpler than formal dinners, with little required beyond the main dish. Crusty bread or a salad can be added, but there's no need for elaborate extras. This chapter includes savoury puddings, pasta and simple pastries. It opens with a dish that has a reputation – quite unjustified – for being tricky. Follow Mrs Beeton's step-by-step instructions for soufflés that rise to the occasion.

PREPARING A SOUFFLE DISH

1 Using a piece of string, measure the height of the dish and its circumference.

2 Cut a strip from two thicknesses of greaseproof paper or non-stick baking parchment that exceeds the height of the dish by 7.5 cm/3 inches and is long enough to go right around the dish with an overlap.

3 Tie the paper around the dish with string. If the dish has sloping sides or a projecting rim, secure the paper above and below the rim with gummed tape or pins. Make sure the paper has no creases and forms a neat round shape.

4 For a hot soufflé, it is not essential to add a collar because the mixture sets and holds its shape as it cooks. However some cooks prefer using a collar for an 'even' shape. Grease the inside of the dish and paper collar with clarified butter or oil.

CRAB SOUFFLE

fat for greasing
50 g/2 oz butter
45 ml/3 tbsp plain flour
250 ml/8 fl oz milk
salt and pepper
4 eggs, separated plus 1 white
200 g/7 oz flaked crab meat
2-3 drops Tabasco sauce
30 ml/2 tbsp dry white wine

Grease a 900 ml/1½ pint soufflé dish. Set the oven at 190°C/375°F/gas 5.

Melt the butter in a saucepan, stir in the flour and cook slowly for 2-3 minutes without colouring, stirring all the time. Add the milk gradually and beat until smooth. Cook for 1-2 minutes more, still stirring. Remove from the heat and beat hard until the sauce comes away cleanly from the sides of the pan. Cool slightly, put into a bowl and add salt and pepper to taste.

Beat the yolks into the flour mixture one by one. Stir in the crab meat and add the Tabasco sauce and wine.

In a clean, grease-free bowl, whisk all the egg whites until stiff. Using a metal spoon, stir 1 spoonful of the whites into the crab meat mixture to lighten it, then fold in the rest until evenly distributed.

Spoon into the prepared dish and bake for 30-35 minutes until well risen and browned. Serve immediately, with hot buttered toast if liked.

SERVES 4

OMELETTE ARNOLD BENNETT

150 g/5 oz smoked haddock
25 g/1 oz unsalted butter
60 ml/4 tbsp single cream
2 eggs, separated
salt and pepper
30 ml/2 tbsp grated Parmesan cheese
parsley sprigs to garnish

Bring a saucepan of water to simmering point, add the haddock and poach gently for 10 minutes. Using a slotted spoon transfer the fish to a large plate. Remove any skin or bones. Flake the fish into a large bowl and add half the butter and 15 ml/1 tbsp of the cream. Mix well.

In a separate bowl mix the egg yolks with 15 ml/1 tbsp of the remaining cream. Add salt and pepper to taste. Add to the fish mixture and stir in half the cheese.

In a clean dry bowl, whisk the egg whites until stiff. Fold them into the fish mixture.

Heat half the remaining butter in an omelette pan. Pour in half the fish mixture and cook quickly until golden brown underneath (see Mrs Beeton's Tip). Sprinkle over half the remaining cheese, spoon over 15 ml/1 tbsp of the remaining cream and brown quickly under a hot grill. Do not fold. Very quickly make a second omelette in the same way. Garnish and serve at once.

SERVES 2

MRS BEETON'S TIP Use a slim spatula to lift one side of the omelette in order to check the colour underneath.

*F*RESH SALMON MOUSSE

oil for greasing
450 g/1 lb salmon fillet or steak (a tail
    piece may be used)
1 litre/1¾ pints Court Bouillon (page 15)
15 g/½ oz gelatine
300 ml/½ pint Béchamel sauce (see Mrs
    Beeton's Tip, page 47)
50 g/2 oz butter, softened
45 ml/3 tbsp double cream, lightly
    whipped
15 ml/1 tbsp medium-dry sherry

Brush a glass or metal fish mould with oil. Leave upside down to drain. Put the salmon in a large saucepan and cover with court bouillon. Bring to the boil, lower the heat and simmer for 15 minutes. Drain, cool and remove the skin and bones. Pound to a paste in a mortar or process in a blender or food processor until smooth.

Place 30 ml/2 tbsp water in a small bowl and sprinkle the gelatine on to the liquid. Stand the bowl over a saucepan of hot water and stir the gelatine until it has dissolved completely.

Tip the salmon into a large bowl and add the cold Béchamel sauce. Mix until thoroughly blended, then add the softened butter, whipped cream, sherry and dissolved gelatine. Mix well, then spoon into the prepared mould. Smooth the top, cover with cling film and chill for 2-3 hours until set. Turn out (see Mrs Beeton's Tip), garnish with cucumber and radish slices and serve.

SERVES 6 TO 8

VARIATION

SALMON MOUSSE (CANNED SALMON) Drain 1 (213 g/7 oz) can red salmon, remove the bones and mash finely with 1 small chopped onion. Alternatively, process briefly in a food processor. Add 125 ml/4 fl oz single cream, 10 ml/2 tsp tomato purée and 75 g/3 oz full-fat soft cheese. Mix well, and season with salt, pepper, paprika and 2-3 drops of hot pepper sauce. Mix thoroughly. Add 15 g/½ oz gelatine, dissolved in water as in the recipe above. Finally, lighten the mixture by folding in 2 stiffly beaten egg whites. (Use very fresh eggs, bought from a reputable source.) Set the mousse in an oiled mould as in the recipe above.

> 🥣 **MRS BEETON'S TIP** Rinse the serving platter in cold water, draining off the excess. Run the point of a sharp knife around the edge of the salmon mould to loosen it, then dip the mould in warm water. Invert the plate on top of the mould, then, holding mould and plate firmly, turn both right side up again. The mould should lift off easily. If necessary, move the mousse to the desired position on the platter – the skin of water remaining on the plate will make this possible. Repeat the process if the mousse does not come out first time, but avoid leaving it in the warm water for too long or the design on the mousse will be blurred.

SAVOURY SOUFFLE

Individual hot soufflés make a very good starter, light main course or savoury finish to a meal. The quantity of mixture below will make 6 individual soufflés in 200 ml/7 fl oz dishes, and will take 20 minutes to bake.

fat for greasing
50 g/2 oz butter
25 g/1 oz plain flour
250 ml/8 fl oz milk
100-150 g/4-5 oz Cheddar cheese,
    grated, or 75-100 g/3-4 oz mixed
    Parmesan and Gruyère cheese, grated
salt and pepper
2.5 ml/½ tsp dry mustard
pinch of cayenne pepper
4 eggs, separated, plus 1 egg white

Prepare a 1 litre/1¾ pint soufflé dish (page 267). Set the oven at 190°C/375°F/gas 5.

Melt the butter in a saucepan, stir in the flour and cook over a low heat for 2-3 minutes without colouring, stirring all the time. Gradually add the milk, stirring constantly until the sauce boils and thickens. Lower the heat and simmer, stirring, for 1-2 minutes more. Remove from the heat and beat hard until the sauce comes away cleanly from the sides of the pan. Cool slightly and put into a bowl. Stir in the cheese, salt, pepper, mustard and cayenne.

Beat the yolks into the mixture one by one. In a clean, grease-free bowl, whisk all the egg whites until stiff. Using a metal spoon, stir one spoonful of the whites into the mixture to lighten it, then fold in the rest until evenly distributed.

Spoon the mixture into the prepared dish and bake for 30-35 minutes, until well risen and browned. Serve immediately with hot buttered toast.

SERVES 4

> **MRS BEETON'S TIP** The flavour of some soufflés, such as those made with fish or white meat, can be bland, so it is a good idea to infuse the milk with plenty of flavouring as when making a Béchamel sauce (see Mrs Beeton's Tip, page 47).

VARIATIONS

CHEESE AND ONION SOUFFLE Add 50 g/2 oz very finely chopped onion cooked in the butter for 2-3 minutes until transparent, to the cheese.

CHEESE AND WATERCRESS SOUFFLE Chop the leaves from half a bunch of watercress and add to the cheese.

LAYERED CHEESE SOUFFLE Put half the soufflé mixture into the dish and add a layer of 75 g/3 oz sautéed mushrooms, or 100 g/4 oz cooked flaked fish, or 45 ml/3 tbsp spinach purée and then the remaining mixture.

OEUFS MOLLETS EN SOUFFLE Soft boil 4 small eggs. Put one-third of the soufflé mixture into the dish. Arrange the eggs on top. Add the remainder of the mixture and bake.

CHICKEN SOUFFLE Add 200 g/7 oz cooked minced chicken, 25 g/1 oz chopped sautéed onion, 30 ml/2 tbsp lemon juice and 5 ml/1 tsp chopped parsley.

POTATO SOUFFLE

butter for greasing
500 g/18 oz potatoes
salt and pepper
50 g/2 oz butter
125 ml/4 fl oz top-of-the-milk
grated nutmeg
3 eggs, separated, plus 1 egg white
30 ml/2 tbsp chopped parsley
100 g/4 oz Cheddar cheese, finely grated

Prepare a 1 litre/1¾ pint soufflé dish (see page 267). Cook the potatoes in a saucepan of boiling salted water for about 20 minutes.

Set the oven at 190°C/375°F/gas 5. Drain and mash the potatoes and put them through a sieve into a bowl. Add the butter and top-of-the-milk, with a generous amount of salt, pepper and nutmeg. Stir in the egg yolks, parsley and cheese. Beat well with a wooden spoon until smooth.

In a clean, grease-free bowl, whisk all the egg whites until stiff. Using a metal spoon, stir one spoonful of the whites into the patato mixture to lighten it, then fold in the rest until evenly distributed. Spoon the mixture into the prepared dish.

Bake for 30-35 minutes, until well risen and browned. Serve at once.

SERVES 4

VARIATION

FISH AND POTATO SOUFFLE
Make as for Potato Soufflé using 350 g/12 oz potatoes. Poach 200 g/7 oz white fish, cod or haddock, for 10 minutes in the milk. Drain, remove any skin or bone from the fish, then flake the flesh. Omit the cheese and add the flaked fish, the milk made up to 125 ml/4 fl oz if necessary, and a few drops of anchovy essence, if liked.

SPINACH SOUFFLE

fat for greasing
25 g/1 oz butter
30 ml/2 tbsp plain flour
125 g/4½ oz spinach purée
125 ml/4 fl oz single cream
50 g/2 oz cheese, finely grated
salt and pepper
4 eggs, separated, plus 1 egg white
grated Parmesan cheese to garnish
    (optional)

Prepare a 1 litre/1¾ pint soufflé dish (see page 267). Set the oven at 190°C/375°F/gas 5.

Melt the butter in a saucepan, stir in the flour and cook over a low heat for 2-3 minutes without colouring, stirring all the time. Stir in the spinach purée and add the cream gradually, still stirring. Cook for 1-2 minutes more, still stirring. Remove from the heat, stir in the cheese, then beat hard until the sauce comes away cleanly from the sides of the pan. Cool slightly and put into a bowl. Add salt and pepper to taste.

Beat the yolks into the mixture one by one. In a clean, grease-free bowl, whisk all the egg whites until stiff. Using a metal spoon, stir one spoonful of the whites into the mixture to lighten it, then fold in the rest until evenly distributed. Spoon the mixture into the prepared dish.

Bake for 30-35 minutes until well risen and browned. Sprinkle with grated Parmesan cheese, if liked. Serve immediately.

SERVES 4

PARSNIP SOUFFLE

butter for greasing
200 g/7 oz parsnips
65 g/2½ oz butter
30 ml/2 tbsp grated onion
45 ml/3 tbsp plain flour
100 ml/3½ fl oz vegetable stock or parsnip
   cooking water
100 ml/3½ fl oz milk
30 ml/2 tbsp chopped parsley
salt and pepper
pinch of grated nutmeg
4 eggs, separated
125 ml/4 fl oz Béchamel sauce (see Mrs
   Beeton's Tip, page 47)

Prepare a 1 litre/1¾ pint soufflé dish (page 267). Cook the parsnips in a saucepan with a little boiling salted water for about 20 minutes until tender. Mash and sieve them into a bowl, working into a smooth purée. Measure out 150 g/5 oz purée, and keep the rest on one side.

Melt 15 g/½ oz of the butter in a frying pan and gently cook the onion until soft. Mix it with the measured parsnip purée.

Set the oven at 190°C/375°F/gas 5. Melt the remaining butter in a saucepan, stir in the flour and cook over a low heat for 2-3 minutes, without colouring, stirring all the time. Mix the stock or water and the milk. Over a very low heat, gradually add the liquid to the pan, stirring constantly. Bring to the boil, stirring, and simmer for 1-2 minutes until smooth and thickened. Stir in the parsnip and onion mixture and parsley. Add salt, pepper and nutmeg to taste. Cool slightly and put into a bowl.

Beat the yolks into the mixture one by one. In a clean, grease-free bowl, whisk all the egg whites until stiff. Using a metal spoon, fold into the mixture. Spoon the mixture into the prepared dish. Bake for 25-30 minutes, until risen and set.

Meanwhile, mix the reserved parsnip purée with the Béchamel sauce, and heat gently. Serve separately in a warmed sauceboat.

SERVES 4

MRS BEETON'S ASPARAGUS PUDDING

fat for greasing
1 (350 g/12 oz) can asparagus tips
50 g/2 oz cooked ham, finely chopped
50 g/2 oz plain flour
salt and pepper
2 eggs, beaten
25 g/1 oz butter, melted
30 ml/2 tbsp milk

Grease a 750 ml/1¼ pint pie dish. Set the oven at 200°C/400°F/gas 6.

Chop the asparagus tips to the size of peas. Put them in a bowl with the ham and flour and add salt and pepper to taste. Stir in the eggs and melted butter with the milk to make a batter.

Turn the mixture into the prepared dish and bake for 25-30 minutes, until risen and golden brown. Serve at once.

SERVES 4

ASPARAGUS CROUSTADES

4 French bread rolls
1 (350 g/12 oz) can asparagus tips
about 50 ml/2 fl oz milk (see method)
25 g/1 oz butter
25 g/1 oz plain flour
1 egg
salt and pepper
5 ml/1 tsp lemon juice (optional)

Set the oven at 220°C/425°F/gas 7. Cut the tops off the rolls. Scoop out the soft crumb; reserve to make breadcrumbs for use in another recipe. Put the rolls, together with the tops, on a baking sheet. Bake for 5 minutes or until they are very crisp. Keep the rolls hot.

Drain the asparagus tips, reserving the can juices in a measuring jug. Make up to 300 ml/½ pint with milk. Melt the butter in a saucepan, add the flour and cook, stirring for 1 minute. Gradually add the milk mixture, stirring until the mixture boils and thickens.

Beat the egg in a small bowl, add a little of the hot sauce and mix well, then tip the contents of the bowl into the saucepan. Stir over gentle heat for 1-2 minutes without boiling, then add the asparagus tips and heat through. Season with salt and pepper and add the lemon juice, if used.

Spoon the asparagus filling into the hot rolls, replace the lids and serve at once.

SERVES 4

CHEESE RAMEKINS

butter for greasing
about 50 ml/2 fl oz milk
about 25 g/1 oz fresh white breadcrumbs
25 g/1 oz Parmesan cheese, grated
25 g/1 oz Cheshire cheese, finely grated
25 g/1 oz unsalted butter, softened
1 egg, separated
salt and pepper
pinch of ground mace

Grease 4 small ovenproof pots or ramekins. Set the oven at 200°C/400°F/gas 6.

Heat the milk in a saucepan. Put the breadcrumbs in a bowl and add just enough milk to cover them. Leave to stand for 5-10 minutes. Stir in the cheeses and butter. Beat the egg yolk into the cheese mixture. Add salt, pepper and mace to taste.

In a clean, grease-free bowl, whisk the egg white until stiff. Using a metal spoon, stir one spoonful of the white into the cheese mixture to lighten it, then fold in the rest. Spoon into the prepared pots or ramekins and place on a baking sheet.

Bake for 15-20 minutes until the soufflés are risen and slightly browned. Serve immediately.

SERVES 4

CHICKEN AND HAM SCALLOPS

25 g/1 oz butter
250 g/9 oz cooked chicken
100 g/4 oz cooked ham
salt and pepper
good pinch of grated nutmeg
60 ml/4 tbsp fine dried white
    breadcrumbs

SAUCE
    25 g/1 oz butter
    25 g/1 oz plain flour
    300 ml/½ pint milk, chicken stock or a
        mixture

Butter 6 deep scallop shells, reserving the remaining butter. Set the oven at 190-200°C/375-400°F/gas 5-6.

To make the sauce, melt the butter in a saucepan. Stir in the flour and cook over a low heat for 2-3 minutes, without colouring. Over a very low heat, gradually add the liquid, stirring constantly. Bring to the boil, stirring, then simmer for 1-2 minutes until smooth and thick. Season and cool.

Remove any skin and bone from the chicken. Chop the meat coarsely and place in a bowl. Chop the ham finely and add it to the chicken. Moisten the mixture well with sauce. Add seasoning and nutmeg.

Fill the prepared scallop shells with the mixture, sprinkle evenly with breadcrumbs and flake the rest of the butter on top. Bake for about 20 minutes, until golden brown.

SERVES 4 TO 6

VARIATIONS

CHICKEN AND CHEESE SCALLOPS

Omit the ham, substitute 5 ml/1 tsp lemon juice for the grated nutmeg and add 5 ml/1 tsp chopped parsley to the mixture. Mix 20 ml/4 tsp grated cheese with the breadcrumbs. Bake as before or place under moderate grill for 4-6 minutes to brown.

BROWNED CHICKEN SCALLOPS

Heat the chicken and ham mixture gently in a saucepan before putting it into scallop shells. Cover with breadcrumbs and butter as before, then put under moderate grill for 4-6 minutes to brown the top.

STUFFED MUSHROOMS

fat for greasing
12 large flat mushrooms
1 onion, finely chopped
25 g/1 oz butter or margarine
50 g/2 oz cooked ham, finely chopped
15 ml/1 tbsp fresh white breadcrumbs
10 ml/2 tsp grated Parmesan cheese
10 ml/2 tsp chopped parsley
white wine
salt and pepper

Generously grease an ovenproof dish. Set the oven at 190°C/375°F/gas 5.

Clean the mushrooms and remove the stalks. Place the caps in the prepared dish, gills uppermost. Chop the stalks finely. Melt the butter or margarine in a saucepan; gently fry the mushroom stalks and onion for 5 minutes.

Add the ham to the onion mixture together with the breadcrumbs, cheese and parsley. Stir in just enough white wine to bind the mixture. Add salt and pepper to taste. Divide the stuffing mixture between the mushroom caps. Bake for 25 minutes.

SERVES 6

CHICKEN JELLY

1.5 litres /2¾ pints vegetable stock
1 (1.1 kg/2½ lb) chicken, skinned and
   jointed
2 celery sticks, sliced
1 onion, thickly sliced
1 carrot, thickly sliced
salt
15 ml/1 tbsp white wine vinegar
2 bay leaves
5 peppercorns
white and crushed shell of 1 egg
30 ml/2 tbsp gelatine
15 ml/1 tbsp chopped parsley to garnish

Bring the stock to the boil in a large saucepan. Put in the chicken pieces, vegetables, salt, vinegar, bay leaves and peppercorns. Bring back to the boil and skim well. Lower the heat, cover the pan and simmer the chicken for 45 minutes until tender. Using a slotted spoon, remove the chicken pieces. When cool enough to handle, cut the meat off the bones in small pieces. Refrigerate in a covered bowl until required.

Return the chicken bones to the stock in the pan and boil until reduced by about half. Remove the bones, then pour the stock into a bowl. When cool, chill the stock until the fat solidifies on the surface and can be removed easily.

Scald a large enamel or stainless steel (not aluminium) saucepan, a piece of clean muslin or thin white cotton, a metal sieve and a whisk in boiling water. Pour the stock into the saucepan with the egg white, crushed shell and gelatine. Bring to the boil over moderate heat, whisking constantly with the whisk until a thick white crust of foam develops on the top of the liquid. Remove the whisk. As soon as the liquid rises to the top of the pan, remove it from the heat. Leave to stand briefly until the foam falls back into the pan, then heat the stock in the same way once or twice more, until the liquid is crystal clear. Strain the stock through the muslin-lined sieve into a perfectly clean bowl.

Arrange the reserved chicken meat in a wetted 1 litre/1¾ pint mould. Pour the stock over gently, taking care not to dislodge the meat. Leave to cool, then chill until set. When ready to serve, turn out the jelly and garnish with the chopped parsley.

SERVES 6 TO 8

🥄 **MRS BEETON'S TIP** To turn out, or unmould a jelly, run the tip of a knife around the top of the mould. Dip the mould into hot water for a few seconds, remove and dry it quickly. Wet a serving plate and place upside down on top of the mould. Hold plate and mould together firmly and turn both over. Check that the mould is correctly positioned on the plate, sliding it into place if necessary. Shake gently and carefully lift off the mould.

CHICKEN RAMEKINS

butter for greasing
175 g/6 oz raw chicken or turkey meat,
    minced
2 eggs, separated
50 g/2 oz mushrooms, chopped
salt and pepper
45 ml/3 tbsp double cream
milk (see method)

Grease 8 small ramekins. Set the oven at 190°C/375°F/gas 5. Put the minced chicken or turkey in a bowl and gradually add the egg yolks, stirring to make a very smooth mixture. Stir in the mushrooms and set aside.

Whisk the egg whites with salt and pepper to taste in a clean, dry bowl until very stiff. In another bowl, whip the cream lightly. Fold the cream into the chicken mixture, then fold in the beaten egg whites. If the mixture is very stiff, add a little milk.

Divide the mixture between the prepared ramekins. Bake for about 30 minutes or until well risen, firm to the touch and browned. Serve at once.

SERVES 4 TO 8

HOT CHICKEN LIVER MOUSSES

butter for greasing ● 15 ml/1 tbsp butter
30 ml/2 tbsp plain flour
150 ml/¼ pint milk
salt and pepper
225 g/8 oz chicken livers, trimmed
1 egg plus 1 yolk
5 ml/1 tsp Worcestershire sauce
45 ml/3 tbsp double cream
15 ml/1 tbsp dry sherry

Grease 4 150 ml/¼ pint ovenproof dishes. Set the oven at 180°C/350°F/gas 4. Combine the butter, flour and milk in a small saucepan. Whisk over moderate heat until the mixture comes to the boil. Lower the heat and simmer for 3-4 minutes, whisking constantly, until the sauce is thick, smooth and glossy. Add salt and pepper to taste. Cover the surface with buttered greaseproof paper and cool.

Purée the livers in a blender or food processor or put them through a mincer twice. Scrape the purée into a bowl and beat in the egg and egg yolk. Add the Worcestershire sauce, cream and sherry.

Divide the liver mixture between the prepared dishes, place them in a deep baking tin and pour in enough boiling water to come half-way up the sides of the dishes. Bake for 25-30 minutes until a fine skewer inserted in the centre of one of the mousses comes out clean. Remove from the water and stand for 2-3 minutes before serving.

SERVES 4

> **MRS BEETON'S TIP** When adding the hot water to the baking tin it is best to use a kettle and to place the tin in the oven before adding the water.

CHICKEN MARENGO

30 ml/2 tbsp plain flour
salt and pepper
1 (1.4 kg/3 lb) chicken, jointed
60 ml/4 tbsp oil
2 garlic cloves, crushed
100 g/4 oz small button mushrooms
2 tomatoes, peeled and chopped
15 ml/1 tbsp tomato purée
150 ml/¼ pint dry white wine

Mix the flour with salt and pepper, then use to coat the chicken portions. Heat the oil in a large flameproof casserole, add the chicken and fry until golden on all sides. Stir in the garlic, mushrooms, tomatoes and tomato purée, with the wine.

Bring just to the boil, lower the heat so that the mixture simmers and cover with a tight-fitting lid. Cook over gentle heat for about 45 minutes until the chicken is cooked through. Sprinkle with parsley and serve (see Mrs Beeton's Tip).

SERVES 4

CHAUDFROID OF CHICKEN

6 cooked chicken joints
125 ml/4 fl oz aspic jelly (see Mrs Beeton's Tip)
375 ml/13 fl oz mayonnaise
lettuce leaves
3 celery sticks, sliced
2 hard-boiled eggs, sliced

GARNISH
stoned olives
tomato slices

Remove the skin, excess fat and bones from the chicken joints, keeping the pieces in neat shapes. Melt the aspic jelly and leave to cool. When it is on the point of setting but still tepid, whisk in half the mayonnaise until smooth.

Place the chicken portions on a wire rack. As soon as the mayonnaise mixture reaches a good coating consistency, pour it over the chicken portions to coat thoroughly.

Arrange the lettuce leaves on a serving dish and place the chicken portions on top. Surround with celery and hard-boiled egg slices and garnish with the olives and tomatoes.

SERVES 6

MRS BEETON'S TIP To make 500 ml/17 fl oz aspic jelly you require 500 ml/17 fl oz chicken stock from which all fat has been removed. Remove all traces of grease from a large enamel or stainless steel saucepan by scalding it in boiling water. Also scald a piece of clean muslin, a metal sieve and a whisk. Put the stock into the pan with 60 ml/4 tbsp white wine, 15 ml/1 tbsp white wine vinegar, 20-25 g/¾-1 oz gelatine, 1 bouquet garni and the white and crushed shell of 1 egg. Heat gently, whisking, until the gelatine dissolves, then bring the liquid to just below boiling point, whisking constantly. A thick white foam crust will form on top of the liquid. When this happens, remove the pan from the heat so that the foam falls back into the pan. Heat the stock in the same way once or twice more, until the liquid is crystal clear. Line the sieve with muslin and place it over a perfectly clean bowl. Strain the crust and liquid through the muslin into the bowl, trying not to break the crust. The aspic should be sparkling clear. If necessary, repeat the process, remembering to scald the equipment again.

CHICKEN OR TURKEY MOUSSE

225 g/8 oz cooked chicken or turkey
  breast meat
275 ml/9 fl oz double cream
275 ml/9 fl oz chicken stock with fat
  removed
15 ml/1 tbsp gelatine
3 egg yolks, beaten
salt and pepper
20 ml/4 tsp mayonnaise

GARNISH
  watercress sprigs
  small lettuce leaves

Remove any skin, gristle and fat from the poultry, mince it finely and put it in a bowl. In a second bowl, whip the cream lightly. Chill until required. Place a mixing bowl in the refrigerator to chill.

Put 100 ml/3½ fl oz of the stock in a heatproof bowl, sprinkle on the gelatine and set aside until sponged. Put the rest of the stock in the top of a double saucepan and stir in the beaten egg yolks, with salt and pepper to taste.

Place the pan over simmering water and cook gently, stirring frequently, until the mixture thickens slightly. Remove from the heat and pour into the chilled bowl. Stand the bowl containing the gelatine over a saucepan of hot water and stir until the gelatine has dissolved completely. Stir into the egg mixture, mixing well. Add the minced chicken or turkey and stir until thoroughly mixed.

Stand the bowl in a basin of cold water or crushed ice, or place in the refrigerator until the mousse mixture begins to thicken at the edges. Fold in the chilled whipped cream and the mayonnaise. Turn into a wetted 1 litre/1¾ pint mould and chill until set. To serve, turn out on to a platter and garnish with wtercress sprigs and small lettuce leaves.

SERVES 4

TURKEY LOAF

fat for greasing
50 g/2 oz long-grain rice
225 g/8 oz cooked turkey meat
4 rindless streaky bacon rashers
salt and pepper
1 onion, finely chopped
about 50 ml/2 fl oz turkey or chicken stock
grated rind and juice of ½ lemon
50 g/2 oz fresh breadcrumbs
2.5 ml/½ tsp chopped fresh thyme
5 ml/1 tsp chopped parsley
15 ml/1 tbsp milk

Grease a 450 g/1 lb loaf tin. Set the oven at 190°C/375°F/gas 5. Cook the rice in a saucepan of boiling salted water for 20 minutes, then drain and set aside.

Mince the turkey meat with the bacon. Put the mixture in a bowl and add plenty of salt and pepper. Stir in the onion, stock, lemon rind and rice. In a separate bowl, mix the breadcrumbs, thyme, parsley and lemon juice. Add a little salt and pepper and mix in the milk to bind this stuffing.

Put half the turkey mixture in the prepared tin, spread with the stuffing, then cover with the remaining turkey mixture. Bake for about 35 minutes, until firm and browned on top. Turn out and serve hot or cold, with Sherried Mushrooms (page 226), if liked.

SERVES 6 TO 8

CHEESE ECLAIRS

CHOUX PASTRY
100 g/4 oz plain flour
50 g/2 oz butter or margarine
pinch of salt
2 whole eggs plus 1 yolk
salt and pepper
pinch of cayenne pepper

FILLING
25 g/1 oz butter
25 g/1 oz plain flour
300 ml/½ pint milk
75-100 g/3-4 oz Cheddar cheese, grated
pinch of dry mustard

Lightly grease a baking sheet. Set the oven at 200°C/400°F/gas 6. To make the pastry, sift the flour on to a sheet of grease-proof paper. Put 250 ml/8 fl oz water in a saucepan and add the butter or margarine with the salt. Heat gently until the fat melts.

When the fat has melted, bring the liquid rapidly to the boil and add all the flour at once. Immediately remove the pan from the heat and stir the flour into the liquid to make a smooth paste which leaves the sides of the pan clean. Set aside to cool slightly.

Add the egg yolk and beat well. Add the whole eggs, one at a time, beating well after each addition. Add salt, pepper and cayenne with the final egg. Continue beating until the paste is very glossy.

Put the pastry into a piping bag fitted with a 1 cm/½ inch nozzle and pipe it in 5 cm/2 inch lengths on the prepared baking sheet. Cut off each length with a knife or scissors dipped in hot water.

Bake for 25-30 minutes until risen and browned. Split the éclairs open and remove any uncooked paste. Return to the oven for 2-3 minutes to dry.

Meanwhile make the filling. Melt the butter in a saucepan. Stir in the flour and cook over a low heat for 2-3 minutes, without colouring. Over a very low heat, gradually add the milk, stirring constantly. Bring to the boil, stirring, and simmer for 1-2 minutes until smooth and thickened. Add the cheese, mustard and salt and pepper to taste.

Cool the éclairs on a wire rack. Fill with the cheese sauce.

MAKES 20 TO 24

VARIATIONS

HAM AND EGG ECLAIRS Omit the cheese. Add 2 chopped hard-boiled eggs, 15 ml/1 tbsp chopped tarragon and 75 g/3 oz diced cooked ham to the filling instead.

SMOKED SALMON ECLAIRS Omit the cheese. Substitute 75 g/3 oz roughly chopped smoked salmon and 2.5 ml/½ tsp grated lemon rind. Smoked salmon offcuts are ideal: up to 100 g/4 oz may be added, depending on flavour and the saltiness of the salmon.

TURKEY ECLAIRS Omit the cheese. Substitute 100 g/4 oz diced cooked turkey and 30 ml/2 tbsp chopped parsley.

FILO AND FETA TRIANGLES

225 g/8 oz feta cheese
5 ml/1 tsp dried oregano
1 spring onion, chopped
pepper
4 sheets of filo pastry
50 g/2 oz butter, melted

Set the oven at 190°C/375°F/gas 5. Mash the feta with the oregano in a bowl, then mix in the spring onion and pepper to taste.

Lay a sheet of filo pastry on a clean, dry surface and brush it with melted butter. Cut the sheet widthways into 9 strips. Place a little feta mixture at one end of the first strip, leaving the corner of the pastry without filling. Fold the corner over the feta to cover it in a triangular shape, then fold the mixture over and over to wrap it in several layers of pastry, making a small triangular-shaped pasty.

Repeat with the other strips of pastry. Cut and fill the remaining sheets in the same way to make 36 triangular pastries. Place these on baking sheets and brush any remaining butter over them.

Bake for about 10 minutes, until the filo pastry is crisp and golden. Transfer the triangles to a wire rack to cool. They are best served warm.

MAKES 36

SHAPES AND FILLINGS FOR FILO PASTRY

The feta filling used in the triangles is a Greek speciality. A variety of other fillings may be used and the pastry may be shaped in other ways.

SHAPES

Instead of cutting strips, the pastry may be cut into squares (about 6 per sheet). The filling should be placed in the middle of the squares, and the pastry gathered up to form a small bundle. The butter coating keeps the bundle closed when the filo is pressed together. For extra strength, the squares may be used double.

Alternatively, squares of filo may be filled and folded into neat oblong shapes.

Oblong pieces of filo (about 4 per sheet) may be folded into neat squares.

FILLINGS

SPINACH AND CHEESE Thoroughly drained cooked spinach may be used with or without the cheese. Flavour plain spinach with chopped spring onion and grated nutmeg.

SARDINE Mashed canned sardines in tomato sauce make a good filling for filo triangles.

CHICKEN OR HAM Chopped cooked chicken or ham are both tasty fillings for filo. Combine them with salt, pepper and a little low-fat soft cheese.

APRICOT Apricot halves (drained canned or fresh) topped with a dot of marmalade make good sweet filo pastries. Dust them with icing sugar after baking.

APPLE AND ALMOND Mix some ground almonds into cold, sweetened apple purée. Use to fill triangles or squares.

PAELLA VALENCIANA

1 kg/2¼ lb mussels, washed, scraped and
  bearded
30 ml/2 tbsp plain flour
1 (1.5 kg/3¼ lb) roasting chicken, cut into
  portions
90 ml/6 tbsp olive oil
2 garlic cloves
675 g/1½ lb risotto rice
pinch of saffron threads
salt

GARNISH
  450 g/1 lb cooked shellfish (prawns,
    crayfish, lobster or crab)
  strips of canned pimiento
  green or black olives
  chopped parsley

Wash, scrape and beard the mussels,
following the instructions on page 11. Put
them in a large saucepan with 125 ml/4 fl oz
water. Place over moderate heat and bring
to the boil. As soon as the liquid bubbles up
over the mussels, shake the pan 2 or 3
times, cover, lower the heat and simmer
until the mussels have opened. Discard any
that remain shut. Remove the mussels with
a slotted spoon and shell them, retaining
the best half shells. Strain the mussel liquid
through muslin into a large measuring jug,
add the cooking liquid and make up to 1.25
litres/2¼ pints with water. Set aside.

Put the flour in a sturdy polythene bag,
add the chicken portions and shake until
well coated. Heat 45 ml/3 tbsp of the olive
oil in a large frying pan, add the chicken
and fry until golden brown on all sides.
Using tongs, transfer the chicken to a plate
and set aside.

Heat the remaining oil in a large deep
frying pan or paella pan. Slice half a garlic
clove thinly and add the slices to the oil.

Fry until golden brown, then discard the
garlic. Add the rice to the pan and fry very
gently, turning frequently with a spatula.
Crush the remaining garlic. Pound the
saffron to a powder with a pestle in a mortar
and sprinkle it over the rice with the garlic.
Season with salt.

Add the reserved cooking liquid to the
pan and heat to simmering point, stirring
frequently. Cook for 5 minutes, still stirring. Add the chicken pieces, cooking them
with the rice for 15-20 minutes until they
are tender and the rice is cooked through.

Garnish with the shellfish, pimiento,
olives and parsley. Replace the mussels in
the half shells and arrange them on top of
the rice mixture. Remove the pan from the
heat, cover with a clean cloth and set aside
for 10 minutes before serving. Serve from
the pan.

SERVES 8

> **MRS BEETON'S TIP** Success
> depends upon correct cooking of the
> traditional risotto rice; the grains should
> be separate and not soggy.

MUSSEL RISOTTO

1.6 kg/3½ lb mussels
50 g/2 oz butter
30 ml/2 tbsp olive oil
1 onion, finely chopped
2 garlic cloves, crushed
225 g/8 oz risotto rice
grated rind of ½ lemon
1 bay leaf
300 ml/½ pint dry white wine
salt and pepper
300 ml/½ pint hot Basic Fish Stock (page 15) or water
75 g/3 oz Parmesan cheese, grated
60 ml/4 tbsp chopped parsley
8 lemon wedges to serve

Wash, scrape and beard the mussels following the instructions on page 11. Discard any that are open and do not shut when tapped. Put the mussels in a large saucepan. Add 125 ml/4 fl oz water and place over moderate heat to bring to the boil. As soon as the liquid boils, shake the pan and cover with a tight-fitting lid. Cook for about 5 minutes until all the mussels have opened, shaking the pan a couple of times.

Heat half the butter with the olive oil in a separate saucepan. Add the onion and garlic, then cook gently, stirring occasionally, for 10 minutes. Stir in the rice, lemon rind and bay leaf. Cook for a few minutes, stirring gently, until all the rice grains are coated in fat.

Pour in the wine, with salt and pepper to taste. Bring to the boil. Stir once, lower the heat and cover the pan tightly. Leave over low heat for 15 minutes.

Meanwhile, strain the mussels and reserve the cooking liquid. Discard any mussels that have not opened. Reserve a few mussels in shells for garnish and remove the others from their shells.

Pour the mussel cooking liquid and the hot stock or water into the rice mixture. Stir lightly, then cover the pan again. Continue to cook for 15-20 minutes more or until the rice is cooked, creamy and moist. Stir in the remaining butter and the cheese. Taste the risotto, adding more salt and pepper if required, then sprinkle in the parsley and place all the mussels on top. Cover the pan tightly and leave off the heat for 5 minutes.

Lightly fork the mussels and parsley into the risotto, turn it into 4 serving bowls and add a couple of lemon wedges to each. Garnish with the reserved mussels.

SERVES 4

CRAB-STUFFED CANNELLONI

fat for greasing
8 cannelloni tubes
salt and pepper
225 g/8 oz crab meat
25 g/1 oz fresh breadcrumbs
3 spring onions, chopped
225 g/8 oz ricotta cheese
600 ml/1 pint Fresh Tomato Sauce (page 352)
225 g/8 oz mozzarella cheese, sliced

Grease a large, shallow baking dish with butter. Alternatively, prepare 4 individual gratin dishes. Cook the cannelloni in boiling salted water for 10 minutes, until tender. Drain and rinse in cold water, then lay out to dry on a clean tea-towel.

Set the oven at 190°C/375°F/gas 5. Place the crab meat in a bowl and shred it with two forks. If using brown meat as well as white, add it after the white has been shredded. Mix in the breadcrumbs, spring onions and ricotta, with salt and pepper.

There are two ways of filling cannelloni: either put the crab mixture into a piping bag fitted with a large plain nozzle and force the mixture into the tubes, or use a teaspoon to fill the tubes. For those who are confident about using a piping bag the former method is less messy.

Lay the filled cannelloni in the prepared baking dish or dishes. Pour the tomato sauce over. Top with the mozzarella and bake for about 40 minutes, until golden.

SERVES 4

SEAFOOD LASAGNE

butter for greasing
12 sheets of lasagne
salt and pepper
25 g/1 oz butter
1 onion, chopped • 1 celery stick, diced
1 bay leaf • 25 g/1 oz plain flour
300 ml/½ pint red wine
45 ml/3 tbsp tomato purée
60 ml/4 tbsp chopped parsley
450 g/1 lb white fish fillet, skinned and cut
    into small pieces
225 g/8 oz peeled cooked prawns, thawed
    if frozen
225 g/8 oz shelled cooked mussels, thawed
    if frozen
100 g/4 oz mushrooms, sliced
600 ml/1 pint Béchamel Sauce (see Mrs
    Beeton's Tip, page 47)
100 g/4 oz mozzarella cheese, diced

Grease a large lasagne dish with butter. Cook the lasagne in a large saucepan of boiling salted water. Add the sheets in-dividually, bending them into the pan as they soften. When tender (after about 10 minutes), drain the lasagne and rinse them immediately in cold water. Lay the sheets out to dry on a clean tea-towel.

Melt the butter in a saucepan. Add the onion and celery, then cook, stirring occasionally, for 10 minutes. Stir in the bay leaf and flour, then gradually pour in the wine, stirring all the time. Add 125 ml/4 fl oz water and bring to the boil, stirring. Stir in the tomato purée and parsley, lower the heat and simmer for 5 minutes. Taste and season the sauce.

Set the oven at 180°C/350°F/gas 4. Remove the wine sauce from the heat. Add the fish, prawns and mussels. Make sure that any frozen seafood is well drained. Lastly, stir in the mushrooms.

Place a layer of lasagne in the prepared dish, then top with half the seafood sauce. Lay half the remaining lasagne over the sauce, then pour on all the remaining sea-food mixture. Top with the rest of the lasagne. Stir the mozzarella into the Béchamel sauce, then pour this over the lasagne.

Bake for 50-60 minutes until golden brown and bubbling hot. If liked, serve with salad and crusty bread to mop up the sauce.

SERVES 6

SPAGHETTI ALLA MARINARA

100 g/4 oz butter
1 garlic clove, crushed
10 ml/2 tsp chopped parsley
15 ml/1 tbsp shredded fresh basil or 5
    ml/1 tsp dried basil
salt and pepper
225 g/8 oz spaghetti, broken into short
    lengths
50 g/2 oz Parmesan cheese, grated
25 g/1 oz plain flour
225 g/8 oz peeled cooked scampi tails
30 ml/2 tbsp oil
pinch of grated nutmeg

SAUCE
    45 ml/3 tbsp oil
    2 rindless streaky bacon rashers, finely
        chopped
    ½ onion, finely chopped
    1 garlic clove, crushed
    ½ red pepper, seeded and finely chopped
    25 g/1 oz plain flour
    50 g/2 oz tomato purée
    4 large tomatoes, peeled, seeded and
        chopped or 1 (397 g/14 oz) can chopped
        tomatoes
    300 ml/½ pint chicken stock
    5 ml/1 tsp thick honey
    15 ml/1 tbsp chopped fresh herbs
        (oregano, basil, rosemary, parsley)

Make the sauce. Heat the oil in a large saucepan, add the bacon and fry for 2 minutes. Add the onion, garlic and pepper and cook gently for 5 minutes, stirring occasionally. Stir in the flour and tomato purée and cook for 5 minutes more.

Add the chopped tomatoes and chicken stock. Bring to the boil, stirring occasionally, then lower the heat and simmer for 30 minutes. Add salt and pepper to taste, stir in the honey and herbs and keep warm.

Cream 50 g/2 oz of the butter with the garlic, parsley and basil in a small bowl. Set aside. Bring a large saucepan of salted water to the boil, add the spaghetti and boil for 10-12 minutes or until tender. Drain in a colander, rinse with hot water and drain again. Turn on to a sheet of greaseproof paper and pat dry.

Tip the spaghetti into a clean pan. Add the remaining butter and half the Parmesan. Season with plenty of salt and pepper and heat through. Transfer to a large shallow flameproof dish and keep warm.

Put the flour in a sturdy polythene bag with salt and pepper to taste. Add the scampi and toss until well coated. Shake off excess flour. Heat the oil in a large frying pan and shallow fry the scampi for 5 minutes. Drain off the oil and add the scampi to the spaghetti. Stir in the herb butter.

Spoon the tomato sauce over the pasta and shellfish, sprinkle with the remaining Parmesan and brown under a moderate grill for 3-5 minutes. Serve at once.

SERVES 4

MRS BEETON'S TIP This sauce is delicious with home-made pasta (see page 354).

DISHES FOR EVERY DAY

Here is a chapter full of family favourites and contemporary dishes for more adventurous cooks. They are all easy to prepare, satisfying and nutritious – and none will stretch the budget to its limits.

*I*TALIAN-STYLE PIZZA

This should be thin and crisp with a slightly bubbly dough base and a moist topping.

fat for greasing
25 g/1 oz fresh yeast or 15 ml/1 tbsp dried
  yeast
5 ml/1 tsp sugar
450 g/1 lb strong white flour
5 ml/1 tsp salt ● 30 ml/2 tbsp olive oil

TOPPING
60 ml/4 tbsp olive oil
2 garlic cloves, crushed
1 large onion, chopped
15 ml/1 tbsp dried oregano or marjoram
1 (397 g/14 oz) can chopped tomatoes
30 ml/2 tbsp tomato purée
salt and pepper
375 g/12 oz mozzarella cheese, sliced

Grease 4 large baking sheets. Measure 300 ml/½ pint lukewarm water. Blend the fresh yeast with the sugar and a little luke-warm water. Set aside until frothy. For dried yeast, sprinkle the yeast over the water, then leave until frothy.

Sift the flour and salt into a bowl, make a well in the middle and add the yeast liquid, remaining water and oil. Mix the flour into the liquid to make a firm dough.

Turn out the dough on to a lightly floured surface and knead thoroughly until smooth and elastic – about 10 minutes. Place the dough in a clean, lightly floured bowl. Cover with cling film and leave in a warm place until doubled in bulk. This will take about 2 hours.

To make the topping, heat the oil in a saucepan and cook the garlic and onion until soft but not browned – about 15 minutes. Stir in the oregano, tomatoes and tomato purée. Bring to the boil, reduce the heat and simmer for 15 minutes. Remove the pan from the heat and add salt and pepper to taste.

Set the oven at 240°C/475°F/gas 9. Knead the dough again, then divide it into four. Roll out each portion into a 25-30 cm/10-20 inch circle. Place a piece of dough on each prepared baking sheet. Top with the tomato mixture and mozzarella, then leave in a warm place for about 5 minutes, or until the dough bases begin to rise slightly.

Bake for about 15 minutes, or until the topping is well browned and the dough is crisp and bubbly. Serve freshly baked.

MAKES 4

SCONE PIZZA

fat for greasing
225 g/8 oz self-raising flour
10 ml/2 tsp baking powder
salt and pepper
50 g/2 oz margarine
5 ml/1 tsp dried marjoram
2.5 ml/½ tsp dried thyme
150 ml/¼ pint milk

TOPPING
1 (200 g/7 oz) can tuna in oil
1 onion, chopped
1 garlic clove (optional)
15 ml/1 tbsp roughly chopped capers
30 ml/2 tbsp chopped parsley
4 large tomatoes, peeled and sliced
100 g/4 oz Cheddar cheese, grated

Grease a large baking sheet. Set the oven at 220°C/425°F/gas 7. Sift the flour, baking powder and salt into a bowl, then rub in the margarine. Stir in the herbs and milk to make a soft dough. Knead the dough lightly.

Roll out the dough on a lightly floured surface into a 30 cm/12 inch circle. Lift the dough on to the prepared baking sheet and turn the edge over, pinching it neatly.

Drain the oil from the tuna in a small saucepan and heat it gently. Add the onion and garlic (if used) and cook for about 10 minutes, until the onion is just beginning to soften. Off the heat, add the capers, parsley and flaked tuna. Spread this topping over the scone base, cover with tomato slices, then sprinkle with the cheese.

Bake for 20-25 minutes, until the topping is bubbling hot and golden and the base is risen, browned around the edges and cooked through. Serve cut into wedges.

SERVES 4 TO 6

DEEP-PAN PIZZA

This is a thick-based, American-style pizza. Pepperoni sausage is a spicy uncooked sausage, available from delicatessens and large supermarkets.

fat for greasing
15 g/½ oz fresh yeast or 10 ml/2 tsp dried yeast
5 ml/1 tsp sugar
225 g/8 oz strong white flour
2.5 ml/½ tsp salt
15 ml/1 tbsp olive oil
flour for rolling out

FILLING
30 ml/2 tbsp olive oil
1 large onion, chopped
1 green pepper, seeded and chopped
1 garlic clove, crushed
salt and pepper
30 ml/2 tbsp tomato purée
100 g/4 oz mushrooms, sliced
100 g/4 oz pepperoni sausage, cut into chunks
100 g/4 oz sweetcorn kernels
75 g/3 oz Cheddar cheese, grated

Grease a 25 cm/10 inch loose-bottomed flan tin or sandwich cake tin. Make the dough following the recipe for Italian-style Pizza (page 285) and leave it to rise.

Roll out the dough on a lightly floured surface large enough to line the prepared tin. Press it into the tin, pinching it around the upper edges to keep in place. Cover and set aside. Set the oven at 220°C/425°F/ gas 7.

To make the filling, heat the oil in a small saucepan and cook the onion, pepper and garlic until beginning to soften – about 10 minutes. Stir in salt, pepper and the tomato purée, then remove the pan from the heat and mix in the mushrooms. Spread this mixture over the dough. Top with the pepperoni sausage and sweetcorn, then sprinkle with the cheese.

Bake for about 40 minutes, until the dough and topping is golden brown and bubbling. Serve cut into wedges.

SERVES 4

PIZZA TOPPERS

Any of the following topping ingredients may be used for an Italian-style Pizza, Deep-pan Pizza or Scone Pizza. They may also be varied according to taste.

SPICY PRAWN PIZZA Seed and finely chop 1 green chilli, then cook it with 1 chopped onion in some olive oil. Add 4 diced peeled tomatoes and 225 g/8 oz peeled cooked prawns (thawed and drained if frozen). Spread over the pizza and top with plenty of sliced mozzarella cheese (more if making 4 Italian-style bases than on a single pizza).

QUICKIE SARDINE PIZZA This one is best on a scone base: arrange canned sardines like the spokes of a wheel on a scone base. Sprinkle with plenty of chopped spring onion, then arrange chopped peeled tomato between the sardines. Sprinkle with plenty of salt, pepper and grated cheese.

ANCHOVY AND OLIVES Chop 1 (50 g/ 2 oz) can anchovy fillets with their oil. Divide between 4 Italian-style bases, sprinkling them over the tomato topping. Add the mozzarella, then top with 50 g/2 oz stoned black olives, either left whole or halved, as preferred. Sprinkle with 30 ml/ 2 tbsp chopped capers before baking.

HAM AND EGG PIZZA Make the 4 Italian-style Pizzas or the dough for 1 Deep-pan Pizza. Spread the tomato topping for Italian-style pizzas over the chosen bases. Top with 225 g/8 oz roughly chopped cooked ham and 225 g/8 oz sliced mozzarella cheese. Make a slight nest in the middle of each Italian pizza or 4 in the deep pan pizza and crack 4 eggs into the nests. Bake as in the main recipes.

SALAMI AND WHOLE FLAT MUSH-ROOM Top the chosen base with tomato purée and cooked chopped onion. Add slices of salami. Remove the stalks from small to medium flat mushrooms, allowing 4 each for individual pizzas, 8-12 for a large pizza. Chop the stalks and sprinkle them over the bases, then arrange mushroom caps on top. Sprinkle the mushrooms with salt and pepper, then top each with a thin slice of mozzarella before baking.

SPICY SAUSAGE TOPPING Place 450 g/1 lb good quality pork sausagemeat in a bowl. Add 1 small grated onion, 2 crushed garlic cloves, 1.25-5 ml/¼-1 tsp chilli powder, 15 ml/1 tbsp ground coriander and 15 ml/1 tbsp paprika. Mix the ingredients really well, with a spoon at first, then wash your hands and knead the sausage mixture. Dot small lumps of the mixture over the chosen pizza, between any mozzarella topping or over any grated cheese so that the meat cooks and browns.

COURGETTE PIZZA Make the tomato topping for the Italian-style Pizza. Spread the tomato mixture over the chosen base, then add a good layer of sliced courgettes and sprinkle them with lots of fresh basil leaves. Drizzle a little olive oil over the top and dust the courgettes with grated Parmesan cheese. Dot with a few pieces of mozzarella but leave at least half the courgettes uncovered so they brown slightly during baking.

CALZONE

A type of pizza pasty, calzone is a pizza which is folded in half to enclose its filling. Often filled with a meat sauce (bolognaise) and mozzarella, the filling may be varied according to taste.

fat for greasing
25 g/1 oz fresh yeast or 15 ml/1 tbsp dried
   yeast
5 ml/1 tsp sugar
450 g/1 lb strong white flour
5 ml/1 tsp salt
30 ml/2 tbsp olive oil
flour for rolling out

FILLING
   225 g/8 oz minced beef
   2.5 ml/½ tsp chilli powder
   salt and pepper
   1 quantity tomato pizza topping (page
     285)
   50 g/2 oz mushrooms, sliced
   225 g/8 oz mozzarella cheese, sliced

Grease 2 baking sheets. Make the dough following the recipe for Italian-style Pizza (page 285) and leave it to rise.

Meanwhile, dry-fry the mince in a heavy-bottomed saucepan over moderate heat until well browned. If the meat is very lean you may have to add a little olive oil. Add salt, pepper and the chilli powder. Stir in the tomato topping and bring to the boil. Cover, reduce the heat and simmer the mixture very gently for about 30 minutes. Set aside to cool. Stir in the mushrooms when the meat has cooled, just before it is to be used.

Set the oven at 220°C/425°F/gas 7. Knead the dough again, then divide it into quarters. Roll out one portion into a 23 cm/9 inch circle. Place it on a prepared baking sheet. Top one side with about a quarter of the meat mixture and a quarter of the mozzarella. Fold over the other half of the dough and pinch the edges together firmly to seal in the filling.

Repeat with the remaining portions of dough and filling. Use the second baking sheet to fill the second calzone, then slide it on to the first sheet next to the first calzone. To shape the last calzone, sprinkle a little flour over the calzone on the baking sheet, then lift the final portion of dough on to the sheet, allowing one half to drape over the filled calzone while filling the opposite side. Otherwise the large calzone can be difficult to lift once filled.

Leave the filled dough to rise in a warm place for about 5 minutes. Bake for 30-40 minutes, or until the dough is golden, risen and cooked. Leave to stand on the baking sheets for a few minutes, then transfer to individual plates.

MAKES 4

Cottage Pie (page 302) with buttered cabbage and mashed swedes

Sweet and Sour Pork (page 305) with Bean Sprout Salad (page 339)

Baked Jacket Potatoes (page 308) topped with Sausage and Chutney, Broccoli and Asparagus, and Southern Special, and served with Coleslaw (page 340), Spinach and Bacon Salad (page 345) and Waldorf Salad (page 346)

Spiced Lentils (page 251) and Lamb Curry (page 313)

Bolognese Sauce (page 314) served with spaghetti and green salad

Seafood Salad (page 336) and Chicken and Celery Salad (page 337)

Savoury Pancakes (page 321) with Smoked Haddock filling, and Fennel and Cucumber Salad (page 340)

Pasticcio di Lasagne Verde (page 318) and Cannelloni with Mushroom Stuffing (page 319)

SARDINE CASSOLETTES

3 large slices of stale bread, each about
    2 cm/¾ inch thick
oil for shallow frying
1 (65 g/2½ oz) can sardines in oil, drained
15 ml/1 tbsp Greek yogurt
15 ml/1 tbsp tomato purée
salt and pepper
few drops of lemon juice
10 ml/2 tsp grated Parmesan cheese
watercress sprigs to garnish

Set the oven at 180°C/350°F/gas 4. Using a 5 cm/2 inch biscuit cutter, stamp out 8-10 rounds from the bread. Mark an inner circle on each bread round, using a 3.5 cm/1¼ inch cutter.

Heat the oil in a large frying pan, add the bread rounds and fry until lightly browned. Remove the rounds with a slotted spoon and drain on absorbent kitchen paper. With the point of a knife, lift out the inner ring on each round to form a hollow case. Put the cases on a baking sheet and place in the oven for a few minutes to crisp the insides. Cool completely.

Make the filling by mashing the sardines thoroughly and mixing them with the yogurt and tomato purée. Add salt and pepper to taste and stir in the lemon juice and Parmesan. Spoon into the prepared cases and garnish with watercress.

MAKES 8 TO 10

TUNA SAUCE

A real quickie to serve with cooked pasta or rice. It also goes well with mashed potato, particularly if the potato is arranged in a ring in a flameproof dish and grilled until brown before being filled with sauce. The sauce may also be ladled into split baked potatoes or into scooped-out crusty rolls.

25 g/1 oz butter
1 (200 g/7 oz) can tuna
1 onion, chopped
25 g/1 oz plain flour
450 ml/¾ pint milk
100 g/4 oz mushrooms, sliced
50 g/2 oz Cheddar cheese, grated
salt and pepper
30 ml/2 tbsp chopped parsley

Melt the butter in a saucepan. If the tuna is canned in oil, drain the oil into the pan with the butter. Drain and flake the tuna and set it aside. Add the onion to the pan and cook gently, stirring occasionally, for about 15 minutes or until soft. Stir in the flour and cook for 1 minute, then reduce the heat to low and slowly pour in the milk, stirring constantly. Bring to the boil, lower the heat again and simmer for 3 minutes.

Stir the mushrooms and cheese into the sauce with salt and pepper to taste. Cook over low heat until the cheese melts, then add the parsley and flaked drained tuna. Stir for 1-2 minutes until the tuna is hot, then serve at once.

SERVES 4

STUFFED CABBAGE LEAVES

fat for greasing
8 large cabbage leaves

STUFFING
   15 ml/1 tbsp oil
   1 onion, finely chopped
   400 g/14 oz minced beef
   1 (397 g/14 oz) can tomatoes
   10 ml/2 tsp cornflour
   15 ml/1 tbsp Worcestershire sauce
   2.5 ml/½ tsp dried mixed herbs
   15 ml/1 tbsp chopped parsley
   salt and pepper

SAUCE
   juice from the canned tomatoes
   15 ml/1 tbsp tomato purée
   20 ml/4 tsp cornflour

Remove the thick centre stems from the cabbage leaves, then blanch them in boiling water for 2 minutes. Drain well.

To make the stuffing, heat the oil in a pan and gently fry the onion for 5 minutes. Add the mince and cook, stirring until the beef has browned. Drain the tomatoes and reserve the juice. Add the tomatoes to the meat mixture. Blend the cornflour with the Worcestershire sauce and stir into the meat mixture with the herbs and salt and pepper. Cover and cook for 20 minutes, stirring occasionally.

Grease a shallow ovenproof dish. Set the oven at 190°C/375°F/gas 5.

Divide the stuffing between the cabbage leaves and roll up, folding over the edges of the leaves to enclose the meat completely. Place in the prepared dish and cover with foil. Bake in the oven for 20 minutes.

Meanwhile make the sauce. Blend the reserved juice from the tomatoes with the tomato purée and make up to 250 ml/8 fl oz with water. Blend the cornflour with 15 ml/1 tbsp of the sauce. Pour the rest of the sauce into a pan and bring to the boil. Pour in the blended cornflour and bring to the boil, stirring all the time, until the sauce has thickened. Add salt and pepper to taste. Pour the sauce over the cabbage leaves just before serving.

SERVES 4

BAKED STUFFED PEPPERS

butter or margarine for greasing
4 green peppers
1 small onion, finely chopped
400 g/14 oz lean minced beef
100 g/4 oz cooked rice
salt and pepper
good pinch of dried marjoram
250 ml/8 fl oz tomato juice
strips of pepper to garnish

Grease an ovenproof dish. Set the oven at 180°C/350°F/gas 4. Cut a slice off the top of the peppers, then remove the membranes and seeds. Blanch in a saucepan of boiling water for 2 minutes.

Mix the onion, beef, rice, salt, pepper and marjoram together in a bowl. Stand the peppers upright in the prepared dish; if any do not stand upright easily, cut a thin slice off the base. Divide the stuffing mixture between the peppers. Pour the tomato juice around the base of the peppers.

Cover and bake for 1 hour. Garnish with strips of pepper.

SERVES 4

BAKED STUFFED MARROW

fat for greasing
1 marrow
1 small onion, finely chopped or grated
200 g/7 oz minced beef
100 g/4 oz pork sausagemeat or 100 g/4 oz
    extra minced beef
25 g/1 oz fresh white breadcrumbs
15 ml/1 tbsp chopped parsley
15 ml/1 tbsp snipped chives
5 ml/1 tsp Worcestershire sauce
salt and pepper
1 egg, beaten

SAUCE
25 g/1 oz butter
25 g/1 oz plain flour
300 ml/½ pint milk, stock or a mixture
    (see method)
75-100 g/3-4 oz Cheddar cheese, grated
pinch of dry mustard

Generously grease a large, shallow casserole. Set the oven at 180°C/350°F/gas 4. Halve the marrow lengthways and scoop out the seeds. Lay each half, side by side, in the prepared casserole.

Put the onion into a bowl with the beef, sausagemeat, if used, breadcrumbs, parsley, chives, Worcestershire sauce and salt and pepper. Mix well. Bind the mixture with the beaten egg.

Divide the stuffing between each marrow half. Cover the casserole and bake for 1 hour.

Strain off most of the liquid in the casserole. Meanwhile make the sauce. Melt the butter in a saucepan. Stir in the flour and cook over a low heat for 2-3 minutes, without colouring. Over a very low heat, gradually add the liquid (the casserole juices may be added), stirring constantly. Bring to the boil, stirring, then simmer for 1-2 minutes until smooth and thickened. Add the cheese, mustard and salt and pepper to taste. Pour the cheese sauce over the marrow and bake, uncovered, for a further 20 minutes, until the sauce is golden brown.

SERVES 4 TO 6

GRATIN DAUPHINOIS

25 g/1 oz butter
1 kg/2¼ lb potatoes, thinly sliced
1 large onion, about 200 g/7 oz, thinly
    sliced
200 g/7 oz Gruyère cheese, grated
salt and pepper
grated nutmeg
125 ml/4 fl oz single cream

Butter a 1.5 litre/2¾ pint casserole, reserving the remaining butter. Set the oven at 190°C/375°F/gas 5. Bring a saucepan of water to the boil, put in the potatoes and onion, then blanch for 30 seconds. Drain.

Put a layer of potatoes on the base of the prepared casserole. Dot with a little of the butter, then sprinkle with some of the onion and cheese, a little salt, pepper and grated nutmeg. Pour over some of the cream. Repeat the layers until all the ingredients have been used, finishing with a layer of cheese. Pour the remaining cream on top.

Cover and bake for 1 hour. Remove from the oven and place under a hot grill for 5 minutes, until the cheese topping is golden brown and bubbling.

SERVES 6

BEEF RISSOLES

In Mrs Beeton's day, when large beef roasts were more common than they are now, this was a popular way of using up leftovers.

450 g/1 lb cold lean roast beef
350 g/12 oz fresh white breadcrumbs
2.5 ml/½ tsp chopped summer savory
2.5 ml/½ tsp chopped thyme or 1.25 ml/¼ tsp dried thyme
grated rind and juice of ½ lemon
salt and pepper
1-2 eggs, beaten
oil for shallow frying
fried parsley (see Mrs Beeton's Tip) to garnish

Mince the beef finely. Put it in a bowl with the breadcrumbs, herbs, lemon rind and juice, with salt and pepper to taste. Add enough beaten egg to bind the mixture, then shape into balls or cones.

Heat the oil in a large deep frying pan and fry the rissoles until they are a rich brown colour. Garnish with fried parsley and serve with a rich Gravy (page 352), Creamed Onions (page 229) and Anna Potatoes (page 231).

SERVES 4

MRS BEETON'S TIP Fried parsley makes a colourful garnish. Select perfectly fresh parsley sprigs, wash swiftly and lightly and dry thoroughly on absorbent kitchen paper. Heat oil for deep frying to 180-190°C/350-365°F. Put a double layer of absorbent kitchen paper on a plate. Drop the parsley carefully into the hot oil and cook for a few seconds until bright green and crisp. Drain on the paper and serve at once.

DORMERS

225 g/8 oz cold roast lamb
75 g/3 oz cooked rice
50 g/2 oz fresh breadcrumbs
salt and pepper
30 ml/2 tbsp chopped fresh mint
about 60ml/4 tbsp gravy, stock or milk
1 egg
50 g/2 oz dried white breadcrumbs
oil for shallow frying

Finely chop the lamb and rice, using a food processor if possible. Add the breadcrumbs with plenty of salt and pepper, and the mint. Stir in enough gravy, stock or milk to just bind the mixture.

Form the mixture into 6 sausage shapes or patties. Beat the egg with 15 ml/1 tbsp water in a shallow bowl. Spread out the breadcrumbs on a sheet of foil. Coat the dormers in egg, then in breadcrumbs. If time permits, chill the crumbed dormers on a plate in the refrigerator for about 1 hour to firm up.

Heat the oil in a large shallow frying pan and fry the dormers for 10-15 minutes until golden brown. Drain on absorbent kitchen paper. Serve with a flavoursome gravy or rich tomato sauce.

MAKES 6

MRS BEETON'S TIP The dormers can be as simple – or as spicy – as you like. Add any of the following, singly or in combinations of three or four: 1 small onion, finely chopped or minced; 2 crushed garlic cloves; 5 ml/1 tsp thyme; 5 ml/1 tsp ground mace; 10 ml/2 tsp ground coriander; 15 ml/1 tbsp green peppercorns, lightly crushed; 15 ml/1 tbsp capers, chopped

CHICKEN AND RICE CROQUETTES

200 g/7 oz risotto rice
450 ml/¾ pint cold chicken stock
salt (optional)
75 g/3 oz butter
1 egg
50 g/2 oz dried breadcrumbs
oil for deep frying

FILLING
175 g/6 oz minced cooked chicken
1 hard-boiled egg, finely chopped
1.25 ml/¼ tsp cayenne pepper
1.25 ml/¼ tsp ground mace
30 ml/2 tbsp double or single cream or
   milk

Put the rice in a saucepan. Pour in the cold stock. Add a little salt if the stock is unseasoned, then bring to the boil. Cover the pan tightly and reduce the heat to the lowest setting. Leave the rice for 15 minutes, turn off the heat and leave for a further 15 minutes without removing the lid.

Add the butter to the rice in the pan and cook over gentle heat until it has all been absorbed and the rice is creamy. Set aside to cool.

Mix the ingredients for the filling in a bowl, adding the cream or milk to bind the mixture. Wash, then wet your hands in cold water. Take a spoonful of rice and flatten it on one palm, then place a small portion of the chicken mixture on top. Mould the rice over the chicken mixture, smoothing it around it to enclose the filling completely. The balls should be about the size of small eggs or tomatoes. Chill the rice balls for about 1 hour to firm up.

Beat the egg in a shallow bowl with 15 ml/1 tbsp water. Spread the breadcrumbs on a sheet of foil. Roll each croquette in egg, then in breadcrumbs. Heat the oil to 180°C/350°F and fry the croquettes, a few at a time, until golden brown. Remove with a slotted spoon, drain on absorbent kitchen paper and keep hot while frying successive batches.

MAKES ABOUT 14

SPICED DRUMSTICKS

15 ml/1 tbsp oil
1 onion, grated
1 garlic clove, crushed
5 ml/1 tsp curry powder
salt and pepper
60 ml/4 tbsp mango chutney
8 chicken drumsticks

Heat the oil in a small saucepan, then add the onion and garlic. Cook, stirring, for 5 minutes. Add the curry powder and plenty of salt and pepper; stir for another minute or so. Remove from the heat. Chop any large pieces of fruit in the mango chutney, then add it to the onion mixture and stir well. Set the oven at 200°C/400°F/ gas 6.

Make two or three slashes into the skin and flesh on both sides of the drumsticks, then place them in an ovenproof dish. Spoon the onion mixture over and cover with foil. Bake for 30 minutes.

Turn the drumsticks over and baste them with the cooking juices, then continue to cook, uncovered, for a further 20-30 minutes, turning once more, until cooked through and well browned. Serve at once. To serve cold, transfer to a cold dish, cover and cool quickly, then chill until required.

SERVES 4

COTTAGE PIE

Illustrated on page 289

Like shepherd's pie, from which it originated, cottage pie consists of cooked meat with onions and sauce, topped with creamy mashed potato and baked in the oven. Where it differs is that whereas shepherd's pie is made from cooked leftover lamb, cottage pie has minced beef.

butter for greasing
50 g/2 oz butter
1 onion, roughly chopped
1 garlic clove, crushed
2 carrots, finely chopped
100 g/4 oz mushrooms, chopped
575 g/1¼ lb minced beef
250 ml/8 fl oz beef stock
5 ml/1 tsp Worcestershire sauce
salt and pepper
675 g/1½ lb potatoes, halved
15-30 ml/1-2 tbsp milk
pinch of grated nutmeg

Melt half the butter in a saucepan and fry the onion gently for about 5 minutes until softened but not coloured. Add the garlic, carrots and mushrooms and fry over gentle heat for 10 minutes or until soft. Using a slotted spoon, remove the vegetables from the pan and set aside.

Add the minced beef to the pan and cook, stirring frequently to break up any lumps, until browned. Drain off excess fat, return the vegetables to the pan and stir in the beef stock and Worcestershire sauce, with salt and pepper to taste. Cook over moderate heat for about 30 minutes, or until the mixture thickens.

Meanwhile cook the potatoes in a saucepan of salted boiling water for about 30 minutes or until tender. Drain thoroughly and mash with a potato masher, or beat with a hand-held electric whisk until smooth. Beat in the remaining butter and the milk to make a creamy consistency. Add salt, pepper and nutmeg to taste.

Set the oven at 220°C/450°F/gas 7. Spoon the meat mixture into a greased pie dish or shallow oven-to-table dish. Cover with the potato. Bake for 10-15 minutes until browned on top. Serve at once.

SERVES 4 TO 6

TOAD-IN-THE-HOLE

450 g/1 lb pork sausages

BATTER
100 g/4 oz plain flour
1.25 ml/¼ tsp salt
1 egg, beaten
300 ml/½ pint milk, or half milk and half
water

Make the batter. Sift the flour and salt into a bowl, make a well in the centre and add the beaten egg. Stir in half the milk (or all the milk, if using a mixture of milk and water), gradually working in the flour.

Beat vigorously until the mixture is smooth and bubbly, then stir in the rest of the milk (or the water). Pour the batter into a jug and set aside.

Set the oven at 220°C/425°F/gas 7. Arrange the sausages, spoke-fashion, in a shallow 1.1 litre/2 pint circular dish. Stand the dish on a baking sheet and cook the sausages for 15 minutes.

Pour the batter over the sausages and bake for 40-45 minutes more until golden brown and well risen. Serve at once with a rich gravy or home-made tomato sauce.

SERVES 4

SHEPHERD'S PIE

butter for greasing
50 g/2 oz butter
2 onions, roughly chopped
15 ml/1 tbsp plain flour
250 ml/8 fl oz well-flavoured lamb stock
   (see Mrs Beeton's Tip)
575 g/1¼ lb lean cooked lamb, minced
salt and pepper
5 ml/1 tsp Worcestershire sauce
675 g/1½ lb potatoes, halved
15-30 ml/1-2 tbsp milk
pinch of grated nutmeg

Melt half the butter in a saucepan and fry the onions until softened but not coloured. Stir in the flour and cook gently for 1-2 minutes, stirring all the time. Gradually add the stock. Bring to the boil, stirring until the sauce thickens.

Stir in the lamb, with salt, pepper and Worcestershire sauce to taste. Cover the pan and simmer for 30 minutes.

Meanwhile cook the potatoes in a saucepan of salted boiling water for about 30 minutes or until tender. Drain thoroughly and mash with a potato masher, or beat with a hand-held electric whisk until smooth. Beat in the remaining butter and the milk to make a creamy consistency. Add salt, pepper and nutmeg to taste.

Set the oven at 220°C/450°F/gas 7. Spoon the meat mixture into a greased pie dish or shallow oven-to-table dish. Cover with the potato, smooth the top, then flick it up into small peaks or score a pattern on the surface with a fork. Bake for 10-15 minutes until browned on top. Serve at once.

SERVES 4 TO 6

HAMBURGERS

If you intend serving the burgers less than well cooked, buy good-quality steak and mince it at home. Bought minced steak should be cooked through before serving.

450 g/1 lb minced steak
2.5 ml/½ tsp salt
2.5 ml/½ tsp freshly ground black pepper
5-10 ml/1-2 tsp grated onion (optional)

Combine the meat, salt and pepper in a bowl. Add the onion, if used, and mix well. Shape the mixture lightly into 4 flat round cakes, about 2 cm/¾ inch thick.

Heat a frying pan or griddle until very hot, add the hamburgers and cook for 2 minutes on each side for rare meat; 4 minutes per side for well done meat. Alternatively, cook under a preheated grill or over coals on a barbecue grill for 6-8 minutes, turning once. Serve plain or in buns, with toppings or fillings as desired.

SERVES 4

VARIATIONS

Offer any or all of the following: lettuce leaves; sliced cucumber; sliced tomatoe; sliced gherkins; sliced raw or fried onions; hamburger relish; German or French mustard; tomato ketchup; mayonnaise; soured cream.

LAMB BURGERS Use good quality minced lamb instead of steak. Add 2.5 ml/½ tsp dried oregano to the mixture.
CHEESE BURGERS Top each hamburger with a slice of processed cheese during the final minute of grilling.
PITTA BURGERS Make 8 burgers instead of 4 and serve them in warm pitta bread pockets, with shredded lettuce, chopped cucumber and chopped tomatoes. Add a dollop of Greek yogurt, if liked.

PORK AND ONION ROLL

fat for greasing
400 g/14 oz lean pork, coarsely minced or
    finely chopped
3 small onions, finely chopped
1.25 ml/¼ tsp dried sage
salt and pepper

SUET CRUST PASTRY
300 g/10 oz plain flour
7.5 ml/1½ tsp baking powder
2.5 ml/½ tsp salt
150 g/5 oz shredded suet
flour for rolling out

Combine the pork, onions and sage, with salt and pepper to taste, in a bowl. Mix well.

Make the pastry. Sift the flour, baking powder and salt into a mixing bowl. Stir in the suet, then add enough cold water (about 75-125 ml/3-4 fl oz) to make a soft but not sticky dough.

Roll out the suet crust pastry on a lightly floured surface to a rectangle measuring 25 × 40 cm/10 × 16 inches. Spread the pork mixture over the rectangle, leaving a 1 cm/½ inch border all round. Roll up from the narrow side, like a Swiss roll, and press the end and sides to seal in the filling.

Wrap the roll firmly in a sheet of greased greaseproof paper and then in foil or a scalded pudding cloth. Bring a large saucepan of water to the boil, add the pork and onion roll and cook for 3 hours. Turn out on to a heated dish and serve with Red Cabbage with Apples (page 213) and Beans with Soured Cream (page 210).

SERVES 6

BAKED HAM LOAF

fat for greasing
100 g/4 oz dried breadcrumbs
350 g/12 oz cooked ham, minced
50 g/2 oz sultanas
1 large cooking apple
15 ml/1 tbsp chopped parsley
5 ml/1 tsp grated lemon rind
pinch of ground allspice
pinch of grated nutmeg
salt and pepper
2 eggs, beaten
milk (see method)

Grease a 450 g/1 lb loaf tin and coat it with some of the breadcrumbs. Set the oven at 150°C/300°F/gas 2.

Put the remaining breadcrumbs in a mixing bowl and add the minced ham and sultanas. Peel, core and grate the apple. Add it to the bowl with the parsley, lemon rind, spices, and salt and pepper to taste. Bind with the beaten eggs, adding a little milk if necessary.

Spoon the mixture into the prepared tin, taking care not to disturb the breadcrumb coating. Bake for 40 minutes. Allow to cool for 5 minutes, then turn out on to a heated serving dish. Serve hot, with Scalloped Potatoes with Onions (page 233) and Italian Spinach (page 234). Alternatively, serve cold with Flageolet Bean Salad (page 257) and Coleslaw (page 240).

SERVES 6

> **MRS BEETON'S TIP** Corned beef may be used in place of ham to make this tasty loaf. Any small amount of leftover cooked meat may be combined with cooked ham or canned meat to make up the quantity of mixture.

SWEET AND SOUR PORK

Illustrated on page 290

675 g/1½ lb pork, trimmed and cut into
  2 cm/¾ inch cubes oil for deep frying

MARINADE
  1 egg white
  40 g/1½ oz cornflour
  30 ml/2 tbsp soy sauce
  30 ml/2 tbsp dry sherry
  salt and pepper

BATTER
  1 egg
  45 ml/3 tbsp plain flour
  45 ml/3 tbsp cornflour
  45-60 ml/3-4 tbsp light beer

SAUCE
  30 ml/2 tbsp oil
  3 spring onions, finely chopped
  1 small red pepper, seeded and cut into
    thin strips
  1 small green pepper, seeded and cut into
    thin strips
  3 canned pineapple rings, chopped
  500 ml/17 fl oz chicken stock
  30 ml/2 tbsp vinegar
  45 ml/3 tbsp tomato ketchup
  45 ml/3 tbsp soy sauce
  25 g/1 oz caster sugar
  30 ml/2 tbsp cornflour

Make the marinade. Beat the egg white in a bowl with the cornflour. Stir in the soy sauce and sherry, with salt and pepper to taste. Add the meat cubes and marinate for 15 minutes, turning frequently. Remove from the marinade and drain well.

Meanwhile make the sauce. Heat the oil in a saucepan, add the spring onions, peppers and pineapple and fry for 2 minutes, stirring all the time. Add the chicken stock, vinegar, tomato ketchup and soy sauce, with sugar and salt to taste. Simmer for 5 minutes.

To make the batter, whisk the egg, flour, cornflour, beer and salt in a bowl. Heat the oil for deep frying to 180-190°C/350-375°F or until a cube of bread added to the oil browns in 30 seconds. If using a deep-fat fryer, follow the manufacturer's instructions. Dip the meat cubes in the batter and fry a few at a time until golden brown. As each batch of cubes browns, remove them with a slotted spoon and keep warm on a serving dish.

Finish the sauce. Put the cornflour in a cup and mix to a paste with a little cold water. Stir the paste into the sweet and sour sauce and bring to the boil, stirring until it thickens. Pour the sauce over the pieces of pork and serve at once.

SERVES 4

VARIATION

SWEET AND SOUR PORK STIR FRY Mix the marinade as suggested above, add the pork cubes and turn to coat in the mixture. Do not allow to stand. Heat 75 ml/5 tbsp oil in a wok. Add the pork cubes and stir-fry over high heat until cooked and crisp. Transfer to a bowl with a slotted spoon and serve with the sweet and sour sauce.

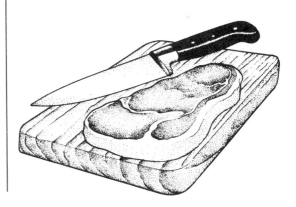

PORK CHOW MEIN

3 dried Chinese mushrooms (optional)
225 g/8 oz lean boneless pork
60 ml/4 tbsp soy sauce
60 ml/4 tbsp dry sherry
225 g/8 oz Chinese egg noodles
90 ml/6 tbsp oil (preferably groundnut oil)
4 spring onions, shredded
1 small green pepper, seeded and cut into
    thin strips
1 small red pepper, seeded and cut into
    thin strips
2 celery sticks, thinly sliced at a slant
50 g/2 oz mushrooms, sliced (optional)
150 g/5 oz drained canned bamboo
    shoots, cut into strips

If using the dried mushrooms, place them in a small bowl or mug and add just enough boiling water to cover them. Put a saucer or second mug on the mushrooms to keep them submerged. Leave to soak for 15 minutes. Drain, discard the tough stalks and thinly slice the mushroom caps.

Slice the pork thinly against the grain, then cut it into strips. Place in a bowl with the soy sauce and sherry. Mix well, cover and marinate for 30 minutes, stirring occasionally.

Meanwhile bring a large saucepan of water to the boil, add the noodles and cook for 2-3 minutes or according to packet instructions. Drain, rinse under cold water until cool, then drain again. Set aside.

Heat half the oil in a large frying pan or wok and add the noodles. Press them out and cook quickly for 2-3 minutes until lightly browned. Turn and cook for another 2-3 minutes, or until the noodles are crisp in places and hot. Turn the noodles out on to a serving plate and keep hot.

Heat the remaining oil. Using a slotted spoon, remove the pork strips from the marinade and add them to the hot oil. Stir fry for 3-5 minutes or until browned, add the spring onions, peppers and celery slices and stir fry for 4 minutes. Add the mushrooms (including dried mushrooms if used) and bamboo shoots with the reserved marinade. Cook, stirring occasionally, for 4-5 minutes, then spoon the mixture over the noodles and serve at once. The noodles and stir fry may be mixed as the chow mein is served.

SERVES 4 TO 6

> **MRS BEETON'S TIP** Stir frying is a quick cooking method and the pan with the cooking oil should be shimmering hot before the meat is added. Groundnut oil is ideal as it reaches a high temperature before smoking, so the pork cooks quickly and browned easily, but other cooking oils may be used. Dried Chinese mushrooms (shiitake) give the chow mein an excellent flavour; however, they are expensive. Look out for fresh shiitake and use them instead of the fresh mushrooms – they have a good flavour. The soaking liquid from the mushrooms may be added to the chow mein or reserved for another Chinese dish.

RABBIT A LA MINUTE

1 oven-ready rabbit, cut into small
    serving portions
salt and pepper
30 ml/2 tbsp plain flour
2.5 ml/½ tsp ground mace
25 g/1 oz butter or 30 ml/2 tbsp oil
100 g/4 oz mushrooms, sliced
300 ml/½ pint chicken or vegetable
    stock
60 ml/4 tbsp sherry
30 ml/2 tbsp chopped parsley

Coat the rabbit portions with the salt, pepper, flour and mace. Melt the butter or heat the oil in a large deep frying pan. Add the rabbit portions and cook, turning frequently, for about 20 minutes, or until well cooked.

Add the mushrooms, distributing them between the rabbit portions, pour in the stock and sherry. Sprinkle the parsley over the rabbit, bring to the boil, then lower the heat and simmer, uncovered, for 15 minutes. Taste for seasoning and serve.

SERVES 4

VARIATION

QUICK CURRIED RABBIT (*Illustrated on page 140*) Substitute 15 ml/1 tbsp curry powder an equal quantity of flour. Omit the mace. Cook 1 chopped onion with the rabbit. Add 1 peeled, cored and diced cooking apple instead of the mushrooms. Stir in 15 ml/1 tbsp mango chutney, 10 ml/2 tsp desiccated coconut, 25 g/1 oz sultanas and 25 g/1 oz blanched almonds. Increase stock to 450 ml/¾ pint; omit sherry. Cooking times as above.

TURKEY AND CHIPOLATA HOTPOT

This is an excellent way of using up leftovers from a roast turkey. Cooked chicken may be used instead of turkey and the chipolatas will extend a small amount of meat to serve 4.

15 ml/1 tbsp oil
225 g/8 oz cocktail or chipolata sausages
1 onion, halved and sliced
2 carrots, diced
2 parsnips, diced
1 bay leaf
5 ml/1 tsp dried sage
45 ml/3 tbsp plain flour
300 ml/½ pint medium cider
300 ml/½ pint turkey or chicken stock
350 g/12 oz cooked turkey, diced
salt and pepper
100 g/4 oz frozen peas

Heat the oil in a large flameproof casserole until it runs easily over the base. Add the cocktail sausages or chipolatas and turn them in the oil. Sprinkle the onion into the pan and cook, turning occasionally, until the sausages are evenly and lightly browned but not necessarily cooked through.

Add the carrots, parsnips, bay leaf and sage to the casserole. Cover and cook gently for 15 minutes. Stir in the flour, then gradually stir in the cider and stock and bring to the boil. Add the turkey, with salt and pepper to taste, then cover and simmer for 10 minutes, or until the vegetables are tender.

Stir in the peas, replace the cover and simmer for a further 10-15 minutes, until the vegetables are all tender. Taste and adjust the seasoning before serving. If using chipolatas, cut them into bite-sized chunks.

SERVES 4

BAKED JACKET POTATOES

Illustrated on page 291

4 large, even-sized baking potatoes
oil for brushing (optional)
butter or flavoured butter to serve

Set the oven at 200°C/400°F/gas 6. Scrub the potatoes, dry them with absorbent kitchen paper and pierce the skin several times with a skewer. If you like soft jackets, brush the potatoes all over with oil.

Bake the potatoes directly on the oven shelf for 1-1¼ hours. Test by pressing gently with the fingers. To serve, cut a cross in the top of each potato with a sharp knife. Squeeze the sides of the potato so that the top opens up. Add a pat of plain or flavoured butter and serve.

SERVES 4

FILLINGS

Make a meal of baked jacket potatoes by cutting them in half, scooping out the centres and mashing them with selected ingredients. Pile the fillings back into the potato shells and heat through, if necessary, in a 180°C/350°F/gas 4 oven for about 20 minutes. Alternatively, reheat in the microwave oven or under a moderate grill.

CHEESE AND HAM Mash the potato. Grate in 100 g/4 oz Cheddar cheese, add 50 g/2 oz chopped ham (use trimmings for economy) and mix with 25 g/1 oz softened butter. Reheat.

KIPPER Mash the potato with 75 g/3 oz flaked cooked kipper. Add 1 chopped hard-boiled egg, with salt and pepper to taste. Thin with a little milk, if necessary. Reheat.

FRANKFURTER Mash the potato with butter. For each potato, add 2 heated chopped frankfurters and 15 ml/1 tbsp tomato relish. Add chopped parsley.

TOPPINGS

The easy option. Cut the potatoes almost but not quite in half and open out. Top with any of the mixtures suggested below.

BLUE CHEESE AND YOGURT Mash 100 g/4 oz ripe Danish blue cheese. Mix with 150 ml/¼ pint Greek yogurt.

SAUSAGE AND CHUTNEY Mix hot or cold sliced cooked sausage with diced eating apple, chopped spring onions and a little chutney.

EGG MAYONNAISE Mash hard-boiled eggs with a little mayonnaise or plain yogurt. Add 5 ml/1 tsp tomato ketchup or tomato purée and some snipped chives.

SARDINE Mash canned sardines in tomato sauce and mix with diced cucumber. Serve with shredded lettuce.

CHICK-PEA Mash 100 g/4 oz drained canned chick-peas. Mix with 1 crushed garlic clove and 15-30 ml/1-2 tbsp Greek yogurt. Top with chopped spring onion and sesame seeds.

CHEESE SOUFFLE Combine 100 g/4 oz grated Cheddar cheese and 1 beaten egg. Cut potatoes in half, pile some of the mixture on each half and grill until topping puffs up and turns golden brown.

PEAS AND BACON Combine 100 g/4 oz cooked petits pois and 3 crumbled grilled rindless bacon rashers. Top with a knob of butter.

BROCCOLI AND ASPARAGUS Mix 175 g/6 oz cooked broccoli with 100 g/4 oz drained canned asparagus tips. Stir in 150 ml/¼ pint soured cream, with salt and pepper to taste.

SOUTHERN SPECIAL Warm 100 g/4 oz creamed sweetcorn. Spoon on to potatoes. Top each portion with 2 grilled rindless bacon rashers and 3-4 banana slices.

☀ **MICROWAVE TIP** Cooking jacket potatoes in the microwave has practically become a national pastime. Prick the potatoes several times with a skewer or they may burst. Cook directly on the microwave rack or wrap in absorbent kitchen paper if a very soft potato is preferred. For crisper potatoes, brush with oil or butter after microwave cooking, then crisp under a hot grill, turning once. Jacket potatoes also cook extremely well in a combination microwave. Follow the instructions in your handbook.

MICROWAVE COOKING TIMES ON HIGH (600-650 WATT OVENS)

Large potatoes (350 g/12 oz)
1 potato .... 8 minutes
2 potatoes .... 15 minutes
4 potatoes .... 27 minutes

Medium potatoes (150 g/5 oz)
1 potato .... 4 minutes
2 potatoes .... 5-6 minutes
4 potatoes .... 10 minutes
6 potatoes .... 18-19 minutes

CAULIFLOWER CHEESE

salt and pepper
1 firm cauliflower
30 ml/2 tbsp butter
60 ml/4 tbsp plain flour
200 ml/7 fl oz milk
125 g/4½ oz Cheddar cheese, grated
pinch of dry mustard
pinch of cayenne pepper
25 g/1 oz dry white breadcrumbs

Bring a saucepan of salted water to the boil, add the cauliflower, cover the pan and cook gently for 20-30 minutes until tender. Drain well, reserving 175 ml/6 fl oz of the cooking water. Leave the cauliflower head whole or cut carefully into florets. Place in a warmed ovenproof dish, cover with greased greaseproof paper and keep hot.

Set the oven at 220°C/425°F/gas 7 or preheat the grill. Melt the butter in a saucepan, stir in the flour and cook for 1 minute. Gradually add the milk and reserved cooking water, stirring all the time until the sauce boils and thickens. Remove from the heat and stir in 100 g/4 oz of the cheese, stirring until it melts into the sauce. Add the mustard and cayenne, with salt and pepper to taste.

Pour the sauce over the cauliflower. Mix the remaining cheese with the breadcrumbs and sprinkle them on top. Brown the topping for 7-10 minutes in the oven or under the grill. Serve at once.

SERVES 4

VARIATIONS

A wide variety of vegetables can be cooked in this way. Try broccoli (particularly good with grilled bacon); small whole onions (see following page for microwave cooking); celery, celeriac; leeks or chicory (both taste delicious if wrapped in ham before being covered in the cheese sauce) and asparagus. A mixed vegetable gratin – cooked sliced carrots, green beans, onions and potatoes – also works well. Vary the cheese topping too: Red Leicester has good flavour and colour; Gruyère or Emmental is good with leeks or chicory; a little blue cheese mixed with the Cheddar will enliven celery or celeriac.

◆

STUFFED ONIONS

salt and pepper
6 large onions
75 g/3 oz cooked ham, finely chopped
30 ml/2 tbsp fresh white breadcrumbs
2.5 ml/½ tsp finely chopped sage
beaten egg for binding
30 ml/2 tbsp butter
100 g/4 oz Cheddar cheese, grated
   (optional)

Bring a saucepan of salted water to the boil, add the unpeeled onions and parboil for 45 minutes or until almost tender. Drain, skin and remove the centres with a teaspoon.

Set the oven at 180°C/350°F/gas 4. Mix the ham, breadcrumbs and sage in a small bowl. Add salt and pepper to taste and stir in enough of the beaten egg to give a fairly firm mixture. Fill the centres of the onions with the mixture.

Put the onions in a baking dish just large enough to hold them snugly. Dot the tops with butter. Bake for 30-45 minutes or until tender, sprinkling the tops of the onions with the grated cheese, if used, 10 minutes before the end of the cooking time.

SERVES 6

☀ **MICROWAVE TIP** Peel the onions. Arrange them around the rim of a round shallow dish, add 45 ml/3 tbsp water and cover. Cook on High for 10-12 minutes or until the onions are tender. When cool enough to handle, scoop out the centres and fill as described above. Return the onions to the dry dish and cook for 4-6 minutes. If a cheese topping is required, sprinkle the grated cheese on top and brown under a grill for 3-4 minutes.

WINTER VEGETABLE CASSEROLE

This simple casserole may be simmered very slowly on the hob, if preferred.

50 g/2 oz butter • 30 ml/2 tbsp oil
2 onions, sliced
1 garlic clove, crushed (optional)
2 leeks, trimmed, sliced and washed
225 g/8 oz swede, cubed
100 g/4 oz turnip, cubed
3 carrots, sliced
100 g/4 oz mushrooms, sliced
100 g/4 oz pearl barley, washed
5 ml/1 tsp dried thyme
1 bay leaf
salt and pepper
450 ml/¾ pint vegetable stock
30 ml/2 tbsp chopped parsley to garnish

Set the oven at 180°C/350°F/gas 4. Melt the butter and oil in a large flameproof casserole. Add the onions, garlic, leeks, swede, turnip and carrots and fry for about 10 minutes, stirring frequently.

Stir in the mushrooms, barley, thyme and bay leaf, with plenty of salt and pepper. Pour in the stock. Cover the casserole and transfer it to the oven. Bake for 1-1½ hours until all the vegetables are cooked and the barley is tender. Fluff up the grains with a fork, sprinkle the parsley over the top and serve at once.

SERVES 4

VARIATION

WINTER VEGETABLE HOTPOT Omit the barley. Cover the vegetable mixture with 450 g/1 lb thinly sliced potatoes. Brush with oil, sprinkle with salt and pepper and bake for the longer cooking time, removing the lid for the last 30 minutes to allow the topping to brown.

PEASANTS' EGGS

salt and pepper
575 g/1¼ lb potatoes, cubed
60 ml/4 tbsp oil
8 rindless back bacon rashers, cut into
    strips
1 onion, chopped
30 ml/2 tbsp chopped parsley
30 ml/2 tbsp butter
4 eggs

Bring a large saucepan of salted water to the boil, add the potatoes and bring back to the boil. Cook for 1 minute, then drain thoroughly.

Heat the oil in a large deep frying pan. Add the bacon and fry for 2-3 minutes until crisp. Using a slotted spoon, remove and drain on absorbent kitchen paper. Add the onion to the oil remaining in the pan and fry for 3-4 minutes until golden; remove with the slotted spoon and put in a baking dish with the bacon. Keep hot.

Add the potatoes to the frying pan and fry gently for 5-6 minutes, turning occasionally, until cooked and brown. Drain and add to the bacon and onion mixture with plenty of salt, pepper and parsley. Mix lightly and keep hot.

Melt the butter in the remaining oil. Fry the eggs. Arrange on the potato mixture and serve at once.

SERVES 4

EGGS MORNAY

1 kg/2¼ lb potatoes, halved
salt and pepper
8 eggs
300 ml/½ pint Béchamel Sauce (see Mrs
    Beeton's Tip, page 47)
75 g/3 oz Cheddar cheese, grated
2.5 ml/½ tsp French mustard
30 ml/2 tbsp butter
45 ml/3 tbsp milk

Cook the potatoes in a saucepan of salted boiling water for 20 minutes, until tender.

Meanwhile bring a small saucepan of water to the boil, carefully add the eggs and cook them for 5 minutes. Plunge them into cold water, leave for 5 minutes, then remove their shells carefully under the water. Leave the shelled eggs under the water. Reheat the Béchamel sauce gently with most of the cheese and the mustard.

Drain the cooked potatoes thoroughly and mash with a potato masher, or beat with a hand-held electric whisk until smooth. Beat in the butter and milk to make a creamy piping consistency. Spoon the creamed potato into a piping bag fitted with a large star nozzle and pipe a border of mashed potato around the edge of a large shallow dish to go under the grill.

Using a slotted spoon, drain the shelled eggs well and arrange in the dish. Coat with the hot sauce. Sprinkle the remaining cheese over and grill until brown.

SERVES 4

> **MRS BEETON'S TIP** When reheating the Béchamel sauce with the cheese, do not allow the mixture to boil or the cheese may become stringy.

DISHES TO COOK AHEAD

Whether you are planning a special dinner party, picnic or buffet, or simply organizing family meals in advance, this chapter offers valuable advice and a selection of recipes.

Cooking or preparing dishes well before they will be needed can be practical and economical but there are a few pitfalls to avoid. Cooking ahead falls into two main categories: either preparing large quantities of a favourite recipe and freezing it in useful batches or preparing a complete dish ready to serve cold, reheat or cook at the last minute. Whichever is the case, it is important to remember food safety.

COOKING, COOLING AND STORING FOOD

Food that is to be stored should be cooled as quickly as possible. Baked items should be transferred to a wire rack in a cool place if possible. Cooked dishes such as casseroles, should be allowed to cool slightly in their cooking container, then transferred to a cold, covered container. If the mixture is left in the hot cooking container, it will take longer to cool.

As soon as the food is cool it should be refrigerated or frozen. Keep food covered in the refrigerator and leave it there until it is heated and served. Freeze cooked food to be kept for more than 2 days.

When cooking ahead, consider the number of portions likely to be required for future meals so that you prepare and chill or freeze practical amounts. Do not chill large quantities of food which will not be consumed within a sensible time period.

REHEATING FOOD

Always reheat food thoroughly before serving it, making sure that the centre is reheated to the original serving temperature. Once the food is hot, serve it promptly. Avoid keeping it warm for long periods.

Reheat cooked food only once; repeated reheating encourages the growth of micro-organisms that may cause food poisoning.

MEATBALLS IN CELERIAC SAUCE

200 g/7 oz minced veal
200 g/7 oz minced pork
1 egg, lightly beaten
50 g/2 oz plain flour
125 ml/4 fl oz milk
2 onions
salt and pepper
2.5 ml/½ tsp ground all spice
600 ml/1 pint vegetable stock
1 large celeriac, diced
25 g/1 oz butter
30 ml/2 tbsp chopped fresh dill or 15 ml/
   1 tbsp chopped fresh tarragon
triangles of fried bread to garnish

Put the veal and pork in a large bowl. Stir in the egg with 45 ml/3 tbsp of the flour. Bring the milk to the boil in a small saucepan. Add it gradually to the minced meat mixture, stirring until all the milk has been absorbed. Grate 1 onion and add it to the meat with salt and pepper to taste. Add the allspice and mix well. Chill for 30 minutes in the bottom of the refrigerator. Wet your hands, then form the mixture into small balls, about 2 cm/¾ inch in diameter.

Bring the vegetable stock to the boil in a large saucepan. Add the meatballs, boil for about 5 minutes, then transfer to a bowl, using a slotted spoon. Add the celeriac to the saucepan and cook for 5 minutes or until just tender but not soft. Again using a slotted spoon, transfer the celeriac to the bowl with the meatballs. Pour the vegetable stock into a jug and make it up to 450 ml/¾ pint with water. Set aside.

Melt the butter in a saucepan. Chop the remaining onion and add it to the pan. Cook, stirring, for 15-20 minutes, until softened. Stir in the remaining flour and cook for 1 minute. Gradually add the reserved vegetable stock, stirring, and cook until the mixture boils and thickens. Add the celeriac and meatballs to the sauce and simmer gently for 5 minutes. Add the dill or tarragon, with salt and pepper to taste. Serve at once with triangles of fried bread, or cool, cover and refrigerate for serving hot next day.

SERVES 4 TO 6

> ☆ **FREEZER TIP** Cool the meatballs quickly in the sauce. Freeze in a sealed container for up to 6 weeks. Reheat from frozen in a preheated 190°C/ 375°F/gas 5 oven for 45-60 minutes.

LAMB CURRY

Illustrated on page 292

1 kg/2¼ lb boneless leg or shoulder lamb,
    cut into 2.5 cm/1 inch cubes
60 ml/4 tbsp lemon juice
450 ml/¾ pint plain yogurt
salt and freshly ground black pepper
75 g/3 oz ghee (see Mrs Beeton's Tip)
2 onions, finely chopped
3 garlic cloves, crushed
5 cm/2 inch fresh root ginger, grated
5 ml/1 tsp chilli powder
10 ml/2 tsp each ground coriander and cumin
8 green cardamom pods
150 g/5 oz tomato purée

Put the lamb cubes into a large non-metallic bowl and sprinkle with the lemon juice. Stir in the yogurt and salt. Cover and marinate for 24 hours or for up to 3 days. Stir the mixture occasionally.

Heat the ghee in a large saucepan, add the onions, garlic and ginger and fry for 4-6 minutes until the onion is soft but not coloured. Add the chilli powder, coriander, cumin and black pepper and fry for 2 minutes, then stir in the lamb, with its marinade. Stir in the cardamom pods and tomato purée, with 300 ml/½ pint water. Bring to the boil, lower the heat and simmer for about 1 hour or until the meat is tender. Serve with rice, chopped tomato and onion, and diced cucumber in yogurt.

SERVES 4 TO 6

> 🪣 **MRS BEETON'S TIP** Ghee is clarified butter. To make your own, heat butter gently until melted, pour into a bowl and allow to stand for 2-3 minutes. Carefully pour off the clear yellow liquid – clarified butter.

*B*OLOGNESE SAUCE

Illustrated on page 293

15 g/½ oz butter
15 ml/1 tbsp olive oil
75 g/3 oz unsmoked rindless streaky
    bacon rashers, diced
1 onion, finely chopped
2 garlic cloves, crushed
1 carrot, finely diced
½ celery stick, thinly sliced
225 g/8 oz lean minced beef
100 g/4 oz chicken livers, trimmed and
    cut into small shreds
1 (397 g/14 oz) can chopped tomatoes
200 ml/7 fl oz beef stock
15 ml/1 tbsp tomato purée
125 ml/4 fl oz dry white or red wine
5 ml/1 tsp dried marjoram
salt and pepper
pinch of grated nutmeg

Melt the butter in the oil in a saucepan. Add the bacon and cook it gently until brown. Add the onion, garlic, carrot and celery. Cook over gentle heat for about 10 minutes until the onion is soft and just beginning to brown. Add the beef and cook, stirring, until browned and broken up.

Add the chicken livers to the pan and cook for 3 minutes, turning the livers over gently to brown them on all sides. Stir in the tomatoes, stock, tomato purée, wine and marjoram. Season with salt, pepper and nutmeg. Bring to simmering point and cook, covered, for about 1 hour, stirring occasionally.

Remove the lid for the final 20 minutes of the cooking time to allow some of the liquid to evaporate. Taste and add extra salt and pepper if necessary. Serve with pasta, rice or baked potatoes.

SERVES 4

*C*UMBERLAND LAMB PIES

300 g/11 oz minced lamb
10 ml/2 tsp dripping or oil
1 onion, chopped
100 g/4 oz mushrooms, chopped
1.25 ml/¼ tsp grated nutmeg
10 ml/2 tsp chopped parsley
pinch of dried thyme
salt and pepper
5 ml/1 tsp Worcestershire sauce
60 ml/4 tbsp chicken or vegetable stock
beaten egg or milk for glazing

PASTRY

300 g/10 oz plain flour ● pinch of salt
150 g/5 oz margarine (or half butter, half
    lard)
flour for rolling out

Set the oven at 190°C/375°F/gas 5. To make the pastry, sift the flour and salt into a bowl, then rub in the margarine until the mixture resembles fine breadcrumbs. Add enough cold water to make a stiff dough. Press the dough together with your fingertips. Place in a polythene bag and refrigerate while making the filling.

Put the minced lamb in a bowl. Heat the dripping or oil in a small frying pan, add the onion and fry for 4-6 minutes until soft but not coloured. Stir into the lamb with the chopped mushrooms, nutmeg, parsley and thyme. Add salt and pepper to taste, stir in the Worcestershire sauce and mix well.

Roll out half the pastry on a lightly floured surface and use to line 6 individual Yorkshire pudding or flan tins, or ovenproof saucers. Divide the lamb mixture between them, adding 10 ml/2 tsp stock to each. Roll out the remaining pastry and cut out six lids. Dampen the edges of the pies, put on the lids and seal well. Brush with beaten egg or milk. Make a hole in the lid of each pie to allow steam to escape (see Mrs Beeton's Tip). Bake for 40-45 minutes, covering the tops of the pies with foil if they begin to over-brown. Serve hot or cold.

MAKES 6

> 🍲 **MRS BEETON'S TIP** To make a hole in the pastry lid, cut a cross in the centre of each lid. Fold back the points of the cross to make a square opening.

STEWED STUFFED BEEF

about 1.4 kg/3 lb top rib of beef or
   braising steak in one piece
1 quantity Mrs Beeton's Forcemeat (page
   349)
salt and pepper
50 g/2 oz plain flour
50 g/2 oz butter
2 blades of mace
30 ml/2 tbsp lemon juice
1.1 litres/2 pints weak veal or beef stock
50 g/2 oz small button mushrooms
60 ml/4 tbsp dry sherry

Slit the beef three-quarters of the way through horizontally. Fold the top portion open and lay the meat on double-thick greaseproof paper. Cover with more paper and beat out the meat to thin it slightly.

Spoon the forcemeat down the length of the meat, then fold the top portion over the stuffing to enclose it completely. Tie the meat firmly in shape. Season the meat well and dust it all over with half the flour.

Melt half the butter in a large flameproof casserole. Add the meat and brown it lightly all over. Add the mace and lemon juice, then pour the stock into the pan. Bring only just to the boil, lower the heat and cover the pan tightly. Simmer the rolled beef very gently for 3 hours, until the meat is very tender. Turn the meat over half-way through cooking. Cream the remaining butter and flour to a paste in a small bowl.

Transfer the meat to a heated serving plate. Boil the cooking juices to reduce them by about a third. Meanwhile, remove the string from the meat and slice it, overlapping the slices on the plate.

Remove the mace from the cooking liquor. Add the sherry, then allow to simmer. Whisking all the time, gradually add knobs of the butter and flour mixture. Bring to the boil, whisking, to thicken the sauce. Add the mushrooms and simmer for 3 minutes. Taste for seasoning.

Ladle some of the sauce over the meat. Pour the rest into a warmed sauceboat and offer separately. Serve at once, with a colourful array of vegetables, such as Glazed Carrots (page 214). Courgettes with Almonds (page 225) or buttered cabbage and Potato Croquettes (page 232) or Anna Potatoes (page 231).

SERVES 6

> 🍲 **MRS BEETON'S TIP** This is an excellent cook-ahead dinner party dish. Cook the beef completely, then allow it to cool in the liquor, with the lid on the pan, for 30 minutes. Transfer the whole piece of meat to a container and pour the liquid over it, discarding the mace. Cover, cool and chill. To reheat, pour the liquid into the pan and bring it to simmering point. Lower the heat slightly and place the meat in the pan. Bring slowly back to simmering point and cook, covered, for 30 minutes. Continue as above.

COUSCOUS

Couscous is a semolina product. It is available prepared from supermarkets and wholefood shops, ready for brief steaming or simply soaking in boiling water before serving.

50 g/2 oz chick-peas, soaked overnight in
    plenty of cold water
45 ml/3 tbsp olive oil
8 chicken thighs, skinned if preferred
2 garlic cloves, crushed
1 large onion, chopped
1 green pepper, seeded and sliced
1 green chilli, seeded and chopped
    (optional)
15 ml/1 tbsp ground coriander
5 ml/1 tsp ground cumin
100 g/4 oz carrots, sliced
100 g/4 oz turnips, cut into chunks
450 g/1 lb pumpkin, peeled, seeds
    removed and cut into chunks
450 g/1 lb potatoes, cut into chunks
1 bay leaf
2 (397 g/14 oz) cans chopped tomatoes
50 g/2 oz raisins
150 ml/¼ pint chicken stock or water
salt and pepper
225 g/8 oz courgettes, sliced
45 ml/3 tbsp chopped parsley
350 g/12 oz couscous
50 g/2 oz butter, melted

Drain the chick-peas, then cook them in plenty of fresh boiling water for 10 minutes.

Lower the heat, cover the pan and simmer for 1½ hours, or until the chick-peas are just tender. Drain.

Heat the oil in a very large flameproof casserole or saucepan. Add the chicken pieces and brown them all over, then use a slotted spoon to remove them from the pan and set aside. Add the garlic, onion, pepper and chilli, if used, to the oil remaining in the pan and cook for 5 minutes, stirring.

Stir in the coriander and cumin, then add the carrots, turnips, pumpkin, potatoes, bay leaf, tomatoes, raisins, stock or water with salt and pepper to taste. Stir in the drained chick-peas. Bring to the boil, then lower the heat and replace the chicken thighs, tucking them in among the vegetables. Cover and simmer gently for 1 hour.

Stir in the courgettes and parsley, cover the pan and continue to cook gently for a further 30 minutes. There are two options for preparing the couscous. The first is to line a steamer with scalded muslin, then sprinkle the couscous into it. Place the steamer over the simmering stew for the final 30 minutes' cooking, covering it tightly to keep all the steam in.

Alternatively – and this is the easier method – place the couscous in a deep casserole or bowl and pour in fresh boiling water from the kettle to cover the grains by 2.5 cm/1 inch. Cover and set aside for 15 minutes. The grains will absorb the boiling water and swell. If the couscous cools on standing, it may be reheated over a pan of boiling water or in a microwave for about 2 minutes on High.

To serve, transfer the couscous to a very large serving dish and pour the hot melted butter over it. Fork up the grains and make a well in the middle. Ladle the chicken and vegetable stew into the well, spooning cooking juices over the couscous.

SERVES 8

> ☕ **MRS BEETON'S TIP** Cubes of boneless lamb may be used instead of the chicken. The vegetables may be varied according to what is freshly available – marrow or green beans may be added or substituted for other ingredients if preferred.
>
> Couscous is usually accompanied by a hot, spicy condiment known as *harissa*. This paste, made from chillies, cumin, coriander, garlic, mint and oil, is deep red in colour and fiery of flavour. It is added to individual portions to taste but should be treated with respect by diners who are unused to it.

MOUSSAKA

Moussaka can be made a day ahead, then reheated, covered, in the oven.

fat for greasing
1 aubergine
salt and pepper
30 ml/2 tbsp olive oil
1 large onion, chopped
1 garlic clove, grated
450 g/1 lb minced lamb or beef
10 ml/2 tsp chopped parsley
2 tomatoes, peeled, seeded and chopped
150 ml/¼ pint dry white wine
300 ml/½ pint milk
1 egg plus 2 egg yolks
pinch of grated nutmeg
75 g/3 oz Kefalotiri or Parmesan cheese, grated

Grease a 20 × 10 × 10 cm (8 × 4 × 4 inch) oven-to-table baking dish. Set

the oven at 180°C/350°F/gas 4. Cut the aubergine into 1 cm/½ inch slices, put them in a colander, and sprinkle generously with salt. Set aside.

Heat the olive oil, and gently fry the onion and garlic for about 10 minutes until the onion is soft. Add the mince and continue cooking, stirring with a fork to break up any lumps in the meat. When the meat is thoroughly browned, add salt, pepper, parsley and tomatoes. Mix well, then add the white wine. Simmer the mixture for a few minutes to blend the flavours, then remove from the heat.

In a bowl, beat the milk, whole egg, egg yolks, salt and a good pinch of grated nutmeg together. Add about half the cheese to the egg mixture, then beat again briefly.

Rinse and drain the aubergine slices and pat dry with absorbent kitchen paper. Place half in the bottom of the prepared dish and cover with the meat mixture. Lay the remaining aubergine slices on the meat and pour the milk and egg mixture over them. Sprinkle the remaining cheese on top.

Bake for 30-40 minutes, until the custard is set and the top is light golden brown. Serve from the dish.

SERVES 4

> ☕ **MRS BEETON'S TIP** To peel tomatoes, hold each tomato on a fork over a gas flame or under a grill until the skin blackens and splits, then skin. Alternatively, place the tomatoes in a heatproof bowl. Cover with boiling water and leave for 1 minute. Drain and skin.

———————— ◈ ————————

*P*ASTICCIO DI LASAGNE VERDE

Illustrated on page 296

Green lasagne or lasagne verdi is pasta into which spinach has been worked at the dough-making stage. A crisp salad is the ideal accompaniment for this dish.

fat for greasing
250 g/9 oz green lasagne
salt and pepper
60 ml/4 tbsp oil
50 g/2 oz onion, chopped
1 garlic clove, chopped
50 g/2 oz celery, chopped
50 g/2 oz carrot, chopped
450 g/1 lb lean minced beef
300 ml/½ pint beef stock
30 ml/2 tbsp tomato purée
75 g/3 oz walnut pieces, finely chopped
50 g/2 oz sultanas
250 g/9 oz tomatoes, peeled, seeded and
　chopped
50 g/2 oz red pepper, seeded and
　chopped
150 ml/¼ pint cold cheese sauce
　(see Baked Cannelloni, right)

Grease a shallow ovenproof dish. Cook the lasagne in a saucepan of boiling salted water for 15 minutes. Drain, rinse under hot water, then place on a slightly dampened, clean tea-towel, side by side but not touching. Leave to dry.

Heat the oil in a frying pan and cook the onion, garlic, celery and carrot for 5 minutes. Add the mince and brown it lightly all over. Add the stock, tomato purée and salt and pepper to taste. Bring to the boil, then simmer for 30 minutes. Set the oven at 180°C/350°F/gas 4.

Line the bottom of the dish with half the pasta and cover with the meat mixture, then sprinkle with the nuts, sultanas, tomatoes and red pepper. Cover with the remaining pasta. Coat with the cold sauce and bake for 20 minutes.

SERVES 4

VARIATIONS

LASAGNE AL FORNO The classic Lasagne is a relatively simple dish, consisting of layers of pasta, meat sauce and Béchamel. You will require 250 g/9 oz lasagne. Make the meat sauce as in paragraph 2, left, and prepare 900 ml/1½ pints Béchamel sauce (see Mrs Beeton's Tip, page 47). Spoon a little of the Béchamel into a shallow ovenproof dish, top with a layer of lasagne (prepared as in the main recipe), then add a layer of meat sauce and more Béchamel. Repeat the layers until all the ingredients have been used, ending with Béchamel. Top with a generous layer of Parmesan cheese. Bake at 180°C/350°F/ gas 4 for about 30 minutes. Allow to stand for 10 minutes before cutting.

RATATOUILLE LASAGNE Instead of the meat, nuts, sultanas, tomatoes and red pepper, layer the pasta with Ratatouille (page 235). Use 300 ml/½ pint cheese sauce.

SPINACH LASAGNE Make a double quantity of Italian Spinach (page 234) to layer with the pasta and top with 300 ml/ ½ pint cheese sauce.

MARROW LASAGNE Make the Marrow with Tomatoes (page 236) to layer instead of the meat, nuts, sultanas, tomatoes and red pepper. Top with cheese sauce as left.

───────── ◆ ─────────

BAKED CANNELLONI

butter for greasing
16-20 cannelloni
15 ml/1 tbsp olive oil
300 g/11 oz frozen chopped spinach
salt and pepper
1.25 ml/¼ tsp grated nutmeg
150 g/5 oz ricotta or cottage cheese
50 g/2 oz cooked ham, finely chopped
25 g/1 oz dried white breadcrumbs
25 g/1 oz Parmesan cheese, grated

CHEESE SAUCE
50 g/2 oz butter
50 g/2 oz plain flour
600 ml/1 pint milk
75 g/3 oz mature Cheddar, grated

Butter an ovenproof dish. To make the sauce, melt the butter in a saucepan. Stir in the flour and cook over a low heat for 2-3 minutes, without colouring. Over a very low heat, gradually add the milk, stirring constantly. Bring to the boil, stirring, and simmer for 1-2 minutes until thick. Add the cheese with seasoning to taste.

Cook the cannelloni in a saucepan of boiling salted water with the oil for 10-15 minutes until *al dente*. Drain well.

Place the frozen spinach in a pan and cook over low heat, stirring frequently. When thawed, cook for 2-3 minutes. Drain thoroughly. Mix together the spinach, salt, pepper, nutmeg, soft cheese and ham. Spoon the mixture into the cannelloni. Place in the prepared ovenproof dish. Pour the sauce over the cannelloni.

Bake for 15-20 minutes. Mix together the crumbs and Parmesan, then sprinkle over the dish. Brown under a hot grill.

SERVES 4

CANNELLONI WITH MUSHROOM STUFFING

Illustrated on page 296

butter for greasing
16-20 cannelloni
15 ml/1 tbsp olive oil
750 ml/1¼ pints Béchamel sauce (see Mrs Beeton's Tip, page 47)
50 g/2 oz butter
200 g/7 oz button mushrooms, thinly sliced
50 g/2 oz Parmesan cheese, grated
50 g/2 oz Gruyère cheese, grated
50 g/2 oz Parma ham, finely shredded
15 ml/1 tbsp fine dried breadcrumbs
15 ml/1 tbsp single cream

Butter a shallow ovenproof dish. Cook the cannelloni in a saucepan of boiling salted water with the oil for 10-15 minutes until *al dente*. Drain well. In a saucepan, simmer 600 ml/1 pint of the Béchamel sauce until well reduced and very thick. Put to one side.

Melt half the butter in a pan and cook the mushrooms for 2 minutes. Add to the sauce with half the Parmesan. Leave to cool for 10 minutes.

Spoon the cooled mixture into the cannelloni. Place in the prepared dish. Sprinkle the Gruyère and ham over the cannelloni, then sprinkle with the breadcrumbs. Add the cream to the remaining sauce and pour over the pasta. Top with the remaining Parmesan and flakes of the remaining butter.

Bake for 15-20 minutes, until lightly browned. Cover with greased foil if browning too quickly.

SERVES 4

SEMOLINA GNOCCHI

This Italian-style dish may be finished in the oven or under the grill. Serve it with a tomato sauce or spicy savoury sauce.

fat for greasing
500 ml/17 fl oz milk
100 g/4 oz semolina
salt and pepper
1.25 ml/¼ tsp grated nutmeg
1 egg
100 g/4 oz Parmesan cheese, grated
25 g/1 oz butter

Grease a shallow ovenproof dish. Bring the milk to the boil in a saucepan. Sprinkle in the semolina and stir over low heat until the mixture is thick. Mix in the salt, pepper, nutmeg, egg and 75 g/3 oz of the Parmesan. Beat the mixture well until smooth. Spread on a shallow dish and leave to cool.

If using the oven set it at 200°C/400°F/ gas 6. Cut the cooled semolina mixture into 2 cm/¾ inch squares or shape into rounds. Place in the prepared ovenproof dish and sprinkle with the remaining cheese; dot with butter. Brown under the grill or in the oven for 8-10 minutes.

SERVES 4

🍲**MRS BEETON'S TIP** Canned chopped tomatoes make a quick sauce. Add them to a chopped onion cooked in butter or oil until soft. Simmer for 5 minutes, then season to taste and add plenty of chopped parsley. Use tomatoes canned with herbs, if liked or add a bay leaf and some marjoram. Garlic may also be added; with a little red wine and longer simmering the sauce is rich and excellent.

POLENTA WITH SMOKED SAUSAGE

The sausages used in this satisfying dish are dried continental ones. They have a high meat content and require a little cooking before eating.

400 g/14 oz polenta
salt and pepper
400 g/14 oz chorizo, cabanos or other small smoked sausages
300 ml/½ pint passata (see Mrs Beeton's Tip)
50 g/2 oz Parmesan cheese, grated
25 g/1 oz dried white breadcrumbs
25 g/1 oz butter

Bring 500 ml/17 fl oz water to the boil in a large saucepan. Stir in the polenta and salt and pepper to taste. Cook for 10-15 minutes, stirring all the time. Leave to cool.

Set the oven at 180°C/350°F/gas 4. Cook the sausages in boiling water for 10 minutes. Remove from the pan and leave to cool. Remove the skins and cut into 2 cm/¾ inch slices.

Put a layer of polenta in the bottom of an ovenproof dish, cover with a layer of sausages, some tomato purée, Parmesan, salt and pepper. Repeat the layers until all the ingredients have been used. Sprinkle the breadcrumbs over the mixture. Dot with the butter. Bake for 25-30 minutes.

SERVES 3 TO 4

🍲**MRS BEETON'S TIP** Passata is a thick purée of cooked, slightly reduced, tomatoes. It may be bought in jars or packs.

SAVOURY PANCAKES

Illustrated on page 295

100 g/4 oz plain flour
1 egg, beaten
200 ml/7 fl oz milk, or half milk and half
    water
salt and pepper
oil for frying

Make the batter. Sift the flour into a bowl, make a well in the centre and add the beaten egg. Stir in half the milk (or all the milk, if using a mixture of milk and water), gradually working the flour down from the sides.

Beat vigorously until the mixture is smooth and bubbly, then stir in the rest of the milk (or the water). Add salt and pepper to taste. Pour into a jug. The mixture may be left to stand at this stage, in which case it should be covered and stored in the refrigerator.

Heat a little oil in a clean 18 cm/7 inch pancake pan. Pour off any excess oil, leaving the pan covered with a thin film of grease. Stir the batter and pour about 30-45 ml/2-3 tbsp into the pan. There should be just enough to cover the base thinly. Tilt and rotate the pan so that the batter runs over the surface evenly.

Cook over moderate heat for about 1 minute until the pancake is set and golden brown underneath. Make sure the pancake is loose by shaking the pan, then either toss it or turn it with a palette knife or fish slice. Cook the second side for about 30 seconds or until golden.

Slide the pancake out on to a warmed plate. Serve at once, with a suitable filling or sauce, or keep warm over simmering water while making 7 more pancakes in the same way. Add more oil.

MAKES 8

FILLINGS

Reheat savoury pancakes in a 180°C/350°F/gas 4 oven for 30 minutes if they have a cold filling; 20 minutes if the filling is hot. Pancakes topped with grated cheese may be browned under the grill.

SMOKED HADDOCK Poach 300 g/11 oz haddock fillets in a little water for 10-15 minutes. Drain and flake the fish. Make 250 ml/8 fl oz Béchamel sauce (see Mrs Beeton's Tip, page 47). Add the fish and 2 chopped hard-boiled eggs, 5 ml/1 tsp chopped capers, 15 ml/1 tbsp chopped parsley, 15 ml/1 tbsp lemon juice and salt and pepper. Fill the pancakes, sprinkle with 25 g/1 oz grated cheese and reheat.

ASPARAGUS Add 30 ml/2 tbsp thawed frozen chopped spinach to the pancake batter, if liked. Place a trimmed slice of ham on each pancake, top with a large asparagus spear and roll up. Cover the rolled pancakes with 600 ml/1 pint Béchamel sauce (see Mrs Beeton's Tip, page 47), reheat, then sprinkle with grated Gruyère cheese and grill to brown.

CHICKEN AND MUSHROOM Sauté 175 g/6 oz sliced mushrooms in 45 ml/3 tbsp butter for 2-3 minutes. Stir in 15 ml/1 tbsp plain flour and cook for 1 minute, then gradually add 150 ml/¼ pint chicken stock. Bring to the boil, stirring. Add 5 ml/1 tsp mushroom ketchup, if liked. Stir in 75 g/3 oz chopped cooked chicken. Fill the pancakes and reheat.

SPINACH PANCAKES Cook 300 g/11 oz frozen spinach; drain well. Add 200 g/7 oz cottage cheese, 50 g/2 oz grated mature Cheddar cheese; 100 ml/3½ fl oz double cream, a pinch of nutmeg and seasoning. Fill the pancakes, sprinkle with 25 g/1 oz grated cheese and reheat.

SCOTCH EGGS

1 egg
50 g/2 oz dried white breadcrumbs
350 g/12 oz sausagemeat
15 ml/1 tbsp plain flour
salt and pepper
4 eggs, hard-boiled
oil for deep frying

Beat the egg with 10 ml/2 tsp water in a small bowl. Spread out the breadcrumbs in a second, shallow bowl. Divide the sausagemeat into 4 equal portions. Pat out each portion into a burger-like shape.

Mix the flour with salt and pepper, and use to coat the hard-boiled eggs. Place an egg in the centre of a circle of sausagemeat. Mould the sausagemeat evenly around the egg, pinching it together to seal the joins.

Mould each Scotch egg to a good shape, roll in beaten egg, then roll in the bread-crumbs. Press the crumbs on well.

Put the oil for frying into a deep saucepan to a depth of at least 7.5 cm/3 inches. Heat to 160°C/325°F or until a cube of bread added to the oil browns in 2 minutes. If using a deep fat fryer, follow the manufacturer's instructions. Add the eggs carefully and fry for about 10 minutes until golden brown. Lift out with a slotted spoon and drain on absorbent kitchen paper. Serve hot or cold, cutting each egg in half lengthways.

MAKES 4

> **MRS BEETON'S TIP** Scotch eggs will keep for a day if chilled when cold; however, do not freeze them as the cooked egg becomes unpleasant, watery and rubbery during freezing and thawing.

CORNISH PASTIES

Cooked Cornish Pasties freeze well.

FILLING
1 large or 2 small potatoes
1 small turnip
1 onion
salt and pepper
300 g/11 oz lean chuck steak

PASTRY
500 g/18 oz plain flour
5 ml/1 tsp salt
150 g/5 oz lard
60 ml/4 tbsp shredded suet
flour for rolling out
beaten egg for glazing

Set the oven at 230°C/450°F/gas 8. To make the pastry, sift the flour and salt into a bowl. Rub in the lard, then mix in the suet. Moisten with enough cold water to make a stiff dough. Roll out on a lightly floured surface and cut into eight 16 cm/6½ inch rounds.

To make the filling, slice all the vegetables thinly, mix together and add salt and pepper to taste. Divide between the pastry rounds, placing a line of mixture across the centre of each round. Place equal amounts of meat on the vegetables.

Dampen the pastry edges of each round. Lift them to meet over the filling. Pinch together to seal, then flute the edges. Make small slits in both sides of each pasty near the top. Place the pasties on a baking sheet and brush with egg. Bake for 10 minutes, then reduce the oven temperature to 180°C/350°F/gas 4. Continue baking for a further 45 minutes, or until the meat is tender when pierced by a thin, heated skewer through the top of a pasty.

MAKES 8

LEEK TURNOVERS

These Welsh pasties make an ideal snack.

10 large leeks, trinmed and washed
5 ml/1 tsp salt
5 ml/1 tsp lemon juice
5 ml/1 tsp sugar
125 ml/4 fl oz single cream
salt and pepper
beaten egg for glazing

SHORT CRUST PASTRY
450 g/1 lb plain flour
5 ml/1 tsp baking powder
100 g/4 oz lard
100 g/4 oz margarine
flour for rolling out

Set the oven at 200°C/400°F/gas 6. Remove the green part of the leeks and slice the white part only into 2 cm/¾ inch pieces. Put into a saucepan with just enough boiling water to cover. Add the salt, lemon juice and sugar. Cook for 5 minutes or until just tender. Drain and leave to cool.

To make the pastry, sift the flour, baking powder and a pinch of salt into a bowl. Rub in the lard and margarine. Mix to a stiff dough with cold water.

Roll out the pastry on a lightly floured surface to 1 cm/½ inch thick and cut into 10 oblong shapes, about 15 × 10 cm/6 × 4 inches. Lay the pieces of leek along the middle of each pastry piece. Moisten with a little cream and add salt and pepper to taste. Dampen the edges of the pastry and lift them to meet over the filling. Pinch and flute the edges to seal.

Place the pasties on a baking sheet and brush with egg. Bake for about 20 minutes.

MAKES 10

PRAWN QUICHE

300 ml/½ pint Béchamel Sauce (see Mrs Beeton's Tip, page 47)
150 g/5 oz Cheddar cheese, grated
200 g/7 oz peeled cooked prawns
juice of ½ lemon

SHORT CRUST PASTRY
100 g/4 oz plain flour
2.5 ml/½ tsp salt
50 g/2 oz margarine (or half butter, half lard)
flour for rolling out

Set the oven at 200°C/400°F/gas 6. Make the pastry. Sift the flour and salt into a bowl, then rub in the margarine until the mixture resembles fine breadcrumbs. Add enough cold water to make a stiff dough. Press the dough together.

Roll out the pastry on a lightly floured surface and use to line an 18 cm/7 inch flan tin or ring placed on a baking sheet. Line the pastry with greaseproof paper and fill with baking beans. Bake 'blind' for 20 minutes, then remove the paper and beans. Return to the oven for 5-7 minutes, then remove.

Reheat the Béchamel sauce if necessary. Stir in half the cheese and all the prawns. Mix well and add the lemon juice.

Pour the mixture into the baked pastry case and sprinkle with the remaining cheese. Brown under the grill.

SERVES 4

LEEK TART

8 small leeks, trimmed and washed
2 eggs
salt and pepper
grated nutmeg
25 g/1 oz Gruyère cheese, grated

SHORT CRUST PASTRY
100 g/4 oz plain flour
1.25 ml/¼ tsp salt
50 g/2 oz margarine (or half butter, half lard)
flour for rolling out

SAUCE
15 g/½ oz butter
15 g/½ oz plain flour
150 ml/¼ pint milk or milk and leek cooking liquid

Set the oven at 200°C/400°F/gas 6. To make the pastry, sift the flour and salt into a bowl, then rub in the margarine until the mixture resembles fine breadcrumbs. Add enough cold water to make a stiff dough. Press the dough together.

Roll out the pastry on a lightly floured surface and use to line an 18 cm/7 inch flan tin or ring placed on a baking sheet. Line the pastry with greaseproof paper and fill with baking beans. Bake 'blind' for 20 minutes, then remove the paper and beans. Return to the oven for 5 minutes, then leave to cool. Reduce the oven temperature to 190°C/375°F/gas 5.

Using the white parts of the leeks only, tie them into 2 bundles with string. Bring a pan of salted water to the boil, add the leeks and simmer gently for 10 minutes. Drain, then squeeze as dry as possible. Slice the leeks thickly.

To make the sauce, melt the butter in a saucepan. Stir in the flour and cook over low heat for 2-3 minutes, without colouring. Gradually add the liquid, stirring constantly. Bring to the boil, stirring, then simmer for 1-2 minutes.

Cool the sauce slightly, then beat in the eggs. Add salt, pepper and nutmeg to taste. Stir in half the Gruyère. Put a layer of sauce in the cooled pastry case, cover with the leeks, then top with the remaining sauce. Sprinkle with the rest of the Gruyère. Bake for 20 minutes or until golden on top.

SERVES 8

☆ **FREEZER TIP** The cooled, filled tart freezes well for up to 3 months. Thaw the tart in the refrigerator for several hours.

QUICHE LORRAINE

1 pastry flan case (see Leek Tart, left)
6 rindless streaky bacon rashers
3 eggs
300 ml/½ pint single cream
salt and pepper
pinch of grated nutmeg
25 g/1 oz butter

Set the oven at 200°C/400°F/gas 6. Bake the pastry case blind. Remove the paper and beans. Reduce the oven temperature to 190°C/375°F/gas 5.

Cut the bacon in strips 2 cm × 5 mm/¾ × ¼ inch. Dry fry for 2 minutes. Drain and scatter the strips over the pastry base. Beat the eggs with the cream, salt, pepper and nutmeg. Pour into the pastry and dot with butter. Bake for 30 minutes. Serve hot or cold.

SERVES 4 TO 6

COOKING FOR ONE

This brief chapter shows that cooking and eating alone does not have to be dull, nor should it mean relying on convenience foods.

If you cook for yourself it can be easy to slip into the habit of opting for a ready-made bought dish or a quick snack instead of preparing a proper meal. On an occasional basis this is unlikely to be a dietary disaster, although it will tax the food budget, but it is not a good idea to eat this way frequently.

BUYING AND STORING FOOD

A certain amount of freezer space, as in a fridge freezer, is a valuable asset since it means that larger portions may be purchased and the surplus frozen.

Selecting your own vegetables at supermarkets means you can buy as little as you need, but meat and poultry are often packed in portions for two. An independent butcher will sell you as little as you want of any cut – if you happen to fancy 4 pork spare ribs or 1 lamb cutlet and 2 sausages, most will happily oblige. A good fishmonger is also worth finding. Some will not only provide individual portions but offer advice on cooking at the same time.

Buying cans and packets is not as significant a problem. If you have sufficient storage space, it is still worth buying larger, more economical, packs of dry foods. Remember to check the best-before date on the packet. Single portion cans, of fish or meat, for instance, can be expensive. The food will keep in a clean, covered container for 24 hours in the refrigerator, so with a little imagination one larger tin can be made into two meals.

CREATIVE COOKING

Cooking double portions of meat dishes, such as sauces or stews, makes sense if you don't mind eating the same style of dish twice. Vary the result by changing accompaniments or adding finishing touches. For example, the ubiquitous meat sauce can be served with baked potatoes, pasta or rice; or it can be topped with a thick layer of breadcrumbs and cheese and grilled until golden before being served with a salad.

Adapting recipes intended to serve four is not necessarily difficult, but there are a few possible pitfalls. Dividing the quantities of main ingredients is fairly straightforward, but quartering a clove of garlic can pose problems. Look for products like minced garlic or garlic salt, which allow tiny amounts to be used. When in season, pickling onions are more convenient than halved or quartered onions, and using a little instant mashed potato as a quick thickening agent for sauces or soups is simpler than messing about with beurre manié, whatever the purists may say.

Another knack to master is that of adjusting cooking methods to suit your facilities. For example food braised in the oven can usually be cooked on the hob. Even the succulent browning effect typical of roasting can be duplicated by cooking on the hob in a heavy-bottomed pan with a tight-fitting lid. A heavy pan with a coated cast-iron base and a lid that fits snugly is a boon. Getting to know your appliances – learning to adjust the heat on an electric ring or gas burner to give a low setting – is also important.

Lastly, with practice and imagination, it is surprising how easy it is to adapt many recipes which incorporate several stages and many pans for one-pot cooking. When attempting to combine stages and ingredients, remember to work out individual cooking times, so you will have a good idea of when to add ingredients to the cooking pot.

MARINATED MACKEREL

1 mackerel
parsley sprig to garnish

MARINADE
    30 ml/2 tbsp olive oil
    5 ml/1 tsp lemon juice
    fresh thyme sprig
    ½ bay leaf
    1 parsley stalk, broken into short lengths
    salt and pepper

Rinse the fish inside and out and pat dry on absorbent kitchen paper. Make 3 diagonal slashes in the flesh on both sides of fish.

Mix all the ingredients for the marinade in a shallow dish just large enough to hold the fish. Add the mackerel, turning to coat it evenly in the marinade. Cover the dish and marinate the fish for 1 hour.

Drain the fish, reserving the marinade, and place on a rack over a grill pan. Grill under moderate heat for 5-7 minutes each side, turning once and basting frequently with the reserved marinade. Serve very hot, garnished with the parsley sprig.

SERVES 1

HADDOCK WITH ORANGE

fat for greasing
1 portion haddock fillet (about 175 g/6 oz)
30 ml/2 tbsp orange juice
salt and pepper
pinch of grated nutmeg
2.5 ml/½ tsp grated orange rind to garnish
knob of butter

Set the oven at 180°C/350°F/gas 4. Lay the haddock fillet in a lightly greased shallow ovenproof dish. Sprinkle with the orange juice and season lightly with salt, pepper and nutmeg. Add the orange rind. Dot with the butter, cover with foil and bake for about 20 minutes.

Alternatively, steam the fish in a suitable dish or between two plates over a saucepan of simmering water for about 20 minutes. Serve the fish with the cooking juices spooned over. A baked potato, some cooked rice or pasta, and a salad of tomatoes with chopped onion are excellent accompaniments.

SERVES 1

☀ **MICROWAVE TIP** Prepare as suggested above, putting the haddock in a covered shallow dish. Cook on High for about 3 minutes, depending on the thickness of the fish.

PRAWNS IN ONION AND TOMATO SAUCE

15 ml/1 tbsp olive oil
1 small onion, finely chopped
1 small garlic clove, crushed
2 tomatoes, peeled and chopped
5 ml/1 tsp chopped parsley
salt and pepper
pinch of dried tarragon
150 g/5 oz peeled cooked prawns
50 g/2 oz cheese, grated

Heat the oil in a frying pan, add the onion and garlic and fry for 7-10 minutes or until soft. Stir in the tomatoes and parsley, with salt and pepper to taste. Add the tarragon, cover the pan and cook gently for 15 minutes.

Stir in the prawns and heat through gently. Spoon into a flameproof dish and sprinkle the cheese over the top. Grill until golden brown. Serve at once, with crusty bread. Alternatively, omit the cheese and use as a filling for a baked jacket potato (see page 308) or serve on rice or noodles.

SERVES 1

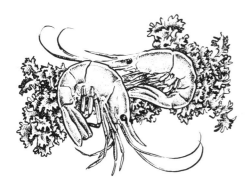

CREAMY GRILLED COD STEAK

1 cod steak
salt and pepper
5 ml/1 tsp French mustard
30 ml/2 tbsp Greek yogurt
15 ml/1 tbsp olive oil
1.25 ml/¼ tsp dried mixed herbs
30 ml/2 tbsp soft cheese with herbs and
  garlic

GARNISH
watercress sprigs
10 ml/2 tsp French dressing (optional)

Trim the fish of skin, if liked, then place on the rack of a grill pan. In a small bowl, mix the salt and pepper, mustard, yogurt, oil and herbs. Use a teaspoon to spread a little of this mixture over the top of the fish. Heat the grill on a medium setting.

Cook the fish steak until lightly browned on one side, spreading a second spoonful of the yogurt mixture over it after 1 minute. Turn the fish carefully using a fish slice, then spread with the half the remaining yogurt mixture. Continue cooking, topping with the rest of the yogurt after about 5 minutes, until cooked through and lightly browned. This should take about 15 minutes in all, depending on the thickness of the fish.

Serve at once, topped with the soft cheese. Garnish with watercress, and spoon a little French dressing over the garnish.

SERVES 1

> ☀ **MICROWAVE TIP** Place the fish and topping mixture in a suitable dish. Cover and cook on High for about 5 minutes, turning once. Top with the soft cheese and serve as above.

*B*RAISED LAMB CHOP WITH BARLEY

15 ml/1 tbsp oil
1 lamb chop, trimmed
½ onion, finely chopped
½ bay leaf
salt and pepper
125 ml/4 fl oz lamb or vegetable stock
45 ml/3 tbsp pearl barley, washed
75 g/3 oz frozen peas

Heat the oil in a small heavy-bottomed saucepan. Brown the chop quickly on both sides, then add the onion, bay leaf and salt and pepper to taste. Pour in the stock, bring to the boil, and lower the heat. Cover tightly and simmer for 15 minutes. Stir in the barley and simmer for 30 minutes more.

Add the frozen peas to the pan, bring the liquid to the boil, then lower the heat and simmer, covered, for 5-7 minutes or until the peas are tender. Serve in a warmed soup bowl, with garlic croûtons (see Mrs Beeton's Tip), if liked.

SERVES 1

MRS BEETON'S TIP To make garlic croûtons, remove the crusts from 2 slices of bread. Cut the bread into cubes. Heat 30 ml/2 tbsp oil in a small frying pan, add 1 crushed garlic clove and fry over gentle heat for 3-4 minutes. Remove the garlic with a slotted spoon. Add the bread cubes to the garlic-flavoured oil and fry until crisp. Drain and serve.

---

*G*RILLED PORK CHOP WITH APPLE

1 pork loin chop, trimmed
5 ml/1 tsp oil
ground pepper
dried sage
dried marjoram
caster sugar
salt
1 sharp eating apple
30 ml/2 tbsp apple sauce

Put the chop on an oiled grill rack. Brush with half the oil and sprinkle with pepper, sage, marjoram and a pinch of caster sugar. Cook under a hot grill until lightly browned.

Using a spoon and fork, carefully turn the chop over. Brush the second side with oil and sprinkle with pepper, herbs and sugar as before. Brown quickly, then lower the heat and cook for 15-20 minutes until cooked through. Sprinkle lightly with salt and keep hot.

Peel and core the apple. Cut 4 thick slices and put them on the grill rack. Brush with the fat in the grill pan and grill lightly until golden brown on both sides.

Put the chop on a heated plate, spoon the apple sauce next to it and fan the apple slices on the other side. Serve at once.

SERVES 1

CHICKEN IN A JACKET

1 (75 g/3 oz) chicken breast, trimmed
15 ml/1 tbsp corn oil
freshly ground black pepper
15 ml/1 tbsp fine cut orange marmalade
5 ml/l tsp sesame seeds
7.5 ml/1½ tsp natural wheat bran

GARNISH
thin slices of fresh orange
watercress sprigs

Wipe the chicken breast and dry it well on absorbent kitchen paper. Brush with oil on both sides, and sprinkle lightly with pepper. Grill under very gentle heat for 15-20 minutes, basting twice with oil. Turn, then grill for 15 minutes more, basting twice.

Remove the chicken from the heat and spread the top with marmalade. Sprinkle with the sesame seeds and bran. Return to the grill and cook very gently for 4-5 minutes, taking care that the coating does not burn. Serve hot, garnished with the orange slices and watercress sprigs.

SERVES 1

CHICKEN IN FOIL

butter for greasing
1 boneless chicken breast
½ small carrot, sliced
1 small onion, sliced
50 g/2 oz mushrooms, sliced
30 ml/2 tbsp white wine
salt and pepper
1 bay leaf

Set the oven at 180°C/350°F/gas 4. Butter a square of foil large enough to wrap the chicken breast. Put the chicken on the foil, top with the carrot, onion and mushroom slices and carefully pour the wine over. Sprinkle with salt and pepper, tuck a bay leaf among the vegetables and close the foil to make a loose parcel.

Put the foil parcel in a baking tin and bake for 45 minutes. Open the parcel carefully to avoid losing any of the juices. Make sure that the chicken is cooked, then transfer it, still in the foil parcel, to a serving plate. Serve with a portion of Italian Spinach (page 234) and a few Glazed Onions (page 228).

CHICKEN AND HAM CHARLOTTE

1 large slice of bread
butter
50 g/2 oz cooked chicken, finely chopped
1 slice of cooked ham, finely chopped
150 ml/¼ pint milk or chicken stock
1 egg yolk, beaten • salt and pepper

Set the oven at 160°C/325°F/gas 3. Remove the crusts, then butter the bread. Put one piece, buttered side up, on the base of an individual ovenproof dish. Cover with the chopped chicken and ham.

Place the second piece of bread, again buttered side up, on top of the chicken. Warm the milk or chicken stock in a small saucepan, remove from the heat and beat in the egg yolk. Add plenty of salt and pepper.

Pour the egg mixture into the dish, put the dish in a small roasting tin, and add enough boiling water to come half-way up the sides of the dish. Bake for 45 minutes.

SERVES 1

ONE-POT STIR FRY

30 ml/2 tbsp oil
1 carrot, halved and thinly sliced
1 thick slice of bread, cut into 2.5 cm/
    1 inch squares
2 small courgettes, sliced
2 spring onions, chopped
50 g/2 oz mushrooms, sliced
50 g/2 oz sliced garlic sausage, cut in
    strips
2 tomatoes, roughly chopped
salt and pepper

Heat the oil in a frying pan or wok. Stir fry the carrot for 3 minutes, then add the bread and continue stir frying for about 5 minutes, or until the chunks are lightly browned in parts.

Add the courgettes, spring onions and mushrooms and continue to stir fry for 3 minutes. Tip in the garlic sausage and cook for a further minute before adding the tomatoes. Once the tomatoes have been added, toss the mixture for just a few seconds as the bread will soon become soft. Add salt and pepper to taste. Serve piping hot.

SERVES 1

KIDNEYS ON CROUTES

2 lamb's kidneys
15 ml/1 tbsp butter
1 shallot, finely chopped
5 ml/1 tsp plain flour
15 ml/1 tbsp sherry or Madeira
60 ml/4 tbsp thin gravy
salt and pepper
Worcestershire sauce (see method)
2 slices of bread, crusts removed
oil for frying
15 ml/1 tbsp chopped parsley

Skin and core the kidneys; slice as thinly as possible. Melt the butter in a frying pan, add the shallot and fry for 2-3 minutes. Add the sliced kidneys and toss gently over moderate heat for 4-5 minutes.

Using a slotted spoon, transfer the kidneys to a small bowl and keep hot. Sprinkle the flour into the fat remaining in the pan, stir and cook for 1 minute. Gradually add the sherry or Madeira and the thin gravy. Cook, stirring, until the mixture boils and thickens. Add salt, pepper and Worcestershire sauce to taste.

Add the kidneys to the sauce and warm through gently. Meanwhile heat the oil in a large frying pan. Add the slices of bread and fry quickly until golden on both sides. Remove from the heat, drain on absorbent kitchen paper and place on a hot plate. Top with the kidney mixture, sprinkle with chopped parsley and serve at once.

SERVES 1

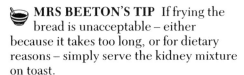 **MRS BEETON'S TIP** If frying the bread is unacceptable – either because it takes too long, or for dietary reasons – simply serve the kidney mixture on toast.

SAVOURY SAUSAGE TOASTS

2 rindless streaky bacon rashers
4 chipolata sausages
4 apple slices
4 tomato slices
15 ml/1 tbsp melted butter
2 slices of bread, toasted

Roll up the bacon rashers and secure with wooden cocktail sticks. Grill the sausages and bacon rolls under moderate heat for about 5 minutes, turning once. Add the tomato and apple slices, brush with butter and cook for 5 minutes.

Brush any remaining butter over the toast, then top each with apple, tomato, chipolatas and bacon rolls.

SERVES 1

BACON OLIVES

50 g/2 oz cooked ham, finely chopped
30 ml/2 tbsp breadcrumbs
2.5 ml/½ tsp finely chopped onion
2.5 ml/½ tsp finely chopped parsley
pinch of dried mixed herbs
pinch of grated nutmeg
salt and pepper
beaten egg or milk (see method)
4 rindless streaky bacon rashers

Combine the ham, breadcrumbs, onion, herbs and nutmeg in a bowl. Add salt and pepper to taste. Gradually stir in enough beaten egg or milk to bind the mixture. Set aside for 30 minutes.

Set the oven at 190°C/375°F/gas 5. Divide the ham mixture into 4 portions. Form each portion into a cork shape, roll in a bacon rasher and secure with string. Put on a baking sheet and bake for 30 minutes.

Serve at once, with wholemeal bread, pasta or brown rice and lightly cooked beans or carrots. Alternatively, serve on toast, with a single portion of Waldorf Salad (page 346).

SERVES 1

> **MRS BEETON'S TIP** If you want to avoid heating the oven, bind the stuffing mixture with milk instead of egg and spread it over the bacon instead of forming the cork shape. Roll up and thread on a metal skewer. Cook under a medium-hot grill until the bacon rolls are cooked through and golden outside. Turn occasionally during cooking.

DEVILLED CHICKEN LIVERS

15 ml/1 tbsp butter
225 g/8 oz chicken livers, trimmed and cut in half
2 spring onions, chopped
1 garlic clove, crushed
15 ml/1 tbsp tomato purée
5 ml/1 tsp French mustard
dash of Worcestershire sauce
pinch of chilli powder

Melt the butter in a saucepan. Add the chicken livers, spring onions and garlic and fry lightly for about 10 minutes over moderate heat, stirring all the time. The livers should be browned and just cooked.

Stir in the remaining ingredients and cook for 1-2 minutes more. Serve on toast, as a filling for a baked potato or with rice.

SERVES 1

SALADS

Refreshing side dishes, interesting light meals or richly dressed main-course combinations: there's a salad to suit every occasion and every palate.

There are one or two golden rules that apply to all salads.

■ The most important is always to use fresh ingredients – good quality vegetables, fruit in prime condition, freshly cooked and cooled meat, poultry, fish or eggs and herbs or flavourings in tip-top condition.
■ Combine complementary ingredients, both in terms of texture and flavour.
■ Choose a dressing that will both balance and marry salad flavours.

SALAD OPTIONS

Salads are generally thought of as cold dishes but there is no reason why a combination of hot and cold ingredients should not be used. For example, hot crispy bacon or sautéed chicken livers may be tossed with salad leaves.

Croûtons, nuts and crispy bacon also add texture and flavour to soft salads; fresh herbs enliven delicate mixtures. There are several ways of serving salad. Some ingredients are best laid out on a platter, others should be well tossed in a large dish while certain mixtures benefit from being layered. Bear in mind the fact that the arrangement is not just for appearance but to combine flavours and textures or separate them so that each can be savoured individually.

DRESSINGS

Suggestions for making dressings are included in recipes or as tips throughout this chapter. There are two basic types of dressing, one based upon oil, as in French dressing or vinaigrette, the other a creamy mixture such as mayonnaise. Here are a few alternatives:
■ Plain yogurt, with herbs and seasoning or blue cheese.
■ Plain tofu, mashed with a little cream or milk and flavoured with herbs. Used generously, this also adds food value.
■ Low-fat soft cheese, thinned with a little milk.
■ Lemon juice and soy sauce.
■ Peanut butter, thinned with oil and lemon juice.

CAMARGUE MUSSELS

2 kg/4½ lb mussels
1 onion, sliced
2 garlic cloves, cut in slivers
1 carrot, sliced
1 celery stick, sliced
1 bouquet garni
125 ml/4 fl oz white wine
chopped parsley to serve

MAYONNAISE
1 egg yolk
5 ml/1 tsp French mustard
salt
cayenne
5 ml/1 tsp white wine vinegar
100 ml/3½ fl oz sunflower oil
20 ml/4 tsp lemon juice

Wash, scrape and beard the mussels following the instructions on page 11. Put them in a large saucepan. Tuck the sliced vegetables among the mussels and add the bouquet garni.

Pour over the wine and add 125 ml/4 fl oz water. Place the pan over moderate heat and bring to the boil. As soon as the liquid bubbles up over the mussels, shake the pan several times, cover, lower the heat and simmer until the mussels have opened. Discard any that remain shut. With a slotted spoon remove the mussels from the stock. Arrange them, on their half shells, on a large flat dish. Strain the cooking liquid into a jug and set aside to cool.

Make the mayonnaise. Blend the egg yolk, mustard, salt, cayenne and vinegar in a bowl. Using a balloon whisk, beat in the oil very gradually, drop by drop. When about half the oil has been added and the mixture looks thick and shiny, add the rest of the oil in a slow thin stream. Stir in the lemon juice.

Add the reserved cooking liquid to the mayonnaise, spoon the mixture over the mussels and sprinkle with chopped parsley. Serve chilled, with a simple salad of lettuce leaves of various types, with snipped chives.

SERVES 5 TO 6

CRAB AND MANDARIN SALAD

50 g/2 oz shelled whole walnuts or walnut
   halves
400 g/14 oz drained canned or thawed
   frozen crab meat
75 g/3 oz celery, sliced
100 g/4 oz drained canned mandarin
   segments
1 lettuce, separated into leaves

DRESSING
  50 g/2 oz blue cheese
  125 ml/4 fl oz soured cream
  2.5 ml/½ tsp grated lemon rind
  salt and pepper
  75 ml/5 tbsp sunflower oil
  20 ml/4 tsp lemon juice

Make the dressing. Crumble the cheese into a bowl. Gradually work in the soured cream until smooth. Add the remaining ingredients and whisk until completely blended. Pour into a jug, cover and chill.

Set half the walnuts aside to use as a garnish. Chop the remaining walnuts finely and place them in a large bowl. Add the crab meat, celery and mandarin orange segments. Toss lightly, breaking up any large pieces of crab meat with a fork.

Arrange the lettuce leaves on a flat salad platter. Pile the crab mixture in the centre. Trickle a little of the dressing over the crab mixture and garnish with the reserved walnuts. Serve the rest of the dressing separately.

SERVES 4

SEA BREAM MAYONNAISE

butter for greasing
575 g/1¼ lb red sea bream fillets, skinned
lemon juice • salt and pepper
125 ml/4 fl oz Mayonnaise (see Camargue
    Mussels, page 332)
1 hard-boiled egg, chopped
10 ml/2 tsp chopped parsley
8 lettuce leaves
tomato wedges to garnish

Grease a shallow ovenproof dish. Set the oven at 190°C/375°F/gas 5. Arrange the fish fillets in the dish, sprinkle with lemon juice, salt and pepper and cover loosely with greaseproof paper. Bake for 20 minutes. Flake the fish with a fork, remove any bones and leave to cool.

Mix the mayonnaise, hard-boiled egg and parsley lightly in a bowl. Stir in the cold fish. Spread the lettuce leaves on a flat platter, top with the fish and garnish.

SERVES 4

BEAN SALAD WITH TUNA

450 g/1 lb dried flageolet beans, soaked in
    water overnight
150 g/5 oz tomatoes, peeled, seeded and
    chopped
2 spring onions, finely chopped
1 (198 g/7 oz) can tuna, drained and flaked

DRESSING
90 ml/6 tbsp sunflower oil
45 ml/3 tbsp white wine vinegar
1 garlic clove, crushed
15 ml/1 tbsp chopped parsley

Drain the beans and put them into a saucepan with fresh cold water to cover. Boil briskly for at least 10 minutes, then lower the heat and simmer for about 1 hour or until tender.

Meanwhile make the dressing by mixing all the ingredients in a screw-topped jar. Close the jar tightly and shake vigorously until well blended.

Drain the beans and put them in a bowl. Add the tomatoes, spring onions and tuna and mix well. Pour the cold dressing over the hot beans and the other ingredients and serve at once on small warmed plates.

SERVES 4

SHRIMP OR PRAWN SALAD

½ cucumber
salt and pepper
2 lettuce hearts or 1 Iceberg lettuce,
    finely shredded
60 ml/4 tbsp Mayonnaise (see Camargue
    Mussels, page 332)
30 ml/2 tbsp plain yogurt
225 g/8 oz peeled cooked shrimps or
    prawns
2 hard-boiled eggs, halved or sliced
    lengthways

Slice the unpeeled cucumber thinly. Put the slices in a colander, sprinkle with salt and leave for 30 minutes to drain. Rinse the cucumber slices, drain well, then pat dry with absorbent kitchen paper. Use the slices to line a glass salad bowl.

Lay the lettuce in the lined bowl. Sprinkle lightly with salt. Mix the mayonnaise and yogurt in a bowl, then spoon the mixture over the lettuce. Pile the shrimps or prawns in the centre of the dish with the hard-boiled egg halves or slices in a circle around them. Grind black pepper over the egg slices just before serving the salad.

SERVES 4

> 🍲 **MRS BEETON'S TIP** Place the cucumber slices side by side, just touching but not overlapping. A layer of radish slices may be added.

HALIBUT, ORANGE AND WATERCRESS SALAD

600 ml/1 pint Court Bouillon (page 15)
4-6 halibut steaks
8 large lettuce leaves, shredded
125 ml/4 fl oz Mayonnaise (see Camargue Mussels, page 332)

GARNISH
orange slices
watercress sprigs

Bring the court bouillon to simmering point in a large saucepan. Add the halibut steaks and poach gently for 7-10 minutes until cooked. Using a slotted spoon transfer the fish to a plate and leave to cool. Remove the skin.

Arrange most of the shredded lettuce on a flat salad platter. Coat the fish in mayonnaise and arrange it on the lettuce. Garnish with orange slices, watercress and the remaining lettuce.

SERVES 4 TO 6

SALAD NICOISE

salt and pepper
225 g/8 oz French beans, topped and tailed
2 hard-boiled eggs, cut in quarters
3 small tomatoes, cut in quarters
1 garlic clove, crushed
1 (198 g/7 oz) can tuna, drained and flaked
50 g/2 oz black olives
1 large lettuce, separated into leaves
1 (50 g/2 oz) can anchovy fillets, drained, to garnish

FRENCH DRESSING
45 ml/3 tbsp olive oil or a mixture of olive and sunflower oil
salt and pepper
pinch of English mustard powder
pinch of caster sugar
15 ml/1 tbsp wine vinegar

Bring a small saucepan of salted water to the boil. Add the beans and cook for 5-10 minutes or until just tender. Drain, refresh under cold water and drain again.

Make the dressing by mixing all the ingredients in a screw-topped jar. Close the jar tightly and shake vigorously until well blended.

Put the beans into a large bowl with the eggs, tomatoes, garlic, tuna and most of the olives. Pour over the dressing and toss lightly. Add salt and pepper to taste.

Line a large salad bowl with the lettuce leaves. Pile the tuna mixture into the centre and garnish with the remaining olives and the anchovy fillets. Serve at once.

SERVES 4 TO 6

———————— ◇ ————————

SEAFOOD SALAD

Illustrated on page 294

450 g/1 lb cod fillet, skinned
30 ml/2 tbsp lemon juice
2.5 ml/½ tsp sugar
salt and pepper
75 ml/5 tbsp olive oil or other salad oil
15 ml/1 tbsp chopped capers
30 ml/2 tbsp chopped spring onion
225 g/8 oz peeled cooked prawns, thawed
   if frozen
100 g/4 oz shelled freshly cooked mussels
4 ripe tomatoes, peeled and diced
30 ml/2 tbsp chopped parsley
1 courgette, diced
¼ Iceberg lettuce, shredded

Steam the cod between two plates over a saucepan of boiling water for 10-15 minutes, until the flesh is firm and white but still moist.

While the fish is cooking, place the lemon juice in a bowl. Whisk in the sugar, with salt and pepper to taste. When the sugar and salt have dissolved, whisk in the oil. Stir in the capers and chopped spring onion.

Flake the cod into large pieces, discarding all skin and bones. Place in a dish and pour the dressing over. Add the prawns, mussels, tomatoes and parsley, then mix lightly, taking care not to break up the cod flakes.

Toss the courgette and lettuce together and arrange on 4 plates. Top with the seafood mixture and serve at once, with hot fresh toast, Melba toast or crusty bread.

SERVES 4

VEAL AND TUNA SALAD

1.8 kg/4 lb fillet of veal
1 carrot, cut into quarters
1 small onion, cut into quarters
1 celery stick, roughly chopped
4 black peppercorns
5 ml/1 tsp salt

SAUCE
   1 (198 g/7 oz) can tuna, drained
   4 anchovy fillets
   125 ml/4 fl oz olive oil
   2 egg yolks
   black pepper
   15-30 ml/1-2 tbsp lemon juice

GARNISH
   capers
   sliced gherkins
   fresh tarragon (optional)

Trim the veal. Tie it into a neat shape, if necessary. Place in a large saucepan with the carrot, onion, celery, peppercorns and salt. Pour over enough water to cover the meat. Bring to the boil, lower the heat, cover the pan and simmer for 1½ hours or until the meat is very tender. Carefully lift it out of the liquid and set it aside on a plate to cool. Boil the cooking liquid quickly to reduce it by half, strain through a fine sieve and reserve.

Make the sauce. Put the tuna in a bowl with the anchovies. Add 15 ml/1 tbsp of the oil. Pound to a smooth paste by hand or use a blender or food processor. Blend in the egg yolks and season with pepper. Add half the lemon juice, then gradually add the oil, as when making mayonnaise. When the sauce is thick and shiny, add more lemon juice to taste. Stir in about 30 ml/2 tbsp of the reserved cooking liquid from the veal to make a thin coating sauce.

Cut the cold veal into thin slices and

arrange them in a dish. Coat completely with the sauce, then cover the dish and refrigerate for up to 24 hours. Before serving, garnish with capers, sliced gherkins and a sprig of fresh tarragon, if liked.

SERVES 6

> 🥄 **MRS BEETON'S TIP** Do not discard the remaining veal cooking liquid. Use it as the basis of a soup or sauce.

PORK AND SALAMI SALAD

1 lettuce, separated into leaves
200 g/7 oz cold roast pork, diced
200 g/7 oz cold boiled potatoes, diced
100 g/4 oz boiled beetroot, diced
2-3 gherkins, sliced
15 ml/1 tbsp capers
salt and pepper
100 ml/3½ fl oz mayonnaise (see
    Camargue Mussels, page 332)
12 slices of salami
1 lemon, sliced
12 stoned green olives to garnish

Wash the lettuce leaves and dry them thoroughly. Use them to line a salad bowl. Mix the pork, potatoes, beetroot, gherkins and capers lightly, then pile the mixture into the lined bowl. Add salt and pepper to taste. Pour the mayonnaise over the top, and arrange alternate slices of salami and lemon around the rim. Garnish with the olives.

SERVES 4

CHICKEN AND CELERY SALAD

Illustrated on page 294

1 large lettuce, separated into leaves
1 celery heart
350 g/12 oz cooked chicken, cut into
    serving pieces
10 ml/2 tsp tarragon or white wine
    vinegar
salt and pepper
150 ml/¼ pint Mayonnaise (see
    Camargue Mussels, page 332)

GARNISH
    lettuce leaves
    2 hard-boiled eggs, sliced or chopped
    stoned black olives and/or gherkin strips

Wash the lettuce leaves and dry them thoroughly. Shred the outer leaves with the celery. Put in a bowl with the chicken and vinegar. Toss lightly and add salt and pepper to taste.

Spoon the chicken mixture into a bowl or on to a platter. Coat with the mayonnaise. Garnish with lettuce leaves, sliced or chopped egg and olives or gherkin strips.

SERVES 6

FRENCH BEAN AND TOMATO SALAD

salt and pepper
225 g/8 oz French beans, trimmed
3 tomatoes, peeled, seeded and
    quartered
15 ml/1 tsp snipped chives

DRESSING
    45 ml/3 tbsp walnut or sunflower oil
    10 ml/2 tsp white wine vinegar
    5 ml/1 tsp lemon juice
    pinch of caster sugar
    pinch of mustard powder
    1 garlic clove, crushed

Make the dressing by mixing all the ingredients in a screw-topped jar. Add salt and pepper to taste, close the jar tightly and shake vigorously until well blended.

Bring a small saucepan of salted water to the boil. Add the beans and cook for 5-10 minutes or until just tender. Drain, rinse briefly under cold water, then tip into a bowl. Immediately add the dressing and toss the beans in it. Leave to cool.

Add the tomatoes and toss lightly. Taste the salad and add more salt and pepper if required. Turn into a salad bowl, sprinkle with the chives and serve.

SERVES 4

MICROWAVE TIP Wash the beans. Drain lightly, leaving some moisture on the pods. Place them in a roasting bag, tie the top loosely with an elastic band and microwave on High for 5 minutes. Shake the bag carefully, set it aside for 1 minute, then transfer the contents to a bowl and add the dressing.

BEETROOT AND CELERY SALAD

450 g/1 lb cooked beetroot
1 celery heart
2 green-skinned eating apples
50 g/2 oz walnuts, roughly chopped
15 ml/1 tbsp chopped parsley
watercress to garnish

DRESSING
    30 ml/2 tbsp olive or sunflower oil
    15 ml/1 tbsp cider vinegar
    pinch of mustard powder
    1.25 ml/¼ tsp brown sugar
    salt and pepper

Peel the beetroot and cut a few neat rounds for the garnish. Dice the rest neatly. Use 1 stick of the celery to make curls (see Mrs Beeton's Tip) and chop the rest.

Make the dressing by shaking all the ingredients together in a tightly-closed screw-topped jar. Quarter, core and dice the apples and put them in a salad bowl. Add the dressing, tossing the apples to prevent discoloration. Add the beetroot, celery, walnuts and parsley. Toss lightly.

Pile the salad into a serving dish and garnish with the reserved beetroot rounds, the celery curls and watercress.

SERVES 6

MRS BEETON'S TIP The easiest way to make celery curls is to cut the celery stick into 7.5 cm/3 inch pieces. Make thin slits in each piece, almost to the end, then place in iced water until the ends curl up. Drain well before serving.

FLEMISH WINTER SALAD

450 g/1 lb cooked potatoes, sliced
350 g/12 oz cooked beetroot, sliced
60 ml/4 tbsp French dressing (see Salad
    Niçoise, page 335)
1 (50 g/2 oz) can anchovy fillets
2 radishes, sliced

Layer the potatoes and beetroot in a glass
bowl, sprinkling each layer with a little
of the French dressing, and ending with
a layer of potatoes. Arrange a lattice of
anchovy fillets on top of the salad, filling
each square with a slice of radish.

SERVES 6

VARIATION

Reduce the quantities of potatoes and
beetroot to 225 g/8 oz each. Add 1 red-
skinned and 1 green-skinned eating apple,
diced but not peeled. Toss these ingredients
with the French dressing.

CELERY AND CHESTNUT SALAD

1 small lettuce, separated into leaves
225 g/8 oz cooked chestnuts, halved or
    quartered
6 celery sticks, finely chopped
1 eating apple
100 ml/3½ fl oz mayonnaise (see
    Camargue Mussels, page 332)

Wash the lettuce leaves and dry them
thoroughly. Line a salad bowl. Put the
chestnuts in a bowl with the celery. Peel,
core and dice the apple and add it to the
bowl with the mayonnaise. Mix well. Pile
the celery mixture into the lettuce-lined
bowl. Serve at once.

SERVES 4

BEAN SPROUT SALAD

Illustrated on page 290

225 g/8 oz bean sprouts
1 small orange, peeled and sliced
100 g/4 oz Chinese leaves, shredded
2 celery sticks, thinly sliced
salt and pepper

DRESSING
45 ml/3 tbsp olive oil or a mixture of olive
    and sunflower oil
15 ml/1 tbsp white wine vinegar
1 garlic clove, crushed
2.5 ml/½ tsp soy sauce
pinch of caster sugar

Pick over the bean sprouts, wash them
well, then dry thoroughly. Cut the orange
slices into quarters.

Make the dressing by mixing all the ingredients in a screw-topped jar. Close the
jar tightly and shake vigorously until well
blended.

Combine the bean sprouts, Chinese
leaves, celery and orange in a bowl. Pour
over the dressing and toss lightly. Season
to taste and serve at once.

SERVES 4

> **MRS BEETON'S TIP** Bean sprouts
> are highly nutritious. To grow your
> own, place dried soya beans, mung peas or
> alfalfa seeds in a clean glass jar. The jar
> should be no more than one-sixth full.
> Cover the jar with a piece of muslin held
> in place by an elastic band. Fill the jar
> with cold water, then drain off the liquid.
> Store in a cool dark place. Rinse the beans
> in fresh water every day. They should start
> to sprout in 2-3 days and will be ready to
> eat in 5-6 days.

COLESLAW

Illustrated on page 291
Coleslaw looks marvellous in a natural cabbage
bowl. Use a sharp knife to cut out the centre of a
Savoy cabbage, using the cut portion for the
coleslaw. Rinse the cabbage bowl under cold
water, shake off excess moisture and dry
between the leaves with absorbent kitchen
paper. Trim the base of the cabbage bowl so
that it stands neatly

450 g/1 lb firm white or Savoy cabbage,
　finely shredded
100 g/4 oz carrots, coarsely grated
2 celery sticks, thinly sliced
½ small green pepper, seeded and thinly
　sliced
150 ml/5 fl oz mayonnaise (see Camargue
　Mussels, page 332) or plain yogurt
salt and pepper
lemon juice (see method)

Mix all the ingredients in a salad bowl,
adding enough lemon juice to give the
mayonnaise or yogurt a tangy taste. Chill
before serving.

SERVES 4

VARIATION

FRUIT AND NUT SLAW Core and
dice, but do not peel, 1 red-skinned eating
apple. Toss in 15 ml/1 tbsp lemon juice,
then add to the slaw with 25 g/1 oz seedless
raisins or sultanas and 25 g/1 oz chopped
walnuts, almonds or hazelnuts.

RUSSIAN CUCUMBER SALAD

4 hard-boiled egg yolks
250 ml/8 fl oz soured cream
few drops of vinegar
1 large cucumber, chilled
salt and pepper
dill sprigs to garnish

Sieve the egg yolks into a bowl, stir in
the cream and vinegar and mix well. Chill
for 30 minutes. Dice the cucumber, pat
it dry with absorbent kitchen paper and
place in a dish. Season well, stir in the
cream mixture. Garnish and serve.

SERVES 4

FENNEL AND CUCUMBER SALAD

Illustrated on page 295

½ large cucumber, diced
6 radishes, sliced
1 Florence fennel bulb, sliced
1 garlic clove, crushed
5 ml/1 tsp chopped mint
2 hard-boiled eggs, quartered, to garnish

DRESSING
30 ml/2 tbsp olive oil
15 ml/1 tbsp lemon juice
salt and pepper

Combine the cucumber, radishes, fennel
and garlic in a salad bowl. Sprinkle with the
mint. Make the dressing by shaking all
the ingredients in a tightly-closed screw-
topped jar. Pour over the salad, toss lightly
and serve with the hard-boiled egg garnish.

SERVES 6

CABBAGE CRUNCH

100 g/4 oz white cabbage, shredded
225 g/8 oz red cabbage, shredded
4 celery sticks, chopped
2 carrots, cut into matchsticks
1 green pepper, thinly sliced
4 ready-to-eat dried apricots, thinly sliced
100 g/4 oz pecan nuts or walnuts, chopped
50 g/2 oz sunflower seeds

DRESSING
1 hard-boiled egg yolk
salt and pepper
1.25 ml/¼ tsp prepared mustard
dash of Worcestershire sauce
pinch of caster sugar
10 ml/2 tsp cider vinegar
15 ml/1 tbsp sunflower oil
30 ml/2 tbsp double cream

Make the dressing. Sieve the egg yolk into a bowl. Gradually work in the salt and pepper, mustard, Worcestershire sauce, caster sugar and vinegar. Add the oil gradually, beating constantly. Whip the cream in a clean bowl, then fold it into the dressing. Mix all the ingredients and toss in the dressing.

SERVES 6

CUCUMBER IN YOGURT

Illustrated on page 222

1 large cucumber
salt and pepper
300 ml/½ pint plain or Greek strained
    yogurt, chilled
5 ml/1 tsp vinegar
30 ml/2 tbsp chopped mint
pinch of sugar

Cut the cucumber into small dice and place it in a colander. Sprinkle with salt, leave for 3-4 hours, then rinse and drain thoroughly. Pat the cucumber dry on absorbent kitchen paper.

Stir the yogurt, vinegar, mint and sugar together in a bowl. Add the cucumber and mix well. Taste and add salt and pepper if required.

SERVES 4 TO 6

> **MRS BEETON'S TIP** Serve within 1 hour of making, or the liquid in the cucumber may thin the yogurt and spoil the consistency of the salad.

GRAPEFRUIT AND CHICORY SALAD

3 grapefruit
3 small heads of chicory
50 g/2 oz seedless raisins
15 ml/1 tbsp grapefruit juice
45 ml/3 tbsp oil
2.5 ml/½ tsp French mustard
salt and pepper
mustard and cress to garnish

Cut the grapefruit in half. Cut the fruit into segments and put them into a bowl. Remove all the pulp and pith from the grapefruit shells; stand the shells upside down on absorbent kitchen paper to drain. Shred the chicory, reserving some neat rounds for the garnish, and add to the grapefruit segments with all the remaining ingredients except the garnish. Toss the mixture lightly together, then pile back into the grapefruit shells. Garnish with the cress and reserved chicory and serve at once.

SERVES 6

ORANGE AND ORTANIQUE SALAD

3 oranges, peeled and sliced
3 ortaniques, peeled and sliced (see Mrs Beeton's Tip)
1 mild Italian or Spanish onion, cut in rings
12 black olives
30 ml/2 tbsp chopped mint to garnish

DRESSING
75 ml/5 tbsp olive oil
30 ml/2 tbsp orange juice
15 ml/1 tbsp red wine vinegar
5 ml/1 tsp soy sauce
5 ml/1 tsp clear honey
salt and pepper

Make the dressing by mixing all the ingredients in a tightly closed screw-topped jar. Close the jar tightly and shake vigorously until well blended.

Put the dressing in a large bowl and add the orange, ortanique and onion slices. Cover the bowl and set aside for 1-2 hours.

When ready to serve, arrange the fruit and onion slices on a large platter, add the olives and drizzle the remaining dressing over the top. Sprinkle with the mint.

SERVES 6

MRS BEETON'S TIP The ortanique – a cross between an orange and a tangerine – was developed in Jamaica. The fruit is easy to peel and segment, and is very sweet and juicy. If unavailable, substitute tangerines, grapefruit or limes.

CAESAR SALAD

As the egg in this salad is only lightly cooked, it is very important that it be perfectly fresh, and purchased from a reputable source.

3 garlic cloves, peeled but left whole
2 cos lettuces, separated into leaves
150 ml/¼ pint olive oil
4 large thick slices of bread, crusts removed and cubed
1 egg
juice of 1 lemon
1 (50 g/2 oz) can anchovy fillets, drained
50 g/2 oz Parmesan cheese, grated
salt and pepper

Cut 1 garlic clove in half and rub it all around a salad bowl. Wash the lettuces leaves and dry them thoroughly. Tear into small pieces and put in the salad bowl.

Heat 60 ml/4 tbsp of the olive oil in a small frying pan, add the remaining garlic cloves and fry over gentle heat for 1 minute. Add the bread cubes and fry until golden on all sides. Remove from the pan with a slotted spoon and drain on absorbent kitchen paper. Discard the garlic and oil in the pan.

Add the remaining olive oil to the lettuce and toss until every leaf is coated. Bring a small saucepan of water to the boil, add the egg and cook for 1 minute. Using a slotted spoon remove it from the water and break it over the lettuce. Add the lemon juice, anchovies, cheese, salt and pepper and toss the salad lightly.

Add the croûtons of fried bread and toss again. Serve as soon as possible, while the croûtons are still crisp.

SERVES 6

RICE SALAD

200 g/7 oz long-grain rice
salt
60 ml/4 tbsp olive oil
30 ml/2 tbsp white wine vinegar
2 spring onions, finely chopped
1 carrot, finely diced and blanched
1 small green pepper, seeded and finely
    diced
2 gherkins, finely diced
30 ml/2 tbsp snipped chives
watercress to serve

Place the rice in a saucepan. Pour in 450 ml/¾ pint cold water. Add a little salt, then bring to the boil. Cover the pan tightly and reduce the heat to the lowest setting. Leave the rice for 15 minutes, turn off the heat and leave for a further 15 minutes without removing the lid. The rice should have absorbed all the liquid. Drain if necessary.

Stir in the oil and vinegar while the rice is still hot. Add the vegetables and chives; mix well. Pile on a dish and garnish with watercress. Serve.

SERVES 4 TO 6

MRS BEETON'S TIP This looks good in tomato shells. Cut the tops off 4-6 beefsteak tomatoes and reserve as lids. Hollow out the centres, saving the pulp for use in soup or another recipe. Turn the tomatoes upside down on absorbent kitchen paper to drain. When ready to serve, fill the tomatoes with the rice mixture and replace the lids at an angle.

POTATO SALAD

salt and pepper
6 large new potatoes or waxy old potatoes
150 ml/¼ pint mayonnaise (see
    Camargue Mussels, page 332)
3 spring onions, chopped
30 ml/2 tbsp chopped parsley

Bring a saucepan of salted water to the boil, add the potatoes in their jackets and cook for 20-30 minutes until tender. Drain thoroughly. When cool enough to handle, peel and dice the potatoes. Put them in a bowl and add the mayonnaise while still warm. Lightly stir in the spring onions and parsley, with salt and pepper to taste. Cover, leave to become quite cold and stir before serving.

SERVES 6

VARIATIONS

FRENCH POTATO SALAD Substitute 100 ml/3½ fl oz French dressing (see Salad Niçoise, page 335) for the mayonnaise. Omit the spring onions, increase the parsley to 45 ml/3 tbsp and add 5 ml/1 tsp chopped mint and 5 ml/1 tsp snipped chives.
GERMAN POTATO SALAD Omit the mayonnaise and spring onions. Reduce the parsley to 5 ml/1 tsp and add 5 ml/1 tsp finely chopped onion. Heat 60 ml/4 tbsp vegetable stock in a saucepan. Beat in 15 ml/1 tbsp white wine vinegar and 30 ml/2 tbsp oil. Add salt and pepper to taste. Pour over the diced potatoes while still hot and toss lightly together. Serve at once, or leave to become quite cold.
POTATO SALAD WITH APPLE AND CELERY Follow the basic recipe above, but add 2 sliced celery sticks and 1 diced red-skinned apple tossed in a little lemon juice.

CHEF'S SALAD

½ cos lettuce, separated into leaves
50 g/2 oz cold cooked chicken, cut in strips
50 g/2 oz cold cooked tongue, cut in strips
50 g/2 oz Gruyère cheese, cut in strips
1 hard-boiled egg, thinly sliced
15 ml/1 tbsp chopped onion
8 black olives

DRESSING
90 ml/6 tbsp olive oil
30 ml/2 tbsp red wine vinegar
2.5 ml/½ tsp lemon juice
2.5 ml/½ tsp French mustard
salt and pepper

Make the dressing by mixing all the ingredients in a screw-topped jar. Close the jar tightly and shake vigorously until well blended.

Wash the lettuce leaves, dry them thoroughly and arrange in a large salad bowl. Add a little of the dressing and toss. Arrange the cold meats and cheese on top of the lettuce, with the egg, onion and olives. Serve the remaining dressing separately.

SERVES 4

PEPPER SALAD

2 large green peppers
2 large red peppers
2 large yellow peppers
1 mild Italian or Spanish onion, thinly
    sliced in rings
100 ml/3½ fl oz olive oil
salt and pepper (optional)

Wash the peppers and pat dry with absorbent kitchen paper. Grill under moderate heat, turning the peppers frequently with tongs until the skins blister, then char all over. Immediately transfer the peppers to a large bowl and cover with several layers of absorbent kitchen paper. Alternatively, put the grilled peppers in a polythene bag. When cold, rub off the skin under cold water. Remove cores and seeds and cut or tear the peppers into thin strips.

Put the pepper strips on a serving platter, arrange the onion rings around the rim, and drizzle the olive oil over the top. Add salt and pepper to taste, if liked. Serve at once.

SERVES 6 TO 8

PASTA, ANCHOVY AND SWEETCORN SALAD

150 g/5 oz pasta shells
salt and pepper
60 ml/4 tbsp mayonnaise (see Camargue
    Mussels, page 332)
15 ml/1 tbsp fruit chutney
1 (50 g/2 oz) can anchovies, drained and
    finely chopped
225 g/8 oz canned sweetcorn kernels
2 spring onions, finely chopped, to
    garnish

Cook the pasta in a large saucepan of boiling salted water for 10-12 minutes or until tender but still firm to the bite. Drain thoroughly. While still warm, stir in the mayonnaise and chutney. Set aside to cool.

Add the anchovies and sweetcorn, with

salt and pepper to taste. Toss the salad lightly and garnish with the chopped spring onions.

SERVES 4 TO 6

> ◉ **MRS BEETON'S TIP** Use any decorative pasta for this dish. Use spirals, bows or tiny cartwheels if preferred. For a touch of colour, use tomato or spinach-flavoured pasta shapes.

TOMATO SALAD

Sun-warmed tomatoes, freshly picked, are perfect for this salad. In the classic Italian version, olive oil is the only dressing, but a little red wine vinegar may be added, if preferred.

450 g/1 lb firm tomatoes, peeled and
   sliced
salt and pepper
pinch of caster sugar (optional)
45 ml/3 tbsp olive oil
5 ml/1 tsp chopped basil
basil sprigs to garnish

Put the tomatoes in a serving dish and sprinkle lightly with salt and pepper. Add the sugar, if used. Pour over the olive oil and sprinkle with chopped basil. Garnish with basil sprigs.

SERVES 4 TO 6

VARIATION

MOZZARELLA AND TOMATO SALAD Interleave the sliced tomatoes with sliced mozzarella cheese. Cover and leave to marinate for at least an hour before serving.

SPINACH AND BACON SALAD

Illustrated on page 291

450 g/1 lb fresh young spinach
150 g/5 oz button mushrooms, thinly
   sliced
1 small onion, thinly sliced
15 ml/1 tbsp oil
6 rindless streaky bacon rashers, cut into
   strips
75 ml/5 tbsp French dressing (see Salad
   Niçoise, page 335)

Remove the stalks from the spinach, wash the leaves well in cold water, then dry thoroughly on absorbent kitchen paper. If time permits, put the leaves in a polythene bag and chill for 1 hour.

Tear the spinach into large pieces and put into a salad bowl with the mushrooms and onion.

Heat the oil in a small frying pan and fry the bacon until crisp. Meanwhile toss the salad vegetables with the French dressing. Pour in the hot bacon and fat, toss lightly to mix and serve at once.

SERVES 4

> ◉ **MRS BEETON'S TIP** If preferred, the bacon may be grilled until crisp and crumbled into the salad just before serving.

SPANISH SALAD

6 firm red tomatoes, sliced
3 cooked potatoes, sliced
2 grilled red peppers (see Pepper Salad,
    page 344), skinned, seeded and sliced
225 g/8 oz lightly cooked French beans
salt and pepper
60 ml/4 tbsp French dressing (see Salad
    Niçoise, page 335).

Arrange the vegetables in neat row on a serving platter. Sprinkle with salt and pepper, drizzle the dressing over the top and serve.

SERVES 4 TO 6

TABBOULEH

This delicious salad is served all over the Middle East. Its central ingredient is bulgur or cracked wheat, which has been hulled and parboiled. It therefore needs little or no cooking.

125 g/4½ oz bulgur wheat
2 tomatoes, peeled, seeded and diced
1 small onion, finely chopped
2 spring onions, finely chopped
50 g/2 oz parsley, very finely chopped
45 ml/3 tbsp lemon juice
30 ml/2 tbsp olive oil
salt and pepper to taste
crisp lettuce leaves to serve

Put the bulgur wheat in a large bowl, add water to generously cover and set aside for 45-60 minutes. Line a sieve or colander with a clean tea-towel and strain the bulgur. When most of the liquid has dripped through, scoop the bulgur up in the tea-towel and squeeze it strongly to extract as much of the remaining liquid as possible. Tip the bulgur into a bowl.

Add the tomatoes, onion, spring onions, parsley, lemon juice and oil, with salt and pepper to taste. Mix well, so that the salad resembles confetti.

Dome the tabbouleh in the centre of a large platter. Arrange the lettuce leaves around the rim to be used as scoops.

SERVES 6 TO 8

VARIATION

TABBOULEH IN PEPPERS Serve tabbouleh in blanched pepper shells for an attractive addition to a buffet table.

WALDORF SALAD

Illustrated on page 291

4 sharp red dessert apples
2 celery sticks, thinly sliced
25 g/1 oz chopped or broken walnuts
75 ml/5 tbsp Mayonnaise (see Camargue
    Mussels, page 332)
30 ml/2 tbsp lemon juice
pinch of salt
lettuce leaves (optional)

Core the apples, but do not peel them. Cut them into dice. Put them in a bowl with the celery and walnuts. Mix the mayonnaise with the lemon juice. Add salt to taste and fold into the apple mixture. Chill. Serve on a bed of lettuce leaves, if liked.

SERVES 4

VARIATION

WALDORF SALAD WITH CHICKEN Make as above, but use only 2 apples. Add 350 g/12 oz diced cold cooked chicken. For extra flavour and colour, add 50 g/2 oz small seedless green grapes.

COURGETTE AND AVOCADO SALAD

salt and pepper
450 g/1 lb courgettes, thickly sliced
1 Lollo Rosso lettuce, separated into
    leaves
2 avocados
3 rindless streaky bacon rashers, grilled,
    to garnish

DRESSING
75 ml/5 tbsp olive oil
30 ml/2 tbsp tarragon or white wine
    vinegar
pinch of caster sugar
1 garlic clove, crushed
salt and pepper

Make the dressing by mixing all the ingredients in a screw-topped jar. Close the jar tightly and shake vigorously until well blended.

Bring a saucepan of salted water to the boil, add the courgettes, lower the heat and simmer for 1 minute. Drain the courgettes and put them in a bowl. While still warm, pour the dressing over. Allow the mixture to cool, then cover and marinate in the refrigerator for 2-3 hours.

Wash the Lollo Rosso leaves and dry them thoroughly. Divide between 6 salad bowls. Drain the courgettes, reserving the dressing, and divide between the bowls.

Peel and slice the avocados, toss them lightly in the reserved dressing, then arrange on top of the salads, using a slotted spoon. Crumble a little bacon over each salad and serve, with the remaining dressing in a small jug.

SERVES 6

STRAWBERRY AND TOMATO SALAD

Illustrated on page 181

450 g/1 lb firm tomatoes, peeled (see
    Mrs Beeton's Tip)
salt
pinch of paprika
15 ml/1 tbsp lemon juice
350 g/12 oz firm strawberries, hulled and
    quartered
30 ml/2 tbsp salad oil

GARNISH
a few whole strawberries
¼ cucumber, thinly sliced

Cut the tomatoes in half and remove the seeds and pulp, reserving these for use in another recipe. Cut the tomato flesh into thin slices, place in a bowl and season with salt and paprika. Sprinkle with the lemon juice, cover and set aside.

Jut before serving, add the strawberries and transfer the mixture to a serving platter or dish. Drizzle with the oil and garnish with the whole strawberries and cucumber slices.

SERVES 6

> **MRS BEETON'S TIP** To peel tomatoes, place them in a bowl and cover with boiling water. Leave for 30-60 seconds, drain and slit the peel with the point of a knife, then it will slide off easily.

ACCOMPANIMENTS

APPLE AND CELERY STUFFING

3 rindless streaky bacon rashers, chopped
1 onion, finely chopped
1 celery stick, finely sliced
3 large cooking apples
75 g/3 oz fresh white breadcrumbs
15 ml/1 tbsp grated lemon rind
salt and pepper

Heat the bacon gently in a frying pan until the fat runs, then increase the heat and fry until browned, stirring frequently. Using a slotted spoon, transfer the bacon to a bowl. Add the onion and celery to the fat remaining in the frying pan and fry over moderate heat for 5 minutes. Remove with a slotted spoon, add to the bacon and mix lightly.

Peel, core and dice the apples. Add them to the pan and fry until soft and lightly browned. Add to the bacon mixture with the breadcrumbs and lemon rind. Mix well, adding salt and pepper to taste.

SUFFICIENT FOR A 4-5 KG/9-11 LB GOOSE, TWO 2.5 KG/5½ LB DUCKS OR 1 BONED PORK JOINT

MRS BEETON'S TIP
Delicatessens and deli counters in supermarkets often sell packets of bacon bits – the trimmings left after slicing. These are ideal for a recipe such as this, and may also be used in quiches, on pizzas and to flavour soups and stews.

WALNUT STUFFING

15 g/½ oz butter
1 small onion, finely chopped
12 whole walnuts or 24 halves, chopped
50 g/2 oz sausagemeat
50 g/2 oz fresh white breadcrumbs
2.5 ml/½ tsp dried mixed herbs
1 large cooking apple
salt and pepper
1 egg, lightly beaten
milk (see method)

Melt the butter in a saucepan, add the onion and cook over very gentle heat for about 10 minutes until soft and pale golden.

Combine the walnuts, sausagemeat, breadcrumbs and herbs in a bowl. Peel, core and chop the apple. Add it to the bowl, with salt and pepper to taste. Stir in the onion with the melted butter and mix well. Bind with the egg, adding a little milk if necessary.

SUFFICIENT FOR 1 × 2.5 KG/5½ LB DUCK; DOUBLE THE QUANTITY FOR A 4-5 KG/9-11 LB GOOSE

SAGE AND ONION STUFFING

2 onions, thickly sliced
4 young sage sprigs or 10 ml/2 tsp dried
  sage
100 g/4 oz fresh white breadcrumbs
50 g/2 oz butter or margarine, melted
salt and pepper
1 egg, lightly beaten (optional)

Put the onions in a small saucepan with water to cover. Bring to the boil, cook for 2-3 minutes, then remove the onions from the pan with a slotted spoon. Chop them finely. Chop the sage leaves finely, discarding any stalk.

Combine the breadcrumbs, onions and sage in a bowl. Add the melted butter or margarine, with salt and pepper to taste. Mix well. If the stuffing is to be shaped into balls, bind it with the beaten egg.

SUFFICIENT FOR A 2.5 KG/5½ LB DUCK; DOUBLE THE QUANTITY FOR A 4-5 KG/9-11 LB GOOSE

MRS BEETON'S FORCEMEAT

100 g/4 oz gammon or rindless bacon,
  finely chopped
50 g/2 oz shredded beef suet
grated rind of 1 lemon
5 ml/1 tsp chopped parsley
5 ml/1 tsp chopped mixed herbs
salt and cayenne pepper
pinch of ground mace
150 g/5 oz fresh white breadcrumbs
2 eggs, lightly beaten

Combine the gammon or bacon, suet, lemon rind and herbs in a bowl. Add salt,

cayenne and mace to taste, mix well with a fork, then stir in the breadcrumbs. Gradually add enough beaten egg to bind.

MAKES ABOUT 350 G/12 OZ

VARIATION

MRS BEETON'S FORCEMEAT BALLS Roll the mixture into 6-8 small balls. Heat oil for shallow frying in a large frying pan, add the forcemeat balls and fry until browned on all sides. Drain on absorbent kitchen paper and serve with roast meat or poultry.

CHESTNUT STUFFING

800 g/1¾ lb chestnuts, shelled (see Mrs
  Beeton's Tip, page 52)
150-250 ml/5-8 fl oz chicken or
  vegetable stock
50 g/2 oz butter, softened
pinch of ground cinnamon
2.5 ml/½ tsp sugar
salt and pepper

Put the shelled chestnuts in a saucepan and add the stock. Bring to the boil, lower the heat, cover and simmer until the chestnuts are tender. Drain, reserving the stock.

Rub the chestnuts through a fine wire sieve into a bowl. Add the butter, cinnamon and sugar, with salt and pepper to taste. Stir in enough of the reserved stock to bind.

SUFFICIENT FOR THE NECK END OF A 5-6 KG/9-11 LB TURKEY; USE HALF THE QUANTITY FOR A 1.5 KG/3¼ LB CHICKEN

 **MRS BEETON'S TIP** Canned chestnuts may be used for the stuffing. You will require about 450 g/1 lb.

WILD RICE STUFFING

350 ml/12 fl oz stock (see Mrs Beeton's
    Tip)
150 g/5 oz wild rice
50 g/2 oz butter
2 shallots, finely chopped
½ small green pepper, finely chopped
1 small celery stick, finely sliced
100 g/4 oz mushrooms, chopped
30 ml/2 tbsp tomato purée

Bring the stock to the boil in a saucepan
and add the wild rice. Lower the heat,
cover and cook gently for 40 minutes until
the rice is almost tender and the majority of
the stock is absorbed. Cover and set aside.

Melt the butter in a saucepan, add the
shallots, green pepper, celery and mushrooms and fry over gentle heat for 3
minutes. Remove from the heat, add to the
wild rice with the tomato purée and mix
well.

SUFFICIENT FOR 2 PHEASANTS OR 1
LARGE GUINEAFOWL

MRS BEETON'S TIP If the stuffing
is used for a bird, use the giblets to
make the stock. To prepare the giblets
from wild birds, cut the small greenish
gall-bladder away from the liver, taking
care not to break it; it will give the giblets
a very bitter flavour. Cut any small sinews
from the liver, and remove excess fat from
the heart and gizzard. Break the neck into
two or three pieces and rinse briefly in
cold water. Cook the giblets in 750 ml/1¼
pints water, with a sliced onion and carrot,
for 45 minutes. Keep the pan covered
during cooking. The liver may be chopped
and added to the stuffing.

SAUSAGEMEAT STUFFING

1 chicken or turkey liver, trimmed
    (optional)
450 g/1 lb pork sausagemeat
50 g/2 oz soft white breadcrumbs
15 ml/1 tbsp chopped parsley
5 ml/1 tsp dried mixed herbs
1 egg, lightly beaten
salt and pepper

If using the liver, chop it finely and put it
in a mixing bowl. Add the sausagemeat
and breadcrumbs, with the herbs. Stir in
enough of the beaten egg to bind the mixture. Season with plenty of salt and pepper.

SUFFICIENT FOR 1 × 1.5 KG/3¼ LB
CHICKEN; TREBLE THE QUANTITY FOR
A 5-6 KG/9-11 LB TURKEY

DUMPLINGS

100 g/4 oz self-raising flour
50 g/2 oz shredded beef suet
salt and pepper

Mix the flour and suet in a bowl. Add salt
and pepper to taste and bind with enough
cold water to make a soft, smooth dough.
With floured hands, divide the dough
into 16 portions; roll into balls. Drop into
simmering salted water, stock, soup or
stew, lower the heat and simmer for 15-20
minutes. Serve with the liquid or with
boiled meat, stew or vegetable.

MAKES ABOUT 16

VARIATION

HERB Add 25 g/1 oz grated onion and 5
ml/1 tsp chopped fresh herbs to the flour
and suet.

BREAD SAUCE

1 onion, studded with 6 cloves
2 bay leaves
600 ml/1 pint milk
100 g/4 oz fresh white breadcrumbs
salt and pepper
freshly grated nutmeg

Heat the onion, bay and milk gently until almost boiling. Simmer for 5 minutes, then remove from the heat, cover and cool.

Strain milk and heat until lukewarm. Add the breadcrumbs and bring slowly to the boil, stirring. Simmer for 5 minutes. Add seasoning and nutmeg.

SERVES 4 TO 6

CRANBERRY SAUCE

150 g/5 oz sugar
225 g/8 oz cranberries

Put the sugar in a heavy-bottomed saucepan. Add 125 ml/4 fl oz water. Stir over gentle heat until the sugar dissolves. Add the cranberries and cook gently for about 10 minutes until they have burst and are quite tender. Leave to cool.

MAKES ABOUT 300 ML/½ PINT

VARIATIONS

CRANBERRY AND APPLE Use half cranberries and half tart cooking apples.
CRANBERRY AND ORANGE Use orange juice instead of water. Add 10 ml/2 tsp finely grated orange rind.
CRANBERRY AND SHERRY Add 30-45 ml/2-3 tbsp sherry with the cranberries.

APPLE SAUCE

Although apple sauce is traditionally served with roast pork, duck or goose, it also makes a very good accompaniment to steamed pudding.

450 g/1 lb apples
15 g/½ oz butter
rind and juice of ½ lemon
sugar (see method)

Peel, core and slice the apples. Put them in a saucepan with 30 ml/2 tbsp water. Add the butter and lemon rind. Cover and cook over low heat until the apple is reduced to a pulp. Beat until smooth, rub through a sieve or process in a blender or food processor. Return the sauce to the clean pan, stir in the lemon juice and add sugar to taste. Reheat gently, stirring until the sugar has dissolved. Serve hot or cold.

MAKES ABOUT 350 ML/12 FL OZ

BENTON SAUCE

Fresh horseradish is very useful. Not only is it the basis of an excellent sauce to serve with roast beef, but it also adds piquancy to seafood cocktail sauces and dips. In Mrs Beeton's day, a little horseradish was also added to apple sauce, which was served with pork or beef.

30 ml/2 tbsp freshly grated horseradish
10 ml/2 tsp prepared mustard
10 ml/2 tsp caster sugar
125 ml/4 fl oz malt vinegar

Pound the horseradish with the mustard and sugar in a small bowl. Gradually add the vinegar, mixing well.

MAKES ABOUT 150 ML/¼ PINT

BEARNAISE SAUCE

The classic accompaniment to grilled steak, especially tournedos, Béarnaise Sauce is also delicious with vegetables such as broccoli.

60 ml/4 tbsp white wine vinegar
15 ml/1 tbsp chopped shallot
5 black peppercorns, lightly crushed
1 bay leaf
2 fresh tarragon stalks, chopped, or
    1.25 ml/¼ tsp dried tarragon
1.25 ml/¼ tsp dried thyme
2 egg yolks
100 g/4 oz butter, cut into small pieces
salt and pepper

Combine the vinegar, shallot, peppercorns and herbs in a small saucepan. Boil until the liquid is reduced to 15 ml/1 tbsp, then strain into a heatproof bowl. Cool, then stir in the egg yolks.

Place the bowl over a saucepan of simmering water and whisk until the eggs start to thicken. Gradually add the butter, whisking after each addition, until the sauce is thick and creamy. Add salt and pepper to taste.

MAKES ABOUT 175 ML/6 FL OZ

◆

FRESH TOMATO SAUCE

30 ml/2 tbsp oil
1 onion, finely chopped
1 garlic clove, crushed
1 rindless streaky bacon rasher, chopped
800 g/1¾ lb tomatoes, peeled and
    chopped
salt and pepper
pinch of sugar
15 ml/1 tbsp chopped fresh basil or 5 ml/1
    tsp dried basil

Heat the oil in a saucepan and fry the onion, garlic and bacon over gentle heat for 5 minutes. Stir in the remaining ingredients except the basil, cover the pan and simmer gently for 30 minutes.

Rub the sauce through a sieve into a clean saucepan or purée in a blender or food processor until smooth. Add the basil.

Reheat the sauce. Check the seasoning before serving and add more salt and pepper if required.

MAKES ABOUT 600 ML/1 PINT

GRAVY

giblets, carcass, bones or trimmings from
    meat, poultry or game
1 bay leaf
1 thyme sprig
1 clove
6 black peppercorns
½ onion, sliced
pan juices from roasting (see Mrs
    Beeton's Tip, below)
25 g/1 oz plain flour (optional)
salt and pepper

Place the giblets, bones, carcass and/or trimmings (for example wing ends) in a saucepan. Pour in water to cover, then add the bay leaf, thyme, clove, peppercorns and onion. Bring to the boil and skim off any scum, then reduce the heat, cover the pan and simmer for about 1 hour.

Strain the stock and measure it. You need about 600-750 ml/1-1¼ pints to make gravy for up to 6 servings. If necessary, pour the stock back into the saucepan and boil until reduced.

Pour off most of the fat from the roasting pan, leaving a thin layer and all the cooking juices. Place the pan over moderate heat; add the flour if the gravy is to be thickened. Cook the flour, stirring all the time and scraping all the sediment off the tin, for about 3 minutes, until it is browned. If the gravy is not thickened, pour in about 300 ml/½ pint of the stock and boil, stirring and scraping, until the sediment on the base of the tin is incorporated.

Slowly pour in the stock (or the remaining stock, if making thin gravy), stirring all the time. Bring to the boil and cook for 2-3 minutes to reduce the gravy and concentrate the flavour slightly. Taste and add more salt and pepper if required.

SERVES 4 TO 6

MRS BEETON'S TIP The quality of the sediment on the base of the cooking tin determines the quality of the gravy. If the meat was well seasoned and roasted until well browned outside, the sediment should have a good colour and flavour. Any herbs (other than large stalks), onions or flavouring roasted under the meat should be left in the pan until the gravy is boiled, then strained out before serving.

GRAVY NOTES

■ If making gravy for a meal other than a roast, for example to accompany sausages or toad-in-the-hole, use a little fat instead of the pan juices and brown the flour well over low to moderate heat. Meat dripping gives the best flavour but butter or other fat may be used.

■ To make onion gravy, slowly brown 2 thinly sliced onions in the fat before adding the flour – this is excellent with sausages or toad-in-the-hole.

■ Gravy browning may be added if necessary; however, it can make the sauce look artificial and unpleasant. Pale gravy is perfectly acceptable, provided it has good flavour.

■ Always taste gravy when cooked. It should be well seasoned. If it lacks flavour, or is rather dull, a dash of Worcestershire sauce, mushroom ketchup or about 5-15 ml/1-3 tsp tomato purée may be whisked in.

■ Gravy may be enriched by adding up to half wine instead of stock.

■ Add 60 ml/4 tbsp port or sherry, and 15 ml/1 tbsp redcurrant jelly to make a rich gravy for duck, game, lamb, pork or venison.

■ Add 2 chopped pickled walnuts and 15 ml/1 tbsp walnut oil to the pan juices to make a delicious walnut gravy.

■ Use vegetable stock to make vegetable gravy. Cook a finely diced carrot and 2 thinly sliced onions in butter or margarine instead of using meat juices. Add 1.25 ml/¼ tsp ground mace and 30 ml/2 tbsp chopped parsley to the gravy.

■ Add 100 g/4 oz thinly sliced mushrooms to the pan juices to make a mushroom gravy. The sauce may be further enriched by adding a little mushroom ketchup.

◈

*P*ASTA

Home-made pasta dough may be used to make noodles, lasagne or stuffed pasta (such as ravioli). Alternatively it may be cut into small squares for cooking.

400 g/14 oz strong white flour
2.5 ml/½ tsp salt
30 ml/2 tbsp olive oil or 40 g/1½ oz
butter, melted
3 eggs, beaten
about 30 ml/2 tbsp oil for cooking
about 50 g/2 oz butter
freshly ground black pepper

Put the flour and salt in a large bowl and make a well in the middle. Add the oil or butter and the eggs, then gradually mix in the flour to make a stiff dough. As the mixture clumps together use your hands to knead it into one piece. If necessary add 15-30 ml/1-2 tbsp water, but take care not to make the mixture soft. It should be quite hard at this stage as it will become more pliable on kneading.

Knead the dough thoroughly on a very lightly floured surface for 10-15 minutes, or until it is very smooth and pliable. Ideally you should be able to work without dusting the surface with flour more than once, provided you keep the dough moving fairly fast all the time.

Cut the dough in half and wrap one piece in polythene to prevent it from drying out. Roll out the dough, adding a dusting of flour as necessary, into a large thin oblong sheet.

To cut noodles, dust the dough with flour and fold it in half, dust it again and fold over once more. Cut the folded dough into 1 cm/½ inch wide strips, then shake them out and place on a floured plate. Cover loosely with polythene to prevent them from drying out until they are cooked. Repeat with the remaining dough.

Bring a very large saucepan of salted water to the boil. Add a little oil. Tip all the noodles into the pan and bring the water back to the boil rapidly, stir once, then regulate the heat so that the water boils but does not froth over. Cook for about 3 minutes. The pasta should be tender but not soft.

Drain the pasta and turn it into a heated bowl. Toss a knob of butter and plenty of freshly ground black pepper with the noodles, then serve piping hot.

MAKES ABOUT 450 G/1 LB

VARIATIONS

PASTA VERDI Cook 225 g/8 oz fresh spinach, or 100 g/4 oz frozen chopped spinach. Drain the spinach thoroughly and purée in a blender or food processor. When making the pasta, use an extra 50 g/2 oz plain flour. Add the spinach purée to the well in the flour and mix it in with the eggs. It will not be necessary to add any water.

TOMATO PASTA Mix 30 ml/2 tbsp tomato purée with the oil or butter, then stir in the eggs before incorporating the mixture with the flour.

COOKING RICE

225 g/8 oz long-grain rice
salt and pepper

If using Basmati rice, plain, untreated long-grain rice or wild rice, start by placing the grains in a bowl. Wash the rice in several changes of cold water, taking care not to swirl the grains vigorously as this may damage them. Pour off most of the water each time, then add fresh water and swirl the rice gently with your fingertips. Finally drain the rice in a sieve and turn it into a saucepan.

Add cold water: 600 ml/1 pint for white rice; 750 ml/1¼ pints for brown or wild rice. Add a little salt and bring to the boil. Stir once, then lower the heat and put a tight-fitting lid on the pan. Cook very gently until the grains are tender: 15-20 minutes for easy-cook varieties and white rice; 20 minutes for Basmati rice; 25-35 minutes for brown rice; 40-50 minutes for wild rice.

Remove the pan from the heat and leave, covered, for 5 minutes, then fork up the grains, add salt and pepper if liked, and serve the rice.

SERVES 4

VARIATIONS

SAFFRON RICE Add 3 green cardamom pods and a bay leaf to the rice. Reduce the amount of water by 50 ml/ 2 fl oz. Pound 2.5-5 ml/½-1 tsp saffron strands to a powder in a mortar with a pestle. Add 50 ml/2 fl oz boiling water and stir well until the saffron has dissolved. Sprinkle this over the rice after it has been cooking for 15 minutes, then replace the lid quickly and finish cooking. Fork up the rice, removing the bay leaf and cardamoms.

PULLAO RICE Cook 1 chopped onion in a little butter or ghee in a large saucepan, then add 1 cinnamon stick, 1 bay leaf, 4 green cardamoms and 4 cloves. Stir in 225 g/8 oz Basmati rice and 600 ml/1 pint water and cook as in the main recipe. In a separate pan, cook a second onion, this time thinly sliced, in 50 g/2 oz butter or ghee until golden brown. Add 30 ml/2 tbsp cumin seeds (preferably black seeds) when the onion has softened and before it begins to brown. Add half the sliced onion mixture to the rice and fork it in. Pour the remaining onion mixture over the top of the rice before serving. Saffron may be added to pullao.

BROWN AND WILD RICE Mix different grains for an interesting texture. Start by cooking the wild rice for 10 minutes, then add the brown rice and continue cooking until the brown rice is tender.

WALNUT RICE Cook the chosen rice; add 100 g/4 oz chopped walnuts and 30 ml/2 tbsp chopped parsley before serving.

LEMON RICE Add the grated rind of 1 lemon to the rice: if it is added at the beginning of cooking it gives a deep-seated flavour; added just before serving it adds a fresh, zesty tang to the rice.

RICE WITH HERBS Add bay leaves, sprigs of rosemary, thyme, savory or sage to the rice at the beginning of cooking. Alternatively, sprinkle chopped parsley, tarragon, dill, mint or fresh marjoram over the rice at the end of cooking. Match the herb to the flavouring in the main dish, with which the rice is to be served.

TOMATO RICE Add 1 finely chopped onion, 1 bay leaf and 30 ml/2 tbsp tomato purée to the rice before cooking.

INDEX